Family in America

Family in America

Advisory Editors: David J. Rothman
Professor of History,
Columbia University

Sheila M. Rothman

The Family and Social Service
In the 1920's

Two Documents

*A*RNO *P*RESS & *T*HE *N*EW *Y*ORK *T*IMES
New York 1972

Reprint Edition 1972 by Arno Press Inc.

Reprinted from copies in
The State Historical Society of Wisconsin Library

LC# 74-169361
ISBN 0-405-03885-2

Family in America
ISBN for complete set: 0-405-03840-2
See last pages of this volume for titles.

Manufactured in the United States of America

CONTENTS

Abbott, Edith and Sophonisba, P. Breckinridge
THE ADMINISTRATION OF THE AID-TO-MOTHERS LAW IN ILLINOIS. *Children's Bureau Publication,*
No. 82. 1921.

Bogue, Mary F.
ADMINISTRATION OF MOTHER'S AID IN TEN LOCALITIES. With Special Reference To Health, Housing, Education, and Recreation
Children's Bureau Publication, No. 184.
1928.

U. S. DEPARTMENT OF LABOR
W. B. WILSON, Secretary
CHILDREN'S BUREAU
JULIA C. LATHROP, Chief

THE ADMINISTRATION OF THE AID-TO-MOTHERS LAW IN ILLINOIS

By

EDITH ABBOTT

AND

SOPHONISBA P. BRECKINRIDGE

LEGAL SERIES No. 7
Bureau Publication No. 82

WASHINGTON
GOVERNMENT PRINTING OFFICE
1921

CONTENTS.

	Page.
Letter of transmittal	5
Introduction	7-17
The funds-to-parents act of 1911	10
The aid-to-mothers act of 1913	12
The aid-to-mothers law as amended in 1915 and in 1917	14
PART I. The administration of the aid-to-mothers law in the Cook County (Chicago) juvenile court	19-124
Methods of making pension grants	19-26
Preliminary investigations	19
The conference committee	23
Investigation by the county agent	23
Court hearings	24
Methods of paying pension grants	25
The problem of supervision	27-47
General policy	27
Pension "stays" or withdrawals of pension grants	39
Changes in amount of pension grants	45
Adequacy of pension grants	48-71
Amount of pension grants	48
Tests of adequacy of pension grants	56-69
Budget estimates as a test of adequacy of relief	57
Comparison between present and past incomes	66
Comparison between public and private relief	68
The supplementing of pensions by private agencies	69
Rejected or dismissed applications	72
Families on the Cook County (Chicago) pension roll during the year 1917	82
Subsequent history of families made technically ineligible by changes in the pension law	95-111
Families broken up	98
Care of Jewish families	100
Families pensioned by private charity	101
Families receiving occasional assistance	107
Families entirely self-supporting	109
Expenditures for mothers' pensions, 1911-1918	112
The aid-to-mothers law in relation to dependency and delinquency	116
PART II. The administration of the aid-to-mothers law outside Cook County	125-166
Introduction	125
The determination of pension policies in the 101 outlying counties	127
Number of counties granting mothers' pensions	131

CONTENTS.

PART II. The administration of the aid-to-mothers law outside Cook County—Continued.	Page.
Expenditures of different counties	134
Use of probation officers for administration of act	136
Investigation of applicants' eligibility	140
Dismissed cases	142
Pension grants to ineligible families	144
Supervision	150
Differences between the pension policy of the Chicago court and that adopted by the down-State courts	156
Adequacy of pension grants	159
Pension records	165
Conclusion	167–171
Precedents for State control	168
Index	173

LETTER OF TRANSMITTAL.

U. S. DEPARTMENT OF LABOR,
CHILDREN'S BUREAU,
Washington, October 1, 1920.

SIR: This report on the administration of the aid-to-mothers law in Illinois was prepared by Miss Edith Abbott and Miss Sophonisba P. Breckinridge of the Chicago School of Civics and the University of Chicago. As residents of Hull-House, both authors have had long practical experience among the poor and neglected children of Chicago. In 1912 they made for the School of Civics a study entitled "The Delinquent Child and the Home," based on material gathered in the Cook County Juvenile Court. Hence this study of the operation of the aid-to-mothers act in Illinois has the advantage of preparation by recognized authorities in the field of social research, who have also been long and intimately acquainted with the work of the Illinois Cook County Juvenile Court. The authors desire that mention be made of the valuable services of Miss Helen Russell Wright and Miss Mary Cantey Preston, who made the field investigations outside Cook County.

Although concerned with a single State, this report is of Nation-wide interest because the family conditions with which it deals are typical and because it shows typical difficulties which have already been surmounted, and points out those still to be overcome in making effective the principle back of the mothers' pension act.

This principle may be stated thus: It is against sound public economy to allow poverty alone to cause the separation of a child from the care of a good mother, or to allow the mother so to exhaust her powers in earning a living for her children that she can not give them proper home care and protection.

In the 40 States which now have mothers' pension laws this principle has undoubtedly been hastened to expression by the results of neglected childhood to be seen in every juvenile court. The earliest laws—of Kansas City, Missouri, and of Illinois—were unquestionably based upon a belief that the juvenile courts revealed facts, not generally known before, as to the injury to the child caused by the inevitable neglect of working mothers and the breaking up of homes because of poverty.

The fact that in 21 States the administration of the aid-to-mothers law is placed in the juvenile courts indicates a purpose to place the power of help in the hands of the judge before whom the trouble is revealed and who must decide the child's future, within the limitations of the resources at his command. Probably a desire to avoid the discredit of the old outdoor poor relief also influenced the plan of placing the juvenile court in charge. On the other hand, the present tendency of expert opinion is undoubtedly toward placing responsibility for actual administration of mothers' pensions in a separate body qualified to deal with the matter scientifically and not in the spirit of the old poor relief.

This report gives the Illinois law and traces legislative changes; it also points out limitations both in law and in operation. The judge of the juvenile court was directed to administer the law, but according to the terms of the first act it was impossible to pay administrative officers out of public funds, and in order to begin operations the volunteer societies in Chicago, working in connection with court cases, contributed agents who formed a working committee to serve under the judge in planning and carrying out an administrative policy.

As this report intimates, the act was loosely drawn. In Chicago, however, the judge and those interested in the problem believed that the wise development of this plan to strengthen rather than pauperize poverty-stricken mothers of young children was worth much effort, and a high degree of scientific skill and humane purpose has been shown in its administration, first by the members of the volunteer committee and now by the paid staff. In the State outside Chicago there is marked unevenness of administration, few qualified officers are available for supervision, and inequality in the amounts of the pensions is great. In brief, the investigators report conditions which lead them to the conclusion that State-wide administration of mothers' pensions is necessary in order to deal justly with those whom the law is designed to aid.

In both city and State the smallness of the pensions is noted, and the need for constant study of fair living standards and necessary budgets is emphasized. The careful budgeting of the Cook County cases is described.

This report adds emphasis to the contention that social legislation can not be static; that it must be based on carefully secured knowledge of the conditions to be remedied; that it must be drawn to establish standards and principles which can be applied to meet changing conditions, rather than to set up fixed rules which are likely to apply for brief periods only, and to require constant revision by successive legislatures; and, perhaps most important of all, that valuable administration must be not only honest and well-intentioned, but primarily scientific.

Respectfully submitted.

JULIA C. LATHROP,
Chief.

Hon. W. B. WILSON,
Secretary of Labor.

THE ADMINISTRATION OF THE AID-TO-MOTHERS LAW IN ILLINOIS.

INTRODUCTION.

The first Illinois statute [1] providing for mothers' pensions was enacted June 5, 1911, as an amendment to section 7 of the Illinois juvenile-court law. The new statute was entitled the " funds-to-parents act " and became operative July 1 of the same year. Its purpose was to keep dependent children under 14 years of age with their own parents, when the parents were unable to provide for them, instead of providing out of public funds for their support in institutions. The administration of the law was placed with the juvenile courts, which were already caring for children declared dependent and delinquent, instead of with the county agents or supervisors of the poor, who were in charge of the public outdoor relief.

This act enabled the court to deal with its wards in a way that had been impossible up to that time. Under the juvenile-court law, which had been passed 12 years earlier,[2] the courts had the authority to commit children to institutions to be supported at public expense. The juvenile-court law provided for the care of two groups of children, those defined as delinquent [3] and those defined as dependent or neglected.[4] For both groups of children, three kinds of treatment were authorized: (1) The return of the child to his own home subject to the

---

[1] Laws of Illinois, Forty-seventh' General Assembly, 1911, p. 126; "Juvenile Courts—Funds to Parents; An Act to amend an Act entitled ' An Act relating to children who are now or may hereafter become dependent, neglected, or delinquent, to define these terms, and to provide for the treatment, control, maintenance, adoption, and guardianship of the persons of such children.' "
[2] Illinois Revised Statutes, July 1, 1899, ch. 23, sec. 169ff.
[3] The statute defines a delinquent child in the following terms: " Any male child who while under the age of 17 years or any female child who while under the age of 18, violates any law of this State; or is incorrigible, or knowingly associates with thieves, vicious, or immoral persons; or without just cause and without that [the] consent of its parents, guardian, or custodian absents itself from its home or place of abode, or is growing up in idleness or crime; or knowingly frequents a house of ill-repute; or knowingly frequents any policy shop or place where any gambling device is operated; or frequents any saloon or dram shop where intoxicating liquors are sold; or patronizes or visits any public pool room or bucket shop; or wanders about the streets in the nighttime without being on any lawful business or lawful occupation; or habitually wanders about any railroad yards or tracks or jumps or attempts to jump onto [any] moving train; or enters any car or engine without lawful authority; or uses vile, obscene, vulgar, profane, or indecent language in [any] public place or about any schoolhouse; or is guilty of indecent or lascivious conduct." [Ill. Rev. Stat., ch. 23, sec. 169.]
[4] The statute defines a dependent or neglected child in the following terms: " Any male child who while under the age of 17 years or any female child who while under the age of 18 years, for any reason, is destitute, homeless, or abandoned; or dependent upon the public for support; or has not proper parental care or guardianship; or habitually begs or receives alms; or is found living in any house of ill fame or with any vicious or disreputable person; or has a home which by reason of neglect, cruelty, or depravity, on the

7

visitation and supervision of a probation officer; (2) the appointing as guardian of the child a "reputable citizen" who became responsible for the custody of the child; and (3) commitment to an institution. Delinquent children were committed to State institutions supported by public funds. Dependent or neglected children were committed to certain quasi public institutions known as industrial schools for girls and manual training schools for boys, organized by private individuals or associations, in accordance with statutes enacted in 1879 and 1883. These so-called training-school statutes authorized the county to pay from the public moneys $15 a month for each girl and $10 a month for each boy committed by court order. No public institution is maintained for dependent children, but nearly 1,000 children each year are committed to private—chiefly sectarian—institutions subsidized by public fund.[5]

No provision was made by any of these statutes for boarding children in private homes. No authority existed for the payment of public money either to enable a parent, such as a widowed mother, to keep her children in her own home; or if the child's own home was unfit but the child capable of being dealt with under home conditions, to board the child in another home carefully selected and supervised. If, in any individual case, either of these forms of treatment approved itself to the court, that treatment was possible only to the extent to which private charitable aid might be obtained.

Thus, if a mother were left destitute because of the death or incapacity of her husband, the law offered provision for her children if she wished to place them in institutions. If she refused to part with them the State made no provision except for outdoor relief under the pauper law. In Illinois, as in many other American States, outdoor relief consists for the most part of spasmodic and inadequate doles, and a widow with a family of small children can not maintain her home with such irregular assistance. In Chicago outdoor relief is given only in kind, and no rents are paid, so that, even if regularly given, the relief consists only of baskets of groceries with occasional allowances of coal and of shoes for school children.

---

part of its parents, guardian, or any other person in whose care it may be, is an unfit place for such a child; and any child who while under the age of ten (10) years is found begging, peddling, or selling any articles or singing or playing any musical instrument for gain upon the street, or giving any public entertainment or accompanies or is used in aid of any person so doing." [Ill. Rev. Stat., ch. 23, sec. 169.]

[5] During the year 1917 the constitutionality of making payments out of public funds for the support of these children in sectarian institutions was raised (See Dunn v. Chicago Industrial School for Girls, 280 Illinois, 613) in view of the constitutional prohibition (article 8) of payments "from any public fund whatever * * * to help support * * * any school * * * controlled by any church or sectarian denomination whatever, * * *" The court held that since the payment made, $15 a month, was less than the alleged cost of the child's support, and less than the cost of children committed to the State training schools, it was not in aid of the institution and, therefore, did not violate the constitutional provision.

Private charitable associations existed, of course, to prevent the breaking up of such families and to mitigate, as it were, the harshness of the law. To many people it seemed anomalous that the law should refuse to pay for the support of the children so long as they remained with the mother, who was their natural guardian, when it stood ready to provide for them as soon as their natural guardian gave them over to the unnatural guardianship of an institution.

The largest private relief society in Chicago spent $298,463 the year before the mothers' pension law was passed and cared for 12,324 families, including families of widows. Those responsible for the administration of this society believed that it was never necessary to break up families solely because of poverty and that if a family was referred to this society provision would be made for keeping parents and children together.

Whether or not before the passage of the mothers' pension law families were broken up because of poverty alone is a controverted question with which we are not now concerned. This study deals only with the administration of the pension law; and a discussion of controversial questions relating to conditions existing before the passage of the law, and, in particular, questions relating to the competency of private relief agencies, need not be undertaken here. Whether or not the advocates of mothers' pensions rested their claims on sound or unsound principles, they were successful in obtaining the legislation for which they asked. It is, therefore, important now to study the effects of the law rather than the reasons for its enactment.

The mothers' pension controversy is perhaps too recent to be dispassionately reviewed. The position has been taken that this new policy was an unwise one in view of the disorganized condition of the administration of outdoor relief in our American States. Many persons, especially the representatives of charitable organizations, have maintained that the wiser policy is to avoid extensions of outdoor relief and to leave the maintenance of the widowed mother and her children to private charitable societies. No attempt will be made here to discuss the merits of any of the arguments for or against the mothers' pension policy. The present inquiry has been carried on solely with the purpose of ascertaining the facts regarding the administration of the oldest of the pension laws. Any social policy can be best tested in practice. This investigation was undertaken in order to test the mothers' pension policy in operation—to find out how the children for whom the law has attempted to provide are actually being cared for in Illinois.[6]

---

[6] A few facts should perhaps be given as to the history of the enactment of the funds-to-parents act. This Illinois law was passed without any preliminary report by an investigating commission. It was passed without any opposition, or at any rate without any

THE FUNDS-TO-PARENTS ACT OF 1911.

The Illinois statute of 1911 was the first of the so-called mothers' pension laws in the United States. Its administration was placed with the judges of the juvenile courts throughout the State because it was primarily a juvenile-court device for caring for dependent children for whom the only State funds available under the old law were funds for institutional support.

The original Illinois statute of 1911 was not called a mothers' pension law but a funds-to-parents law. It was a very loosely drawn statute and consisted of a single brief paragraph, the exact terms of which are as follows:

If the parent or parents of such dependent or neglected child are poor and unable to properly care for the said child, but are otherwise proper guardians, and it is for the welfare of such child to remain at home, the court may enter an order finding such facts and fixing the amount of money necessary to enable the parent or parents to properly care for such child, and thereupon it shall be the duty of the county board, through its county agent or otherwise, to pay such parent or parents, at such times as said order may designate, the amount so specified for the care of such dependent or neglected child until the further order of the court.

It will be noticed that this law vested very wide discretion in the court. It provided for the granting of allowances or pensions to fathers as well as to mothers, and to mothers who were not widows.

---

formal opposition, on the part of the private charitable agencies. The relation of the court to the passage of the law is an interesting question. It has always been the policy of the court to keep families together whenever this was possible without injury to the child. The presiding judge, at the National Conference of Charities and Correction, 1912, made the following statement regarding this policy: " During my term of service in the juvenile court my chief endeavor has been to keep the home intact and when this was impossible through the death of the mother, or through her conceded unfitness, I have sought to substitute another family fireside and the maternal love and care of some good woman." That is, the court stood for the principle that every child has a natural and moral right to home care, and that such care should, if possible, be in his own home.

Poverty presented itself to the court in divers forms, but how often poverty appeared alone as the occasion for separating children from their parents can not be definitely stated. The report of the chief probation officer for the year preceding the enactment of the law contained a plea for some provision that would do away with the necessity of separating children from parents simply on the ground of poverty. (Cook County Charity Service Report, 1910–11, p. 143.) However, no figures are given showing the number of children committed to institutions on the ground of poverty alone.

The funds-to-parents act, which was designed to work a radical change in the method of caring for dependent children, was passed with very little publicity. The approval of the presiding judge of the Chicago juvenile court is said to have been obtained, and he is said to have examined and indorsed the law as passed; but neither he nor the chief probation officer appeared before the legislature on its behalf.

In the juvenile court report of the succeeding year the following brief statement is the only reference to it:

" Mention was made last year as to the need for a law to prevent separation of children of dependent parents where such parents were worthy. A law known as the funds-to-parents act was passed, taking effect July 1, 1911. As no appropriation was made until October, little can be said as to the workings of the law, but we are sure that it is a step in the right direction and will mean much to the families concerned." (Cook County Charity Service Report, 1912, p. 155.)

No qualifications were prescribed for the parents except that they should be proper guardians for the children. Alien and nonresident parents, property owners, and deserted wives were all eligible at this time. For any parents who were, in the words of the statute, " poor and unable to properly care for their children," the court might enter an order finding such facts and fixing the amount of money necessary for the child's care. The amount of the pension was left wholly to the discretion of the judge without any maximum allowance being fixed.

Nothing was said in the act about the ages of children who might become beneficiaries; the definitions of dependent and neglected children in the earlier juvenile-court statute included boys under 17 and girls under 18 years of age. In Chicago, however, in awarding grants to families, notice was taken of the fact that children may lawfully leave school and go to work after the fourteenth birthday and that the great mass of the poor avail themselves of their children's labor after they have reached that age. The presiding judge of the juvenile court of Cook County (Chicago) therefore decided that, except in the case of especially handicapped children, such as those seriously undernourished or undeveloped, or actually crippled, grants would not be made for the support of children over 14 years of age.

This decision was in fact only one of a number of steps taken by the juvenile court of Cook County to supply for its own applicants certain definite tests of eligibility that should have been prescribed in the law. From the beginning, the Chicago court placed certain definite limitations upon its own pension policy, which made the law in practice a very much better piece of social legislation than it appeared to be on the statute book. Thus, although the law permitted the granting of funds without any limitations to almost any parent, the judge of the juvenile court of Cook County, with the advice of a citizens' committee representing the most important social agencies,[7] laid down the following definite rules providing extralegal qualifications for eligibility: (1) No funds shall be granted to any family with relatives able to support them and liable for support; (2) no funds shall be granted to a family who have not resided in the county at least one year; (3) no funds shall be granted to a deserted woman unless her husband has been absent at least two years; (4) no funds

---

[7] This committee was organized by the judge of the juvenile court shortly after the enactment of the law to share with him the responsibility for framing a policy for the administration of this law which gave him such wide discretionary powers. Four experienced relief workers were provided by this committee to assist the court in establishing the funds-to-parents department. They first investigated applicants for pensions with the probation officers. Later the officers did the investigating and the social workers furnished by the committee directed and supervised the work. This extralegal committee continued until April, 1913, when the department organization had reached a point which made outside help no longer necessary.

shall be granted to families (*a*) unless the mother is physically, mentally, and morally fit to care for children, (*b*) unless the children are with the mother, (*c*) unless funds are necessary to save the children from neglect; (5) no funds shall be granted to women with property; (6) funds shall be discontinued for children when they reach the age of 14 years, unless they are chronically ill and unable to work.

Funds were granted to women with incapacitated husbands, and there appears to have been at least one case of a grant to a woman with a husband in the house of correction. A maximum allowance per child was also fixed by the court as a part of its pension policy. Until November, 1912, the maximum granted was $10 a month; after November, 1912, it became $15 for girls and $10 for boys—the sums which the county was authorized to pay for the maintenance of a girl or a boy in an institution. The maximum pension granted for any one family was fixed in general at $40, but certain exceptions were allowed.

THE AID-TO-MOTHERS ACT OF 1913.

The statute of 1911 giving to the 102 judges of the 102 juvenile courts of Illinois the power to grant pensions of any size to any needy parent who was a proper guardian, was obviously a hasty piece of legislation; and in 1913, at the next session of the legislature, the law was radically altered. For the brief paragraph that had formed an amendment to section 7 of the juvenile-court law and had vested in the juvenile-court judges such excessive powers, an elaborate statute was substituted, which was quite separate from the juvenile-court law but which left the administration of the funds-to-parents act in the hands of the juvenile-court judges. It limited the authority of the courts very definitely, however. In the first place the new law was called an aid-to-mothers law; fathers could no longer receive grants. Deserted and divorced wives, alien women, and women property owners were rendered ineligible. The only married women provided for were women whose husbands had been permanently incapacitated for work by reason of physical or mental infirmity. Residence in the county for three years as well as citizenship was required. That is, the law practically restricted the pension grants to destitute widowed mothers who had children under 14 years of age and who could prove citizenship and a residence in the county for a period of three years.

An important addition to the law at this time was the provision that the court might condition the allowance given to a family in which there was an incapacitated wage earner on the removal of the husband and father from home in case he " is permanently incapaci-

INTRODUCTION. 13

tated for work by reason of physical or mental infirmity and his presence in the family is a menace to the physical and moral welfare of the mother or children." A special tax of not more than three-tenths of a mill on the dollar to be known as the mothers' pension fund was provided for in the law of 1913. The new statute also fixed the maximum allowance, or pension, at $15 a month for one child and $10 for each additional child, with the further provision that the total pension grant could not exceed $50 a month to any family.[8] Moreover, the conditions under which pensions might be granted were carefully prescribed under the new statute as follows:

Such relief shall be granted by the court only upon the following conditions: (1) The child or children for whose benefit the relief is granted must be living with the mother of such child or children; (2) the court must find that it is for the welfare of such child or children to remain at home with the mother; (3) the relief shall be granted only when in the absence of such relief the mother would be required to work regularly away from her home and children and when by means of such relief she will be able to remain at home with her children, except that she may be absent for work a definite number of days each week to be specified in the court's order, when such work can be done by her without the sacrifice of health or the neglect of home and children; (4) such mother must, in the judgment of the court, be a proper person, physically, mentally, and morally fit, to bring up her children; (5) the relief granted shall, in the judgment of the court, be necessary to save the child or children from neglect; (6) a mother shall not receive such relief who is the owner of real property or personal property other than household goods; (7) a mother shall not receive such relief who is not a citizen of this country and who has not resided in the county where the application is made at least three years next before making such application; (8) a mother shall not receive such relief if her child or children have relatives of sufficient ability to support them.

The new provisions for eligibility made necessary the withdrawal of a large number of pension grants in counties where the provisions of the law were really enforced. In Chicago there were on the pension list for June, 1913, 532 families with 1,753 children. For the month of July, 1913, only 332 families with 1,075 children remained on the pension list, and the expenditure for pensions fell from $13,418.45 in June, 1913, to $8,231.72 in July, 1913. Between July 1 and November 30, 1913, 263 families, in which there were 895 children,

---

[8] Laws of Illinois, 1913, p. 127. In providing the $15 and $10 grants, the new statute followed the practice of the Chicago court. The presiding judge in Chicago had always felt limited by the provisions of the industrial school and manual training school acts as to the amount he could grant; that is, he felt that he could not allow more to a child at home than the amount which the statute allowed for support in an institution. There seems to have been formulated in the Chicago court in December, 1913, a rule that the total income of a family could not exceed $50 plus one-fourth of the earnings of the children of working age; that is, a working child was counted in the budget only for food, and it was decided that he should turn in three-fourths of his wages to the family income, and that the other one-fourth should be his own. In determining income it was ruled that only three-fourths of the wages of a working child in the family should be counted as part of the family income. The total income therefore might be $50 in addition to one-fourth of the earnings of children of working age.

had their pensions stayed; and although some of these pensioners would have been dropped even if the law had not been changed, the court records show that the names of 696 children, or 79 per cent of the whole number dropped during this period, were taken from the roll because their mothers became ineligible under the new law. The largest number (567) were dropped because they were the children of unnaturalized aliens, 103 because their mothers were deserted women, 16 because they had not been residents in the county for the required period of three years, 7 were the children of divorced parents, and 3 had a father in the house of correction. A point of interest that should not be overlooked is the promptness with which these families were removed from the pension lists. That this change would mean suffering and hardship to these families was inevitable. Those that had been under the care of the private relief agencies before they were granted pensions by the court were, of course, referred back to those societies. A special study has been made of the subsequent history of some of these families in order to determine, if possible, the effect of the court removal order and the value of the pension as a means of safeguarding the welfare of children.[9]

THE AID-TO-MOTHERS LAW AS AMENDED IN 1915 AND IN 1917.

Some minor changes were made in the law of 1913 by the amendments of 1915 and 1917. The law was changed in 1915 [10] because it was found in practice that the amendments of 1913 were unnecessarily rigid with regard to citizenship. The law of 1915 made alien women eligible for pensions when they were the mothers of American-born children under 14 years of age and when they had made formal application for their first citizenship papers, provided, of course, that they could meet the other conditions laid down for eligibility. In 1917, however, the conditions of eligibility were again altered so that only widows of men residing in Illinois at the time of death, or wives of men who became incapacitated while residents of the State could receive grants.

It is of interest that the act of 1915 as introduced in the legislature, also proposed to make deserted women whose husbands had been away two years or more and women whose interest in real property was worth no more than $1,000 eligible for pension grants. These provisions were, however, defeated through the influence of the Chicago court.

The law as passed raised the maximum allowance or pension that could be given to any one family to $60 a month, making possible a

---

[9] See pp. 95 et seq.
[10] Laws of Illinois, 1915, p. 243.

more adequate allowance for large families, and the second proposal was embodied in the legislature of 1917.[11]

Although the law has been made more liberal by its inclusion of alien mothers, there must remain, of course, other cases of real difficulty and hardship not remedied by the law; such is, for example, the case of the wife of an insane alien. Even if the husband has taken out his first papers, the wife is held ineligible for a pension, though neither he nor she can take out second papers, for the United States naturalization law makes no provisions for the naturalization of the wife of an insane alien. Such a woman can become a citizen only if the husband has taken out his first papers while sane and if she later makes "a homestead entry under the land laws of the United States."

Although the aid-to-mothers law has, since 1913, prescribed definite, and even rigid, tests of eligibility, the Chicago court has found it necessary to add further restrictions. Attention was called to the fact that under the loosely-drawn law of 1911 the Chicago court found it necessary to adopt the policy of refusing to pension certain classes of women who would have been eligible under the law. At the present time the Chicago court follows the policy of excluding certain classes of applicants by means of adopting a set of exact definitions for the somewhat indefinite terms used in the law. These rules of administration that are now being followed in the Chicago court include the following:

A man is not considered "permanently incapacitated for work" unless he is totally incapacitated for any work; but if a doctor's statement shows that a man will be unable to work for six months, he is held to be "permanently incapacitated for work."

The possession of more than $50 in money will make a family ineligible on the ground that they have property, but $50 in cash does not make a family ineligible on this ground.

A woman with only one dependent child will not be given a pension unless she is unable to do normally hard work.

A woman who is not a citizen of the United States must have her own "first papers" to get a pension for her American-born children. Her husband's declaration of intention will not render her eligible. That is, a pension will not be granted to an alien widow who has not taken out her "first papers."

A woman who has had an illegitimate child was for a time, considered "morally unfit" for a pension and could receive none even for her legitimate children. Recently this ruling has been changed by the presiding judge, and pensions have been granted to such families for the legitimate children only.

On the other hand, certain provisions in the law are liberally interpreted. Thus, a woman who has been deserted for seven years is held to be eligible on the ground that her husband may be declared legally dead and that she is, therefore, legally a widow and eligible for a pension.

---

[11] Laws of Illinois, 1917, p. 220, secs. 2, 11.

The provision requiring a residence in the county of "at least three years next before making such application" has been liberally interpreted. That is, legal not actual residence is required, and families have been given pensions who had been out of the county for five years preceding their application, in case they could establish the fact that it was their intention to return.

In 1913 the court decided to uphold the county agent in his contention that the total family income should not exceed $50 a month, the maximum pension then allowed by law. Pensions were not granted, therefore, to families having an independent income of $50; nor were pensions granted so as to bring the total income above this figure.[12]

At the close of the first year of the administration of the old funds-to-parents law, in June, 1912, there were 327 families with 1,122 pensioned children on the pension roll of the juvenile court of Cook County, representing a monthly expenditure of $6,963.96 for pensions. In November, 1919, the last month for which the record is available, there were 851 families on the roll with the expenditure of $28,166.65 for that month.

While the number of families and children pensioned has varied with the changes in the law, these figures show that the law has been used extensively in Chicago ever since its passage. In this court the presiding judge and the chief probation officer have been deeply interested in devising methods of administering the law that should promote the well-being of the families for whose benefit it was designed, and should safeguard the interests of the community, which would, of course, have been seriously endangered if the law had been wastefully or unintelligently used or had been allowed to serve partisan or political ends.

The interest in the law and the methods of administering the law in the 101 other counties in Illinois have differed greatly both from Cook County and from each other. It has seemed best, therefore, to present first a study of the administration of the law in the juvenile court of Cook County (Chicago), and then an entirely separate study of the work of the "*down-State*" courts. The Chicago study contains, first, an account of the present methods of administration, which is descriptive rather than statistical. This is followed by a study of the families who were on the pension list at any time during the year 1917. Facts that are not published in the court reports but which are essential in attempting to understand the law in its administration are given in this part.

The Chicago section contains also the results of a study of the later history of 172 families dropped from the pension roll in July,

---
[12] See footnote, p. 13.

1913, because of the change in the law that made alien women ineligible. This study was undertaken in the belief that the situation in which these pensioners found themselves when they became technically ineligible through no fault of their own would throw some light upon the question of the value of this legislation to the beneficiaries. No visits were made to the homes of widows pensioned except for this section. In the case of the women on the pension roll of the Chicago court, the case records of the court and of the charitable agencies to whom so many of the women were known, gave so complete and so accurate a picture of the family life that it seemed an unnecessary intrusion to send investigators to disturb their privacy. It was necessary to make visits to the homes of the pensioned families in the other counties of the State because the records were everywhere so incomplete and unsatisfactory. The material used in the " down-State " part of the study is, however, described later in this report.[13]

[13] See pp. 125–126.

PART I.—THE ADMINISTRATION OF THE AID-TO-MOTHERS LAW IN THE COOK COUNTY (CHICAGO) JUVENILE COURT.

METHODS OF MAKING PENSION GRANTS.

PRELIMINARY INVESTIGATIONS.

After a mother has filed an application for a pension the application is referred to the probation officer in the aid-to-mothers department, who has charge of the investigations for the district in which the applicant lives. The investigation, which must be very carefully made in order to establish technical eligibility, follows the standardized methods pursued by good private case-work agencies everywhere. The case-paper system is used, and a careful record is made of every step taken in the investigation; the same case paper serves, of course, for the later record for those families to whom pensions are granted and who remain, therefore, under the supervisory care of the court.

The first step in the investigation is to clear the name of the family in the confidential exchange, which is known in Chicago as the social service registration bureau. In this bureau all the standardized social agencies in Chicago, both public and private, register the names of the families or individuals with whom or for whom they have been working. It is, therefore, a preliminary inquiry to learn what agencies are already acquainted with the applicant. If the family is found to be already on the books of other social agencies, those agencies are asked to submit a written report summarizing their knowledge of the family before a court officer undertakes any further investigation. The officer may or may not visit the agencies later to consult their records.

This work of clearing with the social agencies by the officer to whom the applicant is assigned is followed by visits to the applicant's home, to relatives, and to other persons to whom the family may be known. When relatives are found able to help and liable for the support of the applicant under the pauper act, they are visited and asked to contribute. If they refuse, the applicant is asked if she is willing to have the relatives who are legally liable for her support prosecuted in the county court. If she refuses, her application for a pension is dismissed and she is left to her own resources. If she is willing that a prosecution should be undertaken, the information that has been obtained is sent to the division of nonsupport of the bureau of social service of Cook County. If a contribution is obtained either by the voluntary action of the relatives or as a result of the prosecution, the court will consider the necessity of making an allowance to supplement what the relatives give; or if the county court, after hearing the evidence, refuses to hold the relatives, the juvenile court again takes up the question of granting the pension. Relatives who are not liable under the pauper act are also asked to help, and if the relatives do not live in Cook County and can not be visited by the officer, letters are written asking them to contribute to the support of the family.

It is now an established part of the routine of the investigation to verify from documents or public records the following facts: The marriage of the parents, the dates of birth of the children, the death of the father, the date of his naturalization or application for first citizenship papers if the process of naturalization had not been completed at the time of his death. If the applicant is a widow whose husband was not naturalized, she must show her own first papers also, since the taking out of first papers by the husband does not, like his naturalization, affect his wife's status. If the husband is living but is permanently incapacitated, a doctor's certificate is required showing that such incapacity exists.

If the desired information can not be obtained from official records, other sources of information are consulted, such as the records of churches, benefit societies, trade-unions, insurance companies, employers, schools, and other institutions with which the family has come in contact.

Verification of all facts relating to the receipt of insurance money and its expenditure is required. If the applicant refuses to make a reasonably exact accounting as to the expenditure of the insurance money, the investigation halts until such an accounting is furnished. Many of the women feel that it is a great hardship to be obliged to tell a public officer how they have spent their money, and they complain that asking for such an accounting is a needless prying into their private affairs. It is not easy for any one who has spent money foolishly to tell about it, and it must be very hard to give an account of unwise expenditures to be presented to an official committee. To the court, however, such an accounting seems necessary, not only because the court must determine whether or not the woman possesses property that would render her ineligible for a pension, but also because the committee must form a judgment concerning her ability to spend money wisely. If the woman is obdurate, however, and to the end refuses any statement, the final decision of the court will not necessarily be adverse, but will be determined by all the circumstances of the particular case. If there is no money left and if there has been no attempt to deceive the court, a pension will not be withheld solely because an accounting is impossible or because the insurance money is shown to be have been unwisely spent. For example, an applicant, who was very indignant when questioned about her expenditures, persisted in defiantly refusing to account for the spending of the $595 that she had received as insurance at the death of her husband in August, 1914. It was finally learned that she had gone to Portland, Oreg., with her mother and her children in October, 1914, and that she had spent, according to her own statement, $108 for railroad fare. Later she told the officer that she had paid $185 freight charges on her piano and the other furniture that she had shipped out and back. These sums added to the $131 paid to the undertaker, the only payment that could be verified by the court officer, brought up the bill of expenditure to $424, leaving finally $171 entirely unaccounted for. The investigation halted in this case for a long time; but ultimately, so important did it seem that the home should be maintained for the three small boys of the widow, a pension was granted. The rule as to accounting for the insurance money was waived. This, however, is rarely done, for very seldom does a woman so resolutely persist in her refusal to furnish a statement of her expenditures. In general statements can be verified, and it is the policy of the court to verify them. To put it briefly, the investigation required by the court follows, in general, the methods common to any good relief agency. The court investigation, however, is much more rigorous as to the verification of certain facts than is any relief agency in Chicago.

A thorough investigation, such as the court requires, necessarily takes a good deal of time. During this period the court gives no emergency relief, and the family is left to its own resources or to the assistance of charitable agencies. If the family needs appear to be very pressing a letter may be given to the mother introducing her to the county agent or to the united charities, and the mother is always told by the interviewer that relief can be obtained from these sources while the investigation is pending.

Table I shows the length of time required for the investigation of the 778 applications of the families on the pension role in January, 1917.

TABLE I.—*Length of time required to investigate eligibility of families on pension roll, January, 1917.*

Time required for investigation of eligibility.	Families on pension roll.	
	Number.	Per cent distribution.
Total	778	100.0
Less than 2 months	121	15.6
Less than 1 month	16	2.1
1 month, but less than 2	105	13.5
2 months and over	655	84.2
2 months, but less than 3	270	34.7
3 months, but less than 4	201	25.8
4 months, but less than 6	113	14.5
6 months, but less than 1 year	61	7.8
1 year or over	10	1.3
Time not reported	2	0.3

These 778 applicants included all those families who were under the care of the court at the beginning of the year 1917. As regards the time required for investigation, they may be considered a "random sample" of those who finally are given pensions. The investigation may take a shorter period of time for the applicants who are refused pensions. This table shows that only 15.6 per cent of these applicants were granted pensions within two months of the time of application and that 84.2 per cent waited for periods varying from two months to one year or longer. To those familiar with relief problems this needs no explanation. The court must choose between making a thorough, which means a slow, investigation, and granting pensions after an incomplete investigation, with the danger of having to withdraw them later. That the court has done well to choose the former method will scarcely be questioned. Those who criticize private charitable agencies for "taking so much time to investigate" have learned that a public agency must follow the same methods if its work is to be well done.

During the investigation every effort is made to protect the family's self-respect. There appears to be no rule against visits to present neighbors, but, in general, the officers seem to understand that such inquiries may injure the applicant's reputation in the neighborhood; and they are undertaken only when no other way can be found of obtaining necessary information. This practice, however, varies with the different officers, some resorting to it more frequently than others. In discussing the subject with a pension officer, the following story was told: This officer, who was formerly on the united charities staff and was therefore experienced in relief work before she went to the court, said that she had rarely made visits to present neighbors in the course of an investigation or in supervising her families, but a recent experience had led her to think she was too careful about it. A pensioned mother, who seemed a most trustworthy woman, had been absent several times when the officer called. The officer did not suspect her of bad conduct, for the woman's sister lived with her and that seemed an adequate safeguard. The officer went to a neighbor merely to ask if she had any knowledge of where the woman was and when she would return. The officer was amazed to be told, " She keeps a man in there." Further inquiry proved the truth of the neighbor's statement. The pension was stayed, and the former pensioner married the man who had been living with her. The officer said she would not have thought of asking the neighbors if they knew anything against the woman's character; and yet in this case, had the inquiry at the neighbor's not been made, she did not know how the information could have been obtained, since there had been no reason to suspect the woman of misconduct.

THE CONFERENCE COMMITTEE.

When the work of investigation has been completed by the court officer, she submits a report to what is called the conference committee, which determines finally whether or not a pension grant will be recommended to the court. This committee consists of the chief probation officer, the head of the aid-to-mothers department, and the county agent, and meets regularly each Thursday morning. Before the report is submitted to the conference committee, however, another step is taken in those cases in which the investigation seems to have produced the facts necessary to establish eligibility. In such cases all information about the family is first submitted to the field supervisor, who is an expert dietitian,[a] and an estimated budget showing the income needed and the amount necessary to supplement the family's own resources is prepared by the supervisor and is submitted to the conference committee with the officer's report of the results of the investigation. The investigating officer appears before the committee in order to submit her report and to answer any questions that may arise during the conference.

INVESTIGATION BY THE COUNTY AGENT.

Unfortunately the investigation is not complete when the juvenile-court officer has established the family's eligibility to a pension. The county agent, through a representative of his office, makes an entirely

---

[a] As a result of changes in court organization, after the date of this study, a dietitian is no longer employed as field supervisor, but the budget method is continued by the use of The Chicago Standard Budget for Dependent Families, prepared by the committee on relief of the Chicago Council of Social Agencies. See Annual Report of the Juvenile Court and Juvenile Detention Home of Cook County, Illinois, for the Fiscal Year 1919, p. 8.

independent inquiry to establish the same facts. In Chicago the county agent is the official in charge of the granting of all public outdoor relief; and the pensions are, under the law, paid by this county officer upon the recommendation of the court. The county agent maintains, however, that he can not legally make payments to such persons as the court recommends except on the basis of an investigation made by his own office. This objectionable double investigation is a great hardship to the family and is a defect in present methods of administration. The county agent's investigation does not often reveal new data, but occasionally this does happen.

The procedure in the matter of awarding grants has come to be as follows: When the conference committee, after hearing reports from the investigators, decides to recommend the awarding of the grant, the name and address of the family are given to the county agent, who, through a member of his own staff, makes an independent investigation and comes to an independent decision. Should the county agent on the basis of his own investigator's report disagree with the conference committee's decision that a pension be awarded, the head of the aid-to-mothers department or the court officer who had charge of the investigation is notified, usually by telephone, that the county agent's office can not approve the committee's decision and is given the reasons for the failure to approve. The case may then be postponed pending further inquiries by the court investigator; or, if there is a difference of opinion merely, the case may go on to presentation in court. The county agent's investigator and the court investigator then present their opposing views to the judge, with whom, of course, the final decision rests.

If the conference committee decides against recommending a pension the case goes no further and the probation officer does not file the formal petition that would lead to a court hearing. The applicant may, however, get a lawyer or some other "reputable citizen" to file a petition for her, but this is very rarely done. The case would then be presented to the court and the judge might, of course, refuse to approve the conference committee's decision to dismiss the case. In practice, however, this has rarely happened.

COURT HEARINGS.

The last step before the granting of a pension is the court hearing and the decision of the judge of the juvenile court as to the mother's application. The head of the aid-to-mothers department and a representative of the county agent's office are present at the hearings which are held regularly on Thursday mornings. The chief probation officer is present only when a case is contested or when some especially difficult questions are involved. The probation officers who have made the investigations in the cases to be heard are also present. Occasionally a representative from the State's attorney's office cross-examines as to common-law marriage or presumption of death. The hearings are on the whole friendly and informal. The mother sits with a little child in her lap and with the other children standing about her while the case is presented. Usually the formal petition is filed and the case presented by the probation officer who has made the investigation, but the family may be represented by a lawyer. Few lawyers have any knowledge of the problems of social treatment, and, therefore, they frequently urge the claims of the applicant as they would urge the case of a client in an action at law. They often fail to appreciate the nature of the task which the judge is performing, which is, in fact, hardly a judicial function. The judge is patient with their persistent efforts and takes pains to explain to them the purpose of the law and the principles upon which it is administered.

In most cases the recommendations of the conference committee are accepted. If, however, the county agent's investigation has revealed new data, their consideration may lead the judge to reject or alter the recommendation made by the committee. When there is a difference of opinion between the county agent and the conference committee, such as opposite views of the mother's character and fitness to care for her children, alleged drinking habits, or similar questions about which direct evidence can not be obtained, the judge considers all the facts and makes the final decision.

After the formal order for the pension has been made, the judge notifies the mother that the probation officer is to supervise the spending of the public money thus allowed to the family. He also charges the mother to keep full and accurate accounts. The supervising officer is usually the probation officer who has conducted the investigation and who is, therefore, already known to the mother.

METHODS OF PAYING PENSION GRANTS.

One further difficulty in the treatment of the pensioned families has arisen from the connection with the county agent's office. The pensions are paid in the office of the county agent instead of in the homes of the beneficiaries. Because of lack of flexibility in the methods of the county agent's office the allowances were at first paid only once a month, although most of the women were in the habit of being paid from the earnings of workers who received their wages once a week or once a fortnight. Since January, 1916, however, payments have been made twice a month—on the 5th and 20th. For some time after the law went into effect the payments were all made down town in the office of the comptroller, in the county building.

Later, the payments were made at the general office of the county agent on the west side of the city. On this subject the citizens' committee [14] made the following recommendation before its final session on April 20, 1913:

> The present method of paying funds is deplorable. The women assemble at the county agent's office, await their turn in just the same way as applicants for county aid have always had to do. The result is gossip among the women and consequent dissatisfaction. Such a public distribution is demoralizing and destructive of self-respect among these people. * * * Moreover, children are being kept out of school to accompany mothers to the county agent's office on the day the funds are paid. * * * It seems to the committee entirely practicable that the payments should be semimonthly instead of monthly and in the homes by mailing a certified check. Failing this, establishing centers in neighborhood banks might solve some of the difficulties of payment.

In response to these recommendations, the judge ordered that the mothers be instructed not to keep their children out of school on such occasions. No change in the method of payment, however, has yet been introduced, beyond the change to semimonthly payments.[b] It is, however, possible for the woman who wishes to avoid the public distribution to go for her check in the afternoon instead of the morning of the day of payment. The women assemble in the morning in large numbers, but by afternoon very few are left. It is probably true that many of the women who receive pensions do not object to the congregate distribution. So limited are they in their social pleasures that they rather enjoy the excitement of the occasion and the opportunity for leisurely gossip. The superior woman has it in her own power to avoid much, at any rate, of the publicity by going for her check after the great mass of the women have left.

---

[14] See footnote p. 11 for an account of the work of this committee.

[b] No change had been made in the method of payment at the time that this report went to press (October, 1920).

THE PROBLEM OF SUPERVISION.

GENERAL POLICY.

The court follows the methods standardized by good private relief societies, not only in the investigation that precedes the pension grant but also in the care of the families after they are placed on the pension roll. Careful supervision of all pensioned families is the policy followed by the court, in order that the public money granted to these families may serve the purpose for which it is appropriated. The kind of supervision depends largely upon the number of families assigned to each officer and upon the training the officers have had for such work. At the time this study was made there were 16 officers in the pension division, so that with 740 families on the pension roll each officer supervised about 46 families. The officers in the pension division vary in training for relief work and in their individual abilities and resourcefulness. They are selected by a severe "merit test," many have had excellent training for relief work, and all are subject, it will be remembered, to the supervision not only of the chief probation officer but also to that of the special head of the aid-to-mothers department.

In order to collect some accurate data regarding the amount of supervision given to the pensioned families, the visits made by the supervising officers were tabulated from the case records of the 212 families who had been under care for a period of two years or longer. These data are as follows: Families visited monthly, 29; visited more frequently, 182; [15] visited irregularly, 1.

These figures show that according to the case records 211 out of the 212 families had been visited regularly once a month or oftener throughout a period of two years or longer, and that only one family had been visited irregularly. The vast majority of the families. 182 out of 212, had, as a matter of fact, been visited oftener than once a month. This is a good measure of supervision, when it is remembered that the families under care are very carefully selected. Only those mothers are placed on the pension roll who seem, after a searching

---

[15] The records showed that four families had not been visited for one period of more than one month, due probably to the officer's vacation; but with the exception of this one month the visits were made more frequently, and these four families seem to belong properly in the class in which they have been placed.

inquiry, to be women who can be trusted to make reasonably wise expenditures and to maintain fit homes for their children. It is obvious that the mere fact of visiting a family regularly does not necessarily mean that the officer made intelligent use of the information that she got as a result of the visit. Regularity of visits is, however, one essential in a system of adequate supervision, and it is clear that the families on the pension roll are given at least that measure of supervision.

In addition to the supervision of the regular probation officer the families are visited by the field supervisor also. The work of the field supervisor is a very important factor in maintaining the best possible care for the pensioned families. Under her direction methods have been worked out for improving the domestic skill of the pensioned mothers and for teaching them the household arts of cleaning, cooking, sewing, and skillful buying. The field supervisor discusses the home conditions of the families with the officers in charge and suggests methods of improving the standards of the homes. The probation officer is then supposed to see that these suggestions of the field supervisor are adopted by the family. The field supervisor also visits the families herself. The study of the records of the 212 families who had been under care for two years showed that the field supervisor had visited these families as follows: Visited once, 44 families; twice, 87 families; three times, 45 families; four times, 17 families; five times, 10 families; six times or more, 4 families; no visits, 1 family; no report, 4 families.

It is, of course, better to have a family remain under the supervision of the same probation officer during the whole of the time that the family is on the pension roll. The officers of the court are assigned to districts, and an officer is usually kept in the same district as long as she remains in the pension department. The officers in charge of pensioned families are changed, therefore, only when a new officer comes into the department, or when a family moves into a new district. During the first two years after the passage of the pension law, the aid-to-mothers department was not well organized, and there seem to have been more frequent changes in the officers supervising individual families. Table II presents such figures as are available for the 212 families who have been on the pension roll at least two years, relating to the number of families that have been under the care of more than one officer.

TABLE II.—*Number of probation officers caring for families on pension roll for two years and over, together with length of time families were under care of court.*

Number of probation officers giving care.	Families under care for specified period.									
	Total, 2 years and over.		2 years, but less than 2 years 6 months.	2 years 6 months, but less than 3 years.	3 years, but less than 3 years 6 months.	3 years 6 months, but less than 4 years.	4 years, but less than 4 years 6 months.	4 years 6 months, but less than 5 years.	5 years or over.
	Number.	Per cent distribution.							
Total	212	100.0	32	33	43	22	58	22	2
1 officer	29	13.7	9	13	5		2		
2 officers	38	17.9	8	6	14	6	4		
3 officers	53	25.0	12	7	9	6	11	8	
4 officers	31	14.6		5	8	4	11	3	
5 officers	31	14.6	2	2	3	4	12	7	1
6 officers	17	8.0			2	1	10	4	
7 or more officers	11	4.2	1		2	1	6		1
Not reported	2	1.0					2		

This table shows that only 13.7 per cent of these families had been continuously under the care of a single officer throughout the pension period. It must be remembered, however, that all these families had been under care for as long a period as two years. The table shows, moreover, that most of the families who had had several supervising officers had been under care for more than two years. In attempting to determine whether or not the families under the care of the court have suffered from being " passed on " from one officer to another the importance of a comparison with the methods of the private relief agencies in the same community should not be overlooked. There can be no doubt that the visitors in the private societies are changed much more frequently than are the court officers, and it would be very difficult to find families that had been regularly visited by a single officer or agent for as long a period as two years, although Table II shows that 29 of the families pensioned by the court had been cared for by a single officer during periods varying from two to four years.

The relationship established between the pensioned mother and the supervising probation officer is one of cooperation to the end that the best possible use may be made of the pension income. If there is any evidence of ill health or poor physical condition a medical examination is insisted upon. Free medical service is not uniformly furnished, but hospital care when needed is secured free of charge. The county agent in his capacity as supervisor of the poor refuses to allow the county doctors to visit the pensioned families, but free service is furnished to those able to attend clinics. The women are also examined free of charge at the county building by the woman physician on the city staff or by the county physician, who is an examining officer at the juvenile court. Medicines are paid for out of the family income; and when a physician visits the home, a doctor's fee is paid. Since free medical service is felt by many persons to be the least objectionable form of relief, the question has frequently been raised as to whether or not these families for whom the county is doing so much should be given free medical care by the "county doctors," who are furnished by the outdoor relief office for destitute families. Such a change must be approved by the county agent before it can be made, and no agreement on this point has been reached. In the estimated budget upon which the pension grant is based, an allowance of 50 cents for each member of the family is nominally made for "care of health"; but as a matter of fact this is not supposed to cover doctor's bills but merely such items as toothbrushes, soap, and occasional medicines or drugs.

Children in pensioned families are placed in the open-air schools and sent to convalescent homes when necessary. School attendance and school progress of the children are carefully watched. School reports giving grade, attendance, deportment, and scholarship are supposed to be obtained monthly and the information entered on the case record. The study of case records showed that this regulation seemed to be very carefully enforced. Reports are obtained directly from the school or by giving the children blanks which must be signed by the teacher. If the mother works outside the home the arrangements made for the care of the children during her absence are carefully scrutinized by the officer. Country outings each summer are arranged by the officers, not only for the children but also for the mothers of the pensioned families.

Living conditions are gradually improved. This is often a difficult problem. Most of the pensioned families have been living in extreme poverty during a long period of illness preceding the death of the husband and father, and sometimes for many months after his death. Decent standards of living have been gradually lowered and are not always easily restored.

Statistics throw little light on a subject such as the improvement in living conditions, but some data are available regarding the improvements in the housing of the pensioned families. A report submitted by the field supervisor to the conference committee in December, 1914, dealt with the care of 313 families who had been under care at least three months. Of these 313 families, 116, or more than one-third of the whole number, had been enabled or persuaded to move to new quarters on receiving the county allowance. Table III shows the reasons for moving in the case of this group of families.

TABLE III.—*Reasons of 116 families for moving.*

Reasons for moving.	Families moved.
All reasons	116
Moral surroundings bad	14
Rents too high	16
Families in furnished rooms	2
Housing conditions bad	84
Dark basement	19
Badly ventilated rooms	37
Low attic rooms	2
Damp rooms	3
Overcrowded quarters	13
Rooms in bad repair	10

Further evidence as to the improvement in housing conditions was furnished by the study of the 212 families who had been under care for two years or longer. Information was available for 210 of these families, showing that 96 had been moved at least once and 10 others two or more times in order to improve the home environment or housing conditions. Tables IV and V show for 195 families the number of rooms in relation to the number in the family at the time when the pension was granted and at the time when this investigation was made two years later.

TABLE IV.—*Number of rooms occupied by 195 families under care two years and over for which information could be secured both at the time of application and at the time of the study, together with the number of persons occupying them at the time of application for pension.*

Number of persons in family.	Families living in specified number of rooms at time of application for pension.							
	Total.	1	2	3	4	5	6	8
Total	195	2	16	33	102	22	19	1
2	1	1						
3	18		4	6	7	1		
4	37		5	9	19	2	2	
5	57	1	4	5	38	6	3	
6	40			8	22	5	5	
7	21		1	3	7	5	5	
8	10				5	2	3	
9	9		2	1	3	1	1	
10	2			1	1			1

TABLE V.—*Number of rooms occupied by 195 families under care two years and over for which information could be secured both at the time of application and at the time of the study, together with the number of persons occupying them two years or more after pension grant.*

Number of persons in family.	Families living in specified number of rooms two years or more after pension grant.							
	Total.	2	3	4	5	6	7	8
Total	195	9	20	114	29	19	2	2
3	18	3	4	9	2			
4	51	2	12	33	1	3		
5	60	4	1	46	8	1		
6	30		1	17	5	7		
7	19		2	5	9	2	1	
8	6			2		3		1
9	9			2	3	2	1	1
10	2				1	1		

These tables deal with a single aspect of housing conditions, the relation between the number of rooms and the number of persons occupying them. Comparing the two periods, it is clear that some progress has been made toward providing more adequate quarters for the families under care. At the time of their applications for pensions, 2 families—1 of them a family of 5—were living in 1-room apartments; and 16 families, including 1 family of 7 and 2 families of 9 persons, were living in 2-room apartments. Taking the numbers cumulatively, 51 families were living in apartments of 3 rooms or less. Table V shows that after these families had been on the pension roll for a period of 2 years or longer, the 1-room apartments had disappeared; 9 families instead of 16 and no families of more than 5 persons, were living in 2-room apartments. At the later period 29 families in contrast with 51 at the earlier period were in apartments of 3 rooms or less. Some further evidence of the improvement in housing accommodations is obtained by means of the heavy zigzag line in the two tables. All families with more than 1 person to a room fall below the heavy line. In the first table 144 families fall below the line and in the second, 125.

It is important to note, however, that housing standards as judged by the number of rooms occupied can not be very greatly improved by the small incomes of these pensioned families. The supervising officers have improved housing conditions most frequently by obtaining better apartments in less congested neighborhoods where more light and air can be had for the same money. That is, housing conditions have been improved by moving families out of basements, damp rooms, and dark rooms rather than by increasing the number of rooms. Some improvement, however, as Tables IV and V indicate, has been made in the number of rooms.

PART I.—ADMINISTRATION IN COOK COUNTY. 33

It must be emphasized, however, that the method or the value to the families of such supervisory work as is done by the court officers can not be measured by statistics. In an attempt to test satisfactorily work of this kind, the statistical method must necessarily be inadequate. Each family represents a complex situation unlike that of any other family, and the services rendered are too varied to be counted as identical units. The supervisory work can, of course, be best understood by a study of case records of individual families. A few of these case records have been summarized, and the summaries are given below to illustrate the supervisory work in different types of families.

SUMMARY OF THE RECORD OF THE A FAMILY.

The A family came to the attention of the court when the father had been dead about three years. He had been a woodworker, American born, earning about $48 a month, and at his death left $900 insurance. There were four children, ranging in age from 2 to 9 years. Both Mr. and Mrs. A had relatives in the city, but they were poor, had large families, and were unable to help much or regularly. After paying funeral expenses and debts, the mother managed to support her family for three years on the remainder of the insurance money and what she could earn at home sewing. She managed to keep the family together without charitable assistance but was doing it at the expense of her health, and the family was not being adequately fed. It was at this time, in January, 1913, that the municipal tuberculosis sanitarium referred the family to the court for a pension. The mother had been found to be tubercular, the three boys had tubercular glands, the children were all undernourished, and the physical condition of the whole family seemed to be going down very rapidly. The doctors said that Mrs. A ought not to work any longer. When this pension of $10 per child was granted she promised to "sew up" what she then had on hand and to stop work until her condition was improved. This $40 a month was the maximum pension that the court was willing to grant at that time; but, as it was not sufficient in view of the tubercular condition of four members of the family, the White Cross League was asked to contribute. It furnished special diet of milk and eggs for nine months. The condition of Mrs. A improved so much that at the end of this period she was able to earn about $7 a month without detriment to her health. In the meantime the family had been moved from four small rooms over a little grocery store to a new and more desirable flat where, in addition to four larger rooms, they acquired an attic, a garden, and a porch which could be used for a sleeping porch. The municipal tuberculosis sanitarium fitted this with blankets and bedding so that the mother and one child were able to sleep out.

During the three years since the family have been pensioned, the officers of the court have cooperated with the municipal tuberculosis sanitarium in restoring them to health. The two younger children were placed in an open-air school and sent to the country in summer. The mother has done her part faithfully, and she is now "paroled" by the sanitarium as a closed case. One child, however, failed to gain as he should, and in the summer of 1916 he was sent to a sanitarium, where he is now improving.

When William, the eldest boy, became 14, the court reduced the pension to $30 a month, as he had sufficiently recovered to be able to work. But the boy had entered high school and was very eager to finish his two-year business course. Since the court could not continue this pension, the probation officer applied for help to the scholarship committee of the vocational bureau. They arranged that he should remain at school and granted a scholarship fund of $14 a month, a contribution to the family's income equal to the amount the boy could have earned. This arrangement is now in its second year and William's progress at school has been very gratifying. In the summer he worked in a railroad office, and at present he is doing errands after school hours. He sometimes earns as much as $3 a week, since a bonus is paid for promptness, and William is both ready and eager. These earnings he faithfully turns over to the vocational bureau to repay them for his scholarship, because both he and his mother feel that no more should be accepted than is necessary to allow him to remain in school. Occasionally, however, the bureau returns some part of his earnings so that he may have some article of luxury such as a warm sweater, and William is always very grateful for what he calls a "present" from the bureau.

Thus this family which at the time the court took charge of it had four tubercular members has been able, because of a steady assured income and the friendly help of the probation officers in cooperation with other societies, to move to better quarters, to improve in health (only one member of the family is now tubercular), and to keep the oldest child in school until he has had a high-school business course. With all the aid the family has received, there is no evidence of any tendency to regard help as their rightful portion, but instead, a sturdy spirit of independence is still so much alive that the boy of 15 is voluntarily and cheerfully turning over his weekly earnings to help pay for his scholarship.

SUMMARY OF THE RECORD OF THE B FAMILY.

The father, who was American born, had been a teamster, earning $48 a month. The court's investigation brought out the fact that the family had previously been known to the Cook County agent, the visiting nurse association, the adult probation department of the municipal court, and to the united charities. The united charities record showed that the family had been first reported to them in November, 1904, when the father was ill and the children were begging from house to house; and again in 1908 this complaint was made about the children. The family at this time were living in a house owned by Mr. B's mother and were not paying rent. When the application for pension was made, however, the family were living in four rooms in a basement, described on the record as "filthy, damp, and dark." Mrs. B, a woman of 35 years, complained of ill health and looked frail, slovenly, and discouraged.

PART I.—ADMINISTRATION IN COOK COUNTY 35

The Teamsters' Union raised a purse of $100 for the family which just covered funeral expenses, as Mr. B had carried no insurance. During the investigation by the court, which lasted a month and a half, the family was dependent upon county supplies and the irregular help of relatives. At the end of this time a pension of $40 a month was granted. This seems to have constituted the family's only income until the two older girls were old enough to become wage earners.

For nearly three years Mrs. B was sick practically all the time. It was difficult to improve her housekeeping, which was very slatternly, and to get the children properly cared for.

In all there were eight probation officers on this case, but each one seems to have given herself to the problems in hand with energy and determination, and gradually the standards of living were raised, and the mother's health began to show a decided improvement. The family was moved from time to time to more desirable rooms. Medical treatment for Mrs. B was secured, and regular dispensary treatment was insisted upon. The diet and buying of the family was carefully supervised, and Mrs. B instructed in the art of keeping a clean home.

The pension for this family has been gradually reduced from $40 to only $24, as the children have become old enough to go to work. Both girls have good positions, one as a stenographer, and the other working for the telephone company. In another year one of the boys will be able to go to work.

In the words of the present probation officer: " This family will soon be self-supporting, has greatly improved in health and standard of living, will probably move into better quarters." This family illustrates the effect that constant, intelligent supervision may have upon the most careless housekeeping habits. The record shows a woman who, when the court began its work with the family, had a miserable home and neglected children, and whose own physical resistance was so low that the slightest ailment incapacitated her. Gradually she has become a woman who washes and scrubs her house, launders her curtains, paints the walls, keeps the children clean and fairly well dressed, and is herself practically discharged from the doctor's care.

SUMMARY OF RECORD OF THE C FAMILY.

In June, 1913, Mrs. C, a Polish woman, applied for a pension for her two children aged 8 and 5 years because she found it impossible to earn enough to support them. Her husband had died of heart disease in 1909, leaving some insurance; but the money had been used for paying funeral bills, debts, and living expenses. The family had been compelled to ask help from the county agent and the united charities a number of times during the four years following the death of the father. A stepson had gone to work at the age of 14, but Mrs. C found him so unmanageable that in 1911 she sent him to his uncle in Tennessee. Mrs. C had been earning only $10 a month by sweeping in a school.

The family budget was estimated at $34, and in October, 1913, the court granted a pension of $10 for each of the two children. With the mother's earnings of about $10 a month, the income of the family was brought up to within $4 of their estimated needs. It was found that the dust raised by sweeping in the school was very bad for the mother, as it caused her to cough so much that she could not sleep. Her work was changed to cleaning in a bank, where she earned $3 a week instead of $10 a month.

The probation officer found that Stephania, the older child, had never gone to school because she was extremely anemic and had very bad teeth. The officer had the mother go with both children, neither of whom were strong, to the municipal tuberculosis dispensary for examination, saw to it that the mother's teeth and eyes received attention, and watched the weights of the children. During the pension period the children had whooping cough, and in 1914 the doctor said that they were likely to become tubercular if they were not very well nourished. However, the fact that in 1916 all of the family were in good health indicated close attention by the officer to the health of the family as well as competent oversight by the mother. Both children are in school, their attendance is regular, and their scholarship and deportment good.

The officer has also secured gifts of clothing and food from the church and parochial school, given the family tickets to settlement parties, and interested Mrs. C in the mothers' club at the Northwestern University settlement. Continuous effort during the past two years has been made by the officer to secure from Mrs. C's mother and brother more generous help for the family. In this the officer has been very successful, since both relatives continued to increase the aid given to the family.

The mother provides a good variety of food and has learned to do her buying in large amounts. The home is reported as being always spotless, the children are well cared for, and a recent comment of the officer is, " Family very happy and comfortable; children exceptionally attractive."

SUMMARY OF THE RECORD OF THE D FAMILY.

A Polish laborer named Henry D lost his life in September, 1911, by falling from a building which was under construction. He had been earning only $40 a month and had a wife and six children to support, but his widow received $1,000 compensation. Two hundred dollars was spent on the funeral, $100 was paid to the doctor, and $50 went toward repaying a loan. Two months after the father's death twin babies were born, who soon died. Their burial cost $50 more. The expenses of the mother's illness and the living expenses for the family of seven soon exhausted the insurance money.

Mrs. D endeavored to carry the family and earned $1 a day at some work given her by the church, on whose building her husband had been killed. Her ability to work was seriously impaired because her hands had been badly crippled since childhood. She managed, however, to do the work, to give her children good care, and to keep her house very clean. In January, 1913, Mrs. D applied for pension, and received her first payment the following May. During that period the united charities paid the rent. The amount granted by the court was $6 a month for each of the six children, the eldest of whom was 12 years and subnormal.

In the D family the standard of living had always been very low and the children were thin and undernourished. When they were examined at the municipal tuberculosis sanitarium it was found that Walter had tubercular glands, three of the others had enlarged tonsils, and Frank, the eldest, had a goiter. The probation officer, therefore, made it her business to watch carefully over the health of the family. After obtaining the mother's consent she had the adenoids removed from two of the children, had the children weighed, and sent them on vacations.

At school Frank was placed in a room for subnormals and made a fine record in basketry, rug making, and manual training. In May, 1916, he was earning $8 a week in a glove factory, and he will probably be able to support himself. A butcher in the neighborhood had accused Frank of being the leader of a gang, and in June, 1916, the case came up in the police court. The complaint was apparently groundless, and the matter was cleared up by the probation officer. The supervisor records: "The subnormal boy, Frank, is holding his position surprisingly well."

Under the care of the court, Mrs. D has learned some English, and although the general capacity of the family is not high, there is no doubt that their standard has been improved. They have at least made an effort to meet requirements. The dietitian has brought about a change in the kinds of food used, although the officer is still working for further improvement here. The dietitian reports: "The income has been at least $10 below the estimated minimum budget since the family has been under the care of the department. Clothing and other help has been received from the church. The children have been found getting coal from the railroad tracks, and the food has always been unsatisfactory."

SUMMARY OF THE RECORD OF THE E FAMILY.

On June 30, 1913, Mr. E died of appendicitis, and promptly on the next day Mrs. E applied for a pension. She received insurance money to the amount of $204, but it was spent on funeral bills, clothes, old debts, and living expenses. There were four children—Charles, aged 6; Henry, 3; John, 2 years; and Anna, 8 months. The father was an American of German descent and the mother was Italian.

At the time of application the family had been living rent free in an attic apartment, in which the ceilings were very low and the bedrooms contained only one window. The house was reported by the probation officer as the dirtiest place she had ever seen. Pending the court's decision on the pension application, the family lived on the remains of the insurance money, the aid of neighbors and relatives, and the ingenuity of the mother, who raffled a quilt, thereby gaining $41.

The necessary budget was estimated at $37.15 a month, and the court awarded a pension of $8 for each of the four children, although the relatives of Mr. E tried to have the children placed in an institution, on the ground that the mother was unfit to care properly for their physical wants. They acknowledged that her character was good but alleged that her house was dirty, as it evidently was. Since the grant the family has lived on the pension, supplemented by occasional gifts of vegetables sent from the farm by Mrs. E's mother and small sums earned at various times by Mrs. E herself.

The family has had little sickness during the pension period, and at present appears to be in good health. The children's school attendance is fair. Mrs. E's housekeeping has improved under supervision, although the children are not yet very neatly kept. The probation officer has suggested changes in diet and insisted on having the house painted inside. At the suggestion of the probation officer, cow's milk was substituted for condensed milk for the baby, clean pans were used for cooking, and the woman learned to buy fresh milk and fruit. Mrs. E has willingly followed advice, but she is undoubtedly subnormal, and is not naturally a good housekeeper. Her mother, a very efficient old lady, frequently has the family spend vacations at her farm, cleans house for her daughter, plans her buying, and helps her as much as Mrs. E's stepfather will allow. Mrs. E's mother showed much more zeal in doing for the family when, with the assistance of the court pension and the cooperation of the probation officer, it seemed possible to maintain a decent standard of living.

SUMMARY OF THE RECORD OF THE F FAMILY.

The F family, at the time of application for a pension, consisted of the mother, aged 31, and three children: Samuel, aged 12; James, 7; and John, 5. The father, who had been a laborer and a hard drinker, had died about four years earlier, leaving insurance which amounted to only $208.40 and which was all used for the payment of hospital and funeral bills. Since his death, Mrs. F had been working as a school janitress, earning from $25 to $30 a month. In November, 1913, when she applied for a pension, she was living with her sister and parents, and her character and thrifty habits were recognized by the family physician and the principal of the school at which she worked. The municipal tuberculosis sanitarium reported that Mrs. F had been examined in October, 1913, and found not to be tubercular, and that although she would be benefited by a rest, she was able to work out.

Besides what she earned, Mrs. F was receiving some aid from a brother, and supplies from the county agent. At times the teachers also helped her a little. After the application for a pension had been made, the dietitian estimated the family budget at $38.50 a month. It was thought that the woman ought to do less work but that her earnings ought to be about $12 a month. In January, 1914, a pension of $8 for each child was granted by the court, and Mrs. F moved out of her sister's home to establish a home of her own.

After the granting of the pension, a brother-in-law, who had quarreled with his wife, came to live in the home of Mrs. F, and, owing to some rumors of drinking and immorality, the conference committee of the court recommended in June, 1914, that her pension be "stayed" and the children sent to an institution for dependent children. The situation was, however, satisfactorily changed by removal to a new neighborhood and the exclusion of the brother-in-law from the home. The probation officer persuaded Mrs. F to sign the pledge, and there seems to have been no further trouble.

One immediate effect of the supervision by the court officer was a marked improvement in the children's school records, which were rather poor when the pension was first granted. The field supervisor gave advice and instructions as to diet and other items of household economy, which seem to have been faithfully followed. At present the mother is happy, takes good care of her children, is very intelligent in her buying, in which she cooperates with several women in the neighborhood, and will soon join a woman's club in her district. Samuel, whose pension was stayed when he became 14, is bright and ambitious. He works as an office boy, earning $6 a week. Arrangements were made for him to attend night school, where he is very much interested in manual training, and devotes a good deal of attention to the furnishings of the household.

Medical aid was secured for Mrs. F, and although there has been illness in the family since the pension was granted, at present all members of the family are apparently in good health. The children's school records have been carefully watched, the diet has greatly improved in variety, and the family's entire standard of living is steadily improving.

PENSION "STAYS" OR WITHDRAWALS OF PENSION GRANTS.

The standard of supervision maintained demands the withdrawal of the pension grants whenever a change in family circumstances has occurred that makes a pension no longer necessary or its continuance undesirable for the good of the children. If the supervision of the pensioned family is adequate the court will be promptly informed of such changes in family circumstances or home conditions.

Table VI shows the number of pension grants "stayed," that is, withdrawn or canceled, during a period of 19 months, together with the reason for the stay and the length of time the family has been on the pension roll. During this period 543 families, including the "stayed cases," were under care.

TABLE VI.—*Reasons for stay of pension in 170 "stayed cases," together with length of time family had been on pension roll.*[a]

Reason for stay of pension.	Total.		Families whose pensions were stayed after receiving pensions for specified period.				
	Number	Per cent distribution.	Less than 3 months.	3 months but less than 6.	6 months but less than 1 year.	1 year but less than 2.	2 years and over.
All reasons	170	100.0	11	10	29	67	53
Pension no longer needed	106	62.4	4	6	18	40	38
Mother's failure	24	14.1	2	2	5	7	8
Family ineligible at time of pension grant	16	9.4	5		2	7	2
Reason ambiguous	24	14.1		2	4	13	5

[a] This table was prepared from material collected by officers of the Aid-to-Mothers Department for a survey of their own work. The period of time covered by the survey was Aug. 1, 1913, to Mar. 1, 1915.

The important questions to be asked concerning the families who are dropped from the pension lists may be summarized as follows: Were they dropped because they were no longer in need of assistance? Were they dropped because the homes failed to come up to the standards set by the court? Were they dropped because the pension had been granted on the basis of an inadequate investigation, and the court discovered facts that would have prevented the grant had those facts been known at the time of the grant? Unfortunately the reasons given in the records for the "stay" of funds are often expressed in a small number of set phrases that are frequently ambiguous. An attempt was made by a careful study of each record, to relate the reason for the stay to the work of the court and in this way to answer the questions suggested above. Further explanation of the reasons for stays given in the table is, therefore, possible. In the first class of families—those in which the reason given is "pension no longer needed"—are included 39 families who were said to be dropped because their income was "sufficient," 32 who "should be self-supporting," 12 who had money that they had received after the pension grant, 12 in which the mother remarried, 5 in which the mother died, 2 in which the mother withdrew voluntarily, and 4 in which the family had left the city. These 106 families, 62 per cent of the total number "stayed," were dropped from the pension roll because the family circumstances had changed; and the fact that this change of circumstances was known to the court and was acted upon by the court is evidence of the fact that the families were being carefully supervised.

In the second class of families, those removed from the pension roll because of some failure on the mother's part, are included the following: Six mothers who were untruthful, 7 who kept roomers, and 11 who were reported as having refused to cooperate. A total of 24, or 14 per cent of the whole number "stayed" were dropped because the mother failed to meet the standards of family care set by the court, and refused to cooperate with the supervising officer in maintaining a proper home or proper care for the children. The woman's refusal to cooperate means that she is unwilling to take those steps which in the judgment of the officer and of the conference committee are essential to the proper care of her children. She may refuse to move from an insanitary house or a demoralizing neighborhood, she may insist on keeping male boarders or lodgers, or the husband may be the victim of an infectious disease, dangerous to the members of his family, and may refuse to leave the home. The court may become convinced that not even with an allowance can the home be kept at that level for which the county is willing to be responsible.

In the third class are included those families whose pensions apparently were stayed because the woman was ineligible at the time the pension was granted. The following were placed in this class: Two mothers who were found to be aliens, four whose relatives were able to assist, three whose marriage could not be proved, two who could not prove the death of their husbands. In all these cases it is obvious that if the preliminary investigation had been adequate, the pension would never have been granted. Included in this group also are five women about whom more ambiguous phrases are used but who probably would not have been granted pensions if the preliminary investigation had been more searching. One had money, another was unfit morally, a third was physically unfit, and the other two had husbands who were not wholly incapacitated for work. In these five cases the pension was stopped before it had run three months, so that it is probably safe to say that there was an inadequate investigation in the first instance.

In the fourth class are included the families who could not be put in any of the foregoing classes because of inadequate information; that is, the reason given for the pension stay was recorded in an ambiguous phrase, "Has money," for instance, may mean that the family either had money undiscovered by the preliminary investigation or at a later date received money from some new source. "Man able to work" may mean that his health has improved, or it may mean a change in the standards of the department. "Mother unfit morally, mentally, or physically" may show deterioration on the part of the mother, it may mean failure to improve as expected under the care of the court, or it may mean an inadequate investigation to begin with. That is, families dropped because they should be self-supporting, because their income was sufficient, or because the mother remarried were dropped after the pension had done the work it was intended to do; while those who lost their funds because of no proof of death, no proof of marriage, etc., were only granted funds because of an inadequate preliminary investigation. But there are other phases used which tell us very much less. That a family is dropped because of an "illegitimate child" immediately raises the question of whether that child was born before the grant of pension or during the time the pension was being enjoyed.

The most important fact in the table is, of course, that 62 per cent of the stays were ordered because the circumstances in the families had changed, that only 14 per cent were dropped because the mother could not be brought up to a proper standard, and only 9 per cent because the family had been found to be ineligible. It is also important to note that of the families whose circumstances had changed, the majority—78 out of 106—had been pensioned for a year or longer.

Most of the mothers who did not come up to the standards required of them had also had pensions for a year or more. This may be interpreted either as showing the patience of the court in dealing with the families whose care it assumes; or it may be taken as an indication of the rising standard set by the court and the gradual weeding out of the unfit, for there is no doubt that a change in pension standards occurred after February 5, 1913.

Of the 16 cases in which the first investigation was obviously inadequate, 5 were dropped within three months; but of the other 11, 9 had been pensioned for a year or longer. This is very probably due to the fact that these pensions were granted in the early period, when the technique of investigation was less fully worked out than at present. Pensions can no longer be stayed because there is no proof of marriage or of the husband's death, since these facts must now be established from public records before a pension is granted.

As has been said, the group called "unknown" includes all those stays in which the reason for staying the funds is given but not in terms which permit the families to be grouped in this scheme. At the same time the reasons given are interesting and Table VII gives a list of these ambiguous reasons, together with the length of time the family had been on the pension roll.

TABLE VII.—*Length of time on pension roll and reason for stay in case of 24 families classed as "reason ambiguous" in table.*

Reason for stay of pension.	Total. Number.	Total. Per cent distribution.	3 months but less than 6	6 months but less than 1 year.	1 year but less than 2 years.	2 years and over.
All reasons	24	100.0	2	4	13	5
Family had money	6	25.0		1	3	2
Man able to work	3	12.5		1	2	
Mother unfit morally	7	29.2	1	1	4	1
Mother unfit physically	5	20.8	1	1	2	1
Illegitimate child	3	12.05			2	1

a See Table VI.

It is probable that some of these families, too, were put on the pension roll because the first investigation was inadequate. Especially is this true of those families dropped because the mother had an illegitimate child. All three had been on the lists for over a year, all three were dropped at the time when the court established the rule that copies of birth certificates must be obtained for children who were already being pensioned. It is also very probable that some of the families who were dropped because they had money were ineligible at the time when the pension was granted, but the investigating officer had failed to discover the savings. In 1914 the county agent began a reinvestigation of families receiving pensions, and he is said to have found that a number of families had money hidden away. The date of the stay of these six cases indicates that their ineligibility was probably discovered in this way. For the other three groups, it is impossible to tell whether their stay was due to a change in their circumstances, to a change in the standards of the court, to the fact that the pension was granted under a misapprehension of the circumstances, or to the fact that the family had been given a trial and had been found wanting.

It appears, then, that the number of families having their funds stayed during the period under consideration was made unduly large by the fact that during this period the court began making an investigation of the families already under its care and demanding of them the same proofs of eligibility and fitness demanded of new applicants. In other words, the court during this particular period was engaged in rectifying the mistakes that had been made at an earlier period when the law was new, the probation staff inadequate and less competent, and adequate investigation the exception rather than the rule. Just how many of these 24 stays were due to these reasons can not be definitely determined; but at the lowest estimate, 20 out of 24 could be accounted for in this way.

One fact remains to be emphasized—the pensions of these families would not have been stayed if the court officers had not been thorough in their supervisory work. It should be made clear, however, that there may often be questions of fact that can not be disclosed by even a searching preliminary investigation and which may lead later to a modification or withdrawal of the pension grant. The possession of such personal property as would disqualify may be concealed for a considerable period; in one case, for example, when the property had been concealed and was later disclosed, the woman said that her conscience was greatly relieved by having the fact finally brought to light. The question of the mother's real fitness, too, is one upon which a later and more intimate knowledge of the family will throw light.

Facts are also available for the pensions stayed at earlier periods. This information throws no light on present pension policies since the methods of administration were so radically changed after February 4, 1913, when the work of reorganizing the pension department was begun. The head of the department has kindly supplied from records the following reasons for the 60 pension stays that were ordered between July 1, 1911, and November 30, 1912:

Pension no longer necessary because of increased earnings in family	10
Mother able to care for family without further outside assistance	5
Money received from insurance company in settlement of damage suit	6
Husband returned to family	5
Remarriage of mother	10
Death of mother	3
Mother insane and placed in hospital	1

Mother in hospital; children placed in homes ———————————————— 4
Mother found to be unfit ———————————————————————— 2
Illegitimate child born after grant of funds ———————————————— 5
Fraudulent statement as to parentage of pensioned child —————————— 2
Improper use of pension funds ———————————————————————— 1
Mother preferred children in institutions ———————————————— 1
Family moved and left no trace of whereabouts ———————————————— 1
Family moved to Europe ———————————————————————— 1
Stayed and afterwards reinstated, pending inquiry ———————————————— 3

Total ———————————————————————————————— 60

For the period between December, 1912, and June 30, 1913, the published annual report shows that 90 families, with 341 children, were removed from the roll. The number removed for each cause is not given, but the following general reasons were given for the removal of all cases for whom the court's care proved impracticable during this time: Pension stayed because the children became 14 years of age, mother remarried, mothers found to have money in the bank, fathers became able to work and found employment, homes were found to be irremediably unfit, and finally those removed because of changes in the law. (See Cook County Service Report, 1913, pp. 293, 294.)

For the years 1915, 1916, and 1917 data are published in the annual reports of the juvenile court (see Cook County Charity Service Reports for these years). In the following statement, showing the reasons for pension stays during these three years, the unit is the pensioned child and not the pensioned family. Similar data for pensioned families can not be obtained.

Reason for stay of pension.	1917	1916	1915
Total	818	652	270
Income sufficient	216	174	57
Mother remarried	133	112	19
Child reached 14 years of age	116	114	70
Has money	47	46	a23
Mother unfit	38	39	22
Family should be self-supporting	36	8	1
Father able to do work	35	14	
Mother would not cooperate	34	19	7
Mother in hospital or sanitarium	23	17	8
Child died	22	14	4
Child in country	20	19	16
Left county	19	13	3
Child in hospital, sanitarium, etc	19	11	
Property interest	13	3	
Mother insane	12	4	5
Mother died	9	19	7
Mother sick	6		
Damage suit settled	4	8	6
Mother withdrew	4	6	15
Family had not accounted for money previous to pension grant	4		
Child in correctional institution	3	4	6
Relatives able to assist	2		
Father died out of county	2		
Child in institution for dependents or defectives	1	6	
Parents not legally married		2	
Child a menace to family			1

a Twenty-one of the 23 received insurance money.

CHANGES IN AMOUNT OF PENSION GRANTS.

Further evidence of adequate supervision is found in a change in the amount of the pension whenever the family income has changed; that is, in some cases the allowance is not taken away entirely, but is merely decreased in amount when family circumstances have changed. For example, if a child becomes 14 years of age, so that he can lawfully work, or if new sources of income appear, the pension allowance may be reduced. If, on the other hand, sources of income are stopped or estimates are proved to be not well founded, the amount allowed may be increased. This has happened in cases where the illness of the mother and her resulting inability to earn has made a larger pension necessary for a time.

Table VIII shows the number of changes that were made in the pension grants of the 212 families who had been under care for a period of two years or longer:

TABLE VIII.—*Number of changes in amount of pension for 212 families under care for two years or longer.*

Number of changes in amount of pension.	Families under care two years or longer.	
	Number.	Per cent distribution.
Total	212	100.0
0	56	26.4
1	60	28.3
2	52	24.5
3	22	10.4
4	18	8.5
5	4	1.9

This study of 212 families who had been on the pension roll for two years or longer shows that only 56 pensions had remained fixed and that the other 156 had been changed at least once during that period. There were altogether 322 actual pension changes ordered for this group of families. One hundred and thirty-five of these orders were pension increases and 187 pension decreases. This does not count the orders of the court which changed the distribution of the pension without altering the total amount. Such changes may occur, for example, when the pension of one child is ordered stayed at his death and the pension of the others increased until the new pension is equal to the old.

The purpose of these orders for pension changes can be best understood by an account of the method of adjusting the pension in a few individual families:

A pension of $16 a month was granted in February, 1912, to the G family, consisting of the mother and four children aged 11, 10, 7, and 6 years. Mrs. G earned $7 a week by cleaning an office building at night. Her housekeeping and care of the children were not satisfactory under this arrangement, and in September the committee recommended that the pension be increased to $32 and that Mrs. G should be told to stop her night work. The court did not grant the full increase recommended by the committee, but granted $28 a month. Evidently Mrs. G did not stop night work at once, for a month later the case was again before the committee who repeated their former recommendation, and this time it was granted by a court order of November, 1912. The mother now did washings and earned from $3 to $4 a week. The pension continued at $32 until March, 1914, when the eldest girl became 14 and her pension was stayed, making the family pension $24. Although the girl of 14 was not so ill as to be pronounced unable to work, she was retarded in growth and underdeveloped, and it did not seem wise to have her go to work at once. The court was not willing to continue her pension, but as the income was thought insufficient in August, 1914, the pension of the youngest child was increased $6, making a total of $30 for the family. This continued until May, 1916, when the second child became 14 and the pension was reduced to $22.

The H family consists of the mother and five children, the eldest 14 years and the youngest 13 months at the time of the application for a pension. The father had been an engineer and earned $16 a week, but he had been sick and unable to work for a year before his death, which occurred in June, 1911. In April, 1912, the family was granted a pension of $36 a month. The 14-year-old girl was attending a trade school and not bringing in any wages. The mother, however, though not strong, worked about three days a week at $1 a day. Thus the total monthly income was $48 a month. In July, 1912, the fourth child, Marie, 3 years old, had infantile paralysis and was sent to the hospital for treatment. She was there two months and during that time her pension was cut off, making the total pension $27 for those two months. In September, 1912, the child came home; the pension was restored to $36. This allowance continued until November, 1913, when Marie was once more sent to the hospital and her pension stayed for a month. For two years after that the pension was $26. In December, 1915, it was withdrawn entirely while the mother went to the hospital for an operation. When it was reinstated the amount was $35 instead of $36. The eldest girl is at work earning $6 a week, making a total income of $59 a month.

The I family was granted a pension of $42 a month in July, 1913. The family consisted of the mother and six children, all under 12 years of age, and the mother's father—an old man of 75, who paid his daughter $5 a week for room and board. The budget as estimated by the dietitian was $66 a month, which meant that the mother must earn only $4 a month by outside work. This she was able to do without any difficulty. In August, 1914, a year after the pension was granted, the baby died, and the pension was reduced to $36 a month. In April, 1915, the eldest child became 14, and her pension was stayed, making the total pension $28. One month later Mrs. I's father died. This meant a substantial reduction of the family income, and the pension was again raised to $36.

PART I.—ADMINISTRATION IN COOK COUNTY. 47

The fact that for the great majority of families the original grant is altered one or more times during the period the family is under care is an indication of thorough supervisory work. In the down-State counties many families were found drawing pensions to which they were no longer legally entitled. This was due to the inadequate probation work. The court was not informed of the changes in family circumstances which made a change in the pension or its withdrawal necessary, and pensions were continued which were no longer needed. The Chicago court, however, is in such close touch with the families under its care that any change in family circumstances is reported at once by the supervising officers, and the pension grant is altered accordingly.

ADEQUACY OF PENSION GRANTS.

AMOUNT OF PENSION GRANTS.

A point of interest and importance is that of the adequacy of the pension grants. The original pension law of 1911 left the amount of the pension to be determined by the court without any limitations as to the maximum or minimum allowance.[17] The amended law of 1913, however, fixed a maximum pension grant at $15 a month for a single child and $10 for each additional child, with a maximum of $50 a month for any one family. By the amendment of 1915, the maximum allowance for a single family was raised to $60 a month. No one of the three mothers' pension statutes of Illinois, however, has made any provision for a minimum allowance. The smallest pension granted by the Chicago court is $4 a month, and the pension allowances from this court, therefore, range from $4 to $60 a month.

Within these limits the amount of the pension grant is determined by such circumstances as the number and ages of the children, the supplementary resources available, and the health of the family, particularly the health of the mother, who is expected to do some work if the officer finds that it can be done without injury to her health or neglect of her home. It has already been pointed out that the field supervisor, who is a dietitian, prepares a budget for each family; and on this budget as a basis the conference recommends to the court that a pension of a certain amount be granted. This amount may, of course, be altered by the judge after he hears in court the discussion between the county agent and the other representatives of the conference committee.

All reports that have been published by the court, by the county agent, or by the comptroller give only the total amount granted monthly or yearly in the form of pensions and the number of families or total number of children receiving these grants. It is impossible to obtain from these reports any further information except the obviously unsatisfactory average monthly pension given per family or per child. In order to determine how far the pension grants furnish adequate relief, information is needed showing the number of pension allowances of definite amounts that have been granted, together with the number of members in the family, and the total income of

---

[17] It will be remembered, however, that the presiding judge in the Chicago court had established a rule of the court, in the absence of a statutory maximum grant, fixing a maximum allowance. This maximum was at first fixed at $10 a month for each child and was later increased to $15 a month for a girl and $10 a month for a boy, the amounts granted by law for the maintenance of dependent children in industrial schools.

PART I.—ADMINISTRATION IN COOK COUNTY. 49

the family. An attempt has been made, therefore, to collect such data. Table IX shows the number of families receiving pensions of specified amounts in the month of January, 1917, together with the number of pensioned children in the family; Table X shows the number of families granted pensions of specified amounts during the period from August 1, 1913, to March 1, 1915, when the officers of the court made their "survey" together with the number of children in each family; and Table XI shows the pension allowances for the families (212) who had been under care for a period of two years or longer. Only for this last group of families has it been possible to obtain data relating to total income.

TABLE IX.—*Number of families receiving pensions of specified amounts during the month of January, 1917, together with the number of pensioned children in the family.* [a]

Number of pensioned children in the family.	Families receiving pensions of specified amounts, January, 1917.													
	Total.	Less than $5.	$5–$9.	$10–$14.	$15–$19.	$20–$24.	$25–$29.	$30–$34.	$35–$39.	$40–$44.	$45–$49.	$50–$54.	$55–$59.	$60.	Not reported.
Total number.	778	1	12	47	115	147	133	107	99	52	29	21	11	3	[b] 1
1 child	31	1	3	5	22										
2 children	203		7	26	50	63	57								
3 children	249		1	10	30	60	51	59	38						
4 children	189		1	5	10	19	19	42	45	30	18				
5 children	82			1	2	4	5	6	15	22	9	12	6		
6 children	18				1		1		1		2	7	4	2	
7 children	5					1						2	1	1	
Not reported	1														[b] 1

[a] Although children over 14 are not usually pensioned, in 13 families there is a child over 14 for whom the pension was continued because the child was unable to work.
[b] Not reported because the record for this family could not be found.

Table IX shows that in January, 1917, when these data were obtained, only 3 families were receiving the maximum pension of $60 a month allowed to a single family, although the 18 families with 6 children and the 5 families with 7 children would have been entitled to pensions of this amount under the provision of the law which permits the granting of $15 a month to the first child and $10 a month to each one of the other children under 14 years of age in a pensioned family; that is, 23 of these families might have been given the maximum pension, but only 3 families had actually been granted this allowance of $60 a month. On the other hand, the pensions for the most part are not doles. Only 1 pension of less than $5 a month was granted; only 12 pensions fall in the group $5–$9; 47 in the group $10–$14; or, taking the numbers cumulatively, 60 pension allowances of less than $15 a month—approximately 8 per cent of the entire number—were being granted at the beginning of 1917. The largest number of families in any one group (147) were receiving pensions of $20–$24 a month; the next largest group, 133 families, were receiving pensions of $25–$29 a month. That is, 280 families, or 36 per cent of the whole number pensioned, fall into a group receiving pensions varying from $20 to $29 a month.

The size of the pension must vary with the size of the family, since the law provides that the pension shall not exceed $15 a month for a single child and $10 for each additional child in the family. The heavy zigzag line in the table is so drawn that all the numbers above the line represent families receiving the maximum pension allowed by law for the number of children pensioned. These include 144, or 19 per cent of the total number of pensioned families.

Adequacy of relief can be tested only by data showing total family income and not by the information presented in Table IX, showing only the amount of pension given. Unfortunately the total income of these families could be obtained only by a detailed study of the case records of all the 778 families under care and such a study could not be attempted. But it must not be overlooked that the data in Table IX throw light on the policy of the court with regard to the amount of relief granted. A study of Table IX indicates that great care is used in determining the amount of the pension grant. The court has not followed an unscientific and careless method of granting a flat rate for each child, but the allowance has been carefully adjusted to the supplementary sources of income available for each family. These outside sources of aid are evidently studied with great care and the pension grant nicely graduated according to the family resources and needs.

Further data showing the actual pension allowances were obtained for the families on the pension roll between August 1, 1913, and March 1, 1915.[18] These data are presented in Table X.

TABLE X.—*Number of families receiving pensions of specified amounts, Aug. 1, 1913, to Mar. 1, 1915, together with the number of children under 14 years of age in each family.*

Number of pensioned children in the family.	Total.	$5–9	$10–14	$15–19	$20–24	$25–29	$30–34	$35–39	$40–44	$45–49	$50
Total number	543	4	39	95	159	55	91	33	52	8	7
1 child	9		4	5							
2 children	117	3	26	29	52	7					
3 children	175	1	7	48	53	8	54	4			
4 children	136		2	10	41	25	20	11	26	1	
5 children	62			2	10	15	10	11	12		2
6 children	29				3		7	6	8	3	2
7 children or more	15			1			1	1	6	4	3

---

[18] This material was taken from the schedules prepared by the officers of the court for their pension survey.

Table X furnishes information similar to that in Table IX. The numbers above the heavy zigzag line in the table represent the number of families receiving the maximum grant allowed by law for the number of children specified at the rate of $15 for the first child and $10 for each additional child. The maximum pension allowed during this period to any one family was $50. The table shows, therefore, that out of 543 families only 24, or 4 per cent of the total number, were given the maximum amount allowed for the number of children specified. Table IX showed that 19 per cent of the 778 families on the pension roll in 1917 in contrast to this 4 per cent for 1913–1915, were receiving maximum grants. The larger number receiving such grants at the later period may indicate a more liberal pension policy or it may indicate the increase in pension allowances made necessary by the rising cost of living.

To make possible a comparison between the size of pension allowances at the earlier and later periods, a table of cumulative numbers and percentages has been prepared showing the number of families receiving pensions of more than certain specified amounts at the two periods.

TABLE XI.—*Number of families receiving pensions of more than specified amounts from Aug. 1, 1913, to Mar. 1, 1915 and in January, 1917.*

Amount of pension.	Families pensioned.			
	Aug. 1, 1913, to Mar. 1, 1915.		January, 1917.	
	Number.	Per cent.	Number.	Per cent.
$60			3	0.4
$55 or more			14	1.8
$50 or more	7	1.3	35	4.5
$45 or more	15	2.7	64	8.2
$40 or more	67	12.3	116	14.9
$35 or more	100	18.4	215	27.6
$30 or more	191	35.2	322	41.4
$25 or more	246	45.4	455	58.5
$20 or more	405	74.6	602	77.4
$15 or more	500	92.1	717	92.2
$10 or more	539	99.3	764	98.2
$5 or more	543	100.0	776	99.8
Less than $5			1	.1
Not reported			a 1	.1

a Not reported because the record for this family could not be found.

Table XI shows that somewhat larger percentages of the pensioned families were getting larger pensions at the beginning of the year (1917) than during the earlier period. Thus, selecting several different points of comparison, 8.2 per cent of the families at the later period in contrast to 2.7 per cent of the families at the earlier period received pensions of $45 a month or more; 27.6 per cent at the later period in contrast to 18.4 per cent at the earlier period received pensions of $35 or more; 58.5 per cent at the later period in contrast to 45.4 per cent at the earlier period received as much as $25 or more.

As a result of a more detailed study that has been made of the 212 families who had been under care for a period of at least two years, some further data are available showing the amount of the pension grants. Data showing the total incomes of the pensioned families were also obtained from this study.

Tables XII and XIII show the amount of the pension grants originally made to the families who had been under care for a period of two years and the amount of pension grants two years later. In both tables the pension grants are given, together with the number of pensioned children; that is, children under 14, in the family.

TABLE XII.—*Number of families receiving pensions of specified amounts at time pension was first granted, together with number of children under 14 years of age.*

Number of pensioned children in the family.	Total.	Families receiving pensions of specified amounts at beginning of grants.									
		Less than $10	$10–14	$15–19	$20–24	$25–29	$30–34	$35–39	$40–44	$45–49	$50
Total a	212	2	8	22	55	30	47	18	22	5	3
1 child	2			2							
2 children	32	2	5	7	15	3					
3 children	62		1	11	17	4	29				
4 children	68		2	2	19	17	10	8	10		
5 children	26				2	6	6	6	6		
6 children	14				2		2	3	5	1	1
7 children	6							1	1	4	
8 children	2										2

a Of the total, 11 cases were found where a child was away from home or approaching fourteenth birthday. Pension was not granted for 1 stepchild.

TABLE XIII.—*Number of families receiving pensions of specified amounts two or more years after pension was first granted, together with number of children under 14 years of age.*

Number of pensioned children in family.	Total.	Families receiving pensions of specified amounts two or more years after first grant of pension.										
		Less than $10	$10–14	$15–19	$20–24	$25–29	$30–34	$35–39	$40–44	$45–49	$50–54	$55–59	$60
Total	212	8	10	28	68	21	37	22	12	3	2		1
1 child	11	5	2	4									
2 children	49	1	8	8	25	7							
3 children	74	2		12	28	8	18	6					
4 children	57			4	12	5	17	10	7	2			
5 children	13				2		1	5	3	1	1		
6 children	5					1	1	1	2				
7 children	2				1						1		
8 children	1												1

In both tables the numbers above the zigzag line represent the number of families who were given the maximum pension grant. Table XII shows that only 8 families out of 212, or 4 per cent of the total number, were originally given maximum allowances. After two years the pensions had been increased so that 20 out of the 212, or 9 per cent of the whole number, were getting maximum allowances. These tables indicate, as did the comparison between Tables IX and X, that pensions of maximum size are more frequently granted than formerly, probably in order to meet the increased cost of living. In general, these tables merely confirm the conclusions already drawn from Tables IX and X, that pensions of the maximum amount are granted with great caution, that the amount of the pension allowance is carefully adjusted to the special needs of each pensioned family, and that no unscientific " flat-rate " allowances are given. Thus, Table XIII shows that 57 families with 4 children to whom the maximum allowance of $45 might be granted were actually given pensions varying from $15 to $45 and that only 2 of the 57 families drew as much as the latter amount.

It has already been pointed out that these tables dealing with the amount of the pension grants do not enable us to determine whether or not the pension allowance is adequate to the family needs. It is impossible to determine the adequacy of pension grants except on the basis of data showing total incomes together with the number in the family. A study of the case records for the 212 families who had been pensioned for at least two years made it possible to obtain the necessary data for determining the total income of these families. It must be explained, however, that accurate statistics of income are difficult to obtain. For example, a pension may be granted on the supposition that supplementary contributions are to be made by relatives or others; but it is impossible to determine accurately just how much these supplementary contributions really are from month to month. Relatives can not always be depended on to make their promised contributions regularly, and the supervising officer does not always know, and does not always record even when she knows, the precise amounts or the regularity of such contributions. Again, the pension may be granted on the supposition that the mother ought to earn a specified amount. But the earnings of women who take in washings or go out for day work are likely to be irregular, and may show a wide variation from week to week. This is true also of families in which there are other wage earners. Children who are supposed to be regular contributors to the family income are in and out of work, and their earnings vary with their periods of unemployment and their changes of jobs. If circumstances lead to a permanent change in the family income, the pension will be altered by the court; but temporary variations in income are inevitable when the entire income is not provided by the court pension and the pension is not altered from week to week to meet such changes in the situation.

It may be said, then, that there are two difficulties in the way of determining the family income: (1) The income in many families is not regular, but varies from week to week and from month to month; (2) the irregular supplementary earnings or contributions are not always recorded, even if known, by the supervising officer. In spite of these difficulties it is believed that as a result of a careful study of the total income of the 212 families who have been under care for a period of two years or longer it has been possible to work out with approximate accuracy for 208 of these families the total actual income for the last month under care.

The income for a single month has been taken, and the most recent month was selected for each family. In many cases it was necessary to estimate the mother's earnings from entries made at other dates, such as statements that the mother earns $3 or $4 a week doing daywork. When such entries were repeated frequently but nothing was said about the earnings in the particular month under consideration, it was assumed that these earnings continued in that month. The estimate of income from relatives or other sources was made in the same way; that is, if the contribution had been regular it was assumed that the same contribution was made in this particular month, even if it was not recorded for this month. In general, the minimum figure has been used in cases of doubt, and the incomes given in Table XIV are probably somewhat below the amounts the families actually received. Another reason for believing that these incomes are slightly below the real incomes is that no attempt has been made to estimate the value of what is sometimes called invisible relief—ice or coal tickets; gifts of food; clothing from probation officers, employers, or friends; or irregular gifts from relatives.

There remains the further question whether earnings for a single month, arbitrarily chosen, may safely be assumed to represent the income for the remaining months in the year. The monthly incomes vary, of course, much more in some families than in others. In a few families the income changes so often that it is impossible to find any month in which the income is like that of any other month for six months or a year, while in other families one month's income is regularly very much like the next. Undoubtedly for some families the income in the month selected was extraordinarily high or low; but it seems probable that for the majority the income was not very different in the selected month from the other months of the pension period. Moreover, an attempt to work out from the case records the yearly income of these families involved the making of so many estimates because of omissions in the records that the yearly income did not promise to be as accurate as the figures for the single month taken.

PART I.—ADMINISTRATION IN COOK COUNTY. 55

The results of this study of the incomes of the 212 families who had been pensioned for two years or more are presented in Tables XIV and XV. For four families the income could not be determined satisfactorily, and the data presented are for 208 families only. The first of these two tables shows the amount of the pension grant together with the total income, and the second shows total income together with the number of persons in the family. A child is, of course, counted as a person, and in general there is only one adult member of the household, since most of the families represent a widowed mother with children not old enough to go to work.

TABLE XIV.—*Monthly income of pensioned families for which information could be secured, together with pension grants.*

Total monthly income.	Number of families having monthly pension of—											
	Total.	$5–9	$10–14	$15–19	$20–24	$25–29	$30–34	$35–39	$40–44	$45–49	$50–54	$60
Total	208	8	9	28	67	21	36	22	11	3	2	1
$20–24.99	3			2	1							
25–29.99	5			2	1	2						
30–34.99	14		2	4	3	3	2					
35–39.99	24		1		11	3	2	7				
40–44.99	38	1		4	11	2	13	4	3			
45–49.99	27	1	1	4	10	2	6	1	1	1		
50–54.99	31			4	8	1	7	5	3	1	2	
55–59.99	10	2	1	1	3	2		1				
60–64.99	19	2	2		7	2	4	1				1
65–69.99	11			2	5	1	1	2				
70–74.99	14		3	3	3	1	1	1	2			
75–79.99	3	1				1			1			
80–84.99	2				1	1						
85–89.99	3				1				1	1		
90–99.99	4			2	2							

TABLE XV.—*Monthly income of pensioned families for which information could be secured, together with number in family.*

Total monthly income.	Families of specified number of persons.								
	Total.	3	4	5	6	7	8	9	10	11
Total	208	21	57	59	34	20	6	9	1	1
$20–24.99	3	2	1							
25–29.99	5	4	1							
30–34.99	14	8	2	4						
35–39.99	24	4	14	4	2					
40–44.99	38	2	21	12	1	1	1			
45–49.99	27	1	11	11	2	2				
50–54.99	31		4	14	8	4		1		
55–59.99	10			5	4			1		
60–64.99	19		2	6	4	4	1	2		
65–69.99	11		1	2	4	2		2		
70–74.99	14			1	7	4	1	1		
75–79.99	3				1	1	1			
80–84.99	2				1				1	
85–89.99	3					1	1	1		
90–99.99	4					1	1	1		1

Adequacy of income can not be discussed on the basis of the data shown in Table XIV, since the size of the family is not given, but the table furnishes some additional information relating to the pension policy of the court. It appears that pensions are granted to families whose income apparently place them above the poorest wage-earning groups. Twelve families, for example, have incomes of $75 a month and over, including the pensions. For these families the pensions ranged from $5 to $49. A family with an income of $70 had its income increased to $75 by the grant of a $5 pension. Two families with incomes of $75 had their incomes increased to $90 or more by pension grants of $15 to $19 a month. Two families with incomes of $70 had their incomes increased to $90 or more by pension grants of $20 to $24 a month. These incomes are probably large because they belong to large families in which there are working children, as well as a number of children under 14 years of age. In such cases the court evidently takes the position that the entire burden of supporting the dependent children should not be placed upon the children who have just gone to work. In any event the table does indicate that the court has shown a willingness to assist in maintaining a decent standard of living, which, with a large family, can be supported only on the basis of a reasonably large monthly income.

It should be noted, on the other hand, that some of the incomes are very low. Thus 3 families have an income of less than $25, 5 other families have incomes of $25 to $29, and, altogether, there are 46 families with incomes below $40. It is clear, however, that a study of incomes alone, without regard to the number of members in the family, is of little value. Table XV shows that the large incomes, in general, go with the large families and the small incomes with the small families. The maximum pension for a family consisting of a mother and two children under 14 years of age is $25. There are two families of this size, however, and one family of four, with an income of less than $25. In these cases the court apparently did not grant the maximum pension because supplementary sources of income were expected, although the table indicates that they were not forthcoming.

TESTS OF ADEQUACY OF PENSION GRANTS.

Statements of income, however, do not serve as a measure of the the adequacy of the pension grants until some tests of " adequacy of relief " or adequacy of income have been accepted. Such tests are, of course, difficult to obtain and it is doubtful whether or not any scientific tests are available. For these Chicago incomes, however, certain tests may be applied with interesting if not wholly satisfactory results. The first of these is the relation between the actual family income and the estimated budget prepared by the field supervisor, and submitted to the conference committee as a basis for determining what the pension ought to be. The field supervisor was a trained dietitian and her budget estimates were prepared after a study of the composition of the family and its special needs. To illustrate the method of making these estimates the following budgets are given. The sample budgets are copies of actual budgets submitted to the conference committee by the dietitian.

Budget estimates as a test of adequacy of relief.

A family: Estimated budget and income.

The following estimated budget was submitted by the field supervisor for a Polish family consisting of a mother, aged 25, and two children, aged 1 and 4 years. The father, who had died six months before the pension was granted, had been an elevator man earning $11 a week.

Estimated monthly budget: A family.

Rent	$8.00
Food	17.00
Fuel and light	4.00
Household supplies	1.75
Clothing (family)	5.00
Care of health	.75
Total	36.50

The mother in this family was working at the time of application earning $6 a week in a restaurant. She worked from 2 o'clock in the afternoon until 11 in the evening, but her sister who lived in the same tenement took care of the children during the mother's absence from home. The conference committee recommended that the mother continue her work and that a pension of $13 a month be given ($7 for the 5-year-old child and $6 for the 2-year-old child). This pension was granted by the court. The income for this family, therefore, may be stated as follows:

Mother's earnings	$24.00
Court pension	13.00
Total income	37.00
Estimated budget	36.50
Surplus	.50

The income for this small family equaled almost exactly the estimated budget prepared by the dietitian.

B family: Estimated budget and income.

In the B family, Russian Jewish, the father, who died of heart trouble six months before the pension grant, had been a presser in a garment factory and had earned about $8 a week. The family consisted of the mother, aged 30 years, and three children, aged 1, 6, and 7 years. The estimated budget for this family submitted by the field supervisor was as follows:

Estimated monthly budget: B family.

Rent	$10.00
Food	19.50
Fuel and light	4.00
Household supplies and furnishings	1.75
Clothing (family)	4.75
Care of health	1.00
Total	41.00

The conference committee estimated that the mother in this family ought to earn $12 a month. The mother, however, is not working now, but the doctor who recently examined her, reports that she is able to work about two days a week. The committee recommended a pension of $27 a month, which was granted. This pension is now being supplemented by the Jewish Home Finding Society, which is giving $8 a month and coal, and this society has reported that this supplementary allowance is to be increased to $13 a month.

The relation between the estimated budget, the pension grant, and income in this family may be stated as follows:

Court pension	$27.00
Jewish Home Finding Society	[a] 8.00
Present income (plus coal)	35.00
Estimated budget	41.00
Present deficit	3.00

That is, there is a present deficit, but when the Jewish Home Finding Society raises its allowance there will be a surplus of $2. It is to be noted, however, that the present income is more adequate than the former income from the father's wages.

C family: Estimated budget and income.

The C family was granted a pension in December, 1916. This family included the mother, aged 31 years, three children, aged 8, 10, and 11 years, and the father, 32 years old, who was in the third stage of tuberculosis, incapacitated for work and living in a sanitarium. The father and the mother were both born in Poland but had been in this country 29 years. The father had been a finisher and had earned $15 a week when he was able to work. The budget for this family included extra diet, for the mother was found to have tuberculosis in the second stage, and the two younger children had had tuberculosis, al-

---

[a] In addition, the society contributed coal; estimated value, $3.

though it was quiescent at the time the pension was granted. The budget estimates which follow are the original budget and a later budget prepared on the basis of the increased cost of living.

Estimated monthly budget: C family.

	Estimated budget on which pension was granted.	New estimate.
Rent	$11.00	$11.00
Food (extra diet)	22.00	26.00
Fuel and light	4.00	4.75
Household supplies and furnishings	1.75	2.50
Clothing (family)	5.75	6.25
Care of health	1.00	1.00
Total	45.50	51.50

The conference committee recommended a pension of $35 a month, the maximum pension allowed by law for a family with three children, and the committee also recommended that the family be granted "county supplies" (the rations given by the outdoor relief department). The pension grant of $35 was allowed by the court, but the county agent refused the request for county supplies on the ground that it is against the rules of the county agent's office to supplement pensions when the family is receiving the maximum pension allowed by law. The mother at the time of application for the pension was working in a phonograph office, earning $6 a week, but she is not able to work now. The present situation of this family is as follows:

```
Income: Pension grant_____ $35.00
        First estimated budget_____  45.50
        Later  estimated budget_____  51.50

        Income deficit _____ 10.50 or 16.50
```

D family: Established budget and income.

The D family consists of the mother, aged 33 years, and three children, aged 8, 10, and 13 years. Both parents were born in Ireland and had been in this country 13 years before the father's death The father died of tuberculosis about eight years before the pension was granted. The mother was in a State hospital for the insane for a time but has recovered. She has tuberculosis of the knee, however, and the knee is in a cast. She also has tuberculosis of the lungs, arrested. The three children all have glandular tuberculosis. The budget estimates for this family were as follows:

Estimated monthly budget: D family.

	Estimate on which pension was granted.	New estimate.
Rent (estimated)	$10.00	$10.00
Food (extra diet)	22.00	24.00
Fuel and light	4.00	4.75
Household supplies and furnishings	1.75	1.75
Clothing (family)	5.75	6.00
Care of health	1.00	1.00
Total	44.50	47.50

The mother of this family was unable to work, and the conference committee recommended the maximum pension for a family of three children, $35 a month. The present monthly income of this family is as follows:

```
Income: Court pension_____ $35.00
First estimated budget_____  44.50
Later estimated budget_____  47.50

    Income deficit_____ 9.50 or 12.50
```

Since the maximum pension for this family can not be more than $35 (that is, $15 for the first child and $10 for each of the other two children), the supervisor of the pension department is asking aid from other charitable sources in order to bring the income up to the budget estimate, but she has no assurance as yet of any regular supplementary allowance although the church is paying the moving expenses and the first month's rent at the new address.

E family: Estimated budget and income.

The E family is typical of the families in which there are several wage earners. This family consists of the mother, aged 43 years, and four children, aged 11, 13, 16, and 18 years. The father died of tuberculosis in August, 1916, and the family was granted a pension in September, 1916. The father was American and the mother German born. The father had been a piano finisher, earning $16 a week. The estimated budgets were as follows:

Estimated monthly budget: E family.

	Budget on which pension was granted.	New estimate.
Rent	$11.00	$11.00
Food (extra diet)	33.50	37.00
Fuel and light	5.00	5.00
Household supplies and furnishings	2.25	3.00
Clothing (family)	5.75	6.00
Clothing (working child)	2.50	3.50
Spending money (working child)	1.00	1.00
Car fare	2.50	2.50
Care of health	1.50	1.50
Total	65.00	70.50

The conference committee recommended a pension of $18 a month for this family since the mother, although she was reported not very well was working and earning about $10 a month, and the two older children were working. The present monthly income for this family may be stated as follows:

```
Mother's earnings_____ $10.00
Boy, 18 years of age, contribution of three-fourths of his
    wages_____  24.00
Boy, 16 years of age, contribution of three-fourths of his
    wages_____  14.00
Court pension_____  18.00
        Total income_____  66.00
Estimated budget_____  65.00
        Surplus income_____   1.00
```

F family: Estimated budget and income.

The F family consists of the mother, aged 37 years, and seven children, aged 4, 6, 7, 9, 12, 14, and 17 years. The father who was born in Germany but who had been in this country 24 years died of heart disease in September, 1916. The family applied for a pension the same month and the pension was granted in October, 1916. The father had been a machinist, earning $21 a week, and had no insurance. The estimated budget for the F family was as follows:

Estimated monthly budget: F family.

Rent	$10.00
Food	38.00
Fuel and light	5.00
Household supplies and furnishings	2.75
Clothing (family)	7.25
Clothing (working child)	2.50
Spending money	1.00
Car fare	2.50
Care of health	2.00
Total	71.00

The mother in this family has not been working and is not working now. The little 14-year-old girl has not yet gone to work, but her future earnings were considered a part of the family income by the conference committee. The present monthly income is as follows:

Pension grant	$35.00
Girl of 16 contribution three-fourths of wages	18.00
Total present income	53.00
Estimated wages to be contributed by 14-year-old girl	12.00
Budget	71.00
Present budget deficit	18.00
Future budget deficit	6.00

G family: Estimated budget and income.

The G family is a colored family, consisting of the mother, aged 31, and four children, aged 8, 10, 11, and 13 years. The father had been a coal miner, and earned from $50 to $60 a month until he became ill with tuberculosis. He died in February, 1913, and the family got $100 insurance from the miners' union. The family had not then been residents of Cook County long enough to be eligible for a pension. The pension was ultimately granted, however, in January, 1917. The following budget estimate for this family was submitted to the conference committee:

Estimated monthly budget: G family.

Rent (estimated)	$12.00
Food	23.50
Fuel and light	4.00
Household supplies and furnishings	2.25
Clothing (family)	7.00
Care of health	1.25
Total	50.00

The mother in this family is not well, but she does day work and earns about $5 or $6 a week. The conference committee recommended a pension of $28 a month, which was granted by the court. The present income of the family may be stated as follows:

Mother's earnings	$22.00
Court pension	28.00
Total income	50.00
Estimated budget	50.00

No surplus or deficit.

H family: Estimated budget and income.

The H family, Russian Jewish, includes the father, who is incapacitated by acute articular rheumatism; the mother, aged 34; and five children, aged 2, 6, 8, 11, and 14 years. The father had been a peddler, earning about $15 a week. The estimated budget which was submitted for this family includes provision for the father, who is living at home as a member of the family.

Estimated monthly budget: H family.

Rent and heat	$16.00
Food	32.50
Fuel and light	2.00
Household supplies and furnishings	2.25
Clothing (family)	9.00
Care of health	1.75
Total	63.50

The mother sews and earns about $3 a week. The estimated income for this family is as follows:

Mother's earnings	$12.00
Court pension	50.00
Total income	62.00
Estimated budget	63.50
Income deficit	1.50

The pension was reduced on November 13, 1916, from $50 to $40, when the eldest child became 14 years of age. The boy has remained in school to graduate from the eighth grade, February 1, 1917. There has been, therefore, for the two months of November and December an income deficit of $11.50 a month, which will continue until work is found for the boy.

These sample budgets show the method used by the Chicago court to determine the amount of the pension grant. The budgets given are for large families with more than one wage earner, and for small families in which there is no one, not even the mother, able to work. No conclusions can be based on these sample budgets, since only a small number are given. Table XVI has, therefore, been prepared showing, for all of the 212 families for whom the information could be obtained from the records,[19] the size of the surplus or deficit after income and estimated budget had been compared.

TABLE XVI.—*Deficits and surpluses of income over last budget for families for which information could be secured.*

Amount.	Families.		
	Deficit.	Surplus.	Even income.
Total number	116	83	6
None			6
Less than $1	11	9	
$1 but less than $2	11	3	
$2 but less than $3	15	11	
$3 but less than $4	13	4	
$4 but less than $5	10	11	
$5 but less than $6	8	5	
$6 but less than $7	9	8	
$7 but less than $8	3	5	
$8 but less than $9	5	3	
$9 but less than $10	7	4	
$10 but less than $15	17	10	
$15 or over	7	10	

A study of Table XVI shows that 116 families, or 56.6 per cent of the whole number for whom the information was obtained, had incomes below the budget estimate prepared by the dietitian. But for the great majority of these families the deficits were very small as the following summary shows:

```
Deficits of—                                               Families.
    Less than $5 _____   60
    $5 but less than $10 _____   32
    $10 or more _____   24
```

The 60 families with deficits of less than $5 may be disregarded, since inaccuracies in estimating income may easily account for a small deficit. There remain 32 families with deficits of $5 but less than $10 a month, and 24 families with deficits of $10 or more. That is, 56 families, or 27.3 per cent of the whole number, have deficits of $5 or more per month. These deficits may be explained as due to one of the following reasons: (1) Temporary circumstances, such as the failure of children of working age to secure work, or temporary loss of work by the mother or some other wage-earning member of the family; (2) the provision of the law which fixes the maximum pension at $15 for a single child and $10 a month for each subsequent pensioned child in the family (this means that very small families in which the mother is so ill or so incompetent that she can

---

[19] For seven of the 212 families no report as to the relation between budget and income could be obtained from the records.

make no contribution to the income may be left with only $15 or $25 a month as the sole income; some method of supplementing such an income will probably be found later by the supervising probation officer, but temporarily the family may be inadequately provided for); (3) the provision of the law fixing the maximum limit of the pension granted at $60 a month. As the limit to the allowance per child may lead to an inadequate income for small families so the limit to the allowance per family may mean an inadequate allowance for very large families. If a family with six or eight small children, for example, has been in a tubercular condition so that extra diet is needed for several members of the family, the $60 a month maximum pension, generous as it may sound, must be inadequate according to the standards set by the careful estimates of the court dietitian, unless supplementary sources of income are available.

A further explanation of the deficits may possibly be found in the fact that the value of the invisible relief already referred to has not been estimated in making up the income totals.

In discussing the adequacy of pension grants or the adequacy of any other form of relief, it is, however, necessary to remember that we have no way of applying a test of adequacy, such as the dietitian's standard, to the incomes of families outside of the pension department. That is, before any judgment can be passed upon the fact that 27 per cent of the families fall approximately $5 or $10 short of what an expert dietitian calls an adequate income, it would be necessary to compare this percentage with the percentage of independent wage earners' families whose incomes fall below a similar standard or with the percentage of families supported by other forms of relief who fall short by a similar test. Unfortunately such a comparison can not be made; and without such a standard of comparison it can only be said that while a certain percentage of pensioned families may not yet have adequate incomes, there is a considerable percentage of the nonpensioned families in the community in the same position.

Some comment should be made on the number of families who have incomes affording a surplus according to the dietitian's standard. The following summary shows that most of these surpluses were very small:

Surpluses of—	Families.
Less than $5	38
$5 but less than $10	25
$10 or more	20

Like the small deficits, the small surpluses may be disregarded since they may be easily accounted for by inaccuracies in estimating income.

The families with the large surpluses are, in general, families whose income is precarious because the help of relatives, or of some other supplementary source, is believed to be uncertain, or they are families whose pensions are being supplemented by the Jewish Home Finding Society.

Comparison between present and past incomes.

A second test of adequacy of income that might be used is a comparison between the present income of the pensioned families and the income of these same families when the husbands and fathers were alive. Although our American relief authorities have long since rejected the old poor-law doctrine that the condition of the family maintained by an allowance from public funds must be "less eligible" than the condition of the independent or self-sustaining family, nevertheless, it is true that the standard of relief for families supported from public funds will be kept within at least measurable distance of the wage levels, not of the lowest independent wage earner, but of the vast majority of the wage earners in the country.

A definite test of the relation of pension incomes to the incomes of the families supported by independent wage earners is furnished by Table XVII which compares for the 180 families for whom the data were available the father's monthly wages and the income of the families after they were put on the pension roll.

TABLE XVII.—*Present monthly income of pensioned families for which information was reported, together with the previous wages of the father.*

Monthly wages of father.	Total	Pensioned families with specified monthly income.													
		$20–24	$25–29	$30–34	$35–39	$40–44	$45–49	$50–54	$55–59	$60–64	$65–69	$70–74	$75–79	$80–84	$85–89	$90–94
Total	180	1	5	11	18	32	23	31	9	18	11	12	1	2	3	3
$20–$24.99	3					2		1								
25–29.99																
30–34.99	4					2	1			1						
35–39.99	6						2		2	1	1					
40–44.99	16		2	1	2	3	1	1		5	1					
45–49.99	30		1	2	2	7	4	3	3	2	2	3		1		
50–54.99	22			2	2	3	4	3		3	4	1				
55–59.99	7		2	1		1	1					1	1			
60–64.99	36	1		3	4	3	5	12	2	2	2	1			1	
65–69.99	10				3	5		1							1	
70–74.99	12				4	1	1	2			2	1			1	
75–79.99	6			1			2	2				1				
80–84.99	12				1	3	2	1		1		2				2
85–89.99	2							2								
90–94.99	2									1		1				
95–99.99	2							1								1
100 and over	10			1			2		2		3		1		1	

Some comment is needed on the data relating to the father's wages. The only record of the father's occupation and earnings is the mother's statement to the probation officer, which is usually entered on the case record. In 32 out of 212 cases the officer either did not ascertain or did not record the father's wages, and Table XVII, therefore, relates only to 180 families. There is, of course, some question as to the accuracy of the statements given by the mother. Some women may give the father's usual earnings or wages and others his maximum or minimum earnings. Some may have overstated earnings and others may have understated. In some cases, too, the father's last occupation and wages may have been given even when the man may have been obliged by illness to give up his usual occupation for light work. In such cases, of course, the normal earnings of the father do not appear. On the other hand, many women gave only the daily rate of wages, and in trades in which employment is irregular the monthly earnings estimated on the basis of the daily rate without any allowance for unemployment represent an overestimate. On the whole the data relating to the father's wages may be said to represent a maximum estimate, since no allowance is made for irregularity in income due to unemployment. The present incomes are much less irregular than the old incomes, as they are based largely, if not wholly, on an absolutely regular allowance from the court.

A study of Table XVII shows that 13 families (those just under the upper zigzag line) have a present income equal to the income represented by the monthly wages of the father when he was alive and at work. It is important to note, however, that the present income for these families represents a larger income per person, even when the income is nominally the same, than in the father's lifetime, for two reasons: (1) The pension income is more regular and not subject to the irregularities due to unemployment; (2) the father's wage supported an able-bodied workingman in addition to the other members of the family. The cost of supporting the wage-earning father is not easy to estimate, but the monthly cost of his food, clothing, lunches, car fare, and tobacco, for example, could not be covered for most men by an allowance of $10 or $15 a week. Taking the lower or $10 estimate, the two heavy zigzag lines in Table XVII have been so drawn as to include between them all the families whose present income equals the former nominal income from the husband's wage, together with all the families whose present income is $5 or $10 less than the old nominal value.

On the basis of this division into groups, the families may be classified as follows: Fifty-three families were above the upper zigzag line and have a larger present income than that represented by the father's nominal monthly wages; 53 other families (those between the two zigzag lines) have a present income which either exactly equals the old nominal income or is not more than $10 less than the old nominal income; that is, 106 families, or 59 per cent of the whole number, seem to be distinctly better off as to the income than during the father's lifetime, if adequate allowance is made for the fact that the present income is more regular and is not charged with the support of the wage-earning man. There remain 74 families below the lower zigzag line who now have an income that is nominally $10 or more than $10 below the income represented by the father's wages. It should be noted, however, that 45 of these families had during the father's lifetime a nominal wage of $65 a month or more, which is, of course, above the maximum pension grant allowed by law. In 10 of these families the father's nominal wage was $100 a month or more, and it appears that these high nominal wages were reported chiefly by women whose husbands were skilled members of the building trades. They were reported at high daily rates, but it would be true, of course, that these high rates were earned very irregularly. Statistics of income therefore seem to indicate that however inadequate the pension incomes may be, if measured by ideal standards they nevertheless measure up satisfactorily to the standard of wages in the groups of the community to which these families belong.

Comparison between public and private relief.

A third test that may be applied to determine the adequacy of the pension grants is a comparison between the amount of relief given in this way by the court and the amount of relief given by the largest private relief agency in the same community. A study was made of the 172 families who were dropped from the pension roll in July, 1913, because of the change in technical requirements for eligibility prescribed by the new law. Many of these familes became charges upon private charity; and in the section [20] in which the study of these 172 families will be found data are given showing the amount of the former court pension and the amount of relief given by the private charitable agency to the same families.

Without anticipating the discussion in these later sections, it may be said here that 55 out of 69 families received smaller allowances after they became a charge on private charity; and those families who lost little or nothing by the transfer from a public to a private agency were the families getting the smaller pensions of $30 or less. Out of 18 families getting large pensions, from $40 to $50, only 1 got as much after the change. That is, these families transferred from the court to a good private relief society lost a considerable

---

[20] See pp. 95 et seq.

percentage of their income by the transfer. Nor did it appear that this change was made because any new sources of income had been discovered. In most cases the mother was working more days than when she had the pension grant.

Scientific tests of what constitutes adequate relief are slowly and with difficulty being developed by our relief societies. It is probably true that until the great majority of independent wage earners have incomes that are adequate, relief will never be really adequate. The point that must be emphasized is that the pensions of the Chicago court, whether really adequate or not, appear to give the pensioned families larger incomes than they enjoyed when they were supported by the husband and father if allowance is made for the fact that there is no adult male wage earner to be supported out of the weekly pension income, and that the pension allowance is absolutely regular and subject to no hazards such as unemployment. Further evidence seems to indicate that the standard of relief maintained by the court is more nearly adequate than that maintained for families who are being supported by one of the best of the private relief societies in the same community.

THE SUPPLEMENTING OF PENSIONS BY PRIVATE AGENCIES.

Those who are familiar with the work of private relief societies know that no test of what constitutes adequate relief has as yet been agreed upon. Judged by the income standards of those families before the wage earner's death, the court pensions are as adequate as the father's wage. It must, of course, be recognized that, judged not by our present wage standards but by reasonable standards of what is necessary to maintain physical and mental efficiency, the court pensions must be inadequate.

Originally the judge of the juvenile court seems to have thought of the pension as a supplementary income merely. The mother's income, he said, should be supplemented with sufficient public funds. But the families asking for pension are many of them families without any income at all, save the precarious earnings of the mother, and in many cases the mother is in poor health and handicapped by the care of small children, so that she really has no earning capacity at all.

There is another method of supplementing the family income— through supplementary grants of aid by other charitable organizations. In Chicago the two most important relief agencies have taken opposite positions on this question. The Jewish societies and the United Charities of Chicago both turned over to the court to be pensioned a considerable number of families whom they had been assisting before the court's allowance was made. There was a definite question raised as to whether or not assistance would be continued for families whose pension income they thought inadequate. The united charities took the position that the welfare of the family demanded the reduction to a minimum of agencies dealing with the family; that the court in estimating the allowance and in making grants should assume entire responsibility for all the charitable aid given the family—for all the income other than such as came from family earnings and from relatives.

The Jewish charities, on the contrary, took the position that adequacy of relief or of income must be sought by every practicable method. If the court's allowance, together with the family's other income, did not prove sufficient the society would contribute the amount necessary to bring the family income up to an estimated minimum. This organization also took the position that a Jewish mother should remain in her home and should not go out to work. Therefore whenever, according to the usual practice of the court, the estimated income includes not only the pension allowance but also a definite sum expected to be contributed from the mother's earnings, the Jewish Home Finding Society makes a contribution not less than the amount the mother is expected to earn.

Data showing the extent to which pensions are known to be supplemented are available for the 212 families that have been under the care of the court for a period of two years or longer. Sixty-one of these families received assistance so regularly that they might be said to be receiving supplementary pensions, and 60 others had received some relief during the period they had been under the court's care. Table XVIII shows the supplementary sources of income for the 61 families whose pension had been regularly supplemented.

TABLE XVIII.—*Supplementary sources of aid for 61 pensioned families.*

Source of aid.	Number.
Total	61
Relatives	27
Jewish aid society or Jewish Home Finding Society	20
Churches	5
Scholarship committee	3
County outdoor relief	1
More than one source [a]	5

[a] Includes Jewish Home Finding Society and a friendly visitor; church, relatives, and county outdoor relief; relatives and Jewish Home Finding Society; relatives and a lodge; relatives and church.

It will be seen that a considerable number of those receiving regular supplementary assistance were being helped by relatives. It should be made clear that the families included in this group are only those receiving definite sums from their relatives regularly each month, either as a result of a county court prosecution or by a voluntary agreement. Many other pensioned families—in fact, the majority of the families cared for by the court—receive some help from relatives, such as irregular gifts of clothing and food. The supplementary aid given by the scholarship committee is in the form of a pension for a child who has reached the legal working age of 14 years and can no longer be pensioned by the court, but who is too delicate to be allowed to go to work or too promising to be allowed to go into unskilled work. It has already been pointed out that the county agent has refused to grant county supplies to pensioned families. The one family receiving supplementary aid of this kind is, of course, a rare exception.

Table XIX shows the kind of assistance received by 60 other families who had had definite supplementary relief after they came under the care of the court.

TABLE XIX.—*Source and nature of supplementary relief received by 60 other pensioned families.*

Source of relief.	Families receiving specified supplementary relief.		
	Total.	Regular.	Temporary.
Total	60	11	49
Hospital	1		1
Employer	4		4
County agent	20	1	[a]19
Scholarship	4	4	
Individuals, clubs, etc	8	2	6
School Children's Aid Society and churches	10	2	[a]8
United charities	8		[a]8
St. Vincent de Paul	2		2
Others	3	2	1

[a] Number includes those also having had other outside aid in addition to that indicated. "Others" includes such organizations as the Volunteers of America, the Woman's Catholic League, and the Waitresses' Union.

REJECTED OR DISMISSED APPLICATIONS.[c]

Rejecting or dismissing applications is a very important part of the work of the pension or aid-to-mothers department of the court; and if the work of the department is to be understood it is quite as necessary to study the rejected applications as those accepted. A woman who is found, upon preliminary questioning, to be plainly ineligible to a pension is not allowed to file her application. If she is destitute and ineligible for a pension, she is told that she must apply to some relief agency and is told where to go. If it is not clear that an applicant is ineligible, the application is filed, the court officer investigates, and the committee, on the basis of this investigation, recommends that the application be granted or dismissed. In some cases, where the home is clearly unfit, not only is the application dismissed but also a petition is filed in order to have the children declared dependent under the section of the juvenile-court law which authorizes the court to remove children from the custody of unfit parents. If this drastic remedy is not taken the cooperation of some other disciplinary agency may be sought.

Valuable data relating to rejected applications are available for the period from August 1, 1913, to March 1, 1915.[21] During this period 532 families with more than 1,400 children applied for pensions and had their applications " dismissed." During the same period 226 new pensions were granted. That is, there were more than two applicants rejected to every new pensioner placed on the roll during this period of 19 months. Table XX shows the marital status of the rejected or dismissed applicants:

TABLE XX.—*Marital status of women whose pension applications were dismissed during the period Aug. 1, 1913, to Mar. 1, 1915.*

Marital status.	Dismissed applicants.	Per cent distribution.
Total	532	100.0
Widows	450	84.6
Husbands living but incapacitated	67	12.6
Deserted or divorced women	14	2.6
Unmarried mothers	1	.2

[c] This section of the report was prepared by Miss Helen Russell Wright.
[21] This material was furnished by the officers of the court, who made the compilation as a part of a survey of the work of their department.

PART I.—ADMINISTRATION IN COOK COUNTY. 73

This table shows that the great majority of the applicants refused are widows. Included with the 450 women classified as widows, however, are 11 women who were unable to prove that they had ever been married. The number of applications from deserted or divorced women is very small, because it is not the practice of the court to allow women to file applications if they are obviously ineligible, and both of these classes of women are ineligible under the present law.

A study of the reasons given for rejecting these 532 applications shows the great care with which pensioned families are selected. In general, the secretary of the case committee uses one of several set phrases in recording the reason for dismissing the case. For the 532 families who were refused pensions during this period, there were 23 such phrases used, of which the most frequently repeated were "Income sufficient," "Should be self-supporting," and "Relatives able." These various phrases may, however, be classified into five large groups.

The first group includes the families who were refused pensions because they were technically ineligible under the law, without regard to the mother's need for regular assistance or her fitness for maintaining a home. The second group includes those women who, in the opinion of the committee, could not come up to the standard set in that section of the law which declares that the mother must be a person morally, mentally, and physically fit to have the care of the children for whom the allowances are granted. The third group of families includes those for whom a pension was not considered necessary to save the children from institutional care or from parental neglect. The fourth group includes those for whom the court, generally because of obstacles put in its way by the women themselves, found it impossible to complete the necessary investigation to prove the right to a pension under the law. Finally, the fifth group of women withdrew their applications so that their eligibility was not passed upon by the committee. Table XXI shows the number of women included in each of these five groups:

TABLE XXI.—*Reasons for rejecting applications of 532 "dismissed cases."*

Reason for rejection of application.	Number.
Total	532
Group I. Pension not needed	293
II. Technically ineligible	98
III. Ineligible because of unfitness of mother	39
IV. Impossible to establish eligibility	49
V. Application withdrawn	a 53

a Included in group V is the case of one mother who died before investigation was complete and one "mother" who proved to be the grandmother.

This table shows that more than half of the rejected cases belonged in Group I and were dismissed because, after a careful investigation, the committee decided that the family did not need a pension. Further information about this group of applicants was sought from the case records in order to determine what circumstances rendered the pension unnecessary. Table XXII shows the more specific reasons for rejecting these 293 applications:

TABLE XXII.—*Reasons for rejecting applicants in Group I, " Pensions not needed."*

Reason for rejection of application.	Number.	Per cent distribution.
Total	293	100.0
Relatives able to support	101	34.5
Income sufficient	90	30.7
Family should be self supporting	46	15.7
Money on hand	50	17.1
Need only temporary	6	2.0

This table shows that 34.5 per cent were rejected because they were found to have relatives able to help them. It must be assumed that these relatives were either legally liable to render assistance or that they were willing to assist, since it is the practice of the court to grant pensions to families with relatives able to help when the relatives can not be compelled or persuaded to assist. It may be assumed, therefore, that in these cases where a pension was refused because of relatives' ability to help, really substantial assistance could be counted on. Thirty of the families were living with relatives at the time they applied for a pension; 19 families were actually being helped by relatives; 7 had relatives boarding in their homes, possibly giving some help in addition to paying board. The relatives of 7 other families agreed to assume the burden of their support, or enough of it to enable the family to maintain a decent standard of life. For 6 families relatives were found who were liable under the law, and these were to be forced to contribute to their support. For about 30 families we have no further information bearing on this question. In two cases only did there seem to be evidence that the help of relatives was not likely to be a dependable source of income. One was the case of a mother who put three of her four children in institutions and found a boarding place for herself and her baby, and the other was the case of a family that was being supported by the Jewish Home Finding Society.

A further analysis was made of two other groups in Table XXII. These are the families whose applications were dismissed because the committee thought that their incomes were already sufficient and the families who, according to the committee, " ought to be self-supporting." This further study showed that in a considerable number of these families the income was so small that they could only be independent with the help of relatives, so that the group of those dismissed because relatives were able to help is even larger than it appears to be. In Table XXIII the families rejected because of sufficient income are classified by income groups and by the number in the family.

TABLE XXIII.—*Size of family and income of families dismissed because " income was sufficient."*

Number in family.	Families with specified monthly income.						
	Total.	Under $30.	$30–$39.99	$40–$49.99	$50–$69.99	$70 and over.	N. R.
Total	90	3	13	8	38	25	3
2	5	2	2			1	
3	13		4	4	4	1	
4	19		5	2	8	2	2
5	16		1	1	11	2	1
6 and over	37	1	1	1	15	19	

The only family in this table that appears to offer a serious problem is the family of six, with an income of less than $30 a month. Further inquiry showed, however, that the family had relatives able to help them and liable for their support. This family was, of course, really dismissed because the relatives were able to assist, but the reason given was income sufficient. The other two families with income of less than $30 were families of only one child, and the court always considers that the mother of an only child should be self-supporting if she is physically able to work. With these exceptions and that of the two families with more than four members who have incomes of less than $40, the income of the family appears, if not adequate, at least not obviously insufficient for the family needs. It should be pointed out, too, that the income figures are, of course, not precise and it is probable that they are too small.

In determining the need for a county pension the source of the family income is as important as the amount of the income. It was found that in 8 families the widowed mother herself contributed more than $50 of the monthly income, in 24 others she contributed between $30 and $50, while in 17 she contributed anywhere from $15 to $29, and in 16 less than $15. In 22 families she contributed nothing at all, and for 3 families we have no information. It is to be regretted that more is not known about those women who were contributing large amounts to the family income, for with women's wages at the present level there are very few untrained women who can earn $30 a month without neglecting their homes and injuring their own health.

Of the 46 families who, in the opinion of the court, ought to be self-supporting, 18 were families in which there was only one child under 14. Of these, 4 were families in which there were older children to help the mother support the younger child; and 14 were families in which the whole burden fell on the mother. As has been said before, it is only when the mother is unable to work that the court considers her unable to support one child; and, of course, with older brothers or sisters it is clearer that the family should support itself. The wisdom of such a ruling may, of course, be questioned, but there are no facts available to show whether or not it worked a real hardship on these families.

Leaving the families who were refused pensions because they were thought to be able with available assistance to support themselves, the next largest group of dismissed cases includes those who were technically ineligible for pension grants under the provisions of the pension law. The specific ground of ineligibility is shown in Table XXIV.

TABLE XXIV.—*Families ineligible for technical reasons.*

Reason for ineligibility.	Families.
Total	98
Mother not a citizen	34
Mother a property owner	20
Husband not incapacitated	20
Mother deserted or divorced	12
Family nonresident	12

As soon as the court investigation reveals a technical disqualification for a pension, the case is dismissed and no further information about the family is obtained. It is true of course that not all those dismissed for technical reasons would have been granted pensions even if the eligibility provisions had been less rigid. Of the 34 women who were refused pensions because of noncitizenship, there were 16 who were evidently in need of this form of relief as they were being cared for by private charity; but there were 10 others who did not need a pension, either because they were able to support themselves, had relatives able to help them, or were expecting money from other sources, such as the settlement of damage suits, etc. Of seven women in this group we know nothing beyond the facts given in the table. About the other groups of those excluded for technical ineligibility we have even less information, but such as we have points in the same direction. There are some in each group who needed regular assistance to keep the homes together and there are others who would not have been given a pension even if the particular provision of the law which excluded them had been inapplicable.

A closely related group includes the families unable to prove their eligibility—families who would not or could not furnish the facts required before a committee decision could be reached. Table XXV shows the more detailed reason found in the case record for the rejection of these applications.

TABLE XXV.—*Families unable to prove eligibility.*

Reason for ineligibility.	Families.
Total	49
Mother refused to cooperate	18
Mother unable to prove marriage	13
Unsatisfactory account of expenditure of money	9
Could not be located	9

In the words of the case record, 18 of these mothers who were applicants refused to cooperate. This may of course mean a number of things. For example, a woman refuses to cooperate when she says that she is too sick to work but will not go to the doctor for examination; or when she will not give such necessary information as the names and addresses of relatives, place of her marriage, or the dates of birth of the children. Not infrequently a woman is placed in the group of refusing to cooperate when she insists upon taking men to room in her home, because the court quite rightly considers this a dangerous practice for the widow with young children.

In other words, a refusal to cooperate is not used to cover that more or less subtle attitude on the part of the mother which resents suggestions and insists on independence, but rather refers to some very definite refusal by which she makes it impossible to establish eligibility or insists upon continuing some practice which the court can not sanction. For 8 of the 18 families the records show the exact point at which cooperation ceased. In 4 cases the father had tuberculosis and refused to leave the home; 2 women refused to give up their lodgers; 1 woman was unwilling to prosecute relatives liable for her support; and the other, contrary to the court's advice, refused to take part-time work.

Very little need be said about the other groups in Table XXV. Thirteen women were unable to prove their marriage to the father of the children. The officers of the court are very resourceful in finding records of marriage when such a record exists, and the court has been very liberal in the kind of proof allowed—two witnesses, for example, are accepted as proof of a common-law marriage. It seems more than likely therefore that most of these 13 women had not been married. In this case they really belonged to the class of those considered unfit morally, but it is worth noticing that the committee considered only 2 of them to be so unfit to maintain a home that steps were taken to break up the family. In these cases the women were considered immoral and were referred to the complaint department of the court for treatment.

Nine women were not able to convince the court that they were without money. Their cases were dismissed because of an unsatisfactory account of expenditure of money, and one woman because she made false statements about her expenditures. Here again the phrase alone does not convey the whole situation, and it is necessary to read a good deal into it to understand just why the court refused a pension. Pensions are not refused on this ground unless a family is known to have had money and unless there are indications that the money is not exhausted. It does not mean that a woman who had $500 three years ago will not be granted a pension unless she can account for it up to the last dollar. Much the same kind of treatment is given the untruthful woman. A single false statement or even several untruths would not cause a woman to lose her chance of a pension if she evidently needed help. A woman who is refused a pension because of her untruthfulness has told so many different and irreconcilable stories that the court is unable to accept her statements and can not, therefore, obtain satisfactory evidence that the family is eligible for a pension. The nine families who could not be located had either given false addresses or had moved without notifying the court of the change of address, so that in any case the family could not be found by the officer assigned to investigate.

Another group of families in Table XXI (group III) includes the 39 women whose applications for pensions were dismissed because the mother was not, in the judgment of the court, mentally, morally, and physically fit to have the care and custody of the children. Of these mothers 30 were refused pensions on the ground that they were morally unfit. The other 9 mothers in this group were refused pensions because they were physically or mentally incapable of caring for their children—3 of these were tubercular and were sent to the county infirmary at Oak Forest; 1 was suffering from "nerves," and the home had already been broken up; and 1 was feeble-minded and was referred to the probation department of the court. In the other 4 cases the nature of the mother's infirmity can not be ascertained from the records, in 1 of them it is not possible to find out what became of the family. Three of these families were left in the care of private agencies or of " benevolent individuals." The reasons for this policy may be questioned on the ground that if a mother is physically and mentally incapable of maintaining a home under the careful supervision of the court and with an income that is steady and comparatively high, she would be no more capable of maintaining it under less rigid supervision and with the smaller allowance of the private organization.

PART I.—ADMINISTRATION IN COOK COUNTY.   79

Of the 30 mothers whose petitions were dismissed on the ground that they were morally "unfit," 7 were the mothers of illegitimate children; and of the 23 other women whom the court regarded as morally unfit 15 were referred by the aid-to-mothers department to other departments of the court, in the belief that the mother should not be allowed the care and custody of the children unless she could be made to change her way of living. The officers from the pension department themselves filed dependent petitions for the children from 2 families; from 2 other families the children were sent to live with the grandparents who had good homes for them; the children of 1 mother were left in the institutions in which they had been placed, and those of another woman were sent immediately to institutions. In other words, in 21 of the 23 cases where the mother was considered morally unfit to have a pension, the pension department took steps to protect the children. Why this was not done in the other two cases does not appear in the material available.

The mothers of illegitimate children, on the other hand, were allowed, with one exception, to keep their families without interference from the court, and four of them were referred to the united charities for the assistance which the court could not give them under the current interpretation of the law.

There are two opposing views of the court ruling that the mother of an illegitimate child, no matter how long ago the child was born, shall be considered morally unfit under the law and, therefore, ineligible for a pension. That such mothers are refused pensions is considered most unfair by some of the officers of the court. As one of them said of a certain woman for whom she had tried in vain to get a pension: " That woman was a good woman and she needed a pension. It does not seem fair to punish her all her life for the sins of her youth." On the other hand, it is pointed out that there are other suitable ways of providing for the needs of the woman and her children, and that so long as there are private charitable organizations willing to assist such families, the court is unquestionably pursuing a wise and safe policy in holding the mother of an illegitimate child technically disqualified for this form of public aid.

Attention should be called to the fact that in addition to the clear cases of ineligibility and of unfitness, there are doubtful cases arising from differences of opinion as to what constitutes fitness. Such a case as the following illustrates the room for doubt and for difference in policy between the probation staff and the court:

A mother whose pension was stayed in June, 1913, because she was an alien, reapplied when the law was changed in 1915, and she became once more eligible. The officer under whom the woman had previously been on probation, though assigned to another district in 1915, was assigned to reinvestigation. It was found that one child in the family was subnormal, one boy was truant, and that the mother drank. The committee decided that the woman's fitness to care for the children was doubtful. The officer was directed to bring the children to court on dependent petitions. These were dismissed by the judge who was sitting temporarily in the absence of the regular juvenile-court judge, with the recommendation that the woman be pensioned. The case committee again discussed the situation. A pension was finally recommended and was granted in court upon the return of the regular juvenile-court judge. The extent to which the court can risk assuming the care of such family groups will depend in large measure upon the amount of time and the degree of skill which the probation staff can bring to bear upon the family situation.

Little if any comment is needed with regard to the other groups of dismissed cases. Fifty-one women either asked to have their applications withdrawn or became ineligible for county funds before the investigation had been completed. Six remarried and their husbands would supposedly support the children; 3 moved out of the county; and the other 42 withdrew their applications. Information is available as to the reasons for the withdrawal of 25 of the 42 applicants—8 women planned to make another attempt to support themselves and their children, 6 decided to rely on the help of relatives, 2 planned to leave the State, 2 preferred to take boarders, 1 expected settlement of a damage suit, 1 decided that she preferred to put her children in an institution, while 5 seem to have withdrawn their petitions when they found that the court would undoubtedly consider their income sufficient.

Table XXII showed that 50 women were refused pensions because they had money at the time of their application. They might be placed in the group of women who were technically ineligible. The court ruling is that possession of more than $50 shall disqualify. The amounts of money possessed by these rejected applicants is not given. Many of them would of course become eligible later when the money had been used.

Six families were found to be only in temporary need. In 4 of these cases the distress was caused by unemployment, and work was found for the person needing it, or the family was referred to the united charities for emergency relief.

There are certain other facts about the rejected families that throw light on the work of the department. Of the 532 dismissed families, 126, or 24 per cent, had applied for funds at an earlier date. Most of them had been refused upon their first application, but 8 had actually had funds at an earlier period and had then been dropped from the pension roll. Of these 8 reapplications 5 at this time were refused because they either were or should be self-supporting, 1 woman refused to cooperate, 1 woman had an illegitimate child, and 1 was thought to be morally unfit. It is not clear whether these last 2 had deteriorated since the stay of their first pension or whether their later rejec-

PART I.—ADMINISTRATION IN COOK COUNTY. 81

tion indicated that the court set a higher standard of what could be accepted as a fit home. On the whole there can be no doubt that a study of the dismissed cases shows the care with which the court chooses the families that are placed on the pension roll, and its scrupulous adherence to the legal requirements as to eligibility.[22]

[22] Through the kindness of the head of the aid-to-mothers department of the court, the following data were obtained showing the reasons for the rejection of 1,248 applications that were dismissed when the law was new and procedure not well standardized. The following data, while not valuable as throwing light upon present methods of administering the law, are of interest because they show the large number of unsuitable applicants that flocked to the court soon after the passage of the law. It should also be pointed out that the reasons given in the following list are not all equally satisfactory. "Referred to the United Charities" or to any other agency does not explain why the applicant was considered unsuitable for a court pension. The data are submitted, however, because they are believed to be interesting, even in the unsatisfactory form in which it is necessary to present them.

Reasons for rejection of 1,248 applications for pensions between July 1, 1911, and November 30, 1912.

Reasons for rejection.	Applications rejected.
Income sufficient	339
Family had money or interest in property	171
Husband alive and able to support	90
Relatives able to support	14
	611
Referred to relief societies	124
Referred to county court or court of domestic relations	13
Referred to other agencies	20
Only 1 child under 14	62
No child under 14	18
Parents dead or insane	9
Application from grandmother or aunt	5
	251
Unfit parents or homes	63
No established home	21
Illegitimate child in family	19
Unmarried mothers	4
No proof of marriage	2
	109
Nonresidents	21
Family could not be found	44
Mother remarried	7
Mother refused information	4
Mother preferred county supplies	3
Mother preferred children in institutions	2
	81
Applications withdrawn	114
Miscellaneous reasons	3
Reasons unknown	16
	133
Total	1188

Attention should be called perhaps to the fact that the annual published reports of the chief probation officer contain statistics of the number of cases dismissed by the court. This is, however, very different from the number of cases dismissed by the conference committee. Cases dismissed in court represent only the cases about which there has not been entire agreement in the conference committee or cases in which the judge fails to approve the decision of the committee. For example, during the year ending Dec. 1, 1916, 41 cases were dismissed in court. The total number of cases dismissed by the committee during this period is not given, but during the nine months from Mar. 1, 1916, to Dec. 1, 1916, the report shows that 318 applications were refused. The report shows the following reasons for rejecting the 41 cases that were dismissed in court: Aliens, 10; money in bank, 8; income sufficient, 3; full amount given to one child, 6; mother withdrew, 2; refused to cooperate, 4; no appearance, 3; no proof of marriage, 2; marriage not legal, 2; over age, 1; total, 41.

FAMILIES ON THE COOK COUNTY (CHICAGO) PENSION ROLL DURING THE YEAR 1917.

An account has been given of the methods used in administering the pension law in the juvenile court of Cook County. Following this discussion of methods of administration, it is important to know the results of the policies that have been described in the number of pensioned mothers and children and certain other facts about the families who have been placed on the pension roll. These facts have been obtained from a study of the pension records of the families on the roll during any part of the year 1917.

In January, 1917, 778 families were on the so-called pension roll drawing allowances under the aid-to-mothers law; and during the year 188 other families were added, making a total of 966. Seventy-three of these families had had pensions at an earlier date, and had been dropped from the pension roll, and then restored. This stay of pension had been due in most cases to the change in the law in 1913 making citizenship a requirement of eligibility, and the return of these families to the pension roll had been made possible by the amendment to the law of 1915.

It is of interest, too, that 182 of these families had made unsuccessful applications for pensions at an earlier date and had later reapplied and been placed on the pension list. The reason for accepting them on a second application was, in most cases, that the families had become eligible in the intervening period because of some change in circumstances; for example, they no longer had money, the required period of residence had been completed, or proof had been found of certain facts necessary to establish eligibility.

Table XXVI shows the length of time the 778 families who were on the pension roll in January, 1917, had been under the care of the court.

TABLE XXVI.—*Time on pension roll of families on the pension roll January, 1917.*

Time on pension roll.	Families on pension roll.	
	Number.	Per cent distribution.
Total	778	100.0
Less than 6 months	170	21.9
6 months and less than 1 year	166	21.3
1 year and less than 1½ years	137	17.6
1½ years and less than 2 years	68	8.7
2 years and less than 2½ years	45	5.9
2½ years and less than 3 years	47	6.0
3 years and less than 4 years	59	7.6
4 years and less than 5 years	79	10.2
5 years to 5½ years	6	.8
Not reported	1	.1

PART I.—ADMINISTRATION IN COOK COUNTY. 83

The change in the pension law in 1915 by which alien women were made eligible to pensions, substantially increased the number of pensioned families. This increase is reflected in Table XXVI, which shows that a large per cent of the total number of pensioned families had been on the pension roll for relatively short periods. Thus 21.8 per cent of the total number of families had been pensioned for less than six months, and 21.3 per cent had been pensioned for periods varying from six months to one year. That is, 43.1 per cent had been on the pension roll for less than one year. Another 17.6 per cent had been on the roll for less than a year and a half. Taking the numbers cumulatively, 60.7 per cent of all the families had been pensioned for less than a year and a half. Only 6 of the families pensioned during the first 6 months after July 1, 1911, when the first pension law went into effect, were still on the pension roll. The families cared for during the year represent a very much larger number of pensioned children. Table XXVII shows the number of pensioned children in each family and the total number of pensioned children.

TABLE XXVII.—*Number of pensioned children in each family with total number of children on pension roll in 1917.*

Number of pensioned children in family.	Number of families.	Total number of pensioned children.
Total [a]	965	3,255
One child	31	31
Two children	232	464
Three children	305	915
Four children	226	904
Five children	112	560
Six children	39	234
Seven children	13	91
Eight children	7	56

[a] Omitting 1 family for which the record was missing.

The 3,255 pensioned children are, with a very few exceptions, children under 14 years of age. It has already been pointed out that the court is very reluctant to pension any child of working age, and such pensions are granted only for children who are reported by examining physicians as physically unfit to go to work. There are a few families in which the child is enabled to remain in school after the fourteenth birthday has been reached because the probation officer has obtained a scholarship stipend from the scholarship committee. In general, however, children in pensioned families have their pensions stayed by court order on the day they reach the age of 14, when the officer finds work for them, or sends them to the vocational bureau, supported by the Chicago Board of Education, for advice or assistance in finding work.

84   ADMINISTRATION OF THE AID-TO-MOTHERS LAW.

In many of these pensioned families there are, in addition to the pensioned children, other children in the family who are at work and contributing to the family support. Table XXVIII shows the total number of children over 14 years of age in the pensioned families.

TABLE XXVIII.—*Number of families on pension roll in 1917 having specified number of children over 14 years of age.*

Number of children over 14 years of age in family.	Pensioned families. Number.	Per cent distribution.
Total	966	100.0
No children over 14	619	64.1
One child over 14	209	21.6
Two children over 14	107	11.1
Three children over 14	29	3.0
Four children over 14	1	.1
Not reported	a 1	.1

a Not reported because the record for this family could not be found.

This table shows that in the great majority of these families—64.1 per cent of the whole number—there are no children old enough to go to work. In these families, of course, the mother is the only possible wage earner. In 209 families—21.6 per cent—one child has reached the legal age of 14; and it is the court rule in such cases that the child must begin to share the burden of supporting the family. In only 14.2 per cent of the families was there more than one child of legal working age.

Certain facts relating to the nationality, marital state, age of the father at time of death, and cause of death, amount of insurance left, and some other facts of interest about the pensioned families will be presented in a series of tables. Table XXIX shows the nationality of the families on the pension roll in the year 1917.

TABLE XXIX.—*Nationality of 966 families on pension roll in 1917.*

Nationality of families on pension roll in 1917.	Families.
Total	966
American	328
White	302
Colored	26
Foreign born	638
Polish	148
German	86
Italian	81
Russian	73
Irish	71
Scandinavian	40
Austro-Hungarian	39
Slavic (miscellaneous)	42
Lithuanian	18
English and Scotch	15
Greek	8
Dutch	6
Canadian	3
Other	8

PART I.—ADMINISTRATION IN COOK COUNTY.   85

In this table the nationality represents the country of birth of the husband. The wife and the husband were usually of the same nationality, but when different the nationality of the husband has been taken. Information as to nationality is supplied by the mother's statements to the investigating officers. No attempt has been made to relate the number of families in each group to the number of each nationality in the population at large, since the question of precisely which families are placed on the pension roll is determined by such questions as length of residence in the country and in the county, number of children under and over 14 years of age, ability of relatives to assist, and other conditions that can not be related to the census returns of nationality.

The present law provides that families are eligible for a pension only after a residence of three years in the county. Table XXX shows the length of time the families pensioned in 1917 had resided in Cook County at the time they made application for pensions. For 17 families there was no report as to length of time of residence.

TABLE XXX.—*Number of families who had resided in Cook County for specified periods of time on application for pensions.*

Length of residence in county.	Number of families.
Total	966
Less than 3 years	14
3 years but less than 10	207
10 years and over	728
10 years but less than 20	354
20 years and over	232
Life	142
Not reported	17

This table shows that the mothers' pension system did not immediately attract a large number of indigent families to Cook County, or if such families came, it is clear that they were not granted pensions. The great bulk of the pensioned families had lived in the county for periods of from 10 to 20 years or longer. Taking the numbers cumulatively, it appears that 728 families, or 75 per cent of the total number, had resided here for 10 years or longer. It will be noted that 14 families had been here less than the 3 years now required for eligibility. These families were pensioned under the old law; and after the new requirement of residence had been established they had become eligible and were therefore not removed from the pension roll. The table, it will be noted, gives the period of residence at the time of application. A few of the families completed the three-year period of residence before the pension was granted.

More interesting questions relating to the families under care are those which throw light on the current pension policy of the court.

The procedure of the court has now become well established, and the data relating to families under care at this time may be assumed to give a very fair picture of the work of the court. Of special interest is the question of the number of widowed mothers on the pension list. Table XXXI shows the marital state of the women receiving pensions.

TABLE XXXI.—*Marital state of pensioned mothers in 1917.*

Marital state.	Pensioned Mothers.	
	Number.	Per cent distribution.
Total	966	100.0
Widowed	864	89.4
Married, but with husbands incapacitated	98	10.2
Deserted	4	.4

It appears from this table that the vast majority, 89.4 per cent, of the pensioned mothers are widows; 98, or 10.2 per cent, are women whose husbands though living are permanently incapacitated for work; 4 are women whose husbands deserted them, but in these cases the husband has not been heard of for 7 years or more, so that he is in the eyes of the law presumed to be dead and his deserted wife is treated as a widow.

Interesting questions arise concerning the group of 98 women with incapacitated husbands. The nature of the "physical or mental infirmity" that has rendered these men unable to support their families is a question of social importance. Since the law authorizes the court to grant an allowance to the wife of an incapacitated husband on condition of his removal from the home when his presence in the family is a menace to the physical or moral welfare of the mother or children, it is also of interest to know how many of the incapacitated men have been removed from their homes and placed in institutions. Table XXXII furnishes this information.

TABLE XXXII.—*Number of incapacitated fathers living at home and outside of the home, according to the nature of their incapacity.*

Cause of incapacity.	Fathers incapacitated.			
	Total.	Living at home.	Living away from home.	Residence not reported.
Total	98	25	72	1
Per cent	100.0	25.5	73.5	1.0
Tuberculosis	37	3	34	
Insanity	32	1	31	
Paralysis	8	5	3	
Locomotor ataxia	5	3	1	1
Heart disease	3	3		
Kidney disease	2	2		
Other[a]	11	8	3	

[a] The other forms of incapacity with the number of cases of each are as follows: Blind, 2; bronchitis and asthma, 2; cancer, 1; epileptic, 1; curvature of spine, 1; multiple sclerosis, 2; gastric crisis of tabes, 1; intestinal trouble, 1.

PART I.—ADMINISTRATION IN COOK COUNTY. 87

This table shows a large proportion of the pensioned husbands, if they may be so described, incapacitated by tuberculosis or insanity. Of the total number, 25, or 25.5 per cent, have been permitted to remain in their homes; and of these 1 is insane and 3 are suffering from tuberculosis. Nearly three-fourths, however, have been removed from their homes. This is due to the fact that a large number of the men are insane and are necessarily under institutional care and to the fact that the court usually requires a man suffering from tuberculosis to leave home and to go to the municipal tuberculosis sanitarium before a pension is granted. It would, of course, be exceedingly interesting to know how far the previous occupations or places of employment of the tubercular men may have been a cause of their incapacity, that is, how far the taxpayers are supporting the families of men who have been incapacitated by bad working conditions. It has not been possible, however, to trace the working histories of these men nor of the fathers who died, leaving their families a charge on the taxpayers.

The age of these permanently incapacitated husbands is another point of interest. The ages of 4 of the men could not be ascertained, but Table XXXIII gives the ages of the 94 for whom this information was available.

TABLE XXXIII.—*Number of incapacitated fathers in different age groups.*

Age of father.	Fathers incapacitated.	
	Number.	Per cent distribution.
Total	98	
Total reported	94	100.0
Under 45 years	70	74.5
Under 40 years	51	54.3
Under 30 years	8	8.5
30 years but less than 35	19	20.2
35 years but less than 40	24	25.5
40 years but less than 45	19	20.2
45 years but less than 50	15	16.0
50 years and over	9	9.6
Not reported	4	

Table XXXIV shows that some of these men were very young; 8 were under 30; 19 between 30 and 35; 24 others were under 40; and 19 more under 45; that is, taking the numbers cumulatively, 70 of these men, 74.5 per cent of the number whose age was reported, were under 45 years of age, and 51, or 54.3 per cent, were under 40. In the tubercular group the proportion of younger men was even higher. It seems to be clear that, in general, the incapacitated fathers were men who should have been at the height of their earning power instead of being supported either in institutions or in their own homes by the aid of State funds.

Further information concerning the 864 mothers who are widowed is also needed. It is important, for example, to ascertain the cause of the husband's death; and in Table XXXIV are presented such data as are available for the 864 families.

TABLE XXXIV.—*Causes of death of fathers of families on the pension list in 1917.*

Cause of death of father.	Families in which father had died.	
	Number.	Per cent distribution.
Total	864	
Total reported	827	100.0
Tuberculosis	247	29.9
Pneumonia	116	14.0
Diseases of heart	103	12.4
Accident [a]	68	8.2
Homicide	42	5.1
Diseases of kidney	40	4.8
Diseases of stomach and liver	29	3.5
Cancer	25	3.0
Suicide	24	2.9
Heat [b]	17	2.1
Paralysis	15	1.8
Appendicitis	13	1.6
Poisoning and infection	12	1.5
Brain trouble	13	1.6
Dropsy	10	1.2
Alcoholism	10	1.2
Typhoid	10	1.2
Syphilis, locomotor ataxia and paresis	6	0.7
Bronchitis	5	0.6
Rheumatism	5	0.6
Other diseases of respiratory system	3	0.4
Other	14	1.7
Not reported	37	

[a] Includes deaths by drowning.
[b] Most of these deaths occurred during the summer of 1916.

The causes of death listed in this table are obviously not scientific. Although the death certificate is examined in order to verify the fact of the father's death, the cause of death on the court record is not copied from the certificate but is merely a record of the woman's statement of the cause of death as she understood it or remembers it.[23]

The table shows that a large per cent of these men who died leaving a widow and young children to be supported at public expense probably died of what may be called preventable causes of death. Since causes of death are recorded as stated by the widow, it is unfortunately impossible to determine how many of the deaths were due to an industrial accident or an industrial disease.

[23] An attempt was made to reexamine the death certificates to ascertain the causes stated by the physician, but many certificates were not on file and those found did not seem to alter the conclusions drawn from the widows' statements.

Equally important with the cause of death is the age of the father at the time of death. Table XXXV shows the ages at the time of death for the 789 fathers for whom this information could be obtained.

TABLE XXXV.—*Age of father at time of death.*

Age of father at time of death.	Fathers who had died.	
	Number.	Per cent distribution.
Total	864	
Total reported	789	100.0
20 but less than 25	15	1.9
25 but less than 30	92	11.7
30 but less than 35	173	21.9
35 but less than 40	219	27.8
40 but less than 45	140	17.7
45 but less than 50	84	10.6
50 but less than 55	41	5.2
55 but less than 60	15	1.9
60 and over	10	1.3
Not reported	75	

Table XXXV shows that the majority of these men were young; 15 were under 25, and 92 were between 25 and 30 years of age. Taking the numbers cumulatively, 107 were under 30 years of age, 280 were under 35, 499 were under 40, and 639 under 45. This table emphasizes the waste of omitting any steps that might be taken to save lives valuable to the community. If the money now expended in supporting the families of these men could have been appropriated for any measures that might have saved their lives by improving living or working conditions, it is unnecessary to say that in the long run the community would have been greatly benefited.

Another question of great interest arises concerning the pensioned families. To what income group did the family belong before the father's death or incapacity? That is, do the pensioned families belong to the very poor groups in the community, or do the widows and wives of men who were once skilled workmen earning high wages become applicants for this form of relief? A second and related question is: How long a period elapses after the death of the father before the mother makes application for a pension? In Table XXXVI is presented such information on the previous occupations of the fathers as is available for the families on the pension roll in the year 1917.

Table XXXVI.—*Occupations of fathers before death or incapacity.*

Occupational group of father.	Families pensioned.	
	Number.	Per cent distribution.
Total	966	
Total reported	914	100.0
Unskilled labor	409	44.7
Skilled labor	328	35.9
Clerical or professional work	32	3.5
Personal service	80	8.8
Miscellaneous	65	7.1
Not reported	52	

The occupations of the fathers as recorded by the officers on the case records would obviously be inaccurate, since the officer gets the information from the mother, who often does not know what her husband's occupation was. She may know where he worked, and she knows quite definitely what he earned, or at any rate what he turned over to her for the family purse, but frequently she has only the vaguest idea of what his occupation was. In general, however, the information seemed to be accurate enough to make possible a classification of the occupations into several large groups that were indicative of the general character of the work done. The table shows that of the men whose occupational group was reported, 44.7 per cent were in unskilled occupations and 35.9 per cent were in what appeared to be skilled occupations. It is believed, however, that the percentage of unskilled men is understated and the percentage of skilled men overstated. A comparison of occupation with earnings seemed to indicate that in some cases when the woman said that her husband was a bricklayer or a carpenter, he must have been only a helper. On the whole, however, there is no question about the fact that a very considerable number of families now on the pension roll were families in which the wage-earning father and husband was a skilled member of a trade.

A great number of the men were unskilled laborers, working with pick and shovel, driving teams, working in the stockyards, etc. But a not inconsiderable number were doing work requiring some degree of training or experience, varying from the very slight skill demanded of a punch presser to that required of electricians and engineers. A smaller group was doing work of a clerical or professional nature, varying from the work of an insurance agent to that of a tight-rope walker drawing $600 a month; a still smaller group of men, porters, waiters, bartenders, etc., was doing work that may be called "personal service."

Table XXXVII throws further light upon the former wage status of the pensioned families.

TABLE XXXVII.—*Number of families pensioned in 1917 in which the father had previously earned specified monthly wages.*

Monthly wages.	Pensioned families.	
	Number.	Per cent distribution.
Total	966	
Total reported	879	100.0
Under $30	9	1.0
$30–$34.99	16	1.8
$35–$39.99	35	3.9
$40–$44.99	114	13.0
$45–$49.99	140	15.9
$50–$54.99	79	9.0
$55–$59.99	47	5.5
$60–$64.99	158	18.0
$65–$69.99	42	4.8
$70–$74.99	85	9.7
$75–$79.99	23	2.6
$80–$84.99	54	6.1
$85–$89.99	10	1.1
$90–$94.99	7	.8
$95–$99.99	11	1.2
$100 and over	49	5.6
Not reported	87	

TABLE XXXVII–A.—*Cumulative series of numbers and percentages.*

Monthly wages.	Pensioned families.	
	Number.	Per cent distribution.
Total	966	
Total reported	879	100.0
Under $30	9	1.0
Under $40	60	6.7
Under $50	314	35.6
Under $60	440	50.1
Under $70	640	72.9
Under $80	748	85.2
Under $90	812	92.4
Under $100	830	94.4
$100 and over	49	5.6
Not reported	87	

An earlier statement has been made as to the accuracy of the data relating to the fathers' wages or earnings,[24] and no further comment will be made on this point. Accepting the data as presented in these tables, it appears that some of the families were supported out of very low earnings. Thus Table XXXVII shows that 9 men

---
[24] See *supra,* p. 67.

earned less than $30 a month, 16 were in the wage group earning $30 and less than $35 a month, 35 in the group earning $35 and less than $40 a month, and 114 in the group earning $40 and less than $45 a month. Looking at Table XXXVII A, which gives a cumulative series of numbers and percentages based on cases for which information was available, it appears that 6.7 per cent of the men, all of whom, it will be remembered, were not only husbands but fathers with small children to support, earned less than $40 a month, 35.6 per cent earned less than $50, and 50.1 per cent earned less than $60. When the earnings are so low, it is not to be expected that savings will be accumulated, and the question at once arises as to the amount of insurance left by these men and the length of time that elapsed between the death of the husband and father and the filing of the application for a pension. No attempt was made to collect this information for the 966 families under care in 1917, since data had already been collected in the course of the survey carried on by the officers of the court for the 470 families under care between August 1, 1913, and March 1, 1915. Table XXXVIII shows the number of families left with insurance of specified amounts.

TABLE XXXVIII.—*Number of pensioned families with insurance of specified amounts: Data for 470 families on pension roll Aug. 1, 1913, to Mar. 1, 1915.*

Amount of insurance.	Pensioned families.	
	Number.	Per cent distribution.
Total	470	100.0
None	201	42.8
Less than $200	77	16.4
$200 to $499	77	16.4
$500 to $999	49	10.4
$1,000 and over	66	14.0

According to this table, 201 of these familes, or 42.8 per cent of the whole number, were left without any insurance at all, and the majority of those who had some insurance received only relatively small amounts. Thus 77 families, or 16.4 per cent, got less than $200; and another 77, or 16.4 per cent, got less than $500. It is well known that a small insurance policy is used largely to pay the funeral expenses, doctor's bills, and other debts incurred during the father's illness. There is very little left out of the insurance policy, therefore, after all these expenses and debts are paid. It is to be expected that many of these families will make application for pensions very soon after the father's death, since in most cases their only source of support in the interval is what the mother can earn or the contribution of a charitable society.

PART I.—ADMINISTRATION IN COOK COUNTY. 93

Table XXXIX shows the length of time that elapsed between the father's death and the application for a pension. The information could be obtained for only 466 out of the 707 fatherless families.

TABLE XXXIX.—*Interval between father's death and application for pension— data for 466 families on pension roll, Aug. 1, 1913 to Mar. 1, 1915.*

Interval between death of father and application.	Pensioned families.	
	Number.	Per cent distribution.
Total	466	100.0
Application before death	14	3.0
Less than one month	78	16.7
One month but less than three	52	11.2
Three months but less than six	38	8.2
Six months but less than one year	65	13.9
One year but less than two	67	14.4
Two years but less than five	97	20.8
Five years and over	55	11.8

Table XXXIX shows that 14 families had made application for pensions before the father's death. These were families in which the father had become mentally or physically incapacitated some time before his death, and the pension had been originally asked on the ground of his incapacity. Seventy-eight families, or 16.7 per cent of the whole number, applied for pensions within a month after the husband's death; 52, or 11.2 per cent, made applications within three months; and 38, or 8.2 per cent, within six months; or, taking the numbers cumulatively, 168, or 36.1 per cent, had applied before the husband and father had been dead six months. The other 61 per cent succeeded in carrying their families without the aid of the court for considerable periods of time.

The tables that have been given in this section show that the fathers of these families were men whose earnings were low, and that many of the widows supported themselves for some time after the death of their husbands. As a result of these circumstances the families that are placed on the court pension roll are often in poor physical condition and are frequently living under conditions that are inimical to health.

Tables have already been given showing certain facts as to the housing condition of the families at the time the pension was granted.[25]

An attempt was made to collect certain other data relating to the health of the families at the time of the granting of the pension. But, although testimony of the officers is unanimous that the families are physically in poor condition, facts as to health are difficult to

[25] See *supra*, p. 31.

obtain. Among the 543 families studied in the survey conducted by the officers of the court, in 113 families, or over one-fifth of the entire number, some member of the family was reported tubercular. The information about other ailments is probably not nearly so complete, but the diseases reported run all the way from general anemia and lack of nutrition, reported for 17 mothers, to the more specific diseases of tumor, varicose veins, goiter, etc. Indeed incomplete as the reports obviously are it is the exceptional family about whom there are no reports of ill health.

The fact that so many of the families are tubercular or are suffering from some other form of ill health has made necessary the allowances for " extra diet " so often met with in the budgets prepared by the field supervisor.[26]

The court has done much to restore these families to normal conditions of health not only by providing the necessary medical care and insisting upon frequent examinations, but also by providing adequate pensions for families in need of special diet.

---

[26] See *supra,* pp. 59, 60, 61.

SUBSEQUENT HISTORY OF FAMILIES MADE TECHNICALLY INELIGIBLE BY CHANGES IN THE PENSION LAW.[d]

Attention has already been called to the fact that the radical amendments of the pension law in 1913 made a large number of families technically no longer eligible for pensions and resulted in the withdrawal of pension grants from 172 families who had been beneficiaries under the old law. What became of these families was a question of interest. Were they able to get on satisfactorily without this public aid? Did the withdrawal of the pension lead to a lowering of the home standards with resulting harm to the children? Or, were the pensioned children promptly placed in institutions for dependent children?

A study of the effects of the withdrawal of the pension upon these families who had been dropped because of technical ineligibility would, it was believed, throw light upon the value of the pensions in sustaining a proper standard of family life. An attempt was made, therefore, to follow the later history of these families, who at the time this study was begun (September, 1915) had been off the pension roll for a period of more than two years. The histories of these families were traced chiefly through the records that were found in the offices of various private agencies to which the families had been referred for help. But the court records were also used, and conferences with probation officers and visits to the families themselves were further sources of information.

Most of the provisions of the aid-to-mothers act of 1913, which replaced the loosely drawn act of 1911, were founded upon the current practices of the Cook County juvenile court;[27] but in several important particulars a change was made, so that some classes of families previously pensioned by the Chicago court were no longer eligible. These were (1) aliens, (2) deserted or divorced women, or women whose husbands were in prison, (3) families who had not had a continuous residence of three years in the county. All such families who were receiving pensions under the old law were summarily dropped from the pension roll on July 1, 1913, when the new law went into effect.

---

[d] This section was prepared by Miss Helen Russell Wright.
[27] See *supra*, pp. 11–13.

95

Immediately after the change in the law a meeting of the citizens' committee was held to discuss the treatment of these families, and it was decided that the court should refer them to private relief societies for care. A list of the families referred to each agency was obtained from the court, together with information as to the amount of the former pension, the date at which the pension had been granted, and the reasons for the stay of the pension. This list contained the names of 172 families with 577 children. Table XL shows the specific ground of ineligibility that led to the removal of each of these 172 families from the pension roll.

TABLE XL.—*Number of mothers dropped from pension roll in July, 1913, because of ineligibility.*

Ground of ineligibility.	Number of mothers.	Per cent distribution.
Total	172	100.0
Mother alien	137	79.6
Mother deserted or divorced	31	18.0
Insufficient period of residence in Cook County	3	2.0
Husband in jail	1	4

Of the 137 women who lost their pensions because they were not citizens, 122 were widows, and 12 had incapacitated husbands living at home. One of the other mothers might be classed with the widows since she was supposed to be widowed, but it developed that she had a second husband. The large number of aliens affected is especially significant since a later amendment to the law, July, 1915, made most of these families again eligible or made it very easy for them to become so.

The length of time these families had been on the pension roll and the amounts of their pensions are facts of importance. Most of the families, as Table XLI shows, had been on the pension roll for periods of nine months or longer, and they had become accustomed to maintaining their homes on the basis of the monthly court allowance.

TABLE XLI.—*Number of families who had been on pension roll for specified periods.*

Time on pension roll.	Number of families.
Total	172
Less than 3 months	18
3 months but less than 6	11
6 months but less than 9	25
9 months but less than 1 year	47
1 year and over	71

PART I.—ADMINISTRATION IN COOK COUNTY.

The pensions relinquished were most of them substantial allowances. Table XLII shows that only 22 of the 172 families were getting less than $20 a month.

TABLE XLII.—*Number of families who had received pensions of specified amounts.*

Amount of pension.	Number of families.
Total	172
Less than $20	22
$20 to $29	60
$30 to $39	60
$40 and over	30

The sudden withdrawal of the pensions from these 172 families involved, in a large number of cases, a readjustment almost as radical as that which followed the father's death. The court referred 124 of the families to the united charities, 27 to the St. Vincent de Paul Society, 21 to the Jewish Home Finding Society, and all the 172 families to the county agent.[28]

A letter concerning each family was sent to the proper organization, and the responsibility of the court for the family came to an end. The private charities, however, did not in all cases consider the letter of reference a request for a visit. Different societies and even different agents of the same society seemed to follow different policies. It should not be overlooked that a very heavy charge had been suddenly placed on the private societies, and the policies must have been to some extent shaped by their available resources both as to visitors and funds.

It was not to be expected that for every family a private charitable pension would immediately be substituted for the old court pension. It was inevitable that in some cases the private society would differ from the court in its view of the assistance the family needed and that some of the families would themselves seek a new method of managing their affairs. The 172 families, therefore, got along without the court pension in a variety of ways. They may be grouped into five main classes: (1) Those whose children were taken away; (2) those who kept the family together by their own efforts, with only irregular assistance from charitable agencies; (3) those who were cared for by means of regular assistance from private charity; (4) those who were cared for in other ways than by a pension in the home, e. g., returned to Europe, given sanitarium care, etc.; and (5)

---

[28] The official in charge of the distribution of public outdoor relief which in Cook County, it will be remembered, is given only in kind. See p. 8 for a statement as to the outdoor relief given in Cook County.

those who apparently had no outside help of any kind. It will be seen that there might be some overlapping of these groups, since a family might have regular relief for a time and then get along with little or no relief, or a family might be helped until the children were placed in institutions.

Since the breaking up of the home and the placing of children in institutions is of special interest, all families who were broken up, either by court order or by private arrangement, have been grouped together without regard to their other history. All families who have at any time received regular relief have been grouped together, leaving in the other groups only those who at no time since July 1, 1913, were given regular material relief.

Table XLIII shows the number of families in these various groups:

TABLE XLIII.—*Number of families assisted or not assisted by private agencies.*

Form of assistance.	Number of families.
Total	172
Pensioned by private agencies	90
Assisted irregularly by private agencies (partially self-supporting)	35
Entirely self-supporting	32
Families broken up	8
Otherwise cared for	3
Not reported	4

FAMILIES BROKEN UP.

Of the 172 women who suddenly lost their pensions while they were still in need of them, only 8 gave up their children. The 8 families in which the children were taken away is a group of special interest. The children of 1 family were sent to their paternal grandmother who had a good home and was able and willing to give them good care. In the other 7 families the children were sent to institutions. One mother made private arrangements for the institutional care of her children without the knowledge of the court. This woman was offered a regular allowance equal to more than half her former pension, and a plan was suggested whereby she might earn the rest; but she was not satisfied to try this arrangement and preferred to put her children in institutions. One family was broken up for a very short time until the mother had had an operation, arranged for by the united charities, and had become physically fit to care for her children. One mother remarried, and she and her new husband were not willing to care for the old family, so they took the simplest means of getting rid of the burden. The other four mothers lost their children because, in the words of the court record, the mother was " unable to give them proper maternal care and guardianship." Further details about these 4 families were secured by a study of the court and the united charities' records.

In two of these cases the united charities refused to support the family because they considered the mother morally unfit to care for her children. The B family had been helped by the united charities from the time of the father's death in 1908. In spite of efforts to improve the home, conditions had never been at all satisfactory. The mother insisted on keeping roomers in quarters too small for her own family, and would not move even when desirable quarters were found for her. The house was exceedingly dirty, and the children were dirty and frequently sick. Moreover, rumors were very frequent that the mother was immoral. The united charities had originally reported the family to the juvenile court, thinking that the court would take the children away, but the court hoped that by further efforts and by means of a regular pension of $40 a month the home could be safely maintained. The task proved none too easy; and when the law changed after she had had her pension for a year, the only improvement noticed was that the house was cleaner. To offset this were the repeated complaints that had come to the department concerning Mrs. B's deportment in the neighborhood. "Sufficient proof of immorality on her part has not been secured. * * * Her quarrelsome habits with the relatives and neighbors are well established," said the letter from the juvenile court to the united charities when the family was referred back to the latter organization. It was also known that at least $50 of her pension money had been spent on clothes for herself and a prospective husband who had later disappeared. When the pension was automatically stayed, the united charities refused to give further assistance, and 3 of the 4 children were sent to an institution for dependent children. The county in this instance paid for the support of the children in institutions instead of supporting them by pensions in the home.

On similar grounds the united charities refused to give further financial assistance to the N family. This decision was not made, however, until it seemed to the visitors of both the united charities and the juvenile protective association that no amount of material relief would benefit the family. The court ordered two of the children sent to institutions, and appointed the county agent guardian of the other three, with power to send them to relatives in Baltimore. The relatives, however, were not located, and later these children also were sent to institutions. In this case also the change in the pension law meant that the children were supported by the county in institutions instead of in the home.

The two other families whose children the court sent to institutions because the mother was unable to care for them had apparently not been dealt with by any private agency after the court pension ceased. One family had three wage earners, and there is reason to think that the four dependent children might have been cared for had a greater effort been made to keep them at home. The mother bore the reputation of being unreliable—she had at an earlier time before the pension grant put three children in an institution, when the family income was $60 a month—and the theory that she was unwilling to carry the family burdens any longer seemed to be well founded. About the other family not enough information could be secured to warrant even a guess as to whether the children should have been kept in the home or whether there was some reason, other than poverty, for the breaking up of the family.

On the whole, therefore, it appears that of the seven mothers whose children went to institutions, two were considered morally unfit, one was temporarily physically unfit to care for her children, three others seemed to be unwilling to make the sacrifices which keeping the children entailed. We have left, therefore, only one other mother whose children were put in institutions, and of this family little is known. It is clear, however, that she did not apply for help to the united charities before she gave up her children.

CARE OF JEWISH FAMILIES.

Passing on to the group of families pensioned by private agencies, these are divided into two groups. Twenty-one were Jewish families cared for by the Jewish Home-Finding Society, and 69 were pensioned by the united charities. Twenty of the 21 Jewish families were given a monthly pension, in all but two cases equal to or greater than the court pension. In the other Jewish family the father was periodically insane, and regular relief was, therefore, given intermittently, varying with his ability to support the family.

After the new pension law of 1915 was passed, most of these families again became eligible for pensions; and 14 have been restored to the pension roll. The net result of the earlier change in the law therefore, so far as the Jewish families were concerned, was a change in the source of their relief, with little if any change in the amount of their income. Since the Jewish Home Finding Society was supplementing their public pensions, even while under the care of the court, there was practically no problem of readjustment for this group of families.

PART I.—ADMINISTRATION IN COOK COUNTY. 101

FAMILIES PENSIONED BY PRIVATE CHARITY.

Out of the 150 non-Jewish families dropped by the court, 69 appear to have received regular assistance from private charity. Sixty-six were pensioned by the united charities for long or short periods; and 3 families through the efforts of the united charities received relief from other sources—1 from an interested individual, 1 from the church, and 1 from a church and township. Of the 69 families regularly assisted, only 9 had children of working age, and in the other 60 families the mother was the sole wage earner. It is of interest, too, that 62 of these families had been known to the united charities before they had been pensioned by the court, and 35 of them had been pensioned during this earlier period.

In general, these families received their private pensions as regularly as they had received their court pensions. There are a few exceptions, for one or two families had different items of relief from different sources, and one or the other was sometimes behind; and in some cases rent was allowed to run until the family was threatened with eviction. But the amount of relief regularly given in the majority of cases appears to have been less than the former court pension. There are, of course, obvious difficulties in attempting to make a direct comparison between the allowances of families who are cared for by different relief agencies. Some difficulties were encountered in determining the precise amount of relief given by the private agency. The court allowance was a fixed and regular cash allowance. In the case of the private society, the rent might be paid from the office, some assistance given in kind, and some cash might also be given. Moreover, the families might also receive assistance from other sources. It is the practice of the united charities, for example, to ask to have its pensioned families put on the outdoor relief list, and the value of the county supplies must also be determined. The county agent gives out several different rations varying considerably in value, and the charity records do not always show the value of the particular ration received nor the estimated value of other relief in kind. An effort was made, however, to make the estimates of the new income on a very liberal basis; and by adding the value of relief in kind to the amounts given the family in money, it is believed that a satisfactory estimate of the new family allowance was arrived at. Table XLIV shows the difference between the former court pension and the value of relief regularly received when the family was under the care of the private agency. It should be made clear, however, that some of these families had additional help in emergencies and that the amount of relief given in the table represents only the estimated regular allowance.

Table XLIV.—*Amount of court pension and estimated deficit in later, private allowances.*

Amount of previous pension.	Families who received regular relief from private agencies.						
	Total.	Estimated deficit in private allowance.					
		None or less than $5.	$5–$9.	$10–$14.	$15–$19.	$20.	Not reported.
Total number of families..	69	15	11	13	12	17	1
$10–$19	3	2		1			
20– 29	23	8	7	3	5		
30– 39	23	4	4	4	5	6	
40– 49	20	1		5	2	11	1

In this table it appears that 17, or 25 per cent, of these 69 families suffered a decrease in income of approximately $20 a month when they became pensioners on a private rather than a public basis; 12 others had a deficit of $15 to $19, making 29 families, or 42 per cent, of the whole number who suffered a decrease of $15 or more. Fifteen families, or 22 per cent, received the same pension or lost less than $5 by transfer to the private relief societies.

It may not be fair, however, to draw the conclusion from this table that the standard of relief maintained by the united charities was as a general policy lower than that of the court. Attention should again be called to the fact that a heavy and unexpected burden had been placed on the private societies by asking them suddenly to support a large number of pensioners, and during the period under discussion, an industrial depression occurred that would, even without this additional burden, have taxed their resources to the uttermost. It is, however, only fair to the court to say that at any rate the aid-to-mothers department apparently was maintaining a standard of relief which, measured by the standards of the best known of the private societies, was liberal and presumably adequate.

Of course a reduction in the amount of relief does not necessarily mean a reduction in family income. Part of the deficit may be made up by increased earnings on the part of the mother or by earnings of children, if there are children in the family who have reached the age of 14. As a matter of fact, there were in these 69 families only four children who began work within six months of the stay of the pension; and of these, two came from families where the united charities relief was equal to the court pension, so that it is evident that the deficits given in Table XLIV were in general not made up by earnings of new child wage earners.

About the increased earnings of the mother, we have, unfortunately, little information. The reports of the mother's earnings are very incomplete both for the pension period and for the later period after the pension had been withdrawn. We are, therefore, too uncertain about both items to attempt a careful comparison. In the comparatively few cases, however, where the mother's earnings both during and after the pension period are recorded, there appears to be little difference in her contribution to the family income. The court policy is to have the mother do all the work she can without injury to her health or to her children's welfare, and in the few cases in which the mother appears to have earned more after the stay of the pension, there is nothing in the records to indicate that the court had made a mistake in its estimate of the mother's earning capacity. Take, for example, the case of Mrs. K. ——, who had incipient tuberculosis as well as tumor. The court required her to do no work except to take care of her four children. On the stay of her pension she received from the charities $5.50 for her rent; $1 a week fairly regularly from a sectarian relief organization; and county supplies. Mrs. K.—— was expected to do enough work to earn the rest of her food. This she attempted to do by washing, and she sometimes earned as much as $3.25 in a week. However, her earnings were not regular; sometimes she did not work because she could not get washings; but more often, she was sick and unable to do the washings she had, or she could not work because of the sickness of the children, which occurred with disturbing frequency. The result was that often the family got entirely out of food, " which," notes our investigator, " was detrimental to her health owing to the fact that she had tuberculosis," and emergency relief seemed to be given tardily. In other words, while the mother was nominally working after the stay of the pension, her work was so interrupted that her earnings were small and there were times of acute distress in the family.

If the difference between what the court gave and what private charity gave was not made up by increased earnings on the part of the family—and there seems to be no evidence to show that it was in any considerable number of cases—the transfer of a family from a public to a private agency was accompanied for the most part by a decrease in the family income. Unless the court pension was more than adequate, the relief given afterwards was less than adequate. It is of course not possible to establish a causal connection between the loss of the pension and later physical deterioration or breakdown. As a matter of fact, some of the families who seem to have suffered most since the withdrawal of the pension are families who were receiving fully as much from the united charities as they had ever received from the court.

Attention should, however, be called to the fact that the health of some of the families seemed plainly to deteriorate. In 8 of the 69 families some member of the family became tubercular; 2, who were tubercular to begin with, grew worse; 3 mothers worked until they broke down—1 before the united charities visited her, 1 for whom the united charities paid the rent regularly, and 1 who was being assisted only in emergencies; 4 families, while they do not appear to have developed any chronic disease or suffered complete breakdown, have had a history which leaves the impression of an almost unbroken succession of sickness. Four families are reported as improved in health; and 3 of the mothers submitted to an operation, so that presumably they, too, have improved. Of the other 44 families we either have no reports of ill-health or reports indicating little change at the later period.

It can not be assumed that all these cases of reported ill-health are to be charged to inadequate relief. Some breakdowns would undoubtedly have occurred even if the court pension had continued. In some cases, however, there does appear to be a connection between physical breakdown and overwork. Take, for example, the story of Mrs. G. Her rent was paid, but she earned the rest of the family support by working six days a week in a laundry. In July, 1915, she was taken sick, was unable to work for two days, and so lost her place in the laundry. The charities visitor notes at this time that work in the laundry has worn her out; she "looks badly, very thin and pale." An examination at the municipal tuberculosis clinic showed that she had incipient tuberculosis; and from that time on, the united charities gave her a weekly allowance of $3 in addition to her rent.

A similar case is that of the mother of the W family, who had been receiving $30 a month from the court. When the pension was withdrawn, she was given only her rent and was expected to earn enough for food for herself and three children. She tried to do this by sewing, but her earnings were irregular, because of her own sickness or that of the children. As a result they were often without food, and the mother was repeatedly forced to ask the united charities for a small grocery order to tide her over. Their whole story is characterized by the investigator as "a dreary tale of sickness." Tuberculosis was discovered in November, 1914, and the rent was then supplemented by a weekly allowance of food.

A number of cases of moral breakdown among these families should also be noted. Here again it is not possible to attach a causal relationship between inadequate relief and bad morals. It is always possible that an old evil, long concealed, has just been brought to light through more intimate acquaintance with the family. Leaving out of account for the present those rumors and suspicions which attach to several of the families, there are in some cases certain definite facts which indicate moral deterioration. From five families whose pensions had been withdrawn children were brought before the juvenile court as delinquent (one as truant); and the daughter of one family had an illegitimate child. Two of these families show no other evidence of low moral standards. There were no complaints recorded about the mother's conduct or the general standard of living of the family. The relief in these two families was much less than had been given by the court, but there may be no relation between this fact and the children's stealing grain from cars on the railroad track. In the other three families which sent children to court as delinquents, as well as in the family where the oldest girl gave birth to an illegitimate child, the delinquent is only one member of a group in which the whole situation is radically wrong. The mother of one delinquent boy is one of those who had an illegitimate child, and F, his older sister, is in grave danger, if not already immoral. The mother of the girl who had an illegitimate child is strongly suspected of immorality, and the united charities has many reports of men being there late at night. The other two come from homes where the standards are generally low, and there are suggestions that one mother may even be immoral. She is known to have men roomers, her housekeeping is haphazard, and the house is unusually dirty.

Aside from these families, where there is evidently some very definite moral failure, there are those other families alluded to above in which suspicion more or less definite attaches to the mother. There are two families not included among those already cited where the united charities felt warranted in discontinuing relief—one, because the mother kept men roomers, and one, because complaints that the mother drank, made her house a rendezvous for drinking men, and was herself immoral were so frequent and came from such trustworthy sources that they could not be disregarded. It is necessary to add that the juvenile court, after a careful investigation, concluded that the charges against this woman were unfounded and regranted the pension in 1916. Unfortunately the report on the investigation is not sufficiently full to explain the situation.

Reports of drinking or immorality are also current about several other families, but their foundation has not been well enough established to make the united charities take any action or stop giving material relief.

It is impossible to say of these difficulties either "They are a new development since 1913," or, "They are not new difficulties, they antedated the withdrawal of the pension." The delinquency of the children is new, but the situation in the home may or may not be new. The birth of the illegitimate children also took place after the withdrawal of the pension, but the lack of moral standards may have antedated even the grant of the pension. This was the situation in the one case of a delinquent boy whose mother had an illegitimate child. The mother's care of her home and children was never satisfactory either to the court or to the united charities. Similar conditions may have existed at an early date in other cases, but may not have been recorded.

A point of interest is the length of time after the withdrawal of the pension before the 69 families began receiving private relief regularly. For some of them there was an interval between the time when the court dropped them and the date when the united charities took them up. Eight families, for example, got along for six months or more without assistance from the united charities. One of these families was visited several times, then lost track of until March, 1915, and at that time the mother, who had supported herself by keeping boarders, was about to have an illegitimate child and needed a good deal of assistance from that time on. Another family was known to the united charities at frequent intervals, but the mother was working for a cleaning firm and seemed to be supporting herself until January, 1915, when she broke down from overwork. One mother who was not visited until January, 1914, was found to have injured her eyes seriously in the meantime; for she had been sitting up late at night " sewing pants " by the light of a kerosene lamp, in a brave attempt to support herself and four little children. Another family was called to the attention of the united charities early in 1915 by a doctor who reported the eldest child ill as a result of underfeeding.

It is of interest that 19 families are still being assisted by the united charities, although the majority of the families dropped in 1913 are either self-supporting now or have been restored to the pension roll. Eight are deserted wives; one woman had been divorced; two alien mothers had insane husbands and, therefore, could not take out their own first papers. There are five families carried by the united charities who, although they satisfy the requirements of citizenship and widowhood, fail to meet other requirements of the law. Two families are, so far as known, eligible in every way; they have applied for a county pension, but their applications have not yet been acted upon (March, 1916). One other family (alien) that is still receiving a private allowance is receiving it from a church and has never taken steps to become eligible for a county pension.

All the five mothers who are classed as ineligible for other reasons have applied for a regrant of pension and have been refused by the court for the following reasons: Two, because in each case the oldest child was found to be illegitimate; one, because a man roomer was discovered; one, because the mother was found to have money; and the fifth, because there was only one child under 14 and the court thought that the family should, therefore, be self-supporting.

In the two cases where there was an illegitimate child there was not any suspicion of the mother's present character; the presence of the roomer on whose account the court dismissed one petition had just been confirmed and the united charities had had no time to decide on their course of action. Undoubtedly they will not continue paying a weekly allowance unless he leaves, although no suspicion attaches to the mother's morality in this particular case. The discovery of one woman's bank account came as something of a shock to the united charities, as this woman had been from all points of view one of the most satisfactory of any of the women in their care. When they talked to her they found that she had saved it little by little from the relief they had given her, and possibly from the county pension. She had not intended to deceive the united charities after they had helped her so much and had no thought of doing wrong when she put away something from each sum that was given her, just as she had done from her husband's wages. She did not want to die and to leave her children penniless, and so was doing her best to provide for them a secure future. She had managed to accumulate $192.75. It was possible for the united charities visitor to make her understand why they objected to what she had done and to persuade her that she could trust the society to look out for her children. She therefore turned over her little savings, which are now being given back to her in small amounts. Probably when this is gone she will reapply for a county pension.

The mother of the family in which there is only one child under 14 is able to do some work, but she has not been able to do steady work, so that her earning capacity is small. The eldest girl is 14 but is not strong, and the united charities thinks it far better that she remain in school. The court doctor will not certify that she is unable to work, so the court does not feel justified in pensioning the family.

FAMILIES RECEIVING OCCASIONAL ASSISTANCE.

There remain two other groups of families whose pensions were withdrawn: (1) Thirty-five families who managed to get along with only occasional assistance; and (2) 32 families who apparently were entirely self-supporting.

Were these families as well off as they were under the pension system? With regard to the families who had occasional assistance, our discussion must be confined to the families who finally asked help from the united charities. Other families were assisted by churches, by the county agent, or by some minor charitable agency; but their records were not so easily available as those of the charities. In general the 35 families in this group were families with only a few pensioned children and with correspondingly small pensions; and in 13 families there were other sources of income than the mother's earnings. The readjustment, therefore, was not so difficult.

Fourteen of these families who asked or received very little help were found on later investigation apparently to need more assistance. To five of these who had become eligible the court had re-granted their pensions before our investigator visited them. Five families were found by the investigator to be in such obvious need that three of them were reported to the united charities and the other two were told to reapply for pensions at once. The records show with regard to the other four families that the mother either broke down completely or was frequently ill and showed unmistakable signs of overwork.

It is very easy to understand why the mother should have overworked, since in 12 of the 14 families she was the sole contributor to the family income, and since in most of these families there were several children to be provided for. One mother had six children to care for, one mother had five children, four mothers had four children each, five had families of three children, while only one mother had a small family of two children. To support families of this size meant a heavy portion of work; and as these mothers were not equipped to do any kind of skilled work, it meant for every case but one spending long hours over the washtub or scrubbing on her knees.

Of the families who seemed able to support themselves with slight assistance, seven were families in which at least one child was helping the mother care for the family; and in three of the families relatives also were helping to some extent. In one family a mother and one child cared for six people. They had a hard struggle, and it has been possible for them to succeed only because the mother was an excellent seamstress. She had a little help immediately after the pension was withdrawn and is very resentful that she ever became a "case" on the records of a private charity. She said it was through no fault of hers, as she would "rather die than take charity," but because the court had sent in her name. She did not consider the court pension charity. There were two families of two children each in which the mother was the sole wage earner. They live quite comfortably when work is plentiful and no one in the family is ill; but in time of emergency one woman falls back on the united charities, and the other relies on the help of a brother who lives with her. He apparently does not fail her, though he has had to pawn his clothes to help her out. In normal times, too, the board of this brother and another roomer is a great help in eking out the scanty income. The other mother also had help from relatives, although of a different kind. Her father takes care of the children, leaving her free to go to work.

There are a number of families who could not be located and about whom the records contained little information. In a few cases the woman is known to have remarried, and in a few others in which the pension was small there was a child within a few months of working age. Apparently the family managed with credit until this new wage earner began to contribute to the family income.

In general, it may be said that in some of these families the change of circumstances that occurred would have led to a discontinuance of the pensions, even had there been no change in the law; that in at least 14 families in which the mother tried to manage with only occasional help the burden seems to have been too heavy for her. Of the other families we lack complete information in many cases. We have no evidence that they did not get on satisfactorily. Eight families, however, about whom the records gave considerable information, seemed to have managed very well with the occasional help they received.

FAMILIES ENTIRELY SELF-SUPPORTING.

Out of the 172 families, there were only 32 who, so far as we know, managed without any assistance from charitable resources. Some of these were helped by relatives, but in most cases the mother and children maintained the family by their own efforts. Like the preceding group these families were for the most part those with few children and small pensions. Some of them were families with children over 14 and some with children nearly 14, who were able to work shortly after the discontinuance of the pension. These facts undoubtedly go far toward explaining why this particular group of families was able to get along without assistance.

The manner in which they lived and the exact means by which they supported themselves immediately following the stay of their pensions is not known. They are families about whom charitable agencies have no record, and two years had passed before they were visited in the course of this investigation. The information obtained, therefore, is more complete for the recent than for the more remote past. Valuable as this information is, the period of readjustment is the one with which we are directly concerned.

Eleven mothers were the sole contributors to the family income, but six of these had only three people to support. Of those who had more, one was granted a county pension again within six months; another worked for a time scrubbing at night and then remarried; a third woman had a brother in Norway, who sent for her and her three children to come home.

A colored family of five was supported entirely by the mother, who was exceptionally skilled and competent. There was a defective girl of 15 in this family who, though she could not work herself, was able to relieve her mother of the household duties. The mother was an excellent cook and laundress, in good health, and a good wage earner. The court hoped that this family would succeed without assistance; and after the change in the law in 1915, when the mother asked for a pension again, it was refused on the ground that her income was sufficient.

Some other families, however, maintained their independence at heavy cost. For example, Mrs. R, an extremely plucky Swedish woman, supported a family of five, but they all became tubercular. Mrs. R was a deserted woman who, before she was granted a court pension, had been helped by the charities, had done night scrubbing in the county building and also some washing. Later, however, after a county election, the new administration made a clean sweep of all county employees, even the scrub women. Efforts were made to get Mrs. R reinstated, but fortunately for her, they failed, so that she applied for a pension under the aid-to-mother's act and was granted $20 a month. The court soon found that Mrs. R was tubercular. They increased her pension to $40 a month to enable her to rest; and after three months of this treatment she was so much improved that she was once more able to do light work and her pension was cut to $28. When the law changed in 1913 and the court was forced to withdraw her pension, she was referred to one of the private societies with the recommendation that she continue light work. Instead of applying for aid, Mrs. R began scrubbing again in the county building, where for the next two years she earned $60 a month. In March, 1914, her husband, who had not been heard of since his desertion in 1908, was killed on the railway tracks at Highland Park, where he had been at work and had accumulated property. After the funeral bill, some claims against the property, debts, etc., were paid, his wife received $500, which she, probably overthrifty, put in the bank in trust for the children while she continued scrubbing. When the family was visited by the investigator, they were living in a dark apartment in a rear tenement, crowded in between two higher buildings. The children who were at home were frail and delicate, and their mother said they were tubercular. In verifying this statement at the municipal tuberculosis sanitarium, the records showed that the mother herself was in the second stage of tuberculosis, moderately advanced, two of the children were glandular and in need of treatment; and one girl was in the first stage in need of sanitarium care. Here obviously the costs of "independence" had been too great.

Five mothers who supported themselves and two children without assistance were exceptionally vigorous and well, and the children too, with a single exception, have apparently been equally well. Even in these families, however, independence has been maintained with a struggle which for women less fortunately endowed physically would have been disastrous. Two women did washings away from home; one earned $5 to $6 a week, and the other worked four or five days a week at $2 a day. One woman worked in a tobacco factory, standing at a labeling machine 10 hours a day six days a week, and earned a dollar a day. Another earned the same amount as a waitress.

Thirteen mothers shared the duty of supporting the family with children of working age, and most of them according to their own stories get along without any special distress, although the long, hard pull had left its mark on some of the mothers. One Italian woman who seems quite worked out, and who is now supported by her two boys, expressed great indignation because her pension had been cut off in the time of their greatest need, and she had been forced to go to work again in spite of serious heart trouble.

In two of these families independence has been accompanied by moral disaster, although the moral breakdown was clearly not caused by the withdrawal of the pension in either case. One mother gave birth to an illegitimate child in 1914, but the father was a boarder who had been living with her a long time, unknown to the court, while she was still a county pensioner. Another woman drinks, and although three children are now of working age, not one of them is a good wage earner, and the eldest boy, according to his sister, is a " plain bum." But this family had a very unsatisfactory history before the court pension was granted, the children had been sent out to beg and the mother was incompetent.

In conclusion, looking back over the histories of the majority of these families, it appears to be true that the families, on the whole, suffered a serious loss when the pensions were withdrawn. In general, their incomes were not so large or so regular, even when they had the assistance of private charity, and many of the mothers suffered from overwork. In a few cases the families became sufficiently self-supporting and managed to get on with a struggle, but without any disastrous results. Can it be said that these families should never have been placed on the pension roll? On the contrary, it would probably be nearer the truth to say that these families were in grave danger—danger of overwork on the mother's part and danger of neglect of home and children. A few exceptionally competent women were able to take grave risks and succeed in spite of them. The community, however, can not safely refuse aid to mothers on such grounds. The few women of exceptional health and skill who were able to be self-supporting would doubtless have maintained better homes with the help of the pension from the court and have given their children a better start in life.

EXPENDITURES FOR MOTHERS' PENSIONS, 1911-1918.

Every social experiment should be considered on its merits as a social institution, entirely apart from the question of cost. The community can afford to pay to have its children trained to be useful citizens if it can be persuaded that the money will bring these results. The question, "How much will it cost?" is, nevertheless, an interesting if not a determining factor in the problem. In Cook County during the eight and a half years since the installation of the pension system in July, 1911, $1,477,960 has been expended for pensions, exclusive of the cost of administration. This has been distributed as follows:[29]

1911 (six months)	$2,784	1916	$219,004
1912	86,249	1917	263,291
1913	128,380	1918	259,767
1914	100,236	1919	281,213
1915	137,036		

The section of the aid-to-mothers act providing for a fund to be raised by a special tax was declared unconstitutional in 1915 (People v. C., L. S. & E. Ry., 270 Ill., 477). Between 1911 and 1916, although the county board had made an annual appropriation for mothers' pensions, the court was not limited by this appropriation, for the board was obliged to honor the pension orders until the amount brought in by the special tax was exhausted. This amounted to over $300,000 a year, and the entire sum has never been used, the nearest approach to it being in 1916, when the pension expenditures rose to $219,000. The appropriation for this year had been only $185,000, but, although the court did not keep within the appropriation, the special-tax fund would not have been exhausted had not the supreme court decision invalidated the special tax. After this time the court was limited in making pension grants by the county board appropriation, but the latter became more generous.

For the fiscal year 1917 the appropriation made was $260,000. While this was almost $45,000 greater than the expenditure for the year preceding, it failed to allow for the necessary increase in pension expenditures. The increase of 1916 over 1915 had been nearly $82,000.

---

[29] Data are for calendar years and are computed from the Cook County Comptroller's Report for 1916 and from figures supplied by his office. Data for 1918 and 1919 are from published reports of the Cook County agent. They are slightly higher than the comptroller's figures for the same period, as they include all checks issued and there are always some that are not cashed. Comptroller's figures for these years were not available.

The officials of the court realized that the appropriation of $260,000 was inadequate; and for some time they hoped that when the need for more money became apparent to the board some means would be found of increasing the appropriation for this purpose. For some months, then, the court continued to grant pensions without regard to the probable inadequacy of the appropriation. When it finally became apparent that the county board could not or would not find any money with which to increase the appropriation, the court had to find some way by which it could keep down expenditures. It was decided to continue the pensions for the families under care, but to discontinue the granting of pensions to new families except to fill vacancies. As there were already more than enough applications pending to fill such vacancies, further applications were refused. Between May, 1917, and December, 1917, the court referred all applicants to the united charities or other relief organizations. There were in May, 1917, 162 applications on file on which the investigation had not been made. The court decided to complete the investigation in these cases and have the committee consider them. No cases were actually brought before the judge, however, until there was a pension vacancy. Whenever a family already on the list was dropped these new families were taken on, not in order of priority of application, but in order of their need as determined by the committee. Not all vacancies thus created could be filled, however, as it was necessary to reduce the monthly expenditure in order to keep within the appropriation. In place of 158 pensions stayed, only 100 new pensions were granted. Even with this rigid economy the department found itself with a deficit of $12,000 at the close of the year. Fortunately a surplus in the outdoor relief department balanced this deficit. The year 1918, however, brought similar difficulties.

The appropriation for mothers' pensions for 1918 was $260,000, the same as for 1917, and the outdoor relief appropriation was cut down on the basis of the surplus of the preceding year. In the last half of 1917, 798 mothers were turned away without being allowed to file their applications, because of the inadequacy of the appropriation. In December, 1917, the beginning of the new fiscal year, all these women were notified that they might now make application for pensions. The great majority of them did so, and those applications were investigated and pensions granted in cases of urgent need. During the first months of the year 1918 the rate of expenditure was beyond that allowed for in the appropriation, but the judge hoped that the county board could be persuaded to take money from some other appropriation for this purpose. This hope failed, however; and since April, 1918, new applications have not been accepted, and women in need have again been referred to the united charities or other relief organizations.[30]

The continued failure of the county board to provide the funds necessary to pension the mothers made eligible by the legislature is an interesting example of the ease with which our American legislatures record their good intentions in the form of laws which are left to the local authorities to enforce. The legislature of Illinois has continued to add to the list of eligible beneficiaries under the mothers' pension act without taking steps to see that pensions will be provided for the mothers who have been made eligible.

County boards throughout the State have failed to make appropriations adequate for the pensioning of all mothers with legal claims under the aid-to-mothers act. In a few counties all pensions have been summarily ordered discontinued because the pension fund was exhausted. Fortunately, in Chicago it has never been necessary because of lack of funds to withdraw any pensions already granted; nor has the Chicago court been willing to adopt the policy of granting a larger number of small pensions. The plan of maintaining adequate care for the families who were already dependent on pension grants was the only wise course under the circumstances. The burden has inevitably fallen heavily on the united charities, charged with the unexpected burden of caring for most of the deferred applicants for an uncertain period of time; but the society has always found a way to meet the increasing charge.

The cost of administration should be added to the cost of the pensions. At the time of the study, the salaries of the 4 clerks, 16 officers, and the supervisor in the department amounted to $2,100 a month. To this must be added an additional $320 a month, the salaries of 1 clerk and 2 investigators in the county agent's office; and $125 a month for a clerk in the circuit court office. It seems unnecessary to add any portion of the salary of the chief probation officer and the judge, since no additional expense has been added here by the pension work. Without any allowance, however, for the salaries of these two officials, the expense for administrative service amounts [31] to $2,545 a month, or $30,540 a year.

---

[30] This situation continued until July, 1919, when an amendment, free from the constitutional difficulties of the early law, providing for a tax of four-fifteenths of a mill (Illinois Session Laws, 1919, p. 781) brought relief. At this time the list of the women who had been turned away without being allowed to file applications contained about 1,000 names. When it became apparent that the law would pass, these women were notified to come in and file applications and the department proceeded at once with the work of investigation. As the work was more than the department could handle with dispatch and as the united charities, which had been supporting many of the women, announced that it could not continue this support after January, 1920, the district superintendents of that organization were commissioned volunteer probation officers, and their investigation of the families was accepted. In April, 1920, the head of the department stated that they were now up with their work and had no more old cases to investigate.

[31] In January, 1919.

It is of interest that, along with the increasing expenditure on pensions, there has gone not a decrease but an increase in expenditures on county outdoor relief and county subsidies for the maintenance of dependent children in institutions.

Total expenditure on outdoor relief increased from $188,773 in 1910, the year before the passage of the pension law, to $242,030 in 1919. The cost of supporting dependent children in institutions rose from $61,981 in 1910 to $292,248 in 1919.

THE AID-TO-MOTHERS LAW IN RELATION TO DEPENDENCY AND DELINQUENCY.

Interesting questions arise as to the effect of the mothers' pension law upon the commitment of children to institutions and upon the number of widows with children remaining under the care of public or private relief agencies. Statistics are available only for Cook County. It has already been said that the number of pensioned widows increased month by month, except when changes in law and policy rendered ineligible some families who had in consequence to be removed from the pension roll. The following statement shows the numbers on the pension roll at the end of each six months' period, beginning with July, 1912:

	Number of families.	Number of children.	Monthly expenditure for pensions.		Number of families.	Number of children.	Monthly expenditure for pensions.
July, 1912	382	1,306	$8,145	July, 1916	681	2,106	$18,403
January, 1913	501	1,663	12,413	January, 1917	780	2,355	21,0ᵉ4
July, 1913	332	1,075	8,232	July, 1917	802	2,449	22,409
January, 1914	338	1,096	8,185	January, 1918	768	2,332	22,0 7
July, 1914	346	1,121	8,320	July, 1918	733	2,288	22,422
January, 1915	362	1,191	8,902	January, 1919	646	1,978	19,6ᵣ5
July, 1915	439	1,431	11,731	July, 1919	709	2,195	22,681
January, 1916	580	1,845	15,363				

The changes in the pension law in 1913 and 1915 are reflected in this statement. In 1913, when women who were not citizens were made ineligible, the number of pensioners dropped very suddenly; and in 1915, when women of this class were once more declared to be eligible, the number of pensioners rapidly increased. Except for these changes the increase in numbers up to 1918 probably represents a normal increase, due to the gradually increasing knowledge of the generous provision that is being made for mothers who are charged with the support of young children. The decrease in 1918 has been explained as due to the failure of appropriations.[32] The increasing confidence of the community in the aid-to-mothers department undoubtedly tended to increase the number of pensioners. Women who would not have applied or would not have been advised by charitable organizations to apply for outdoor relief were told of the work of the pension department and encouraged to ask for this assistance,

---
[32] See section on Expenditures for Mothers' Pensions, 1911–1918, pp. 113–114.

that was adequate on the one hand and was so administered as to encourage the self-respect of the beneficiaries instead of humiliating or degrading them.

Curiously enough, along with the increase in the number of mothers and children pensioned there went, for a time, an increase in the number of dependent children committed to institutions. The following statement shows the number of court commitments to institutions for dependent children with the amount paid to these private institutions from the county treasury from 1911 through 1919:

Year.	Number of dependent children committed.[a]	Public money paid to institutions.	Year.	Number of dependent children committed.[a]	Public money paid to institutions.
1911	894	$73,119	1916	867	$297,652
1912	1,327	183,223	1917	789	290,077
1913	1,109	267,542	1918	895	294,210
1914	1,048	307,558	1919	839	292,248
1915	916	302,101			

[a] Figures compiled from Cook County Charity Service Reports. Figures include commitments to all institutions for dependent children. They do not include commitments to hospitals, or homes for defectives, child-placing societies, or homes for friendless which provide only temporary shelter.

Although the number of committed children increased in 1912 and remained for 1913, 1914, and 1915 larger than in 1911, when the pension law was passed, the change was more apparent than real. It has already been explained that, by the industrial school law of Illinois, institutions for dependent children may, by qualifying as industrial schools, receive a county subsidy of $15 a month for each dependent girl and $10 for each dependent boy committed by the court. Before the passage of the pension law, only four institutions in Cook County received such grants, two Catholic institutions, one for boys and one for girls (St. Mary's Training School for Boys at Feehanville and the Chicago Industrial School for Girls), and two nonsectarian schools (Glenwood Manual Training School for Boys and Park Ridge Industrial School for Girls). After 1911, a number of schools which had been in existence for some years but which had never received public money went through the form of qualifying as industrial schools under the State law and immediately asked public money for the children they were supporting. This meant, in effect, that some institutions brought into court the children who had had institutional care, in some cases for years, and asked to have the children formally recommitted under the industrial school acts, in order that the institution might receive the $10 or $15 a month per child allowed to the other four institutions that had qualified and were receiving subsidies under those laws.

It is not possible to determine how many of the children who, on the face of the court record are dependent children committed to institutions were, as a matter of fact, dependent children who had been receiving institutional care but for whom the institutions had not previously received public money. That is, there may have been an increase in the number of children committed by the court without there having been an increase in the number of institutional children. In so far as this explains the increase in the institutional population it is only indirectly connected with the operation of the mothers' aid law. The discussion of mothers' pensions in the newspapers and the wide publicity given to the fact that some institutions were being given large grants of public money may have led other institutions that had not hitherto known of this subsidy to make application for similar subsidies. It may even have led to the organization of some new institutions that hoped to be able to support themselves with the assistance of the public grant.

It is clear, however, that the mothers' pension law could reduce the number of children committed to institutions only if children had been committed to institutions before the passage of the pension law because of the poverty of their mothers. It is believed that this had not been happening in Chicago except in occasional, exceptional cases in which the mother had not been put in touch with the good relief agencies of the city. There were large relief societies in Chicago whose policy was the keeping of children with their mothers except when the mother was not fit. Some difference of opinion might exist as to what constituted a " fit " mother. A relief organization might, of course, refuse to support a home on the ground that it was unfit and on the theory that the children could be given suitable care only if they were taken away from their home when the court, or some other agency, or some private individual interested in the family might disagree with the relief society and feel that a wrong was being committed when the children were sent to institutions. In the view of the relief society the children were being committed because the home was unfit; from the other point of view the children were being committed because of poverty. Such cases of disagreement, however, were apparently not numerous; and since children were not committed because of poverty, except in these rare instances, a reduction in commitments could not be expected because of the introduction of the pension system.

Another point as regards the effect of the aid-to-mothers' law is how far delinquency and truancy among children may have been prevented. Unfortunately, this is not a subject on which satisfactory statistics can be furnished. It is true that statistics are sometimes published to show that there are very few delinquent children among the pensioned families; but, of course, it is not possible to say how many children would have been delinquent in these families if there had been no pension system. A careful examination of the records of the 212 families who had been on the pension roll in Chicago for at least two full years showed only 3 families of the 212 in which a child had been brought into court as delinquent and only 1 family in which a child had come in as truant. This seems to be an exceedingly good two-years' record; but again it must be pointed out that no estimate can be made of the number of children who would have become delinquent if these families had not been pensioned.

Earlier studies of juvenile delinquency have laid stress on the fact that neglected homes with wage earning mothers were an important contributing cause of delinquency among children.[33] And it is only reasonable to assume that the policy of providing adequate pensions for destitute mothers with children, and of keeping more mothers at home where they can look after their children, has undoubtedly prevented a considerable number of homes from becoming unfit, and has probably kept more mothers alive and in good health than the old system did. In so far as an adequate pension means a better standard of living, less work for the mother outside of her home, and better care for the children in the home, there will probably be fewer commitments of children because of delinquency and truancy; but this would be a long-time effect of the pension system and one that in any event could never be established statistically.

One of the interesting questions with regard to the effects of the aid-to-mothers law is whether a new class of families in need were discovered and provided for by the machinery created by this statute, or whether the law merely set up new machinery for doing work that was already being done, or at any rate being attempted, by other relief agencies. This can be determined on the basis of available data, showing how many of the pensioned families had been assisted before the granting of the pension by other private or public charitable agencies.

The records of the social registration bureau of Chicago were consulted in order to ascertain how many of the families on the court pension roll had been registered prior to the granting of the pension by some social agency. Table XLV summarizes this information for the families added to the pension roll in 1917, who had been assisted by other agencies before the court pension was granted. The table also shows the number of families registered by agencies giving services and not relief.

---

[33] Russell Sage Foundation. Delinquent Child and the Home, Breckinridge and Abbott. Charities Publication Committee MCMXII, Ch. V, pp. 95–97.

TABLE XLV.—*Number and per cent of pensioned families who had been registered in the social registration bureau prior to pension grant.*

Registered by—	Number.	Per cent distribution.
Total	188	100.0
United charities	112	59.6
Other relief-giving agency	31	16.5
Other type of agency	10	5.3
Unknown to any agency	35	18.6

The information in this table relates only to the social agencies of Chicago which register their families with the social registration bureau. According to this table all but 18.6 per cent of these recently pensioned families had been on the records of some one of the social agencies of the city, and 76.1 per cent had been on the records of one of the relief-giving agencies (59.6 per cent registered by the united charities and 16.5 per cent by other relief societies).

Data on this point were first gathered for the pension survey conducted by the officers of the court, and it is of interest to note that the per cent of families unknown to any agency seems to have been increasing. This survey covered 543 families on the pension roll during the period between August 1, 1913, and April 1, 1915, and 532 families whose applications for pensions were rejected during this period. Table XLVI shows the number and per cent of the pensioned families who had been registered prior to the granting of the pension.

TABLE XLVI.—*Number and per cent of families pensioned between Aug. 1, 1913, and Apr. 1, 1915, who had been registered in the social registration bureau.*

Registered by—	Number.	Per cent.
Total	543	100.0
United charities	a 393	72.4
Other relief-giving agency	84	15.5
Other type of agency	35	6.4
Unknown to any agency	31	5.7

a Most of these were known to other agencies as well, such as the county agent, the municipal tuberculosis sanitarium, the visiting nurse association.

Of these 543 pensioned families it appears that 393, or 72 per cent of the entire number, were known to the united charities. How much or how little had been done for them by that agency we are not told; but the united charities had registered their names in the social registration bureau. Most of these "charities" families had also been registered by various other agencies, such as the county agent, the municipal tuberculosis sanitarium, the visiting nurse association, etc. Besides this group of 393 families who had been on the charities records there was a group of 84 families registered and presumably helped by other relief-giving agencies; 35 more were known to social agencies that give services only; while only 31 families, that is, 6 per cent of the 543, had not been registered by any social agency at the time of their application for aid from the juvenile court. It is probable, too, that some of these families may have received aid from organizations that do not register in the social registration bureau. Some of the sectarian relief organizations, for example, do not register the families whom they assist. It is clear, however, that the evidence of the survey indicates that, in general, it is not a new group of dependents who are receiving aid under the aid-to-mothers act.

A study was also made of the 532 families who applied for pensions but whose applications were rejected during the period of the survey. Table XLVII shows the per cent of the dismissed applicants who were on the social registration bureau in comparison with the per cent of successful pension applicants who had been registered.

TABLE XLVII.—*Per cent of dismissed applicants registered by social agencies compared with the per cent of pensioned applicants registered.*

Registered by—	Applicants dismissed.	Applicants pensioned.
Total	100.0	100.0
United charities	45.9	72.4
Other relief-giving agency	16.7	15.5
Other type of agency	13.5	6.4
Unknown to any agency	23.9	5.7

This table shows that a considerably larger per cent of the pensioned families than of the dismissed families had had charitable assistance before they were given relief in the form of pensions. This may be explained in part by the court requirement that the family shall be without property and with not more than $50 in money before eligibility for a pension can be established. That the court scrupulously adheres to the tests laid down is indicated by these figures. Families who are not destitute, who have been getting on without charitable assistance in the past, are left to continue in the way of independence until their resources are exhausted, when they may reapply for a court pension. The larger per cent of rejected families known to the nonrelief giving agencies is probably due to the fact that the unfit applicants are included among those rejected and that these unfit applicants have probably been registered by corrective agencies such as the juvenile protective association.

Questions invariably arise as to just how much assistance had been given to the families by the relief-giving organization that had registered the families in the social exchange. No information on this point is available for the large group of families included in the court survey, but certain facts were found for the group of 212 families who had been under care for two years.

The reports for these families made by the agencies to the court before the granting of the pensions furnishes some evidence of the care they had been giving to the families they registered. One hundred and fifty-three of these 212 families, or 72 per cent of the whole number, had been registered by the united charities. The reports of the united charities do not show what had been done for 82 of these families. For the other 71 the reports show that the society had given little or no material relief to 18 families; 39 families had been given relief irregularly; and only 4 families had been pensioned. It is probable that this is not an understatement of the number of families who were being pensioned, since a fact of this kind would almost certainly be included in their report to the court. It is also probable that the 82 families for whom the amount of relief is not specified had been assisted only irregularly.

Some attention should, perhaps, be given to a question that may arise from a study of the data in Tables XLV and XLVI. The theory on which the law was based was that children who might otherwise be separated from their parents because of poverty should be enabled to remain under the care of their natural guardians. On that theory, it may be asked whether the enactment of the law was really called for since private organizations had apparently already made provision for maintaining the integrity of these homes. That is, it may be asked whether the families to whom pensions were given should not have been families not otherwise adequately cared for.

In this connection two facts should not be overlooked. The first is that being registered by a social agency and being adequately cared for by the agency are not the same thing. It has already been shown that only a small percentage of the registered families were really being pensioned. Another fact of importance is that some of the private charitable agencies turned over to the court the families they were assisting.

Thus the records of the united charities show that during the first year after the enactment of the pension law 387 families previously under their care were told by officers of the society to apply for pensions. Similarly, the Jewish societies referred about 100 of their families to the court; while the St. Vincent de Paul Society referred to the court approximately 365 families during the first year and a half after the enactment of the law.[34] In such cases, it is evident that no new dependent groups are formed, but those formerly relying on private now depend on public aid.

---

[34] These figures were obtained from the executive officers of the several societies.

PART I.—ADMINISTRATION IN COOK COUNTY. 123

The original policy of referring to the juvenile court all families who appear to be eligible for mothers' aid appears to have been consistently followed by the private relief societies down to the present time. In reply to an inquiry as to whether they now had on their relief lists any pensionable families, both the Jewish aid society and the united charities prepared for our investigator a list of families with children of pension age who were being given relief by these societies instead of pensions by the court. The united charities list contained 26 names. Of these, 12 were widows then ineligible because they were aliens. Two other widows were technically ineligible because they owned a very small interest in some property in Italy; the property brought them no income but rendered them ineligible for pensions. In 7 other cases the husband and father was alive but unable to work. In these 7 cases, however, the man was not totally and permanently incapacitated, and his children were therefore ineligible for pensions. The remaining 5 families were being supported pending the court investigation and were to be transferred to the court roll if found eligible.

The Jewish aid society was similarly supporting seven families with small children, all of whom were technically ineligible for pensions, three because they were not citizens and four because the husband and father was not totally incapacitated. It is clear therefore that the large private relief organizations are not now supporting families eligible for pensions and that they must have found the aid-to-mothers law a substantial relief to their treasuries. It has, however, already been pointed out that some new charges would have accrued to both societies in so far as the law had created or tended to help in the discovery of new applicants for assistance, many of whom became a charge on the private societies pending investigations by the court or chargeable permanently because they were found ineligible by the court. It seems fair to assume further that these were cases of legitimate need for whose discovery the community and the private agencies must feel grateful.

As regards public outdoor relief the county agent's attitude toward the pension department is apparently somewhat uncertain. The county agent, it will be remembered, is a member of the committee which passes on the pension applications, and he makes an independent investigation of the applicants' eligibility. Although his department must inevitably suggest to many applicants for outdoor relief that they go down to the court and apply for pensions, this does not appear to be the consistent policy of the outdoor relief department. A study of the records in the county agent's office in one important district showed, for example, 165 families with children of pension age (i. e., below 14 years) in receipt of outdoor relief.

Sixty were widows with young children, and 105 were classified as married couples with young children. The case records were then examined in order to discover why they had not been sent to the court for pensions, with the following result: 114 were technically ineligible for pensions, 5 were below the court standard of fitness, and 23 were in need of temporary relief only, leaving 21 families who appeared to be eligible for pensions and in need of such assistance. Among the families termed technically ineligible there were 32 aliens, 4 property-owners, 28 married couples in which the husband was not totally incapacitated but was unable to support his family entirely, 35 in which the husband was not permanently incapacitated, and 15 families with the husband in jail.

In the group classified as needing only temporary relief were 3 married couples in which the man was unemployed, 3 widows who had just received insurance money, 13 in which there was only one dependent child, and 4 in which there were children of working age.

Five families were classified as below the court standard of fitness for the following reasons: In 2 the mother was physically or morally unfit to care for her children at home, and in 3 others some member of the family who refused to leave the home for sanitarium care was considered a menace to the health of the other members.

The 21 families who appeared to be eligible and in need of pensions were studied further. Seven families have since been pensioned, 9 were merely being aided pending investigation. Five families remained who appeared not to have applied for a pension although the investigator was told that in 2 of the families the mothers preferred to work regularly and support their children with occasional aid from the county agent rather than apply for a pension. But the other families apparently did not know of the aid-to-mothers law, and the county agent's office had not informed them of this source of regular and adequate aid. A similar study of the records in another district office of the outdoor relief department brought to light 11 other widows who were eligible for pensions and who had not applied for mothers' aid. Here again the investigator was told that 9 of these widows were able to support their families with occasional doles from the outdoor relief department, and that there were only 2 widows, therefore, in need of regular aid who had not been told to apply for pensions. On the whole, then, although there are a few families in need of help who might become pensioners if the county agent's office suggested an application at the court, there are apparently not many who do not in course of time discover for themselves the possibility of this more adequate form of relief.

PART II.—THE ADMINISTRATION OF THE AID-TO-MOTHERS LAW OUTSIDE COOK COUNTY.

INTRODUCTION.

The Illinois aid-to-mothers law makes no provision for State supervision or control over the administration of the law. Each county in the State is an independent administrative unit. The law prescribes, of course, that pensions shall be granted only on certain conditions; but if a county disregards these conditions and grants pensions to persons not legally entitled to them, there is no State department with authority to see that the law is enforced.

Since there are 102 different counties in Illinois, which represent nearly 102 different pension policies, few general statements can be made about their methods of administering the law.

The material relating to the administration of the law in the "down-State" counties, which is presented in this section, has been secured from the following sources: (1) The data secured from the replies to an inquiry conducted by correspondence with the county judges of the State. Through the cooperation of the State charities commission, a schedule was sent out by the secretary of the commission to each county judge in the State, asking for certain facts as to the use of the pension law in his county. Schedules were returned from 77 counties only, for some of the judges refused to send any reply even after follow-up letters had been sent to them. (2) Further data were secured by correspondence with the representatives of various private charitable organizations in the outlying portions of the State. Twenty-three schedules were returned by representatives of such agencies. (3) After this preliminary survey of the field by correspondence, further data were secured through a special investigator who visited 14 counties, all except 1 that had pensioned thirty or more families during the preceding year and a number of other counties selected for special reasons. The counties selected to be visited were in different sections of the State, some poor and some rich, some mining, some manufacturing, and some rural. Twenty-three counties had only five families or fewer than this number pensioned, and no investigation was made in any of these counties.

The schedules collected by correspondence with the county judges were sent out in August, 1915, and the data relate, therefore, largely to the autumn of 1915. The visits of the special investigator were made in the months of October, November, December, 1916, and January, 1917. As has been pointed out, the Illinois law provides no State supervising agency with control over the administration of the pension law, and no reports are submitted by the 102 different local authorities to any central office. It is very difficult, therefore, to ascertain either the extent to which the law is being used or the methods of administration that have been adopted. The State charities commission has obtained such information as it has published by correspondence with the judges, many of whom refused to answer letters, and by reports sent in by the State inspector of county almshouses and jails during her investigations in 1913 and in 1915. Information as to the number of counties that have made use of the law is, however, probably complete. But although the preliminary inquiries of the State inspector have been a useful basis for further inquiries, she visited none of the pensioned families, and her inquiries as to methods of administration were very limited.

In addition to this material, use has been made of three reports on the use of the aid-to-mothers law published by the State charities commission in the Institution Quarterly in September, 1913, December, 1914, and September, 1916.

THE DETERMINATION OF PENSION POLICIES IN THE 101 OUTLYING COUNTIES.

The judge of the juvenile court, who is also the county judge in the 101 counties outside of Cook County, is the person in each county who has the right to grant pensions; and if he does not approve of the law, he may nullify it simply by refusing to grant any pensions. But the judge who approves of the law and wishes to put it into operation can do so only after the county supervisors have voted to appropriate money for this purpose. That is, both the judge and the supervisors must agree as to the desirability of providing pensions or none will be granted. Thus in five counties the supervisors have made appropriations, but the judge has granted no pensions. On the other hand, some counties have not used the law because of the unwillingness of the county commissioners to add to the taxes. The judge in one county, for example, reported that the county board would not levy a tax for the purpose of providing this fund unless compelled to do so by a mandamus suit, and the judge added that in his opinion such a suit should be brought " if for no other reason than to convince the county board that the laws of Illinois apply to them as to any other body of public servants."

In another county the judge actually granted a few pensions, but the supervisors obtained legal advice to the effect that the constitutionality of the law was doubtful and refused to pay them. Further evidence of the unwillingness of the county supervisors to make the necessary appropriation is found in several other letters. Thus the judge of County X wrote: " Our board of supervisors have so far failed to levy the tax under the mothers' pension law * * * so we have been unable to personally test the law." Appropriations were made later on in this county and pensions actually paid. Similarly the judge of County Y, where an appropriation of $2,000 had just been made, wrote: " I have tried heretofore to have our county board appropriate some money to be used for this fund, but was never successful until now. * * * Since the law was passed I had a number of applicants, some of whom I knew to be worthy, but have had to deny them all as there was no money to be used for them." [1]

---

[1] It is of interest that a letter from the probation officer in this county contains the following statement : " The matter stands thus at the present time, but public sentiment is getting better and there is a prospect that this law may be carried out in the county. Just now there are no cases calling for a mother's pension that are not being taken care of, only in such cases as those in which a mother refused to take help in the old way for fear it will be thrown up to her children at school by their playmates."

In other counties, as has been pointed out, the law has not been put in operation because the county judge does not approve of the law or is not sufficiently interested in the law to grant any pensions. In one county the probation officer of the court wrote briefly: "This county does not approve of mothers' pensions." In five other counties appropriations have been made but no pensions granted; in one county the clerk is supplied with the necessary blanks; while from another county the judge wrote in reply to our inquiry: "We have had applications for help where the mothers' pension act should have been invoked, but no one has seen fit as yet to invoke it. * * * The county board has in some instances aided parties who could have made proper proof, but who were aided as paupers."

In one county the judge reported that there had been numerous applications under the act, but that he has adopted the policy of asking the local supervisors of the poor to be present at the hearing. In every instance, he reported, the supervisors were "able to furnish the aid required." "This plan," continued the judge, "seems to me to be in the interests of economy, as necessaries rather than money are furnished the applicant; and I think I can safely say in every instance thus far the wants of the parties in need have been supplied." This judge—and he is no doubt in some instances typical—saw no difference between the purpose of the mothers' pension law and the old outdoor relief system.

This judge also added that in his opinion the principal objection to the law was that the applicants received money, which they could spend as they pleased; whereas, if the aid were "furnished through the supervisor, as local poor master, they get no money and only the necessary supplies." There undoubtedly are other judges in the State equally unintelligent with regard to the purpose of the pension law. In fact, a letter published two years ago in the Institution Quarterly contains a very similar statement. The judge of Z County wrote to the secretary of the State charities commission as follows:

Will say in reply to your inquiry concerning the mothers' pension law that I do not think it is a good one. For this reason, there is a supervisor in each township who is the overseer of the poor, and he is far better acquainted with the mother who lives there about 365 days in the year than the county judge can possibly be, and the supervisor can look after and see that the tax money is being spent for the necessities of life instead of frivolities for which some mothers would use the money.

I think that every supervisor in Z County would see to it that no family would suffer in his township if he were given any notice at all concerning their circumstances. If we have a hearing, the mother wishing to be pensioned comes into court with a few of her friends; and of course if the court listens to the evidence there is nothing left to do except to grant to her a pension, which she may need a part of the year and a part of the year she does not. Many mothers claim a pension under the mistaken idea on their part that they do not become county paupers if they take under this law, and seem to think they have as much right to a pension as any of our war veterans, while they are just as much county paupers as those residing at our county home.

For counties like our own, where the population is not so numerous, I think the supervisor is well enough acquainted with the families and can deal out better justice to the poor and the taxpayer than can the county judge, and that we are not in need of the mothers' pension law.

In another county, where 11 pensions were being granted, the judge also believed that the families would better be left to the overseer of the poor, and wrote to the secretary of the State charities commission:

In this county we do not have very many who are receiving support under this law, but during the time that it has been on the statute books we have had a large number of applications, considering the population of our county. The most of them could not comply with the strict requirements of the law and the most of them were ones who were not entitled to support under this law. In most cases in our county in which provision is being made in the family under this law, are families who were receiving support from the county through the supervisor or overseer of the poor. And in a county like this one I am of the opinion that the better way to take care of these is through the overseer of the poor in each township. The supervisor who is the overseer of the poor has better opportunity to know of the conditions in these families than has the county court or any agents appointed by it. There is a tendency among a great many people to think that when the term " pension " is used it is a matter of right and they are entitled to ask and receive this pension, no difference as to their physical or financial condition.

There is sometimes, too, confusion not only with respect to the purpose of the law but also with respect to the actual requirements of the law. This is well illustrated by the following extract from a letter from the judge of R County, in reply to a questionnaire sent out by the State charities commission in August, 1914.

When the law was first enacted and was published by the newspapers throughout the State, a number of mothers made application for aid under this law, and I directed the probation officer to make the investigation as required by the law and granted three or four of these pensions. When the orders came to the county clerk, the question was raised as to what fund the money was to be paid from; and on examination of the law I found that the board of supervisors could levy a tax, which should not exceed a certain per cent, and that that money raised by that tax should be placed in a special fund and be used for the mothers' pension. There was no provision in the statute that the board of supervisors might make an appropriation and place it in this fund, so I changed the orders from aid under the aid-to-mothers act to aid under the dependent and neglected children's act, and then I began to observe and study this law.

I am not favorably impressed with this law at all. In the first place, I do not think that there was any necessity whatever for this law. The dependent and neglected children's act covers the whole field, and I believe in a better way than the mothers' pension law does. Of course, I understand that you people who favor the mothers' pension law are making the claim that the mother would be more independent and would not feel that she was receiving funds from charity so much if it were under the mothers' pension law than if it were under the dependent and neglected children's act, because under the dependent and neglected children's act the probation officer visits the home once in each month and then recommends to the judge how much should be paid to them for the succeeding month, while under the mothers' pension law the money is paid monthly from the county treasury to the mother, and she spends the money as she sees fit.

It is unnecessary to point out the inaccuracies in this letter, which is interesting solely as indicating that some of the judges are very much confused not only as to the purpose but as to the actual provisions of the pension law. It is interesting that a later judge in County R has adopted the same interpretation of the law. A letter from the probation officer of this county, received on July 14, 1916, contained the following statement:

In reply to your letter addressed to Judge ―――, of R County, will say that we have not used a dollar from the mothers' pension fund. A number of monthly allowances have been granted. But the children were declared dependent, and an average of $5 per month for each child was given from the pauper relief fund. These people needed help, but did not comply with the law regulating the mothers' pension fund.

NUMBER OF COUNTIES GRANTING MOTHERS' PENSIONS.

In spite of the opposition of county judges and county supervisors to the law, pensions were being granted in 1916 in 71 out of the 101 down-State counties. The cost of these pensions was, in 1916, approximately $349,200; and as nearly as can be estimated 1,583 families with 4,850 children were provided for out of this fund. Information is not available as to why the law is not being used in the other 30 counties that are not granting pensions. But, in general, they seem to be the poorer and more backward counties of the State.

During the first year following the enactment of the pension law only 16 counties outside of Cook County made any use of it. No reasons have been found to explain the prompt adoption of the law by these 16 counties, or its neglect by the remaining 85 counties of the State. The counties using the law represent no one geographical section of the State, since they range from the extreme northwestern to the southeastern section; 4 of them are counties in which are found 4 of the 11 large cities of the State; but an equal if not greater number are counties that are rural communities of farms and small towns. Nor can the adoption of the pension law be explained on the ground that these 16 are the communities most progressive in their care of the poor, for the reports of the State board of charities show that some of these 16 counties are extremely backward in their outdoor and even in their indoor relief. The use of the pension law in 1911–1913 in these 16 counties could only be explained separately for each county by a study of special local conditions.

No additional information as to the number of counties using the pension law is available until December, 1914, when 63 counties were granting pensions under the act.

Before the 1st of January, 1916, 10 other counties were using the act; and 5 more counties had indicated an intention of using the law by making an appropriation for this purpose, although no pensions had actually been granted. This increase in the number of counties in which pensions are being granted is shown in the following summary:

	1912	1913	1915
Total	101	101	101
Counties using pension law	16	63	72
Counties not using	85	35	a29
No report		3	

a Five of these counties had made appropriation for a "pension fund."

It is not possible to find any general reasons that explain satisfactorily the failure of 29 counties to make use of the law. The failure is due in some counties to some accidental situation, such as the lack of interest or opposition of a county judge or of some members of the board of supervisors. It should be noted, however, that, although these 29 counties represent no one geographical section exclusively, yet by far the greater number of them are in the southern and poorer portion of the State; while with the exception of a group of 6 counties in the center of the State, they are all counties either on the border or extremely close to it. That is to say, they are in general the outlying districts and river counties.

Another point of interest about these counties is that in all 29 there is only one city of 10,000 inhabitants. It is of interest, too, that these counties which are backward in applying the aid-to-mothers act are in general counties in which the administration of other outdoor relief is relatively worse than in the rest of the State. This is indicated by the fact that only 7 out of these 29 counties required written orders for relief and itemized bills; while in the other 72 counties, 36, or one-half the number, did make these slight requirements.[2]

With the increase in the number of counties granting pensions there has been of course a corresponding increase in the number of persons receiving aid under the law. Unfortunately there are no figures available that show exactly the growth in the number of beneficiaries. In 1912 there were 50 mothers aided, and more than 150 children pensioned (the exact number could not be obtained). For 1913 no accurate information is available either as to the number of families or the number of children receiving help under the law. The State charities commission estimates the number of children at about 1,200. For the year 1915 the figures are more exact. By August of that year there were 1,042 families getting aid under the pension law; and during that year at least 282 additional families were pensioned, making a total of 1,324 families with approximately 3,700 children pensioned during the year ending August 1, 1915.

The number of families pensioned varies, of course, from county to county. Table XLVIII shows the number of families pensioned in the different counties in a single month in 1915. The number pensioned in a given month is much easier to determine than the number pensioned during the year, since the policy of the counties

---

[2] These figures may not be complete. They are compiled from the Institution Quarterly of March, 1916; but as no uniformity was observed in the details reported for the various counties, it is possible that some counties required written orders and itemized bills but did not report this procedure.

PART II.—ADMINISTRATION OUTSIDE OF COOK COUNTY. 133

varies as to the number of months that individual families are kept on the pension roll.

TABLE XLVIII.—*Number of counties giving aid to specified number of families, August 1, 1915, or nearest date thereto.*[a]

Number of families pensioned by county.	Counties granting pensions.	
	Number.	Per cent distribution.
Total	72	100.0
1- 4 families	18	25.0
5- 9 families	19	26.4
10-14 families	9	12.5
15-19 families	7	9.7
20-29 families	10	13.9
30-49 families	6	8.3
50 families or more	3	4.2

[a] The figures do not all refer to one date, since they are compiled from two sources, our own schedules from 56 counties giving the figures on August 1, 1915, and the Institution Quarterly of March, 1916, in which the date to which the figures refer falls somewhere between April and December, 1915.

This table shows that most of the counties pensioned very few families. Only 3 counties pensioned as many as 50 families; and in these 3 counties, three of the largest cities of the State are located. Eighteen counties, or 25 per cent of the total number, pensioned fewer than 5 families; and 19 other counties, 26.4 per cent, from 5 to 9 families. That is, 37 counties, or 51.4 per cent, did not have 10 mothers pensioned on the date for which the information was collected.

A comparison between the number of families on the pension roll August 1 and the maximum number of families pensioned at any time during the year was possible for the 58 counties from which schedules were obtained. In the majority of these counties there was no difference between the number on the August pension roll and the maximum number pensioned in any other month.

Only 6 counties reported a maximum number for the year greater by more than 5 families than the number pensioned on August 1. In one county the number dropped from 164 to 5, and in another county from 105 to 70 because the pensions were discontinued during the summer months on account of lack of funds.[3] Further study of the administration of the law in these two counties suggests that a more judicious expenditure of funds would have rendered unnecessary any such drastic reduction during the summer months. In H County the difference, which is not so great, is accounted for by a change of probation officers and a consequent " cleaning up." No explanation of the difference in the other 3 counties has been found.

---
[3] See p. 135.

EXPENDITURES OF DIFFERENT COUNTIES.

Further information as to the extent to which the pension law is used may be obtained from a statement of the amount of money spent by the different counties on mothers' pensions. On the schedules sent to the county judges they were asked to state the exact amount spent during the year ending August 1, 1915, or during the last fiscal year. Only 53 of the 58 counties returning schedules answered this question, and some of those answering the question explained that their figure was an estimate. No information is available as to the expenditures of the other counties in which the law was used. The report of the State charities commission does in some instances give the amount of the appropriation for this purpose, but there is no statement as to whether or not this appropriation was actually expended, and the figures given refer in some cases to the year 1914–15, in others to the year 1915–16, and in still others to the current year. It is not possible, therefore, to make any satisfactory estimate of the expenditure of these 14 counties.

The total expenditure for mothers' pensions in one year for the 53 counties for which information is available was $118,148, which was $12,000 less than the expenditure in Cook County in the same year. The population of Cook County in 1910 was 2,405,000; the total population of the other 53 counties was 2,110,000. Thus the per capita cost of the pensions in Cook County was $0.0541, and in the 53 other counties it was $0.056; that is, the per capita cost of the relief was actually lower by $0.0019 in Cook County than in the other 53 counties taken as one unit.

The expenditure varied in the different counties just as the number of families varied. Table XLIX shows the amounts expended by the 53 counties sending in definite replies to the schedule question relating to expenditure.

TABLE XLIX.—*Number of counties with specified expenditure for mothers' pensions.*

Expenditure for pensions by county.	Counties providing pensions.	
	Number.	Per cent distribution.
Total	72	
Total reported	53	100.0
$100–$499	9	17.0
500–999	12	22.6
1,000–1,999	11	20.8
2,000–2,999	7	13.2
3,000–3,999	4	7.5
4,000–4,999	4	7.6
5,000 or more	6	11.3
Not reported	19	

This table shows that no one of these 53 counties spent very large sums on mothers' pensions. The expenditure depended to some extent upon the size of the counties. The 9 counties spending less than $500, the 12 counties spending from $500 to $1,000, and the 11 counties spending from $1,000 to $2,000 are all counties with a population of less than 60,000 persons. The 6 counties reporting an expenditure of $5,000 and over are all counties with a population of over 60,000. In these counties are found the large industrial centers of the State. The largest sum expended by any one of these counties was $11,900. The per capita cost in this county was $0.099, which is considerably higher than the $0.0560 average per capita cost for the 53 counties, and yet this county was one of those that had almost no pension list during the summer because the funds were exhausted.

Table L, which gives the expenditure together with the population of the counties, shows, however, that expenditure did not always vary with population.

TABLE L.—*Number of counties of given population spending specified amounts for mothers' pensions in 1915.*

Population of county.	Counties reporting specified expenditure for mothers' pensions.						
	Total.	$100–499	$500–999	$1,000–1,999	$2,000–2,999	$3,000–3,999	$4,000–4,999	$5,000 & over.
Total	53	9	12	11	7	4	4	6
10,000–19,999	13	2	7	4				
20,000–29,999	10	2	2	5	1			
30,000–39,999	12	3	3	2	3		1	
40,000–59,999	7	2			2	3		
60,000–79,999	4				1		2	1
80,000–99,999	5					1		4
100,000 or more	2						1	1

USE OF PROBATION OFFICERS FOR ADMINISTRATION OF ACT.

The failure to use the law in more than one-fourth of the counties in the State and the extent to which the law is used in the other counties are perhaps less important than the methods of administration in the counties in which pensions are actually being given. The law definitely requires that, before a pension is granted, an investigation be made by a probation officer; and there seems to be an attempt at an investigation as required by law in all the counties. Information is needed, however, as to the kind of probation officers appointed by the courts, since the character of the investigation and of supervising care given to families depends upon the ability of the officers to render intelligent service.

In very few counties is there a probation officer giving full time to the probation work, which includes not only the pension work but all other forms of probation service. In the other counties there are part-time officers, or there is some one appointed a probation officer to comply with the law; but the so-called probation officer is a judge or sheriff or supervisor of the poor or some one whose chief duties are of another sort. Table LI shows the different types of officers appointed for the mothers' pension work.

TABLE LI.—*Number of counties having specified kind of probation officers.*

Persons acting as probation officers.	Number of counties.
Total	72
Probation officer on yearly salary	[a] 30
Full-time officers	4
Part-time officers	19
Time not given	7
Other probation officers	17
Officers paid per diem	7
Officers paid per case	2
Volunteer probation officer	5
Salary and time not reported	3
Supervisor or overseer of the poor	13
Special officer for each family	7
States attorney	2
Judge	1
Sheriff	1
Not reported	1

[a] In two of these counties investigations are also made by the supervisor, and in one the judge also investigates.

PART II.—ADMINISTRATION OUTSIDE OF COOK COUNTY. 137

Some further account of the activities of the persons described in this table as probation officers is probably needed. The table shows that only 4 counties had full-time probation officers. In 19 counties the officers who are classified as regular probation officers on a yearly salary give only part time to the work of the court, variously reporting their other duties as: Probation officer of the circuit court; work for private relief societies; policeman; policewoman; secretary to the judge; county coroner; truant officer; investigator of the applications for outdoor relief; lawyer; school-teacher.

In discussing the Cook County work, it was pointed out that upon the probation officers fell the very difficult work of determining which applicants met the tests of eligibility prescribed by law. This work can probably not be well done by State's attorneys, judges, or even volunteer or occasional probation officers. Nor are officers paid for casual work on a per diem basis likely to render the services needed. Of the two officers paid per case, one is paid $10 for every case investigated, and one is paid $10 for every case that gets a pension.

The amount of work carried by some of the officers who are paid a regular yearly salary for part-time work makes it impossible that the officer should have adequate time either for the investigation or for proper supervision of pensioned families. In D County, for example, the probation officer who had 33 families to supervise in 1915 was also secretary of the local charitable society, which handled some 1,500 cases during the year.[4] Again, in another county, the probation officer, who has 13 pensioned families and all other cases brought before the juvenile court, is supervisor of the poor and truant officer as well. This officer reports that she has so much to do that she can not supervise families as she should, "especially those in the country," and she suggests that the court needs a full-time probation officer and a clerical assistant. Another example of an overworked officer is found in T County. There, the supervisor of the 19 pensioned families is, in addition to the other probation work, supervisor of the poor for the township, which has a population of 17,000; truant officer for the county; and superintendent of the associated charities. She has one paid assistant; but, even so, there is little time available for the pension work.

Not only are the part-time officers so fully occupied as to be unable to do the pension work adequately, but the full-time officers who do all the other probation work are most of them left with little time for the pension service. Thus in K County the probation officer has charge of 36 pensioned families, in addition to all the other juvenile court work of a city of 45,000 inhabitants. She complains

---
[4] Since that time she has been relieved of the work in the associated charities, but has added the work of truant officer. She stated that she "tries to visit each family every month" but has no time for the additional services that might be rendered her families.

that she is overworked and is especially in need of clerical assistance. She has tried to supplement her visits to the pensioned families by visits from " friendly visitors," but does not find this system of volunteer assistants entirely satisfactory. In H County there are three probation officers, but its county seat is a large city, and there, too, it has proved necessary to use volunteer visitors for the pensioned families.

The need for an adequate number of regular salaried probation officers is too apparent to need discussion. What is not so apparent, however, is that the regular salaried officer may also be extremely unsatisfactory. This is due chiefly to two circumstances: (1) That the salary is so low that properly qualified persons will not accept the position; (2) that appointments are made by the judge, often for personal or political reasons instead of for merit.

One or both of these situations seem to be found rather generally in the counties of Illinois. Some data as to the salaries of the officers were collected; but, since it was not always clear how much time was being given to the work, the information furnished did not appear to be valuable.

On the subject of the method of appointing probation officers there is much to be said. The appointing power is left in the hands of the county judge; and although, in Cook County, the judge of the juvenile court used the power thus conferred upon him to select the officers by competitive examination, and called on persons of recognized experience in child-caring work to conduct the examination, in all other counties the judge has used his personal discretion in appointing the probation officer. Many of the judges undoubtedly appointed the person whom they believed to be best qualified for the work. In five counties, for example, the person appointed was the secretary of the local charity organization society; in two other counties the officer had had experience in social work; in another county she had had long experience as a probation officer before the aid-to-mothers act was passed. In another county the officer appointed had had training in a professional school of philanthropy.

Although some judges selected persons apparently well qualified for their work as probation officers, other judges have not done so. Attention has already been called to the fact that a county coroner, a policeman, a clerk from the assessor's office, a doctor, a lawyer, and a school teacher are among the persons appointed to act as probation officer in different counties.[5]

---

[5] The following item taken from a daily paper of one of the down-State cities indicates the method of appointment. The item is headed " New Probation Officer ": " Mrs. X, a widow with one child about 5 years old, was appointed county probation officer for the north portion of N County yesterday by County Judge Z. Judge Z said he believes a mother will have the spirit of maternal love which will enable her to make the best probation officer. Mrs. X succeeds Miss A, who resigned and will engage in religious work with a traveling evangelist."

In 10 counties there were persons acting as probation officers, some on full-time and some on part-time basis, who appeared to have had special training and experience for probation work, or who at any rate appeared to be well qualified for such work. Unfortunately, however, in 6 of these 10 counties the officers had so much to do in addition to the pension work that the latter could not be properly done. That is, there seem to be only four counties in which conditions appear to be such that intelligent aid to the families is possible, and two of these counties have very small pension rolls—one county pensions one family and the other county pensions seven. The other two counties have a larger number of pensioned families. Only one of these four counties was visited by the special investigator, and it was disappointing to find that even in this county, where conditions appeared to make good pension work possible, good work was, nevertheless, not being done. In L County, which was visited, the county was found to be divided into three districts, with a different probation officer for each district. While the officer in one district, who is also a visitor for the associated charities, does give intelligent help to her families, such as finding work for the mother or children, supervising school attendance, etc., the other two officers make no attempt at anything of the kind, and their services stop with a perfunctory monthly visit to the family.

INVESTIGATION OF APPLICANTS' ELIGIBILITY.

The kind of investigation that is made depends largely on the intelligence of the person making the inquiries, and sufficient comment has already been made on this point. Further information as to precisely what is done in the way of investigation has been obtained from the schedules returned by county judges, the 24 schedules returned by social workers, and the visits of the special investigator. The schedules that were returned all reported that, before a pension was granted, it was the practice to have the home visited as required by law. In some counties, however, this represents the intention of the court rather than the uniform practice. Thus the report from one county is, "As to the investigation, the officer calls at the home in almost all cases; in a very few he may not." In another county, one of the two probation officers makes no pretense of visiting the home but interviews the women in his office. In other counties in which it seemed to be the usual practice to visit the home, some families were found who were not visited until after the pension was granted.

A single visit to the home seems to be all that is done in the way of investigating the applicant's eligibility. Most counties report that relatives are visited; but five counties report definitely that they are not " visited," and two more report that they are visited " sometimes " or " not always." The visits to the relatives, if made, seem to be wholly perfunctory ones, since no report has been made from any county and no case could be found by the investigator of any relative who had been either persuaded or compelled to assist an applicant or a pensioner.

In reply to the question as to whether any verification is made of other facts needed to establish eligibility, such as the marriage, death of husband, birth of children, and possession of property, the claim was made in most counties that this was done. In counties visited by the special investigator, however, it appeared that this verification really was not made. Officers when questioned were vague and indefinite and qualified their answers with " usually," " sometimes," " in some cases." No records of any steps in the investigation could be found. The officers' reports usually read " Your officer has investigated and has found"; but it seems to be the practice to consider an investigation complete when the applicant has been visited and interviewed, and the findings of the investigating

PART II.—ADMINISTRATION OUTSIDE OF COOK COUNTY. 141

officer seem to be based on the unverified statements of the applicant. The testimony of the applicant on oath in open court is held in many counties to furnish sufficient evidence of her eligibility. On the whole, the only general statement that can be made as to the practice of the outlying counties in the matter of the preliminary investigation is that usually the home is visited and that some officers believe that they make an attempt to verify the facts necessary to prove eligibility. The methods of verification are not on record and apparently can not be found, and it is clear that in many places the verification is that offered by the applicant herself in court, while, in other counties, "community knowledge" is accepted. From no county has any evidence been obtained of a uniform practice of verifying by legal records, such as has been adopted in Cook County.

Two results may usually be expected if a careless preliminary investigation is made: (1) A very small number of applications will be rejected or dismissed, since very few will be found by an inadequate investigation to be ineligible; (2) ineligible persons will be found on the pension lists. Each of these points will be discussed.

DISMISSED CASES.

In Cook County in the course of a year a great many more applications are rejected after investigation than are finally granted, notwithstanding the fact that it had been customary from the first to refuse to take applications from persons who are clearly ineligible. In the other counties of the State, about which we have information on this point, this rule does not appear to hold good.

Table LII shows the number of mothers whose applications were rejected or dismissed in a year in 49 counties from which reports could be obtained.

TABLE LII.—*Number of counties in which a specified number of applicants were refused pension grants.*

Number of pension applications rejected.	Number of counties.
Total	72
None	13
1–4 families	19
5–9 families	8
10–19 families	4
20–29 families	3
30–49 families	1
50 families or more	1
Not reported	23

It thus appears that 13 of the pension-granting counties rejected no applicants in a year and a considerable number of other counties rejected very few applications.[6] A list of reasons for dismissing

[6] The following table showing the relation between the number of families refused aid and the number in receipt of aid in the various counties may be of interest:

Number of counties refusing pensions to a specified number of families, together with number of families pensioned.

Number of pensions granted.	Applications refused.						
	Total.	None.	1–4	5–9	10–19	20–29	30–49	50 or more.
Total	49	13	19	8	4	3	1	1
1–4	12	5	6	1				
5–9	13	6	4	1	1	1		
10–19	11	1	8	1		1		
20–29	8	1			4	2		1
30–49	3		1	1	1			
50 or more	2					1	1	

PART II.—ADMINISTRATION OUTSIDE OF COOK COUNTY. 143

cases was given for the rejected applicants in Cook County. No such reasons could be obtained for the outlying counties. A great majority of the counties keep no record of the reasons for refusal to grant pensions. Officers when questioned could give no more definite reasons than that the applicants were refused " for legal reasons," or " for not complying with the law." There are so many requirements prescribed by the law that these reasons are too indefinite to be satisfactory.

The pensioning of every applicant who applies may be due to one of several reasons: (1) Lack of care in receiving and registering applicants; (2) inadequate investigation of applicant's eligibility; (3) failure to devise other methods of solving problems of family distress; (4) a willingness on the part of the court to disregard the provisions of the law and to grant pensions to ineligible applicants even when this ineligibility has been ascertained.

PENSION GRANTS TO INELIGIBLE FAMILIES.

One result of an inadequate preliminary investigation is the granting of pensions to families who are not legally eligible for this form of relief. In Illinois this condition is made worse by the fact that the county judges not infrequently refuse to be bound by the law and seem to take the position that they may grant pensions to any person whom they consider a suitable applicant. Twelve judges expressly said that they did not observe the requirements that had been added to the old vague law of 1911 by amended laws of 1913 and 1915. The legislature, when it passed the law of 1913, did not repeal the 1911 act by name but merely by the general phrase of "all acts or parts inconsistent herewith." That the new law was intended to replace the old one is not open to doubt; it was so interpreted in Cook County, and, it will be remembered, something like 200 families who did not comply with the new requirements were dropped from the rolls. But in some other counties the judges say that the funds-to-parents act of 1911 was not repealed by the later law; and 12 counties were in 1915 granting funds under that act. The investigator in suggesting to different judges that certain persons on his lists were ineligible under the present law, received more than once such a reply as: "Well, perhaps that is so, but I am operating under the old 1911 law." One judge said that he used the 1911 law instead of the amended law because he considered the earlier law a better one. Another judge told the investigator that he knew that a certain one of his pensioners was not legally entitled to a pension, but it would have "taken a heart of stone," he said, "to refuse what she asked."

In all but three of the counties outside Cook County visited by the investigator, pensions were being granted to persons who were legally ineligible. This may be due to the lawless attitude of the judges or to their lack of intelligence more than to the inability of the probation officer to discover and to report the applicant's ineligibility. But whatever the cause, the evidence clearly shows that, although the law specifically excluded deserted women, divorced women, and women property owners, such persons were frequently granted pensions in the outlying counties.

The requirement of the law most frequently ignored was that which provided that the mother who is the "owner of real property, other than household goods," shall not be eligible for a pension.[7] Four counties reported that they were in the habit of granting pensions to property owners, and family visiting by the investigator showed that it was also done in 8 additional counties. That is, in 10 of the 14 counties visited by the investigator it was found that pensions were granted to women property owners, although the schedules sent in by correspondence reported this practice in only 2 of these counties. Had it been possible to visit the other counties in which pensions are granted, there is reason to believe that the practice of ignoring the property disqualification would have been found to be even more widespread than it appears to be from the evidence. The value of the property owned by these pensioners varied greatly—some of the mothers owned only a little home representing a very small investment, but occasionally the property was more valuable.

For example, one such case in B County was that of a woman with two children over 3 and under 14 years of age. She owns property valued at from $4,000 to $5,000 with a $2,200 mortgage on it. Her home was very well furnished with good rugs, piano, etc. Her husband was a saloon keeper and a well known local politician. After his death she ran for town constable but was defeated, and a pension of $30 a month was almost immediately secured for her in spite of local opposition. The investigator was told that the pensioner was locally known as a financier, and it was charged that her pension was due to political influence. In any event, the ownership of property made her technically ineligible for this particular form of public aid.

Another case in the same county is that of a widow who was granted in October, 1915, a pension of $10 a month for two children. She owned the house in which she was living, valued at $800, and an adjoining 3 acres of land, which she sold to pay the mortgage on the two pieces of property. Her ownership of the property was a fact well known in the small community. In May, 1916, one of the pensioned children died. His pension was not stayed and the mother thought that the full pension was continued because the judge wished to help her a little more. In addition to the pension, the supervisors gave her coal and groceries. This is an especially interesting case, since at the time of the visit the woman had only one child under 14 and one child over 14 living with her. She had also three married daughters.

In the same county a pension of $10 a month was granted in January, 1914, to another widow for her one child. She owned the house in which she was living, valued at $700, but with a mortgage of $200. A local minister who has taken great interest in the pension law explained to the investigator that the court granted the pension on the ground that she is " such a deserving woman."

---

[7] Illinois Revised Statutes, 1917, ch. 23, sec. 308. This provision has since been altered; see *supra*, p. 15.

Still another case is that of Mrs. G, in C county, a Lithuanian woman, who was receiving a pension of $5 a month for four children and was buying the property where she was living from a building and loan association. The property was valued at $1,200, and she had paid more than half its value in monthly installments of $6.

Again, in F County in October, 1911, a pension of $6 a month was granted to the B family, consisting of the mother, one boy of 15, who was in a city outside the State, and four children under 14. They owned a small, three-room "box" house, built of bare boards and unplastered, valued at about $250. The present judge, who has come on the bench since the law of 1913 was passed, intended to discontinue the pension for this family because they owned property; but he said that so much pressure was brought to bear by fellow-townsmen of Mrs. B that he was unable to do this. That the law was being violated did not seem a sufficient reason for action.

Another propertied family was found in L County. A widow received a pension of $20 a month for six children. She owned property worth $1,500, which she was buying from a building and loan association and in which her equity was worth about $700. She was paying $6.50 a month to cover payments on the property, taxes, and interest.

Whether or not the law should have prohibited the granting of pensions to women who owned or were buying property is not the question here. Doubtless the "homestead" disqualification worked what seemed at any rate to be greater hardships in the country districts than in Chicago, and it is of interest that several down-State judges, in replying to a questionnaire sent out by the State charities commission asking their opinion as to the working of the law, suggested in their reply that ownership of a home should not render a woman ineligible for a pension.[8]

The law has already been amended in this respect and, as has been pointed out, now provides that when the mother is entitled to homestead rights under the exemption laws of the State or holds dower interest, and the value of either interest is not greater than $1,000, she shall not be thereby disqualified for relief under the mothers' aid provision. The judges who thought that the law should be altered in this respect administered the law as they thought it should be rather than as it was.

But it should be remembered that the law definitely prohibited the granting of such pensions, and every judge who, prior to July 1, 1917, granted a pension to a property owner, violated the law.

The down-State courts appear to be lax also about the enforcement of the provision relating to personal property. The Chicago court has ruled that a woman who has more than $50 in hand or in the

---

[8] Institution Quarterly, December, 1914, pp. 13–15.

PART II.—ADMINISTRATION OUTSIDE OF COOK COUNTY. 147

bank shall be considered ineligible under this provision. The down-State courts do not seem to have made any definite ruling as to the amount of property that disqualifies, but cases were found of women who were granted pensions when they still had a considerable sum of money. A case in point is that of the X family in N County. This family consisted of the mother and five children between the ages of 1 and 4. The father, who had been a miner earning $60 a month, died of appendicitis in May, 1915. He left $1,000 insurance. In October, 1915, the mother was granted a pension of $10 a month at a time when she still had $700 of the insurance money left. The county agent, who acts as probation officer, knew of this and the court also knew of it. The county agent is said to have told Mrs. X to use this money to supplement her small pension and to have promised her that when this was used the pension would be increased.

Other women who were pensioned, although they were not eligible, were women whose relatives were able to assist in their support. The law clearly says that a mother shall be eligible for a pension only "if her child or children has or have relatives of sufficient ability, and who shall be obligated by the finding and judgment of a court of competent jurisdiction, to support them." It has already been pointed out as a weakness of the down-State methods of investigation that little if anything is done to determine the liability of relatives for the support of the mother or her children, as is done, for example, in the Chicago court. Nor does any attempt seem to be made by the county judges to enforce such liability if it is known to exist. Thus pensioned families were found down State with relatives who were liable for their support but who had never been forced to comply with the support provisions of the law.[9]

For example, a woman in C County, Mrs. Y, who had been divorced by one husband and deserted by another, had lived in another State for five years, where her last child had been born. Her husband became ill, and was sent to a sanitarium, and in 1915 she was sent back to her former home in Illinois by the public authorities, but probably at her own request. She then sold her piano, and with the proceeds brought her husband to Illinois; but he soon deserted, and she was given a pension of $6 a month, $3 for each of her two children. She lived in a house adjoining her mother's, and the mother with the two unmarried sons owns the home. These unmarried brothers were both working, and they and the mother were abundantly able to support the pensioner, who was technically ineligible not only because she was a deserted and divorced woman but also because she had not been in the county for three years previous.

A somewhat similar case is that of Mrs. Z in B County, who had a pension of $15 a month, one child under 14, one child over 14, two married daughters, and one married son. Mrs. Z lived with one

---
[9] See Illinois Revised Statutes, ch. 23, sec. 308.

daughter in a very comfortably furnished house, but the other married daughter and son had given her no help, and had never been asked to do so.

A similar case in M County is that of Mrs. A, a woman with one dependent child. This pensioner was living with her mother and her stepfather, who owned a good house in a good neighborhood. The house was well furnished, and they had a piano and a telephone. There was a cottage at the rear of the lot that was rented. The mother and the stepfather ran a kind of catering business, and the widowed daughter sewed and earned about $15 or $20 a month. The woman was technically ineligible for a pension, because she had not lived in the county three years, and it seemed to be clear that in any event the pension of $6 was not needed in the household. The paternal grandfather and uncles were also able to contribute, should help have been necessary. Incidentally, it may be noted that it is against the practice of the Chicago court to grant a pension to any able-bodied woman with only one dependent child, so that in the case given above the woman would not have received a pension in Chicago even if she had had no relatives able to assist and had met the residence qualifications.

Another group of ineligible pensioners not infrequently found down State were the deserted wives who were eligible under the 1911 law but have been ineligible since 1913. Reports from two counties showed that pensions were granted to deserted wives, and deserted wives were also found receiving pensions in eight of the counties visited.

Another case of the pensioning of a group of women in violation of the law was found in M County. Here the judge had granted pensions to women whose husbands were in the National Guard and had been sent down to the Mexican border with their regiments. The investigator called attention to the fact that these soldiers' dependents were not eligible for pensions under the aid-to-mothers act, but the judge said that he acted in these cases under the clause in the law which provided for the pensioning of women whose husbands were permanently incapacitated for work by reason of mental or physical infirmities. Only two such pensions were granted, and they were discontinued after a G. A. R. fund had been raised to care for soldiers' wives.

Another illegal practice that seems to be countenanced by some of the down-State judges is the pensioning of children who do not live with their mother. The law clearly says that "the child or children for whose benefit the relief is granted must be living with the mother of such child or children." In two counties pensions were granted to grandparents, and in another county to other guardians, but in these three counties the judges claimed that they were operating under the "old 1911 law." In other counties pensions were granted nominally to the mother who then used the money to board out the child or children, a practice clearly illegal. For example, Mrs. B, of C County, with a pension of $6 for one child only, worked out as housekeeper for a widower and boarded her child with a friend.

PART II.—ADMINISTRATION OUTSIDE OF COOK COUNTY. 149

Mrs. D, of G County, received a pension for three children, two of whom she placed in a church institution, apparently with the consent of the judge. The boys ran away from this institution and have now been sent to an institution for delinquents; but no change has been made in the pension.

Mrs. E, of P County, with one child, 6 years old, was granted a pension of $5 a month. Mrs. E is a strong, vigorous woman who works as a domestic, leaving the child with her own parents in another village.

The list of ineligible pensioners is greatly increased by the lack of supervision after the family is pensioned. One result of this lack of supervision is that families who were eligible at the time of the granting of the pension may become ineligible through the remarriage of the mother, or her removal from the county, or because a child has reached the age of 14 and has gone to work, or because of some other change in the family situation. Unless the supervision of the families is thorough enough to insure that the pension will be stopped with the change in circumstances, families who have become ineligible for pensions will be found on the pension rolls.

SUPERVISION.

The importance of proper supervisory care for pensioned families has already been discussed.[10] Supervision is of course necessary, not only that pensions may be stopped when they are no longer needed, but also in order that the court may be assured that the public funds are being wisely expended and that the mothers may be assisted in maintaining a good home for the pensioned children. Proper supervisory care, however, can be provided only by competent, responsible—and this probably means salaried—probation officers. If the probation officer for the pension work is not really a probation officer at all but a supervisor of the poor, deputy sheriff, county judge, State's attorney, or even a volunteer visitor, adequate supervision can hardly be expected. It has already been pointed out that in 25 counties the probation work is carried on by persons who are probation officers in name only.

In reply to the schedule questions relating to supervision, 27 of the 64 counties sending in replies reported that no attempt was made to provide any supervision of pensioned families.

Of the eight counties from which no schedules were returned only two have regular probation officers, and one of these counties pays a salary of $10 a month, the other, $40. In three counties the supervisors act as probation officers; in one the officer is paid $3 per diem; in one a special officer is appointed for each case; while the other is the county which pays the officer for each case pensioned. It seems probable, therefore, that all these counties should be added to the list of those not providing supervision. Nine other counties report that supervision is provided, but the families are not visited in their homes. Thus, in at least 36, and probably 43, of the 72 counties granting pensions there is no visitation of the pensioned families.

Twenty-nine counties, on the other hand, report that their families are visited by the probation officer, but 5 add qualifying statements, such as " at times," " when necessary," " frequently," etc. Thus, G County reports that visits are made " when desirable "; but out of 10 families in this county visited by our special investigator not 1 reported even a single visit of the officer since the grant of the pension. In this county a substitute for visits had been devised. The judge called the pensioned mothers into court " about every six

---

[10] See *supra*, pp. 27 et seq.

PART II.—ADMINISTRATION OUTSIDE OF COOK COUNTY. 151

months" and reexamined them as to their need of a pension. Six other counties report that the probation officer visits the families, but the frequency of the visits is not reported. In two of these counties the officer is paid on a per diem basis, in two the officer is not paid for his services, but in the other two there is a regular officer on a salary—in one case of $360 a year, in the other $600. It is possible that these last two officers may visit at regular intervals, but it is extremely unlikely that this is done in the other four counties.

Five counties reported that the families were visited three or four times a year. Thirteen reported that families were visited once a month. Five of these 13 counties, however, were visited by our special investigator, and in only 1 were visits actually made regularly every month. In A County there were three probation officers, all volunteers; and while two of them appeared to visit some of their families very frequently, the other was unable to get round more than three or four times in a year. In D County the officer visited only every second or third month but saw her families every month when the pension was drawn. In H County the probation officer herself is unable to visit oftener than two or three times a year, but the family is visited by "friendly visitors" who are supposed to go once a month. In I County the probation officer, a young daughter-in-law of the judge, had not yet made the rounds of her pensioned families, because, as she explained, "it was extremely hot last summer." Two of the counties which reported that visits were made only two or three times a year have these visits supplemented by reports from the mother to the probation officer every month, and a third county has the family visited by volunteers, supposedly monthly.

Such data as are available, then, show that there were nine counties in which the probation officer visited monthly; three in which the probation officer saw the mother every month but visited only every second, third, or fourth month; four in which she visited three or four times yearly, but in two of these the family was nominally visited every month by a volunteer; the practices of the three officers in one county varied; and one county which reported monthly visits was found to be one of those in which the officer visited "when desirable."

The various forms of service that may be rendered by intelligent supervising officers have already been discussed in the section of this report dealing with the work of the Chicago court. It is unnecessary to say that such work can not be done by the probation service provided for in the down-State counties.

The facts about the supervision of pensioned families in the 63 counties for which information was secured are summarized in Table LIII.

TABLE LIII.—*Number of counties providing different degrees of "supervisory care."*

Methods of supervision reported.	Number of counties.
Total	63
No supervision	27
Supervision without visits	8
Visits "when necessary"	6
Probation officer visits monthly	8
Probation officer visits three or four times yearly	[a] 7
Frequency of visits varies with officers	1
Frequency of visits is not reported	6

[a] In three of these counties the mothers reported to the officer every month, and in two others the families were visited by volunteers every month.

Abundant evidence of the lack of supervision was collected by our special investigator in the 14 counties in which she visited some of the pensioned families. This investigator found, for example, that women were having pension checks forwarded to them through the mail, although no one at the court knew exactly where they were living.

Thus Mrs. I, with four children and a pension of $10 a month, received her pension at the Z postoffice; but our investigator found that her present address was unknown to any one, that she was pregnant with an illegitimate child, and that she was supposed to have moved to another city.

A similar case in another county was that of Mrs. N. Her name was given to the investigator as receiving a pension of $5 a month. The investigator was unable to find the woman at the address which was on the county treasurer's list. Neighbors either did not know or would not tell anything of her whereabouts. The landlady was consulted and explained that she had moved about two years ago; that she had said she was going to a city in another State to live with her two older daughters. She was getting her checks forwarded by mail. Neither the adult probation officer nor the overseer of the poor knew anything of this family.

Again, the investigator found it difficult to locate a woman in C County. The neighbors said that they had not seen her for months. They explained that "she moved round a good deal." The woman, who was finally found, had just returned from a six months' stay in a neighboring State; she had returned reluctantly, but she said that she was afraid if she stayed away much longer her pension would be revoked. While out of the State she had worked in a hotel and had boarded one child in an institution for dependent children and two boys in a newsboys' home. These boys, aged 10 and 12 years, sold papers and were allowed to keep what they made after their board was paid. The older of the boys went across the river to his home in Illinois each month and got the

PART II.—ADMINISTRATION OUTSIDE OF COOK COUNTY. 153

mother's pension check, cashed it, and brought the money back to her. The 10-year-old boy said that he had attended school a few weeks while he was away. This woman had been a widow three times. The pension was granted before any of the children were old enough to work. At the time of the visit the family income was $55 a month, and the total income with pension $65. The officer in this county is supposed to visit every pensioned family once a year.

A serious result of the lack of supervision was the finding of a large number of families who had been put on the pension roll and then had not been removed, although family circumstances had changed and the pensions were no longer needed.

Thus, Mrs. M of G County, who was receiving a pension of $15, was found by our investigator to have been remarried. This was reported back to the court, and she was then taken off the pension roll.

In the same county Mrs. N, with one child, had been receiving a pension of $10 a month for more than two years. The investigator called at the address given in the county treasurer's book, found that Mrs. N had been a servant in this house; that she had never had the child with her there; and that she had used her pension to board out the baby. No one knew where Mrs. N had gone, but people thought that she was married and that the baby was still boarded somewhere. When this was reported back to the court by the investigator, a clerk in the office then said that he had seen a notice of the pensioner's marriage in the local newspaper and had expected to tell the judge to discontinue the pension but had forgotten to do so. He added that no more checks would be mailed to her.

Most frequently the change in circumstances is due to the fact that children who were pensioned when they were under 14 years of age have grown old enough to go to work. This is a change that could easily be discovered if there were a responsible person keeping the records, for the exact ages of the children should be on record at the time the pension is granted, and the exact date when the pension should be stayed should also be a matter of record. Some of these families had very good incomes in 1917, but the pensions were still going on.

Thus, in M County, Mrs. O, the widow of a farmer, was granted a pension four years before, when she had living at home four children under 14 and three children over that age. At the time of the visit of the investigator there were only two children under 14, and five children living at home were working and earning $153 a month. Included in the family, moreover, was the illegitimate child of one of the daughters, born after the pension was granted.[11] The children

---

[11] It should be added that the investigator reported that the home was beautifully clean and that it seemed to be a good one in spite of the older girl's delinquency.

paid $64 a month board out of their earnings. Although the probation officer was supposed to visit the family once in three months, she had not recommended any change in the pension, in spite of the fact that the family's situation had changed radically. Nothing had been done to compel the father of the illegitimate child to contribute to its support, and nothing had been done to compel a daughter in a neighboring town to contribute to the mother's support, although she is abundantly able to do so if it were necessary.

In K County two families were found in somewhat similar circumstances. In one there were six children over 14, and their earnings were about $140 a month, but the pension of $24 was still continued. In the other there was only one child under 14, while there were four children at work, whose earnings were $163 a month, but the pension of $5 was still going on. This is an abuse that is bound to increase if something is not done to keep a careful watch of the pension rolls and to compel the withdrawal of pensions for children who have gone to work and are above the age at which pension grants can legally be made.

One result of this lack of supervision on the part of the probation officer and constituted authorities that was noted by the investigator who visited the selected counties in 1916 was the peculiar importance of the county clerks, county treasurers, or whoever in their offices may have had charge of making out the monthly pension checks or of mailing them or handing them to the pensioned mothers. These clerks were sometimes the only persons who were in any way in touch with the pensioned families after the grant had been made, and the investigator found that they were often better informed on the family circumstances and more interested in the pensioners than any other officials in the county. They saw to it, so far as it was done at all, that pensions were stayed when children became 14 or when the mother remarried. In some places there was an attempt to do this systematically, as in B, where the clerk has recently adopted a card catalogue, showing the date on which each pensioned child became 14; more often, however, the families were watched only in haphazard fashion, and pensions were stayed only when something happened to call it to the attention of the clerk. Thus, it was not uncommon for the clerk in going over the records with our investigator to remark, "Why, Johnnie is 14 now, we will have to stay his pension," or "I saw in the papers that that woman is remarried, I guess she won't need a pension any longer." Occasionally also other violations of the law were noticed by members of the office staff. In P County, for example, the sister of the county clerk, who was herself a clerk in the office, learned that one of the pensioners (Mrs. A) had placed her child with its grandparents. The county clerk's sister thereupon sent for Mrs. A before sending out the pension check, since the law clearly states that the pensioned child must be living with the mother. In this instance the efforts of the clerk proved futile, since the mother appealed to the judge, who continued the pension in defiance of the law. But the clerks in the office can not be expected to carry the sole responsibility for staying pensions, and it is a result of the lax administration that they not infrequently send checks to women who are no longer entitled to them. Cases have been already given from C and G Counties of pensions going to women who had left the State. Similarly, it has been noted that checks went to women who had remarried; for the women are not all so honest as one woman in F County who did not claim her checks after remarriage, so that they were finally returned through the post-office authorities.

Another weakness in the administration of the law discovered by our investigator in the course of her visits to the counties was the lack of responsibility which was felt by one judge or probation officer for the acts of his predecessors. One judge was found who was evidently trying to administer the mothers' pension law strictly according to the terms of the law, and who explained that the ineligible families on his lists had been granted pensions by the former judge. The possibility of staying these illegal pensions either did not occur to him or he did not think that he ought to be required to incur the unpopularity of correcting his predecessor's mistakes. Similarly, in a few counties the probation officer visited the families who had been granted funds since her term of office began, but seemed to feel that she had no responsibility for the families who were on the lists before she began her work.

DIFFERENCES BETWEEN THE PENSION POLICY OF THE CHICAGO COURT AND THAT ADOPTED BY THE DOWN-STATE COURTS.

Certain differences in policy are to be found in the different courts and, in particular, differences between the down-State courts and the Chicago court. Certain rules, it will be remembered, have been laid down in the Chicago court that either define more accurately the terms of eligibility or add new requirements. The differences between the Chicago court and the down-State courts may be due to the latter's failure to formulate any policy at all rather than to the adoption of a policy that is unlike that of the Chicago court. But whether due to accident or to design, differences in policy do exist. The most important of these relate to the following points: (1) The pensioning of an able-bodied mother who has only one child under 14 years of age; (2) the refusal to continue pensions for children who have reached the legal working age and who are not "ill or physically incapacitated for work."

1. The Chicago court, as has been explained, holds that an able-bodied mother should be able to support herself and one child; and in Chicago, therefore, pensions are infrequently granted to such women. Only 31 of the 778 families in Cook County for whom this information was secured had but one child. There seems to be no other court which has adopted such a policy. In many counties pensioned families with only one dependent child were found in which there were older brothers and sisters to help to support the family. In the down-State counties 138 of the 690 pensioned families about which data were obtained were families with only one child under 14.

Out of 106 families for whom schedules were obtained by the investigator, 26, or approximately one-fourth, were families with only one child under 14, and in 15 of these 26 families there were also older children, sometimes as many as three or four. Certainly these families should have been self-supporting according to any reasonable standard. For example, a typical case is that of Mrs. P, of B County, who had one child under 14 and a pension of $10. She had also living at home a daughter, 21 years of age, who worked in a piano factory, and a son, 24 years of age, who was a printer. The mother kept two boarders and four "mealers." The total income without any contribution from the son was about $142 a month.

A similar case is that of Mrs. Q, of K County, who received a pension of $15 a month for one child who was under 14. She had two sons, aged 16 and 22, living at home, both of whom were working. Mrs. Q also supplemented the income by doing work at home for the knitting factory. The family income here was $100 a month, and the pension $15 a month.

In another family in M County there was one child under 14 and two children above this age, a daughter earning $5 a week in a tinsel factory and a boy of 15 attending high school. The mother worked, too, and earned from $20 to $24 a month. The mother's health was not good, and the investigator discovered that no medical examination had been made. The pension of $15 a month was granted when there were two children under 14. The probation officer was supposed to visit, as she said, "about a couple of times a year."

Although opinions may differ as to the justice of requiring or expecting under the present standard of women's wages that a woman should provide support for herself and her child when she has no resources except her ability to work, the investigator in her visits to these families felt that the Cook County policy was a reasonable one, and that the "one-child" families might properly have been expected to be self-supporting. When such mothers were working full time, as most of them were, and were not earning enough to support themselves and one child, the court pension might be looked upon as a "subsidy in aid of wages."

2. For children who have reached the legal working age of 14, the Chicago court follows the policy of staying the pension. The court holds that a child who is legally old enough to work must be counted a wage earner and must contribute his share to the family income, provided always that he is not "ill or physically incapacitated for work." A normally strong child in a pensioned family in Chicago is allowed to remain in school after he is 14 only on condition that the amount he would contribute to the family income is forthcoming from some other source. As a result, children leave school and go to work before they are fit for work; but so long as the laws of the State sanction this proceeding, and so long as the vast majority of wage-earning families are obliged to sacrifice their children in this way, public-relief agencies almost inevitably have to follow a similar policy.

Outside of Cook County, however, pensioned children of working age and physically able to work were found still in school. It is not clear whether the outlying courts have adopted the policy of allowing these children to remain in school or whether the continuing of the pension is due to the lack of supervision and the failure to take notice of the fact that the child had become old enough to go to work. The families themselves explained the fact that the children were still in school as due to the few opportunities for children of that age to find work. If this is true, and there is every reason to think it is, especially in the smaller communities, it constitutes an excellent reason for raising the age at which all children are allowed to leave school; whether it is also a sufficient reason for pensioning a few such children must remain a matter of opinion.

There are certain other questions of policy on which the down-State practice seems to differ from that of the Chicago court, but they are less important since they affect a smaller number of families. Few down-State courts, for example, seem to have formulated any definite policy relating to the presence of an incapacitated father in the house, when his presence is a menace to the children. In most cases the court has not the information on which to decide whether or not the man should be required to go to a sanitarium; and places to which the man might be removed are perhaps less easily found in the down-State counties. In Chicago, again, a man is not considered incapacitated except on the basis of the physician's statement that he is "totally incapacitated for work." In the outlying counties a family may be pensioned even if the man is not totally incapacitated; nor does the degree of the incapacity which entitles a man to ask for a pension for his wife and children appear to have been defined.

Two other classes of down-State pensioners who would be excluded according to the rules of the Chicago court include the woman who has ever had an illegitimate child and the woman who partially supports herself by taking men boarders and roomers. This may, of course, be the only way in which a widow finds it possible to contribute to the support of her family, but the Chicago court takes the position that the woman who earns her living in this way is in morally dangerous surroundings for which the court can not assume the responsibility. In visiting the down-State families, however, the investigator found that this practice was not disapproved of by the courts.

Whether or not the down-State courts have erred in failing to adopt the policies formulated by the Chicago court on the basis of its wider experience is a question on which opinions may not agree. Conditions in Chicago are, of course, very different from conditions in many of the down-State cities and counties. It does not seem probable, however, that these differences in policy are due to any differences in down-State conditions but rather to the failure on the part of the down-State courts to formulate any principles or policies of administration.

ADEQUACY OF PENSION GRANTS.

An attempt was made to collect data relating to the size of the pension grants in the different down-State counties. No published data were available except the figures collected by the State charities commission showing the total amount paid out for pensions and the total number of families pensioned, from which it is impossible to determine the size of the pension granted to any individual family. Further information on this subject has been obtained from the following sources: (1) From material gathered by our special investigator, who reported on the practice of fixing the pension allowances in the counties she visited; (2) from data collected by correspondence showing the pension pay roll totals for 41 counties for a single month; (3) from data, also collected by correspondence, showing the exact pension allowances of 690 families in 53 different counties, together with the size of the families. Such information as was collected indicates that in general the pensions are inadequate and that in some counties they are little more than doles.

The reports of the investigator as well as the schedules collected by correspondence indicate that the practice of granting pensions on an unscientific "flat rate" basis is very common. The most usual flat rate is $5 per child per month; eight counties make a practice of granting this rate, although in five of the counties the rule is occasionally broken. Two counties pension at the rate of $2.50 a child; one county gives $5 for an only child, another county gives $2 for each child, while still another gives $2 a week per child. Other counties make a difference between the first and other children. Thus, one county gives $8 for the first child and $1.50 for every other child, while another county gives $8 for the first and adds $4 for each additional child. U County gives from $12 to $15 to families with one child, but $10 per child to larger families.

Three counties have adopted the unfortunate practice of granting a flat rate per family, which is, of course, even more inequitable than a flat rate per child. Two counties give $10 a month to every pensioned family, and one county gives $5 a month to 24 out of 27 families, while to the other 3, which are unusually large families, it gives $10 each month.[12]

---

[12] The answer of the clerk of one of these counties to the question whether they found this "sufficient to cover the needs of families of all sizes" was: "This is not looked upon as an entire or independent support but merely as an assistance. Ten dollars is not sufficient for all the needs of any family, nor is $100 sufficient for all the needs of some families."

While it is apparent from this that there were a few counties which fixed a rate that was fairly liberal, it is also evident that the great majority of counties which granted pensions at a fixed rate established a rate that was obviously too low to insure a desirable standard for living of most of their families.

It should perhaps be noted that the flat rate is due in part to the fact that the court, as a result of the inadequate preliminary investigation, does not know the earnings of supplementary wage earners nor other sources of income.

TABLE LIV.—*Number of counties with average monthly pensions of specified amounts per child and per family.*

Average pension per child.	Number of counties.	Average pension per family.	Number of counties.
Total	41		41
Less than $2	3	$5 to $9	6
$2 to $3	6	10 to 14	19
$4 to $5	13	15 to 19	8
$6 to $7	10	20 to 24	4
$8 to $9	6	25 to 29	1
$10 to $11	2	30 to 34	3
Not reported	1		

It is perhaps unnecessary to explain that "average pension" is in many respects an unsatisfactory term. In the down-State counties, however, the practice of granting a flat rate per child or per family is so common that the "average pension" is more significant than it would be in Cook County. It is obvious that the practice of granting pensions at a flat rate, without regard to other family circumstances, must result in inadequate relief to some of the families; and a study of Table LIV confirms the report of the investigator in showing that some of the rates are very low. Thus the average pension per child was less than $2 a month in 3 counties, from $2 to $3 in 6 other counties, and $4 to $5 in 13 other counties. That is, in 22 of the 41 counties the average pension per child was $5 or less; and the average pensions per family, it will be noted, were also extremely low.

The data obtained from schedules showing the pension allowances granted to 690 families in 53 counties [13] are presented in Table LV, together with similar data from Cook County. The Cook County data are for the families pensioned during the period August 1, 1913, to March 1, 1915, when the officers of the court made their survey of

---

[13] The 690 families are not all the families aided by those 53 counties Aug. 1, 1915, nor were all of them on the roll at that date. Thirty-eight counties, with 361 families, give the data for every family pensioned at that date, and no further information; 10 counties give data for only 123 of the 285 families pensioned; 4 counties give data for every family pensioned in the year; while 1 county gives data for some families not on its roll on Aug. 1, but not the total for the year. Since the question of interest is the amount of money each family receives, the fact that they do not relate to the same date is not significant.

PART II.—ADMINISTRATION OUTSIDE OF COOK COUNTY. 161

the pension work. The Cook County pensions, it will be remembered, were higher at a later date.[14]

TABLE LV.—*Number of families receiving pension grants of specified amounts in Cook County and in 53 other counties.*

Amount of pension.	Number of families.		Per cent distribution.	
	Cook County.	53 other counties.	Cook County.	53 other counties.
Total	543	690	100.0	100.0
Less than $5		4		.6
$5–$9	4	199	.7	28.8
$10–$14	39	258	7.2	37.4
$15–$19	95	126	17.5	18.3
$20–$24	159	56	29.3	8.1
$25–$29	55	23	10.1	3.3
$30–$39	124	21	22.8	3.0
$40 and over	67	3	12.4	.5

TABLE LV–A.—*Cumulative numbers and percentages.*

Amount of pension.	Cook County.		Other counties.	
	Number.	Per cent.	Number.	Per cent.
Less than $5			4	0.6
Less than $10	4	0.7	203	29.4
Less than $15	43	7.9	461	66.8
Less than $20	138	25.4	587	85.1
Less than $25	297	54.7	643	93.2
Less than $30	352	64.8	666	96.5
Less than $40	476	87.6	687	99.5
$40 and over	67	12.4	3	.5

Table LV shows very clearly that in comparison with the Cook County standard, the down-State pension policy might be called a niggardly one. There were no pensions of less than $5 a month granted in Cook County, and only four families, or less than 1 per cent of the total number of families, fell into the $5 to $9 group, whereas 28.8 per cent of the down-State families were in this group.

The cumulative series shows that whereas only 7.9 per cent of the Cook County families got less than $15 a month, 66.8 per cent of the down-State families got pensions of less than $15; 25 per cent of the Cook County families and 85 per cent of the down-State families were getting less than $20 a month. Again, 12.4 per cent of the Cook County families in comparison with one-half of 1 per cent of the down-State families got pensions of $40 or more than $40. No families were found down State who got a pension as high as the old $50 maximum allowed by law or the $60 maximum now allowed, although in the discussion of the Cook County pensions, it appeared that a number of families received these maximum grants.

---

[14] See *supra*, Tables IX and XI, pp. 49, 51.

Differences in pension grants are, of course, more significant if they relate to families of the same size, and Table LVI has therefore been prepared, showing the pension grants only for families with two or three children, both in Cook County and down State.

TABLE LVI.—*Number of families with two or three children receiving pensions of less than specified amounts in Cook County and in 53 other counties cumulative numbers and percentages.*

Amount of pension.	Cook County. Number.	Cook County. Per cent.	Other counties. Number.	Other counties. Per cent.
Less than $5			1	0.3
Less than $10	4	1.4	98	26.3
Less than $15	37	12.7	253	67.8
Less than $20	114	39.1	333	89.3
Less than $25	219	75.0	363	97.4
Less than $30	234	80.1	367	98.4
Less than $35	288	98.6	370	99.2
$35 and over	4	1.4	3	.8

This table only serves to confirm what has already been said about the down-State pension grants. The comparison here is a more accurate one since it relates to families of the same size, but it shows again that very much larger percentages of the down-State families get small pensions, and very much smaller percentages get large pensions, when the down-State and the Cook County pensions are compared.

The cost of living is probably somewhat higher in Chicago than it is in the smaller cities and rural communities in which the 690 families live, and it may not be necessary for other counties to give pensions so large as those given by the Cook County juvenile court in order to make their relief adequate. It must be remembered, however, that, if the cost of living is higher in Chicago, industrial opportunities are probably more abundant, and wages higher, so that the income aside from the pension is likely to be greater. Taking everything into consideration there seems to be no reason to doubt that the differences found between the size of the pensions in Cook County and in other parts of the State do represent very real differences in the adequacy of the relief granted.

Another point to be noted is the insecurity or uncertainty of the down-State pension grants. The pensions may be paid regularly each month, or they may be paid for part of the year only.

Serious results sometimes follow from the differences between the pension-granting and pension-appropriating authorities. Thus in one county the total expenditures for mothers' pensions in the fiscal year ending May 1, 1915, exceeded the appropriation for this purpose by $5,000. This deficit was paid with demoralizing results to the 134 pensioned families, for the deficit had to be made up from the next year's appropriation, which meant that all pensions were stopped in May and not resumed until the next fall. In C County the appropriation was not adequate to cover the pension grants, more than half of which were suddenly cut off in May, and the families were left to shift for themselves for the remaining four months of the year. In F County all pensions were withheld for one month for the same reason in 1915, and it seemed probable that some such step would have to be taken again in 1916, since the appropriation was $800 and the amount required to take care of the families pensioned was $900. Again in L County we learn that " by reason of the insufficient appropriation by the county supervisors no pensions have been paid in the county since April 1, and it is not likely that payments will be resumed before September 1." In this county the families were not allowed to suffer, as private relief agencies substituted their relief, at least " in most pressing cases."

It should not be overlooked, however, that in all these counties the appropriation might have covered the necessary expenditure for pensions if it had been more wisely used. If pension lists are padded by the carrying of ineligible families and families whose pensions ought to have been stayed, appropriations will probably never be adequate. In at least two of these counties, families not infrequently are pensioned who clearly could be self-supporting if all the possible sources of income were utilized. That is, some of the counties seem to have an entirely haphazard pension policy. Almost any person who applies is placed on the pension roll, and the families are allowed to continue on the roll long after their circumstances have so changed as to render them ineligible for pension grants. Then, when the pension appropriation is used up, all the families alike are left without any relief until the new appropriation is made.

Some evidence of the inadequacy of the down-State pensions is indicated by the fact that many mothers continue to do more work than they should after the pension is granted. For example, in one city, out of 11 pensioners selected at random off the pension list and visited, 4 worked all day long six days in the week. The report of the investigator on these families is as follows:

Mrs. R works every day in a factory and is at home only in the evening. One child; $8 pension.

Mrs. S works every day in a clothing factory; children have dinner in a day nursery. Five children; $15 pension.

Mrs. T works all day in a factory. One child; $8 pension.

Mrs. U works all day every day in a laundry as forelady. She has three children, one over 14. The pension is $12 a month. The house is frightfully untidy, and the small children, aged 9 and 12, look very desolate and uncared for. The mother and the oldest and youngest children are thought to be tubercular. The probation officer thinks the pension should be large enough to permit the mother to stay at home.

The record seems somewhat similar in A County, thus: Mrs. V works every day in a factory, earns about $4 a week; gets $20 pension for two children.

Mrs. W works 10 hours every day in a laundry for $4 a week. She gets $20 pension.

In B County Mrs. M works in a factory six days in the week. She has only one child and earns only $26 a month; but she owns her home, valued at about $1,000, and received $2,000 insurance when her husband died six years before. But her mother, and a feeble-minded sister who should be in an institution, live with her; and the pension of $10, although not legal since she is a property owner, is, nevertheless, useful in supporting this household.

PENSION RECORDS.

The various statutes contain no requirements as to the records to be kept for each pensioned "case," or family, other than to prescribe certain legal papers that must be used, a petition, summons, etc., and to provide that the report of the probation officer, after an investigation has been made, must be submitted in writing to the judge with a recommendation regarding the application. These legal papers are usually filed, and in most cases serve as the only record of the family aside from the entry, in a ledger, of the name of the mother, the number of pensioned children, and the amount of the pension. Such records are quite inadequate even for describing the family situation at the time the grant is made.

The form of such papers is not uniform, but the same points are covered in all counties. The application usually states that the undersigned mother of such and such children under 14 years of age (here follows the exact age of each child) respectfully submits that she is a citizen of the United States; that she has resided in the county for three years past; that her husband is dead or permanently incapacitated for work; that said children are living with her; that she is a person mentally, physically, and morally fit to have the care and custody of said children; that in the absence of such relief she would be required to work regularly away from home, etc. In brief, the applicant fills out a blank form stating in general terms that she complies with each and every provision of the law, but giving little of her individual circumstances except her name, address, and the names and ages of such of her children as are under 14 years of age. No information is given as to her present occupation and earnings, the other wage earners in her family, her income from other sources, or the names and addresses of relatives. The report of the investigating officer is somewhat more detailed, and space is provided for the specific findings of the probation officer with regard to such points as the mother's qualifications and her need of relief, but the points covered are the same as those covered in the application and the omissions are also the same.[15] The petition is in general still more vague, as the petitioner merely states his own qualifications to act in that capacity, with the additional statement that an investigation has been made and aid recommended. The order of the court follows along the same lines as the application, for the court must find that every provision of the law is complied with.

---

[15] It would probably be possible to fill out one of these reports so as to give all the facts desirable; but there is nothing in the form or the instruction which requires such specific information, and it is obviously easier to fill it out in general terms.

As legal papers, these forms may be entirely satisfactory, but they can not, of course, serve as the basis for constructive work with the family. They are equally useless as a record of what was done during the investigation, since it is impossible to find out from any one of the papers whether or not a real attempt was made to learn the family's need for a pension or its eligibility under the terms of the law. These papers, moreover, contain no record of such changes in the family situation as occur from time to time. Obviously, such facts must be recorded in a supplementary record. It is impossible to say how many counties keep records other than the legal papers. From all the evidence, however, it appears that the great majority of counties keep no record but the ledger and legal papers.

A few counties appear to have devised some kind of supplementary record. The forms used vary from a simple card index, such as has been recently adopted in B County, to the elaborate case record which has been described in connection with the work of the Chicago court. These case records are in use in only four of the down-State counties.

In other counties there is some form of monthly report to be filled in by the mother, as in E County, or by the visitor, as in K County. Although such records as these are more valuable than the legal papers that are filed away and never looked at again, or the meager record that goes on the clerk's ledger, they are still very far from being satisfactory records upon which to base constructive work for the family.

A further objection to the down-State records is that they are often carelessly and incompletely filled out and are put away in such form that they can not be found. In fact, the investigator thought it worthy of comment when she found the court papers and the ledger neatly and accurately kept. The records of families whose pensions have been stayed or withdrawn are especially difficult to find. The books in many instances fail to show even the number of families who have had their pensions stayed, and it was the exceptional county that could give the reasons for the stay of each pension. Even in the four counties in which case records with forms similar to those used in Chicago are kept the actual recording is not uniformly complete—probably because of the lack of clerical assistance, which was complained of by more than one probation officer. The records that were seen by the investigator did not give so much information as was desirable about the work done in investigating, and in some of them the running reports of visits were little more than a note that the family was visited on a given date. It may be said, therefore, of the records kept outside of Cook County that they are uniformly either imperfect in form or poorly kept, or both. Even the records in H County, which are better than those elsewhere, are incomplete as to the investigation.

CONCLUSION.

A study of the Illinois situation reveals grave defects in the administration of the aid-to-mothers law. These evils are inseparable from irresponsible local administration. That a great public relief experiment could be safely left to 102 different local authorities to administer without any centralized supervision or control was inconceivable. In this, its fatal defect, the law copies the old pauper law with its principle of local responsibility rather than the new principle of State control, which has been adopted for the care of the insane and of other special groups.

The experience with the mothers' pension legislation in Illinois followed that of other forms of legislation left to the various counties to support and enforce. Some counties have refused to grant any pensions; other counties have granted pensions illegally; and so diverse are the methods of administration that there may be said to be not one pension system but many different systems in Illinois. There is, for example, the very successful and admirable pension department of the Cook County court; and there are, supposedly established under the same law, pension departments in the down-State counties that are a disgrace to the State. Even in Cook County, the present system rests upon the tenure in office of a single individual, the circuit-court judge, who is annually assigned or reassigned to the juvenile-court bench. The judges who have presided in this court since the pension law has been in operation have followed closely the fine standards set by the man who was responsible for the initial experiment, but there remains each year the possibility of the appointment of a judge who will destroy the merit system. It is a favorable precedent that thus far the merit system has been voluntarily adhered to in the appointment of probation officers.

It may, perhaps, be said briefly that the most important lesson to be learned from the Illinois experiment is merely an old lesson to be learned over again—namely, that all social legislation that is left to 102 different local authorities to enforce without any supervision and without any help from the State must fail. The mothers' pension law can only be administered by good social workers, and in some of the rural counties there is no one within the borders of the county who knows anything about social work; other counties will never be willing to provide money for salaries to pay those who do. If the State wants its mothers' pension law to be properly administered, State aid must be provided in some form, a pooling of social resources so that the rich counties can help the poorer and more backward counties.

PRECEDENTS FOR STATE CONTROL.

There have been precedents in Illinois both for State administration and for State support. The long struggle for a free-school system (1818–1855) was won only by the creation of a State school fund. The rural counties in the southern part of the State claimed they were too poor to raise the necessary taxes for free schools, and the free-school law of 1855 was passed when provision was made for a State fund by which the resources of the wealthy northern counties were shared with the poorer counties of the south.

A precedent for State administration is to be found in the labor code. The compulsory-education law unfortunately has been left to the local authorities to enforce; but when the first child-labor law was passed in 1893, it was not left to 102 different counties to enforce indifferently if they pleased. Instead, a State department of factory inspection was created in order that the same standards of administration might be maintained throughout the State.

More recently the care of the insane has been transferred from the Illinois counties to the State. A shameful standard of provision for the insane was maintained in many of the counties of Illinois until in 1912 the State undertook to provide support and care for all persons legally committed for custodial care. A similar movement is under way for the better care of prisoners. The county jails of the United States have been a national scandal. In 1917 Illinois followed the lead of a few progressive States and passed a law for the establishment of a State farm for misdemeanants. This will ultimately mean that all the misdemeanants now supported in idleness by the separate counties in 102 miserable county jails will be transferred to the custody of the State and be cared for at State expense.

The presiding judge of the Chicago court in an address made before the National Conference of Charities and Correction in 1912, after a year's experience in Chicago with the first mothers' aid law, said: "All the evils found by experience to be inherent in any plan for public outdoor relief seemed to beset, at the beginning, the successful administration of the act." The evils that beset the administration of the law in Chicago at the beginning of its administration seem still to continue in most of the other counties of the State.

The heaviest responsibility for the maladministration of the law may be said to rest upon the county judges. They have it in their power to appoint efficient probation officers, and, without such appointments, good administration is impossible; they can also decide all general questions of policy—whether, for example, to use the money appropriated in small doles for many families or for constructive work in fewer families.

The responsibility of the judge is not always apparent; for the judge may seem intelligent and anxious to do his duty, and the responsibility may be shifted upon some one else. For example, a young woman who worked for some time in one of the counties where the pension work is very unsatisfactory has nothing but blame for the probation officer, who is a local politician totally unfit for his work, and nothing but praise for the judge who appointed him. That the judge who had misused his appointing power was really responsible for the maladministration of the law in his county was not apparent.

This criticism of the county judges brings us back once more to the fact that no social legislation which is left to the independent administration of 102 county officials can possibly be successful. That 102 different county judges should have the social intelligence needed for administering, on their sole responsibility, a new form of public outdoor relief is not to be expected. That 102 different county boards can be made socially intelligent enough to appropriate adequate salaries for an adequate number of probation officers and adequate sums for family pensions is also not to be expected. The only solution appears to lie in an amendment to the law providing for State assistance and State control. The probation service should probably be entirely supported by State funds and appointments to the service should be made by the State civil service commission.

A point of great importance that should be raised here is the relation between the juvenile courts and the mothers' pension administration. One reason for suggesting that a divorce between pension work and the juvenile courts may be necessary is that the Illinois Supreme Court [1] has held unconstitutional the section of the juvenile court law which provided for the appointment of probation officers on a merit basis. This decision, defending and upholding the independence of the courts, may stand in the way of any State administrative control of any branch of the court work.

The administration of the pension laws was in most States placed with the juvenile courts for two reasons:

(1) Mothers' pensions were suggested as a means of protecting children from institutional life. The advocates of mothers' pensions wished to have the public funds used to keep children at home with their own mothers instead of being used to subsidize children's insti-

---

[1] Witter v. Cook County, 256 Illinois Reports, 616.

tutions. On this point they were mistaken, since institutional subsidies have not decreased since the pension system began. But they may have been right in thinking that a juvenile-court judge, who, in Illinois, had the power to commit children to institutions, was the proper person to determine which were fit homes and who were fit mothers to be given pension grants.

(2) The profound distrust and dissatisfaction felt with the old outdoor-relief agencies formed another reason for placing the administration of the law with the juvenile court. The county outdoor-relief system appeared so hopeless that it seemed easier to abandon the problem in despair instead of attempting to solve it. But the outdoor-relief problems must sometime be dealt with. The aged and the sick, the deserted wife, and others temporarily destitute who are now left to the incompetent services of the local outdoor-relief authorities, are in need of the kind of competent and intelligent help that is now being given to the pensioners of the Cook County juvenile court under the aid-to-mothers law. Whether a new State-administered public assistance system should be created or whether, under an existing State department, some better form of State aid and State control can be devised, could be discussed satisfactorily only on the basis of a study of the administration of mothers' pension laws in those States in which the law provides for some form of State supervision. Such a discussion obviously leads beyond the scope of this report. It is only possible, as a result of this inquiry, to emphasize the need of State assistance in some form.

The importance of perfecting the mothers' pension law on the administrative side has been insisted on because, in the mothers' pension system, if properly organized and safeguarded, may lie the nucleus of a new form of State aid vastly superior to any form of public assistance which our American States have known, and capable of being very considerably extended. But the problem of a better administration is all important, since it would be obviously unwise to attempt to extend the scope of the law when not 1 of the 102 counties in the State has provided adequate funds for pensions or for the necessary investigations and supervision of mothers eligible under the present law.

Even in Cook County, which for so long has set an admirable standard both as to liberality of pensions and efficiency of administration, hundreds of eligible mothers in dire need of pensions have been thrown back during the past two years on the private societies and on the Cook County agent because the county board has refused to provide the large appropriations needed if all mothers who are eligible to become beneficiaries under the act were actually granted the pensions to which they are legally entitled. It is useless for the legislature solemnly to add alien women or small property owners or any other mothers to the legally eligible list when parsimonious county boards can render such changes ineffectual by refusing to provide the funds necessary for additional pensioners. Legislation increasing the number of beneficiaries must be accompanied by legislation guaranteeing a State subsidy or support from State funds to provide the new pensions, or the statute will remain, in its neglect of provisions for enforcement, an official mockery of the needs of the poor.

Further extensions of the pension law are likely to be asked in behalf of women whose husbands are temporarily incapacitated. For example, the family of the tubercular man who is not certified as permanently incapacitated must depend for help on the joint assistance of private charity and public outdoor relief. Unless a system of health insurance should in the near future make provision for sick benefits, mothers' pensions would seem to be as necessary here, while the man is slowly recovering his health, as in the case of families in which the chief wage earner is permanently incapacitated. Such extensions of the scope of the act, however, should not be made until adequate funds can be assured, and such extensions can not be safely made until an efficient system of administration, including intelligent investigations and supervision, can be devised. Neither of these conditions can be secured except on the basis of State control and State aid.

INDEX.

Administration of aid-to-mothers law. *See* Aid-to-mothers law, administration of.
Administration of funds-to-parents act. *See* Funds-to-parents act, administration of.
Agencies, relief. *See* Relief societies.
Aid-to-mothers department:
  administration of_____ 116–117
  data obtained from_____ 39, 81
  duties of_____ 72, 79
  duties of chief of_____ 23, 24, 27
Aid-to-mothers law (1913):
  administration of (Cook County) _____ 15–17, 19–124
    adequacy of pension grants _____ 48–71
    dismissed applicants _____ 72–81
    method of making pension grants _____ 19–26
    supervision of pensioned families _____ 27–47
  administration of (outside Cook County) _____ 16, 125–166
    by whom administered_____ 169
    extent of_____ 125, 126
    method of obtaining data concerning_____ 125–126
    variance in_____ 16, 125, 167
  amendment to (1915)—
    maximum pension granted under _____ 14, 48, 49
    provisions for eligibility under _____ 14
  amendment to (1917), provisions for eligibility under_____ 14
  amendment to (1919), provision for tax under_____ 114
  effect of—
    upon certain groups___ 95, 96, 116
    upon commitment of children to institutions_____ 116
    upon number of pensioned families _____ 119–120
  inadequacy of pension records required under_____ 165–166
  maximum pensions granted under_____ 13, 16, 48, 51
  need of amendment to, providing for State control____ 169, 170, 171
  number of pensioned families under (Cook County)___ 116
  opposition to (outside Cook County) _____ 127–132, 144, 146
  provisions of_____ 12, 13, 95
  relation to dependency and delinquency_____ 116–124
  restrictions of_____ 12, 13
  under rules of administration (Cook County)___ 15, 156
  violations of (outside Cook County) _____ 144–149, 152–155
Alien women, status of:
  under aid-to-mothers law (1913) _____ 12, 13, 14, 16, 17, 85, 95, 96, 106, 116, 123, 124
  under aid-to-mothers law (1915) __ 14, 15, 79, 83, 96, 116
  under Chicago court ruling____ 15, 16

Applications, pension. *See* Pension applications.
Associated Jewish Charities of Chicago. *See* Relief societies (private).
Budget:
  by whom prepared_____ 23, 48
  relation between family income and_____ 56–65
Case records:
  illustrating—
    budget estimates as a test of adequacy of relief (Cook County) _____ 57–63
    condition of families receiving occasional or no assistance (Cook County)_107–111
    inadequacy of pensions (outside Cook County)_ 163–164
    lack of supervision of pensioned families (outside Cook County)_____ 152–155
    method of adjusting pensions (Cook County)___ 45–46
    pensioning of ineligible families (outside Cook County) ____ 145–149, 156–157
    relation of withdrawal of pension to physical and moral deterioration (Cook County) _____ 103–105
    supervisory work (Cook County) _____ 27, 33–39
  school records entered on_____ 30
  See also Pensioned families.
Case-paper system, use of (Cook County)_____ 19
Citizens' committee:
  duties of _____ 11, 96
  organization of_____ 11
  revised method of payment advocated by_____ 26
Conference committee:
  personnel of _____ 23
  recommendations by _____ 23, 24, 48, 57, 58, 59, 60, 61, 62, 80
Counties granting pensions:
  average monthly grant per child and per family__ 159–160
  by specified number of families and period_____ 132–133
  location of_____ 132
  number of_____ 131
  varied expenditures in_____ 134
Counties in Illinois, number of_____ 125
Counties of given population, number spending specified amounts for pensions in 1915_____ 135
County agent (Cook County):
  duties of _____ 24, 30, 123
  investigation of cases by___ 23–24, 123
  power of, regarding source of pension _____ 123–124
  See also Outdoor relief, public.
County judge (outside Cook County):
  opposition of, to pension law___ 127–132, 144, 146

INDEX. 173

County judge (outside Cook County)—
Continued. Page.
  power of _____ 127, 169, 170
  responsibility of, for maladministration of the pension law _____ 168–169
County outdoor relief. See Outdoor relief, public.
County supervisor (outside Cook County):
  opposition of, to pension law ___ 127
  power of _____ 127

Delinquency:
  definition of _____ 7
  relation of aid-to-mothers law to _____ 116, 118, 119
Dependency:
  definition of _____ 7
  relation of aid-to-mothers law to _____ 116, 117, 118, 119
  relation of funds-to-parents act to _____ 10
Dependent children, maintenance of, in institutions _____ 115, 117
Dependent or neglected children, commitment of, under juvenile-court law (1899) _ 7–8
Deserted women, status of:
  outside Cook County _____ 144, 147
  under aid-to-mothers law (1913) _ 12, 13, 14, 73, 95, 106
  under aid-to-mothers law (1915) _ 14
  under Chicago court ruling _____ 15
  under funds-to-parents act _____ 11
Dietitian. See Field supervisor.
Divorced women, status of:
  outside Cook County _____ 144, 147
  under aid-to-mothers law (1913) _ 12, 13, 14, 73, 95, 106
Dower interest, effect of, upon eligibility for pension _____ 146

Eligibility for pensions, lack of verification of (outside Cook County) _____ 140–141
Employment of mother, gainful _____ 33, 35, 36, 38, 43, 46, 53, 54, 57, 59, 61, 62, 63, 102, 103, 104, 106, 108, 109, 110, 111
Expenditures for pensions (Cook County, 1911–1918) ___ 112–115
Expenditures for pensions (outside Cook County) _____ 134–135
  compared with Cook County ___ 134
  relation of population to _____ 134–135
  variance in _____ 134

Families:
  ineligibility of. See Pensioned families, ineligibility of; see also Pension applications, dismissal of.
  pensioned. See Pensioned families.
Fathers. See Pensioned families on roll in 1917.
Field supervisor, duties of _____ 23, 28, 48, 57
Funds-to-parents act (1911):
  administration of _____ 7, 10
  rules by Chicago court for aiding _____ 11
  amendments to. See Aid-to-mothers law (1913).
  enactment of _____ 7
  number of families pensioned under, by Chicago juvenile court _____ 16
  pensions granted under _____ 11, 12
  power of courts under _____ 10, 11, 12, 48
  provisions of _____ 10, 11
  purpose of _____ 7, 10

Funds-to-parents act (1911)—Con. Page.
  relation of juvenile court to passage of _____ 10
  text of _____ 10
Funds-to-parents department (Chicago juvenile court):
  duties of _____ 11
  personnel of _____ 11

Health conditions at time of granting pension _____ 93, 94, 106
Health conditions, effect of withdrawal of pension upon _ 103, 104
Homestead exemption, effect of, upon eligibility for pension ___ 146
Housing conditions at time of granting pension _____ 30–34, 93, 99
Housing conditions, effect of supervision upon _____ 30–34, 99

Illegitimacy, status of, under Chicago court ruling _____ 15, 77, 79, 80, 158
Illinois juvenile-court law (1899).
  See Juvenile-court law.
Incapacitation for work, permanent, interpretation of _____ 15, 158
Income compared with budget:
  deficit _____ 58, 59, 60, 62, 63, 64
  no surplus or deficit _____ 63, 64
  surplus _____ 57, 61, 64, 65, 66
Incomes, comparison between present and past _____ 66–68
Increase in pension. See Pension, change in amount of.
Industrial schools. See Training schools.
Ineligibility for pension. See Pension applications, dismissal of; see also Pension families, ineligibility of.
Institutional care for children:
  causes necessitating _____ 118, 119
  effect of aid-to-mothers law upon _____ 116, 118
  of families made ineligible by changes in the pension law _____ 97–100
Insurance money, expenditure of ___ 20–21
Investigations by the county agent_ 23–24
Investigations, preliminary:
  inadequacy of (outside Cook County) _____ 140–141, 143, 144
  length of time required for ____ 21–22
  method of procedure in _____ 19–23

Jewish Charities of Chicago, Associated. See Relief societies (private).
Jewish Home Finding Society. See Relief societies (private).
Judge, county. See County judge.
Juvenile court:
  administration of aid-to-mothers law by, reasons for ___ 169–170
  administration of the funds-to-parents act by _____ 7, 10, 11
  power vested in—
    under the aid-to-mothers law (1913) _____ 12, 25
    under the funds-to-parents act (1911) _____ 7, 10, 11, 12
    under the juvenile-court law (1899) _____ 7
  relation of, to passage of funds-to-parents act _____ 10
Juvenile court of Cook County:
  hearings in, with reference to granting pensions _____ 24–25
  maximum pension granted by _ 16
  method used by, in determining pension grants _____ 57–63

174 INDEX.

Juvenile court of Cook County—Con. Page.
 number of families pensioned by, under funds-to-parents law 16
 pension policy of, as compared with that of other counties 156–158
 provisions for eligibility under. 11–12, 15, 16
 rules of administration formulated by—
  under aid-to-mothers law (1913) 15
  under funds-to-parents act. 11, 12
Juvenile-court judge (outside Cook County). See County judge.
Juvenile-court law (1899):
 amendment to. See Funds-to-parents act.
 pensions granted institutions under 8
 power of courts under............... 7
Juvenile-court officer. See Probation officer.
Juvenile protective association, registration of unfit pension applicants by 121

Manual training school act. See Training school statutes.
Married women, status of:
 under aid - to - mothers act (1913) 12, 13
 under aid - to - mothers act (1915) 14
Maximum allowance. See specified acts — pensions granted by.
Medical supervision of pensioned families 29–30, 33–34, 35, 36, 37, 39
"Morally unfit," definition of ___ 15, 77–78
Mothers' pension fund. See Pension fund, mothers'.
Mothers' pension laws. See Funds-to-parents act; see also Aid - to - mothers act (1913).

Neglected child, definition of........ 7

Opposition to aid-to-mothers law (1913). See Aid-to-mothers law (1913), opposition to.
Outdoor relief, public:
 assistance given by............... 8, 30, 59, 97, 101, 107, 113, 115
 expenditures for specified period............... 115
 inefficiency of............... 170
 refusal of, to pensioned families 59, 71
 relation of county agent to..... 24, 97
See also County agent.

Pauper act, provisions of............ 19
Pensions:
 adequacy of (Cook County)..... 48–71
  budget estimates as a test of 56–65
 adequacy of (outside Cook County)............... 159–164
  source of data concerning...... 159
 amount of (Cook County)...... 48–56
  method of determining..... 48, 50
 amount of (outside Cook County)............... 159
 by whom granted (Cook County)............... 24
 by whom granted (outside Cook County)............... 127
 change in amount of (Cook County)............ 45–47, 56, 63
  increase, reasons for.... 45–46, 56
  reduction, reasons for.. 45–46, 63

Pensions—Continued. Page.
 comparison between allowances of, at earlier and later periods (Cook County).. 51
 comparison between amounts of, in and outside Cook County............... 161, 162
 differences between granting and appropriating authorities—
  evil effects of (Cook County)............... 170–171
  evil effects of (outside Cook County)......... 127, 162
 expenditures for (Cook County, 1911–1918)............ 112–115
 expenditures for (outside Cook County).......... 131, 134–135
 maximum number of families receiving (Cook County)_ 49, 50, 51, 52, 53
  See also under separate laws.
 methods of paying (Cook County)............... 25
 number of families receiving, by specified periods (outside Cook County).......... 131, 132
 number of families receiving specified amounts of, for specified periods (Cook County)............... 49–52
 procedure before granting (Cook County)............... 19–24
 recommendation for revised method of paying (Cook County)............... 26
 refusal of court to grant. See Pension applications, dismissal of.
 refusal of private agencies to grant (Cook County) ___ 99
 relation between income, budget, and (Cook County)..... 57–65
 supplementing of, by private agencies (Cook County).. 69–71
 tests of adequacy of (Cook County)............ 50, 56–69
 withdrawal of (Cook County) .. 13, 14
  interval between, and private relief (Cook County) 106
 moral effect of (Cook County)............... 104, 105
 physical effects of (Cook County)............... 103, 104
 reasons for (Cook County)_ 39–44, 68, 82, 95, 96, 106–111
Pension applications:
 dismissal of (Cook County)—
  marital status of women refused 72–73, 106
  number of families refused_ 72, 121, 142
  reasons for...... 72–81, 106, 113
 dismissal of (outside Cook County)—
  number of families refused_ 142
  reasons for............ 142–143
 relation between number of families refused and number receiving aid........ 142
Pension department. See Aid-to-mothers department.
Pension fund, mothers', provision for, under aid-to-mothers law:
 1913............... 13
  unconstitutionality of 112
 1919 (amendment) 114
Pension policies:
 determination of (outside Cook County)............ 127–130
 differences between Chicago and down-State courts concerning............... 156–158

INDEX.

Pension records: Page.
inadequacy of (outside Cook
County)_____ 166
inadequacy of, under pension
law_____ 165–166
Pensioned families:
case records of (Cook County)_ 27,
33–39, 45–46, 57–
63, 103–105, 107–111
case records of (outside Cook
County) _____ 145–149,
152–155, 156–157, 163–164
changes in amount of grant to.
See Pension, changes in
amount of.
housing conditions of (Cook
County)_____ 30–34, 93, 99
ineligible—
grants to (outside Cook
County)_____ 144–149
number having received
pensions of specified
amounts (Cook County)_ 87
number on roll for specified periods (Cook
County)_____ 96
provision for (Cook County) 97–100
ineligibility of (Cook County)—
through change in family
circumstances _____ 39–44,
47, 149, 153, 154, 163
through change in the law_ 12, 13,
14, 15, 16–17, 68, 82,
95, 96, 123, 124, 144
liability of relatives for support
of _____ 11,
13, 19–20, 140, 147–148
medical supervision of (Cook
County) _____ 29–30,
33–34, 35, 36, 37, 39
mothers of—
gainful employment of (Cook
County) _____ 33–36,
38, 46, 57, 61, 62, 63,
101, 102, 103, 104
gainful employment of (outside Cook County)_____ 148,
149, 157, 163–164
nature of assistance given, by
private societies (Cook
County)_____ 122
nature of supplementary relief
for (Cook County)_____ 70–71
number of—
effect of changes in aid-to-mothers law upon (Cook
County) _____ 116
receiving assistance prior
to court pension (Cook
County) _____ 119–122
receiving grants by specified periods (outside
Cook County)____ 131, 132, 133
receiving maximum pensions
(Cook County)___ 50–51, 52, 53
receiving no assistance prior
to court pension (Cook
County)_____ 120, 121
receiving specified amounts
at time pension was first
granted (Cook County)_ 52
receiving specified amounts
for specified periods (Cook
County)_____ 49–51
receiving specified amounts
(in and outside Cook
County)_____ 161, 162
receiving specified amounts
two or more years after
pension was first granted
(Cook County)_____ 52
number of probation officers caring for (Cook County)__ 29
number visited and how often
(Cook County)_____ 27, 28

Pensioned families—Continued. Page.
pensioning of children over 14
in (outside Cook County)
149, 153, 154, 156, 157
relation between income and
budget of (Cook County)_ 56
relation between monthly income and number of persons in (Cook County)__ 55–63
relation between pension and
number of children in
(Cook County) _____ 49,
50, 52, 53, 57–63
size of, by number of rooms occupied (Cook County)__ 31–32
supervision of (Cook County)__ 27–47
results of, as shown by case
records _____ 33–39
supervision of (outside Cook
County)_____ 137,
139, 149, 150, 151, 152, 153, 154
vacation provisions for (Cook
County)_____ 30, 34
wage earners in (outside Cook
County) _____ 153–154, 156, 157
Pensioned families on roll Aug. 1,
1913, to Mar. 1, 1915
(Cook County):
amount of father's insurance___ 92
interval between father's death
and application for pension _____ 93
Pensioned families on roll in 1917
(Cook County):
nationality of_____ 84, 85
number of_____ 83
number of (January)_____ 22, 82
period of residence at time of
application _____ 85
children, pensioned, number of_ 83
children, pensioned, number over
14 years_____ 84
fathers, age at time of death of_ 89
causes of death of_____ 88
incapacitated, ages_____ 87
incapacitated, number_____ 86
incapacitation of, causes__ 86
nationality _____ 85
occupations of, before death
or incapacity_____ 90
wages of, specified amounts
previously earned by___ 91, 92
mothers, marital state_____ 86
Pensioned families. See also Case
records.
Probation officer:
appointment of (Cook County)_ 138
appointment of (outside Cook
County)_____ 138
chief, duties of (Cook County)_ 16,
23, 24, 27
duties of (Cook County)_____ 11, 19,
25, 136, 137
duties of (outside Cook
County) _____ 136, 137
need of full-time, qualifying
(outside Cook County)__ 138,
139, 150, 151
number of, caring for same families two years or more
(Cook County)_____ 29
opposition of, to pension law
(outside Cook County)__ 128
types of persons acting as (outside Cook County)_ 136–139, 150
Property owner:
provision for pensioning_____ 146
status of—
outside Cook County_ 144–147, 164
under aid-to-mothers law
(1913)____ 12, 13, 123, 124, 146
under aid-to-mothers law
(1915)_____ 14
under Chicago court ruling _____ 12, 15

176　　　　　　　　　　INDEX.

Public outdoor relief. *See* Outdoor relief, public.
Reduction in pension. *See* Pension, change in amount of.
Relatives, liability of, for support_ 11, 13, 19–20, 140, 147–148
Relief, comparison between public and private____ 68–69, 100–105
Relief societies (private) :
　activities of_____ 9, 78, 100
　Associated Jewish Charities of Chicago—
　　Jewish Aid Society, activities of_____ 70, 123
　　Jewish Home Finding Society, activities of_____ 58, 70, 74, 97, 100
　　view of, as to supplementing pension aid_____ 69, 70
　churches _____ 70, 71, 106, 107
　St. Vincent de Paul, activities of _____ 71, 97
　supplementing of pensions by___ 69–71
　United Charities of Chicago—
　　activities of_____ 9, 71, 79, 97, 98, 100, 103, 104, 106
　　amount of relief compared with court grant_____ 68
　　families refused support by_____ 99, 105
　　view of, as to supplementing pension aid_____ 69, 70
Relief, supplementary, nature of, given pensioned families_ 70–71
Residence, required length of :
　under aid-to-mothers act (1913) _____ 12, 13, 85, 95
　under Chicago court ruling____ 16
　under funds-to-parents act_____ 11

St. Vincent de Paul. *See* Relief societies (private).
School records, entering of, on case records (Cook County) __　30
Social service registration bureau (Cook County), administration of _____　19
Societies, relief. *See* Relief societies.
State charities commission, cooperation of, in obtaining data (outside Cook County)_____ 125, 126, 128, 129–130, 159
Supervision of pensioned families :
　Cook County_____ 27–47
　outside Cook County_____ 137, 139, 149, 150, 151, 152, 153
Supervision, State, lack of_____ 125, 126, 155, 167, 170
　precedents for_____ 168–171

Tax provided by aid-to-mothers law (1913)_____　13
　failure to levy (outside Cook County) _____　127
　unconstitutionality of _____　112
Tax provided by amendment to law (1919)_____　114
Training-school statutes (1879, 1883), provisions of__ 8, 13, 117
Training schools, number receiving public grants _____　117

United Charities of Chicago. *See* Relief societies (private).
Unmarried mothers, status of, under Chicago court ruling_ 15, 77, 79

Withdrawal of pension. *See* Pension, withdrawal of.

O

U. S. DEPARTMENT OF LABOR
JAMES J. DAVIS, Secretary
CHILDREN'S BUREAU
GRACE ABBOTT, Chief

ADMINISTRATION OF MOTHERS' AID IN TEN LOCALITIES
WITH SPECIAL REFERENCE TO
HEALTH, HOUSING, EDUCATION, AND RECREATION

By

MARY F. BOGUE

Bureau Publication No. 184

UNITED STATES
GOVERNMENT PRINTING OFFICE
WASHINGTON
1928

CONTENTS

	Page
Letter of transmittal	VII
Purpose and method of the study	1
The laws and general administration in the localities studied	4
Scope and purpose of mothers' aid laws	4
Attitude toward mothers' aid	5
Investigation	6
Adequacy of grants	6
Qualifications and salaries of administrative staffs	9
General findings	11
Health	11
Physical health	11
Mental health	14
Housing	15
Education	16
Education and employment of the children	16
Educational activities for the mothers	22
Recreation	23
Budget allowance for recreation	23
Policies of agencies in regard to recreational activities	23
Some strong and weak points in the administration of mothers' aid	25
Mothers' allowances in Allegheny County, Pa.	29
Provisions of the law	29
State supervision	30
Administration of the law	31
Administrative agency	31
The staff	32
Appropriation and volume of work	32
Procedure in making allowances	33
Use of a standard budget	34
Supplementing of mothers' aid	40
Visiting	40
Health	40
Physical health	40
Mental health	46
Housing	47
Education	48
Cooperation with the schools and facilities for education	48
Schooling and work of children 14 and 15 years old	50
Educational activities for the mothers	52
Recreation	52
Mothers' allowances in Berks County, Pa.	53
Administration of the law	53
Administrative agency and staff	53
Appropriation and volume of work	53
Use of a standard budget	54
Supplementing of mothers' aid	55
Visiting	56
Health	56
Physical health	56
Mental health	60
Housing	60
Education	61
Cooperation with the schools and facilities for education	61
Schooling and work of children 14 and 15 years old	63
Educational activities for the mothers	64
Recreation	64

CONTENTS

	Page
Mothers' allowances in Cook County, Ill	67
Provisions of the law	67
Administration of the law	68
Administrative agency and staff	68
Appropriation and volume of work	69
Procedure in making allowances	70
Use of a standard budget	71
Supplementing of mothers' aid	74
Visiting	75
Health	75
Physical health	75
Mental health	81
Housing	82
Education	83
Cooperation with the schools and facilities for education	83
Schooling and work of children 14 and 15 years old	87
Educational activities for the mothers	89
Recreation	89
Mothers' allowances in Erie County, N. Y.	91
Provisions of the law	91
State supervision	92
Administration of the law	93
Administrative agency	93
The staff	93
Appropriation and volume of work	94
Procedure in making allowances	94
Use of a standard budget	94
Supplementing of mothers' aid	96
Visiting	96
Health	97
Physical health	97
Mental health	103
Housing	104
Education	105
Cooperation with the schools and facilities for education	105
Schooling and work of children 14 and 15 years old	107
Educational activities for the mothers	109
Recreation	109
Mothers' allowances in Hamilton County, Ohio	111
Provisions of the law	111
Administration of the law	112
Administrative agency and staff	112
Appropriation and volume of work	112
Procedure in making allowances	113
Use of a standard budget	113
Supplementing of mothers' aid	114
Visiting	115
Health	115
Physical health	115
Mental health	118
Housing	120
Education	121
Cooperation with the schools and facilities for education	121
Schooling and work of children 16 and 17 years old	124
Educational activities for the mothers	127
Recreation	127
Mothers' allowances in King County, Wash	129
Provisions of the law	129
Administration of the law	129
Administrative agency and staff	129
Appropriation and volume of work	130
Procedure in making allowances	130
Determination of allowances	131
Supplementing of mothers' aid	131
Visiting	132

CONTENTS

	Page
Mothers' allowances in King County, Wash.—Continued.	
Health	132
Physical health	132
Mental health	135
Housing	136
Education	137
Cooperation with the schools and facilities for education	137
Schooling and work of children 14 and 15 years old	138
Educational activities for the mothers	140
Recreation	140
Mothers' allowances in New Bedford, Mass	143
Provisions of the law	143
State supervision	144
Administration of the law	145
Administrative agency and staff	145
Appropriation and volume of work	145
Procedure in making allowances	146
Use of a standard budget	146
Visiting	147
Health	147
Physical health	147
Mental health	150
Housing	151
Education	151
Cooperation with the schools and facilities for education	151
Schooling and work of children 14 and 15 years old	152
Educational activities for the mothers	153
Recreation	153
Mothers' allowances in San Francisco, Calif	155
Provisions of the law	155
State supervision	155
Administration of the law	156
Administrative agencies	156
Staff of the widows' pension bureau	157
Amount of allowances and volume of work	157
Procedure in making allowances	158
Use of a standard budget	159
Supplementing of mothers' aid	160
Visiting	160
Health	161
Physical health	161
Mental health	165
Housing	166
Education	167
Cooperation with the schools and facilities for education	167
Schooling and work of children 14 and 15 years old and work of children over 16	168
Educational activities for the mothers	169
Recreation	169
Mothers' allowances in Wayne County, Mich	171
Provisions of the law	171
Administration of the law	171
Administrative agency and staff	171
Appropriation and volume of work	172
Procedure in making allowances	172
Use of a standard budget	173
Supplementing of mothers' aid	175
Visiting	175
Health	176
Physical health	176
Mental health	180
Housing	182
Education	183
Cooperation with the schools and facilities for education	183
Schooling and work of children 14 and 15 years old	184
Educational activities for the mothers	186
Recreation	188

CONTENTS

	Page
Mothers' allowances in Manitoba, Canada	189
Provisions of the law	189
Administration of the law	190
Administrative agency	190
The staff	190
The friendly visitors	190
The public-health nurses	192
Appropriation and volume of work	192
Procedure in making allowances	193
Use of a standard budget	193
Supplementing of mothers' aid	196
Visiting	196
Health	196
Physical health	196
Mental health	200
Housing	201
Education	202
Cooperation with the schools and facilities for education	202
Schooling and work of children 14 and 15 years old	203
Educational activities for the mothers	206
Recreation	206

LETTER OF TRANSMITTAL

UNITED STATES DEPARTMENT OF LABOR,
CHILDREN'S BUREAU,
Washington, May 29, 1928.

SIR: Transmitted herewith is a report on the administration in 10 localities of public aid to mothers in their own homes. The study was made by Miss Mary F. Bogue, State supervisor of the Mothers' Assistance Fund, Pennsylvania Department of Welfare, who has also written the report. Acknowledgment is made of the help received from officials in the localities studied, who not only cooperated at the time the information was being gathered but also read the sections of the report dealing with their own work.

Respectfully submitted.

GRACE ABBOTT, *Chief.*

Hon. JAMES J. DAVIS,
Secretary of Labor.

ADMINISTRATION OF MOTHERS' AID IN TEN LOCALITIES

PURPOSE AND METHOD OF THE STUDY

The study covered by this report was undertaken at the request of the committee on public aid to mothers with dependent children in their own homes, first called "mothers' pension committee," which was organized in 1921 at the request of public officials in the mothers' aid field, as a subcommittee of the family division of the National Conference of Social Work. At the conference of mothers' aid officials held in Washington, D. C., in May, 1923, the committee recommended that the United States Children's Bureau be requested to make further studies of standards relating to health, housing, and education, in the belief that such studies would encourage public agencies to evaluate their present policies more carefully and would lead to the definition of minimum standards of fundamental importance in child care.

During 1921–22 the committee made a study by questionnaire of the use among mothers' aid agencies of household budgets as the basis for determining the allowances, and a report was made at a meeting of mothers' aid officials in Providence, R. I., June 28, 1922, at the National Conference of Social Work.[1]

The extension of mothers' aid in the United States is indicated by the increase in the number of States that have enacted mothers' aid laws, in the funds appropriated, and in the number of children benefiting under them.[2]

Because of these facts and the request of the committee this study was undertaken to gather material bearing upon standards and policies of administration with particular reference to health, housing, education, and recreation. In each of the 10 localities included in the study a general schedule was filled out covering the policies and standards of the agencies on these four points. Case records selected by the agencies as representative of their practices in the four fields under consideration were given intensive study. Visits were made by the representative of the Children's Bureau with the family visitor or the agency executive to the homes of selected families in each locality. As the children 14 and 15 years old (16 and 17 in

---
[1] See Proceedings of Conference on Mothers' Pensions, held under the auspices of the mothers' pension committee, family division of the National Conference of Social Work, and the Children's Bureau, U. S. Department of Labor (U. S. Children's Bureau Publication No. 109, Washington, 1922).
[2] The U. S. Children's Bureau estimated in 1923 that about 130,000 children in the United States on a given date were recipients of aid. It was estimated in 1927 that at any given date in that year approximately 200,000 children were receiving public aid in their homes (Public Aid to Mothers with Dependent Children, p. 21, U. S. Children's Bureau Publication No. 162 (revised) Washington, 1928).

1

one locality) were those who in case of emergency in the home would be compelled to leave school to go to work, and the data in regard to those of this age who were eligible for employment certificates would indicate therefore the policy of the agency administering mothers' aid, a special study of the records was made on this point. Individual schedules were filled out for all children of these ages in families in which allowances had been granted. Such items were ascertained as grade and school in which each child was enrolled; basis on which schooling was continued; grade completed and age at leaving school; occupation, wages, and contribution to the family support if the child was working; and some data on physical and psychological examinations and the vocational and educational advice given.

It was desired to make this study as representative as possible in regard to geographical location, the unit covered, and the type of administrative agency. The following types of unit were studied:[3]

1. Six counties in which a large city was included: Cook County, Ill. (including Chicago); Wayne County, Mich. (including Detroit); Allegheny County, Pa. (including Pittsburgh); Erie County, N. Y. (including Buffalo); Hamilton County, Ohio (including Cincinnati); and King County, Wash. (including Seattle).

2. One county coterminous with a large city: San Francisco County, Calif.

3. One county including a small city: Berks County, Pa. (including Reading).

4. One city: New Bedford, Mass.

5. One Province of Canada: Manitoba, with especial reference to the city of Winnipeg.[4]

Four types of administrative agency were represented by the 10 localities, as follows:

1. Administration by an unpaid commission or board with a paid executive: Allegheny and Berks Counties, Pa.; Erie County, N. Y.; and Manitoba, Canada.

2. Administration by the paid board of public welfare (formerly called the overseers of the poor) under the immediate direction of a paid executive secretary: New Bedford, Mass.

3. Administration by the juvenile court with or without advisory committees: Cook County, Ill.; Wayne County, Mich.; Hamilton County, Ohio; and King County, Wash.

4. Administration by a bureau directly responsible to the finance committee of the county board of supervisors: San Francisco, Calif.

---

[3] In the 42 States and the District of Columbia providing in 1927 for the granting of mothers' allowances the local administrative agencies were as follows: A court having juvenile jurisdiction, 19 States; county officials granting poor relief, 13 States; county or city boards having other functions, 5 States and the District of Columbia; special county board, 3 States; local school board, 1 State; in 1 State administration is solely in the hands of a State agency.

[4] This Canadian locality was selected for study rather than the one small State in the United States that has a similar method of administering mothers' allowances (Delaware) because in addition to illustrating the method of administration in general, Canada's administration of mothers' aid holds much of interest to our own country.

As it was necessary in such a study to become somewhat familiar with the community resources in the four fields covered by the study, about one-third of the time was spent in conferences with the social agencies that in one way or another touched the mothers' aid agencies.

The investigation for the study was made within the period October 15, 1923, to April 15, 1924.

(For convenience the name of the chief city in the counties containing a large city, rather than the name of the county, is used in some instances in the pages following.)

THE LAWS AND GENERAL ADMINISTRATION IN THE LOCALITIES STUDIED

SCOPE AND PURPOSE OF MOTHERS' AID LAWS

The experiment of granting public aid to children in their own homes under a State law, which may be said to date from 1911, has met with prompt legislative approval.[1] Its administration has not kept pace with legislation, but this is due largely to the fact that public interest in many States diminished when the law had been passed and appropriations were inadequate in all except a few States. It may be said that the principle of home care for dependent children is generally accepted in this country, even though the need has not yet been met fully. The fundamental principles that must be observed if such laws are to be effective child-welfare measures are in general the following:

1. Application broad enough to permit aid whenever by such aid a suitable home may be maintained.
2. Age limitation to conform to education and child-labor laws.
3. Determination of the amount of aid by the need of each individual family, with due regard to other available resources.
4. Inquiry in each case to determine the home conditions and the assistance needed for the proper care of the children.
5. Continued oversight in order to protect the welfare of the children and to adjust the aid to meet changing conditions.
6. Safeguards to protect the public treasury against fraudulent or unwarranted claims and against burdens that should be borne by other communities or by individuals legally responsible and able to furnish support.
7. Administration by the public agency best fitted to carry out the provisions of the law as a constructive child-welfare measure.
8. Appropriation adequate to carry out the purpose of the law, with respect both to funds required for aid and to expenses of administration.

---

[1] As early as 1906 the juvenile courts of some counties of California granted aid to children in their own homes, and in 1911 the State began to reimburse counties for such aid given to half orphans. An Oklahoma law of 1908 provided for "school scholarships" to be paid by counties upon recommendation of the school authorities to children whose widowed mothers needed their earnings. A Michigan law of 1911 also authorized payment from school funds to enable children of indigent parents to attend school. The first definite legal provision of aid to mothers of dependent children was passed by the Missouri Legislature in 1911, applying only to Jackson County (in which Kansas City is located) and later in the same year extended to the city of St. Louis. The first state-wide mothers' aid law was enacted in Illinois in 1911.

9. Some form of general oversight by the State combined with educational activities to develop high standards in the work of the local administrative agencies.

The earlier laws generally limited the aid to children of widows, but the trend of legislation has been toward widening the application of the law, either permitting aid to be granted to any mother with dependent children or defining the circumstances, so as to include those in which the father is dead, deserting, divorced, physically or mentally incapacitated, or imprisoned, with necessary restrictions pertaining to cases of desertion and divorce. A few States give aid to relatives or guardians having custody of dependent children.[2]

The eligibility requirements as to citizenship and residence vary considerably in the different States, as do also those in regard to the ownership of property. The conditions determining the granting of aid refer mainly to economic need and the mother's ability to give proper care to the children. The most important consideration in regard to the age to which a child may be granted aid is that it shall be in conformity with compulsory school attendance and child-labor laws.

ATTITUDE TOWARD MOTHERS' AID

Among all the agencies the point of view was taken that mothers' aid is given in the interest of future citizenship and that it is much more than a relief measure in that the test of its worth and efficacy is not wholly and primarily the alleviation of material distress but also the well-being of the children under supervision, as expressed in terms of adequate mother care, health, both physical and mental, school progress, and preparation for effective manhood and womanhood. The agencies, the public, and the beneficiaries recognized that by the passage of these laws the State acknowledged the inviolability of the relation of mother and child, its own stake in the preservation of the home, and the unique social value of the service rendered by mothers in maintaining their homes when fathers " drop out."

To this interpretation of the mothers' aid laws was doubtless due in large measure the attitude of the mothers receiving assistance. It was the testimony of the workers in the field and of the executives that the aid did not tend to develop a spirit of dependency but on the contrary developed self-confidence, initiative, and generally a desire for economic independence at as early a date as possible. This is illustrated by the following letter written by a mother in Chicago, who with a crippled 17-year-old daughter was offering to assume the full financial responsibility for the family of four, including one girl in high school:

CHICAGO, ILL.

Judge ———,
 Juvenile Court, Chicago, Ill.

YOUR HONOR: I am writing to inform you that we will not need the pension I am receiving any more. The pension certainly helped me to clothe the

---

[2] In 1927 only 5 States limited the grant to children of widows, although the 42 States then granting aid included widows directly or by implication; and 8 States and the District of Columbia gave aid to any mother with dependent children. A few States and the District of Columbia gave aid to relatives or guardians.

children and give them a fairly good education. Helen has a very nice position now and is getting along very well. Ruth will perhaps be able to do something this summer, which will help a great deal. Frank will soon be able to do something during the school vacation.

Judge ———, I want to thank you for what you have given me in the past years, and also Mrs. ——— [the probation officer]. I was always glad to see her coming, and the children surely loved her. She did so much for them, and I can never thank her enough.

Thanking you again, I am,
Yours truly, ———————.

Since the mothers' value as caretakers of their children is the corner stone of mothers' aid this principle gives to the relation established between them and the State a professional status that they are quick to apply and that enhances their sense of personal worth.

INVESTIGATION

In every agency a social-history sheet or blank was filled out, which called for and gave reasonably full social data. Facts regarding residence, property, the father's death, commitment, or divorce were always verified; generally, but not always, dates of children's birth, of marriage, and of citizenship (not all the laws required citizenship) were verified. It sometimes seemed that the emphasis upon technicalities of the law obscured the need of social investigation. The standards of the social investigations varied among the agencies. Usually not much was learned about the father unless he had been abusive. The interviews with the relatives were apt to be perfunctory and to relate solely to their financial ability to assist the family; they did not open the door to future cooperation. More complete investigations of the background, so far as the records showed it, including such facts as the circumstances surrounding the childhood, youth, and married lives of the parents, their standards of living, ambitions for themselves and their children, and qualities of character and temperament would have been valuable.

The social-service exchange was generally consulted as a preliminary step, and the social agencies which had known the families were communicated with where the best standards of work prevailed. This was followed by visits to school-teachers, the family physician, the minister, one or more references, and at least one relative and often two. The summaries which the workers in Pittsburgh sent to the State office included a statement covering the problems the investigation brought to light and a tentative plan for meeting them.

It was unfortunate that in a number of communities the stenographic facilities were so meager that the dictation had to be reduced to a minimum, and the case workers often had to give time to typing their own records.

ADEQUACY OF GRANTS

The ability of an agency to provide adequate aid for the majority of the families under its care was influenced by the amount of the maximum grant provided by the law as well as by the adequacy of the appropriations. The laws of Massachusetts and Manitoba did not specify the maximum amount of aid that could be given. The New York law required that the maximum grant should not exceed the cost of institutional care. In each of the seven remaining localities studied the State had defined the maximum grant.

In Pennsylvania the maximum allowed was $20 for the first child and $10 for each additional child in the family; this was inadequate for between one-third and one-fourth of the families assisted. When supplementary aid could not be secured the mothers in families so affected were compelled to spend too much of their time and strength in contributing to the income (sometimes to the hurt of the children), or the families were falling below the minimum standard of living necessary for health and efficiency.

The Washington law provided a maximum of $15 for the first child and $5 for each additional child. This assistance was often meager and even pitifully insufficient for the maintenance of a standard of family life that would allow the mother a reasonable minimum of time and strength to devote to the care of her children. To meet the economic need some mothers worked all day away from home; sometimes adolescent boys and girls were placed in private homes where they went to school and worked for their board and lodging; and two families were living at a home for destitute mothers and their children, where the children were cared for while the mothers worked because they could not maintain a home on the grant from the court and such wages as they could make and at the same time care for their young children.

The California law allowed $10 a month per child from the State, the county at its own option to supplement this by a sum up to $10. At the time of the study San Francisco County was supplementing by the sum of $7.50 per child (though for some cases no supplement was given, the State only being drawn upon).

The laws of Illinois, Ohio, and Michigan made the most adequate provision of the localities studied in which a maximum was specified. Illinois made a higher provision for counties having more than 300,000 inhabitants than for less populous counties, granting $25 a month for the first child and $15 for each additional child in the family. Ohio provided $35 for the first child and $10 for each additional child in the family. Michigan provided $43.33 a month for the first child and $8.67 for each additional child in the family.

The average monthly grant per family [3] in each of the 10 localities studied was reported to be as follows:

Pittsburgh (Allegheny County, Pa.)	$39.10
Berks County, Pa	39.50
Chicago (Cook County, Ill.)	50.31
Buffalo (Erie County, N. Y.)	51.81
Cincinnati (Hamilton County, Ohio)	30.71
Seattle (King County, Wash.)	20.00
New Bedford, Mass	[4] 43.00
San Francisco, Calif	37.41
Detroit (Wayne County, Mich.)	42.45
Manitoba, Canada	57.40

In connection with the foregoing figures consideration should be given not only to the grants allowed by law but also to the average number of children per family, which varied from 2.7 in Cincinnati to 3.9 in New Bedford. The grants were affected also by the amounts contributed to the family income by the members who worked.

---
[3] As reported for some month in 1924 in Allegheny, Berks, Cook, and Hamilton Counties; for some month in 1923 in Erie, Wayne, and San Francisco Counties and in Manitoba; and for 1922 in New Bedford. For King County the year was not specified.
[4] Plus fuel, shoes, and medical attendance.

In all except 1 of the 10 localities the needs of the family were established on the basis of a budget,[5] and an effort was made to provide within the limitations of the law an allowance that together with other resources of the family would cover their needs. Because of insufficiency of appropriations or limitations set by law many of the agencies found it necessary to seek for families under their supervision some supplementary aid from other public agencies (such as outdoor relief) or from private social agencies.

The following table shows for seven localities the amount of aid contributed by public and private relief agencies, the number of families receiving allowances and on the waiting list, and the number given aid:

Supplementary aid contributed by public and private relief agencies for families receiving allowances, number of families receiving allowances, and number given aid; seven localities

Locality	Agencies giving aid		Families receiving allowances			Families on waiting list		
	Public	Private	Total on given date	Aided in year	Amount [1]	Total	Aided	Amount [1]
Pittsburgh (Allegheny County, Pa.)	1	4	477	36	[2] $6,300.53	425	156	[2] $37,427.10
Chicago (Cook County, Ill.)	1	3	1,207	186	[3] 14,850.63	([4])	350	[3] 48,375.94
Buffalo (Erie County, N. Y.)	2	1	354	6	934.18			
Cincinnati (Hamilton County, Ohio)		3	470	([5])	[6] 17,791.40	500	([5])	([5])
Seattle (King County, Wash.)	1	5	453	44	([5])			
San Francisco, Calif.		3	481	([5])	[7] 3,600.00			
Detroit (Wayne County, Mich.)	2		999	166	([5])			

[1] Figures for calendar year 1923 or a fiscal year ending within that year except as otherwise specified.
[2] Figures for contribution of 1 private agency were for a period of 14 months.
[3] Figures for 2 private agencies; the third gave aid but no figures were reported.
[4] From 500 to 600 families were on the waiting list, and some of these received aid from a public agency.
[5] Figures incomplete or not reported.
[6] Figures for 1922; 1 agency gave medical service also. Although the figures for 1923 were not available it was reported that 1 of the private agencies that in 1922 gave $6,000 was giving material relief only and to only 6 families.
[7] Estimated.

In two localities no supplementary aid was reported. In Berks County, Pa., the families needing such aid were cared for through private benevolences and various other resources, and in New Bedford the only aid in addition to allowances was the occasional furnishing of milk for delicate children—generally by private relief agencies. In Manitoba any needed aid was obtained through the efforts of the " friendly visitors " and ladies' auxiliary assisting the mothers' allowances commission.

[5] The budgets used were based upon the following: Pittsburgh and Chicago—the standard budget issued by the Chicago Council of Social Agencies in 1920; Berks County, Pa.— the Chicago standard budget and also that issued by the New York Nutrition Council in 1922; Manitoba—the Chicago standard budget and also a budget prepared by the public welfare commission's dietitian; San Francisco—for food, the budget prepared by Professor Jaffa, of the University of California, and for other items, figures furnished through the State department of finance; Buffalo—a budget compiled by the Westchester County (N. Y.) Department of Child Welfare; Cincinnati—a budget based on a schedule prepared by a local social agency; New Bedford—a budget based on several standard budgets and also budgets in use in certain localities; Detroit—a budget prepared by the Visiting Housekeeper Association. In Seattle the judge of the juvenile court determined the amount of the allowance for each applicant, and no budget was used.

LAWS AND GENERAL ADMINISTRATION 9

QUALIFICATIONS AND SALARIES OF ADMINISTRATIVE STAFFS

The standards of the 10 agencies in regard to training and experience of the field staffs varied greatly. The educational background of the workers was generally good. Among them were 2 physicians, 3 graduate nurses, and 22 college or university graduates, also a number of workers who—though not graduates—had had some college training. Three had been well educated in Europe. Previous training in social case work was reported for 32 of the 73 staff members (excluding the clerical force). The number of persons on the staff varied from 1 to 24. The visitors took their work very seriously and gave themselves to it with enthusiasm and devotion.

The organization of the administrative agencies and the volume of work reported at given periods are shown in the following tabulation:

Organization of the administrative agency and the volume of work, 10 localities

Locality	Administrative agency	Executive officer	Field workers	Clerical force	Families receiving allowances
Pittsburgh (Allegheny County, Pa.).	Board of trustees	Executive secretary	10	3	477
Berks County, Pa	do	do	1	1	87
Chicago (Cook County, Ill.)	Mothers' pension division, juvenile court.	Head, mothers' pension division.	24	1	1,207
Buffalo (Erie County, N. Y.)	County board of child welfare.	Executive secretary	6	3	354
Cincinnati (Hamilton County, Ohio).	Department of mothers' pensions and neglected children, juvenile court.	Supervisor	² 2	(³)	470
Seattle (King County, Wash.).	Mothers' pension department, juvenile court.	Commissioner	3	1	453
New Bedford, Mass	Board of public welfare	Executive secretary [6]	1	(⁵)	96
San Francisco, Calif	Widows' pension bureau	Director [6]	⁴ 3	1	473
Detroit (Wayne County, Mich.).	Mothers' pension department, juvenile court.	Chief probation officer for women and girls.[7]	10	2	999
Manitoba, Canada	Mothers' allowance commission.	Executive secretary	3	(⁵)	611

[1] Devoted part time to field work.
[2] Designated probation officers.
[3] Probation officer giving part time to mothers' aid work.
[4] Assistance in field work was given by certain other public officers or by specified private relief agencies.
[5] None reported.
[6] Giving only part time.
  Also referee of the juvenile court.
[8] Including a supervisor. The department had also the services of an interpreter and a psychiatric social worker (part time) and of a volunteer worker.

Even with the various additional services there were only 4 of the 10 localities in which the visitors were not overburdened with an excessive volume of work. This point should be taken into consideration in the later discussions of the extent and quality of the supervision given to the families. Adequate supervision of the physical and mental health, education, and recreation of each member of a family requires much more time than can be given by a visitor supervising the large number of families that were assigned to each field worker in many of these localities.

Apparently the staffs as organized consisted generally of the one executive officer and the field workers. In the three localities having 10 or more visitors, supervisors would have been desirable to aid in directing the case work and training inexperienced and untrained workers, but none were employed, nor were the more expert visitors so used. Hence the quality of work performed within a single agency varied, and the agencies were dependent upon outside sources for filling their ranks, if they required trained staffs. As there were few or no positions of intermediate rank there was a lack of incentive to qualify for higher grades of work within the respective agencies. From the point of view of efficiency, quality of case work, training, and staff morale the question might be raised as to the possibility and advisability in the large cities of effecting an organization similar to that commonly existing in charity-organization societies; that is, with a superintendent in charge of each district, with district visitors (case workers) in the field, with workers in training also, and, if possible, students in training, provision being made for close supervision by the director or an assistant director. Under such a method of organization salary advances would be made not solely on the basis of length of service but on that of quality of service as well, and workers could not assume responsibilities for which they were not qualified. There would also be the attraction of greater executive responsibility for qualified workers. The wisdom of making salary advances contingent upon the workers' enrollment in specialized short courses in schools of social work and their attendance at State and national conferences, and of conducting staff meetings in such a way as to render them of educational value if regular class instruction is not given should be considered.

The salaries of directors or executive secretaries of mothers' aid agencies were approximately $2,500 in five communities; in one agency the director received $2,700; in three the salary was less than $2,500. The salaries of the field workers varied from $1,200 to $1,800. The majority were in the neighborhood of $1,500.

GENERAL FINDINGS

HEALTH

PHYSICAL HEALTH

Physical examinations.

Five of the 10 agencies studied required that the children in each family applying for an allowance be given a physical examination before the grant would be made. All except one of the five required that the mother be examined also. The examinations in these five localities were generally made by public agencies or officers or by private individuals, as follows:

Berks County, Pa_____ Family physician.
Chicago (Cook County, Ill.)_____ Juvenile-court physician.
Erie County, N. Y.:
    Buffalo_____ City clinics.
    Rural districts_____ County health officer.
New Bedford, Mass_____ City physician.
Cincinnati (Hamilton County, Ohio). Cincinnati General Hospital.[1]

One agency (Detroit) required that examinations preliminary to grants be made only of the children of preschool age whose families lived in Detroit, and of mothers who gave evidence of need or who were known to have been exposed to tuberculosis; but it required that the visitors consult the reports of the school physical examinations for those children who were attending school in the city of Detroit. Therefore it may be assumed that practically all the children in this locality also received a preliminary examination. In one locality (San Francisco) in which no preliminary examination was required the investigator on the agency's staff was a physician; and although no medical-report blank was filled out, this physician, on the occasion of her first visit to the family, recorded the height and weight of the children and made note of obvious defects. In the remaining three localities (Pittsburgh, Seattle, and Winnipeg) there was no formal requirement that an examination precede the granting of the allowance. This does not mean, however, that the physical condition of the children under supervision of the agencies in these localities received no attention; for at least the school children in these cities who were members of mothers' aid families had such medical attention as the public schools gave to all their pupils, and the mothers' aid workers put forth special efforts in behalf of any child having obvious or extreme physical handicaps. In Pittsburgh three hospital clinics had offered to make examinations of mothers' aid children under 12 years of age in the city, and at the time of the study about two-fifths had been examined.

---
[1] The examinations made here were of the children only.

Periodic physical examination after the granting of the allowances was not the rule in the localities studied. Erie County, N. Y. (Buffalo) was the only locality in which yearly physical examinations for all mothers and children in families receiving allowances were required by the administrative agency. In Chicago no examination was made after the allowances had been granted unless the physical condition of the children or of the mother made such examination clearly necessary; but here the agency had the advantage of the Elizabeth McCormick Memorial Fund's thorough supervision of groups of children. This organization weighed and measured about a third of the children in families in Chicago receiving allowances and enrolled part of these in nutrition classes. In the remaining eight localities the only members of mothers' aid families for whom the workers tried to make arrangements for physical examinations after the granting of the allowances were those in obvious need of medical attention. Of course children in school had the benefit of such periodic medical inspection or examination as the respective school systems afforded, and the yearly physical examinations of school children would have included each year a number of the boys and girls in the mothers' aid families.

Often the health resources of the child-health centers could have been used to better advantage. Such centers were accessible in all the more populous communities, and they generally were recommended to mothers of children under 6 years of age; but it would seem desirable that the agencies stimulate regular attendance at such centers and that they make sure that the instructions received there are carried out by the mothers. Only one agency (in Buffalo) had arranged to receive from the child-health centers reports concerning the attendance of mothers receiving allowances. A more systematic consultation of school medical reports might well be made also, following the example of workers in Detroit and Pittsburgh. Although reports of school medical inspections may offer only a rough index of the children's health they at least would have been helpful in the absence of better information. A number of agencies were planning to consult these reports in the future.

Follow-up of special problems.

The facilities for care of tuberculosis cases or suspects, venereal-disease cases, orthopedic and cardiac cases, and ear, eye, nose, and throat affections, and the work done by the schools and by local clinics and health centers in the several localities are mentioned briefly in the sections of this report dealing with the respective localities, whether or not any members of mothers' aid families were known to be having care through these facilities at the time of the study. All the agencies (with possibly two exceptions) were careful in their attention to the correction of physical defects, and it was the intention of all of them that no mother nor child should go without necessary medical care for lack of knowledge as to the medical resources available. The discrepancy between the desire of all the agencies to have proper attention given and the actual practice of some of them was due largely to the excessive case load carried by many workers, which made intensive and protracted supervision of health cases extremely difficult. Careful follow-up work was done to see that defects were corrected, and the mothers were urged to have themselves and their children put in good physical condition. Sometimes withdrawal of the grant was threatened, but generally explanation of the advantages that would accrue from the suggested correction was enough to obtain the mother's consent for it.

Some agencies were careful to see that every mother and child who had been exposed to tuberculosis should be examined and that incipient tuberculosis cases should be under regular supervision of tuberculosis clinics. The orthopedic work with children was taken care of excellently in practically every locality, and there was much fine individualizing of the needs of crippled children. In general where there was an acute health situation it was well handled; but where the defect or disease was chronic and required protracted medical treatment it sometimes happened that no reports were recorded over long periods of time. This would seem to indicate that the workers had forgotten to keep in touch with the medical agency and the patient concerned or failed to make entries in the record.

The agencies in all the communities except Seattle, San Francisco, and Winnipeg make provisions either for routine physical examinations or for the consultation of the school medical inspection reports which uncovered conditions of malnutrition and anemia and possibilities of tuberculosis among mothers and children under their supervision. Some facilities for the supervision of undernourished children were available in most of the cities, but such resources were not universally used by the mothers' aid workers. In Chicago, in addition to taking advantage of the opportunities offered through the Elizabeth McCormick Memorial Fund, the juvenile court enrolled a few children from mothers' aid families in nutrition classes conducted by the municipal tuberculosis clinics and various hospitals. In Buffalo a domestic educator on the staff of the county board of child welfare conducted three nutrition clinics in parts of the city previously without any and had nutritional supervision of individual families. The schools in most of the cities in the localities studied had nutrition classes. Perhaps the mothers' aid workers should follow up underweight children more closely and make sure of their placement in nutrition classes at school or elsewhere. So far as the records showed, the treatment on the part of the agencies generally consisted of extra diet and some personal instruction of the mother and child by the physician or the social worker. But it would have been well if the record had stated whether the child who was diagnosed as undernourished by the physician giving the routine examination had already been so diagnosed by the school medical inspector and placed in a nutrition class by the teacher or the nurse. Some workers assumed that as the schools placed underweight children in nutrition classes no follow-up by the agency was necessary, but it is hardly safe not to make sure by actual checking that the need is being met. The records were often lacking in a conclusion to the diagnosis of malnutrition or underweight, so that it was not clear when the child was brought up to weight.

MENTAL HEALTH

There has been a marked growth of appreciation of the value and need of providing accurate diagnosis and special training for retarded and mentally defective children. At the time of the study the importance of such care had not been fully realized by many mothers aid workers. Possibly the agencies assumed that seriously retarded and mentally defective children would be given psychological tests in the schools and that recommendations would be made for their care. Yet at the time of the study several agencies knew of children in mothers' aid families who were considered mentally defective but had not had tests. In a few of the records studied there were reports of retardation and failure of promotion growing steadily worse over a period of years, to which little attention had been paid until they were complicated by delinquency so that court action was required. A poor school report, retardation, or failure of promotion may be preceded, accompanied, or followed by so many serious factors other than mental subnormality that they are to be construed as symptomatic in the absence of other well-established causes, such as ill health. They should be counted serious enough to warrant careful follow-up by the agency, including a psychological examination, a personality study, and an attempt to remedy environmental causes. Buffalo was the only locality studied in which mental examinations were obtained as a matter of routine for children whose fathers were insane or in whose families there was a recent history of mental defect or disease. However, all the agencies obtained medical attention for obvious cases of mental disease. The records studied showed many examples of excellent work done for and with psychopathic or emotionally unstable mothers and a few instances of similar work for children.

The agency in Detroit had the part-time service of a psychiatric case worker under the immediate direction of the psychologist attached to the court, to whom were brought for examination psychopathic or emotionally unstable children and mothers. Such families, if requiring particularly careful supervision, were turned over to the psychiatric worker, who was given great latitude in the plans she made on their behalf and who accomplished remarkable reorientations in their mental attitudes. In the matter of behavior problems of children the most skillful workers made excellent use of the psychiatric clinics in the attempt to discover the underlying causes of the child's abnormal behavior and so to set about intelligently remedying the conditions that accounted for them.

It seems especially desirable that all mothers' aid workers should be acquainted (many are already acquainted) with the relations which often exist between conditions in the home causing mental conflict in children (and adults as well) and the conduct patterns through which the conflict expresses itself. Then they could help to prevent harsh judgments, undue punishments, and unwise recourse to the courts by scientific analysis of the facts and modification of the children's environment so as to bring about harmony in their emotional lives, and hence conduct that conforms to the social sanctions.

HOUSING

All the agencies gave serious consideration to the housing of mothers' aid families with respect to the desirability of the neighborhood, the sanitary condition of the houses, and the availability of as much room space, yard or garden space, and open air and sunshine as local conditions permitted. Good houses or good flats were not everywhere to be had at reasonable rentals. Except in one large city, where housing conditions left much to be desired, the families were for the most part in decent, sanitary dwellings or flats in respectable neighborhoods; many were in comfortable one-family houses, and a considerable number had flower gardens. If families were found living in too congested quarters, under insanitary conditions, or in neighborhoods whose morality was questionable, the courts required them—or the agencies persuaded them—to move to better locations. Two localities had housing conditions that permitted the agencies to take into consideration the accessibility to playgrounds and other recreation facilities for mothers' aid families; and in another locality this was done " when possible "; but in two others it was stated that giving as much attention to play space and accessibility of playgrounds as would have been desirable was out of the question. In most of the localities the agencies apparently had to devote most of their efforts to approximating such standards of sanitation, room space, and environment as they wished they could enforce.

A point was made of having enough rooms so that adolescent boys and girls should have separate bedrooms, even if this required that the living room be used for sleeping purposes. Usually the furnishings were sufficient for decency and often for comfort. Many families had plants blooming in the house.

The fact that a large number of families were living in houses which they owned or were paying for when the father died helped to maintain their original social status and the security and self-respect that come from long-continued residence in one home and neighborhood; it helped also to carry over into the new life memories of the father and to preserve the continuity of the family spirit. The policies in regard to home ownership and other assets were for the most part very liberal.[2] The two extremes observed were in Detroit and in New Bedford. In the former an allowance might be granted to a mother having as much as $3,500 equity in a home. In the latter an allowance could not be granted to a mother who had more than $500 equity in a home. The amount of equity in real property or of value of real property owned, the amount of savings or other assets allowed, and the percentage of mothers' aid families

---

[2] Restrictions in regard to home ownership had been incorporated in the law governing only one of the localities studied (Chicago). One locality (San Francisco) was governed by a ruling made by the State department of finance, one (New Bedford) by a ruling of the State department of public welfare, and two others (Allegheny and Berks Counties, Pa.) by a ruling made by the State supervisor of the mothers' assistance fund. In Manitoba the provincial commission, which was also the administrative agency, had established the restriction. The local administrative agency formulated the rulings or established the policy in the remaining four localities studied (Buffalo, Cincinnati, Seattle, and Detroit).

owning their own homes or having an equity in them in the 10 localities studied are shown in the following table:

Amount of equity in real property or value of real property owned, amount of savings or other assets allowed, and percentage of mothers' aid families owning their own homes or having an equity in them; 10 localities

Locality	Equity or real property allowed	Savings or other assets allowed	Percentage of families owning homes or having an equity in them
Pittsburgh (Allegheny County, Pa)	$1,500	$400	8
Berks County, Pa	1,500	400	37
Chicago (Cook County, Ill.)	1,000	None.	(¹)
Buffalo (Erie County, N. Y.)	2,500	300	18
Cincinnati (Hamilton County, Ohio)	3,500	200	14
Seattle (King County, Wash.)	3,000	300	49
New Bedford, Mass	² 500	³ 200	3
Detroit (Wayne County, Mich.)	3,500	500	43
San Francisco, Calif	2,500	⁴ 500	28
Winnipeg (Manitoba, Canada)	2,000	(⁵)	(⁵)

[1] Not reported. Since the Illinois law had been amended in 1921 to allow the equity of $1,000, the number of new families with equity in the home that had been granted allowances was negligible.
[2] In house the assessed value of which is not more than $2,500.
[3] But not more than $500 total equity plus other assets.
[4] If there was no real property the other assets might total $1,000.
[5] Not reported.

EDUCATION

EDUCATION AND EMPLOYMENT OF THE CHILDREN

Contacts with the schools.

Seven of the agencies had developed systems for obtaining school reports at regular intervals. These were made by the schools on blanks furnished by the agencies covering attendance, grade, scholarship, and conduct; spaces were left also for remarks in regard to health, punctuality, neatness, and any other items. The blank used in Buffalo, which was especially good, requested information on the child's aptitudes, habits, and personality also. Such reports were received at least twice a year in Pittsburgh, in Berks County, Pa., and in Detroit; and yearly or twice a year in Seattle. In Chicago, Buffalo, and Winnipeg they were received quarterly (sometimes every two months in Chicago). In Cincinnati a semiannual report was made to the Cincinnati Associated Charities in accordance with a juvenile-court requirement, and the mothers' aid workers were expected to examine these reports. No report was required in San Francisco nor in New Bedford.[3] In every locality studied it was stated that the mothers' aid workers maintained more or less close contact with the schools, except possibly in San Francisco (where the children themselves frequently reported their grades and progress to the mothers' aid workers); and in every locality special visits and special reports were made in case any difficulty or problem arose in the schools concerning a child in a mothers' aid family.

[3] In New Bedford a system of regular reports from the schools was established in 1926.

GENERAL FINDINGS

Education of children of legal working age in mothers' aid families.
It was the well-established policy and practice of the agencies in the 10 localities studied that the compulsory-education and child-labor laws should be observed scrupulously in all that concerned children in families receiving mothers' aid. The laws affecting each locality allowed assistance to children at least to the age at which they were eligible for employment certificates under certain specified conditions, and the majority allowed aid to a higher age.

In Michigan an employment certificate for work during school hours (with certain negligible exceptions) could not be issued to a child under the age of 15 years, and in Washington an employment certificate [4] could not be issued at 14 unless the child had completed the eighth grade or, in the judgment of the superintendent of schools, could not profitably pursue further regular school work. With the exception of these two States and of Ohio, where children could not obtain certificates for work during school hours until they were 16,[5] and of the Province of Manitoba, where girls under 15 years of age might not work in factories. the child-labor laws in all the localities studied permitted the issuance of employment certificates at 14 if certain grade and health qualifications were met.[6]

There were 1,652 children 14 and 15 years of age under the care of the agencies administering mothers' aid in the localities studied—excluding Cincinnati, where school attendance was required up to 16 years of age.[7] Of this number 1,281 (78 per cent) were in school. The following table shows the number of children 14 and 15 years old in these nine localities and the number in each of the nine localities attending school at the time of the study:

Number of children 14 and 15 years old in mothers' aid families and number attending school at the time of the study; nine localities

Locality	Children 14 and 15 years old Total	Attending school	Locality	Children 14 and 15 years old Total	Attending school
Total	1,652	1,281	Buffalo (Erie County, N. Y.)	160	139
			Seattle (King County, Wash.)	154	144
Pittsburgh (Allegheny County, Pa.)	203	164	New Bedford, Mass	26	14
			San Francisco, Calif	187	181
Berks County, Pa	35	10	Detroit (Wayne County, Mich.)	255	198
Chicago (Cook County, Ill.)	521	347	Winnipeg (Manitoba, Canada)	111	84

[4] This certificate was required where continuation schools were established, as in the city of Seattle.
[5] High-school graduates under 16 and children determined incapable of profiting by further school instruction were exempted.
[6] In California the need of child's earnings had to be shown also.
[7] In Cincinnati (Hamilton County, Ohio) there were 167 children 16 and 17 years of age in the families receiving mothers' aid and 40 (24 per cent) were attending school.

The 1,281 school children among the 1,652 children 14 and 15 years old in mothers' aid families were enrolled in the following grades or types of school:

	Number of children		Number of children
Total	1,281	High school—Continued.	
		Fourth year	2
Elementary school:		Year not reported	1
Below the seventh grade	232	Vocational school [8]	25
Seventh grade	205	Business school	19
Eighth grade	272	Special class	27
High school:		Industrial training school	1
First year	205	Agricultural training school	1
Second year	87	Not reported	[9] 183
Third year	21		

That many of these children were not eligible for employment certificates on account of failure to meet grade requirements is evident from the number that were attending the lower grades. All the localities except Manitoba had specific requirements, the lowest being completion of the sixth grade and the highest completion of the eighth grade. In addition to grade requirements most of the localities required a physician's certificate of physical fitness before employment certificates could be issued. Although information was not obtained as to the number of children actually kept in school because of physical disability, there must have been some such children.[10]

Several other factors besides eligibility for employment certificates also affect the decision whether children of legal working age in the mothers' aid families shall continue in school or go to work. Probably the most important of these is the approval of continuance in school and the granting of an allowance by the administrative agency for a child who is eligible for an employment certificate. Another is the availability of scholarship funds to supplement the allowances granted by the agencies or to take their place. The extent to which the schools foster or create a desire for further education through the development of a liberalized curriculum is undoubtedly another element in holding in school many children who otherwise would go to work because of lack of interest in their studies and in their school connections. A less easily measured condition but one that nevertheless may be important is the value placed upon secondary or higher education by the various social groups with which the respective boys and girls are associated.

It is impossible to estimate the extent to which any of these factors may have influenced the individual children or dominated the situation in each of the localities studied. In some localities the policy of the agency administering the allowances was apparently a dominating factor, whereas in others, such as Seattle and San Francisco,

---

[8] Includes 2 children taking prevocational and special courses.
[9] Includes 181 children in San Francisco for whom data in regard to grade or type of school attended were not obtained.
[10] Information on this point was obtained for Chicago: Among 187 children reported ineligible for employment certificates in February, 1924, were 96 who were physically unfit; and among 90 who had not completed the required grade a number (not specified) were physically unfit also. All except 2 of the 187 children were attending school.

GENERAL FINDINGS 19

the community conditions would seem to have been of nearly equal importance.[11]

The proportion of the mothers' aid children fully eligible for employment certificates can not be calculated from the data obtained, as a number of those of legal working age who had completed the required grade were ineligible because of physical disability or still other reasons on which complete figures were not available; but figures indicating the proportion of the children 14 and 15 years of age who were eligible, so far as age and grade completion were concerned, but who, nevertheless, were continuing in school are presented in the following table for seven of the nine localities in which children of this age could legally work:[12]

Number of mothers' aid children 14 and 15 years old eligible in age and grade for employment certificates, and number and per cent of such children attending school; nine localities

Locality	Children 14 and 15 years of age			
	Total	Eligible for employment certificates as regards age and school grade completed		
		Total	In school	
			Number	Per cent
Total	1,652			
Reporting age and grade	1,354	911	615	68
Pittsburgh (Allegheny County, Pa.)	203	155	128	83
Berks County, Pa.	35	32	7	(¹)
Chicago (Cook County, Ill.)	521	430	² 259	² 60
Buffalo (Erie County, N. Y.)	160	95	81	85
Seattle (King County, Wash.)	154	78	74	95
New Bedford, Mass.	26	20	8	(¹)
Detroit (Wayne County, Mich.)	255	³ 77	³ 36	47
Not reporting	⁴ 298			

¹ Percentage not shown where base is less than 50.
² Of these children 162 (49 per cent) were eligible in other particulars as well as in age and grade.
³ These children were 15 years old. Children 14 years old were not eligible for regular employment certificates.
⁴ Information as to grade completed was not obtained for the 187 children 14 and 15 years old in families receiving allowances in San Francisco nor the 111 of these ages receiving allowances in Manitoba.

Policies of agencies as to continuance of aid for children of legal working age. In States where mothers' aid might be allowed beyond the age at which children could legally work it became necessary that the agencies formulate policies as to the conditions under which aid might be so continued.

In Pennsylvania no State ruling had been made and the county boards were free to use their own judgment. The majority granted

---

[11] In 1926 only 10 children 14 years old and 153 children 15 years old took out employment certificates in San Francisco, according to figures furnished to the U. S. Children's Bureau by the San Francisco Bureau of Attendance and Guidance (Board of Education). In 1920 the total number of children 14 and 15 years old in San Francisco was 11,239 (Fourteenth Census of the United States, 1920, vol. 3, Population, p. 127, Washington, 1922).

[12] Employment certificates could not be issued in Cincinnati to children under 16 years of age (with certain exceptions). Of the 167 children 16 and 17 years of age in this locality 164 were eligible for employment certificates as regards grade completed and 38 (17 per cent) of them were attending school.

aid to the age of 16 to children who would profit by further school advantages if the family could thereby get along without the child's earnings, and the State department of public welfare encouraged this practice.

In Illinois, where children could obtain employment certificates at 14 years of age, aid might be allowed to the age of 16. It was the policy of the juvenile court in Cook County to continue aid for children over 14 who were physically handicapped or who were up to normal grade and had an average of B in scholarship and wished to continue in school.

In New York no State ruling had been made, and aid was granted in Erie County, N. Y., to the age of 16 to a child who would profit by further schooling, provided this would enable the family to get along without the child's wages.

In Ohio the children were required to attend school until 16 years of age, and mothers' aid could be granted until children were eligible for employment certificates. The juvenile court of Hamilton County encouraged children to remain in school, a continuance of grant for younger members of the family frequently permitting the older children to complete high school or to receive special or further training.

In Washington, where children 14 years old could obtain employment certificates, the law allowed aid to be granted to 15 years of age. Ambitious children of legal working age were encouraged in Seattle to continue in school if the family could get along without their aid in its support, and the family was helped through the allowance of aid for younger children.

In Massachusetts the intent of the law evidently was that children in mothers' aid families should go to work as soon as they were eligible for employment certificates, and the policy of the State department of public welfare and of the mothers' aid administrators in New Bedford was in conformity with it. However, the State department had ruled that when in industrial depressions children under 16 could not find work, although legally permitted to work, the aid might be continued, as the children in such cases were required to attend day school.

In California the law permitted aid to be granted to 16 years of age. Children in San Francisco eligible for certificates were encouraged to continue in school unless their families were in need of the wages they could earn. All except 6 of the 187 children in this group under supervision of the widows' pension bureau were attending school.

In Michigan the law permitted aid to be granted to children under 17. Usually the allowance was not continued beyond 15 years of age; but for a child who was frail or physically handicapped or who was finishing a unit of education the allowance could be continued until he was 16.

In Manitoba many children had been permitted to remain in school up to 16 years of age, but in 1924 the commission ruled that grants should continue to the age of 15 only.

Community provision for special types of children.

Provision for handicapped children.—As the number of children in the families receiving allowances who had one or more physical defects or who were subnormal or mentally defective or diseased did not seem large, information in regard to the work of the agencies in behalf of such children and reports concerning the numbers receiving special training were not obtained in detail from all the localities studied. A brief general description of the facilities available, private as well as public, is given in the sections of this report dealing with the separate localities, however, and such figures and further details as were reported are also included.

Provision for children wishing further education.—Most of the agencies were actively interested in obtaining for children of unusual ability or ambition such opportunities for further education as were within reach. Generally their activities consisted in giving the children information concerning scholarships and other aid that was available in the respective localities, putting them in connection with the authorities determining the grants of such scholarships or other aid, or seeking the cooperation of private relief agencies that were in a position to arrange for such connections. Sometimes they acted merely as advisers to the ambitious children or their families, suggesting ways and means by which the desired education could be attained in the near future if not immediately accessible. Lastly, a method followed in a number of agencies was continuance of the allowances; that is, allowances were granted for the younger children in a family so that the older boys and girls might continue in school instead of being obliged to go to work to assist in the support of the younger children—as they would be expected to do if this special arrangement were not made.

Vocational and educational counseling.—Some of the cities in the 10 localities studied were well equipped to give adequate vocational guidance to children of legal working age; among them may be mentioned especially Pittsburgh, Chicago, Cincinnati, Seattle, and Detroit.[13] Vocational advice had been given to many of the mothers' aid children by interested persons also, including mothers' aid workers, school officials, and friends. Educational advice had been given to a number of mothers' aid children by various persons; school officials and psychologists giving mental tests had given the most authoritative advice reported. In the larger number of cases their recommendation was continuance in school, whether to complete a unit of education, to transfer to special courses or classes, or to take specialized training that would lead to wage-earning vocations.

It would appear that much more intensive use could be made in some communities of the vocational service available. The span of years that can be devoted to educational and vocational preparation for the responsibilities of adult life are for the dependent child so short at best that the fullest use should be made of every facility that will enable him to make the most of his natural gifts, to capitalize his interests and aptitudes in choosing an occupation offering opportunity for acquirement of skill, security of employment, and advancement in wages.

---
[13] For details in regard to this work in Chicago, Pittsburgh, Cincinnati, and Seattle see Vocational Guidance and Junior Placement, pp. 157 ff., 191 ff., 267 ff., 317 ff. (U. S. Children's Bureau Publication No. 149 and U. S. Employment Service Publication A, Washington, 1925).

Children at work.

Of the 1,652 children 14 and 15 years old in the families receiving allowances 314 (19 per cent) were working. Information concerning the occupations of the working children and their contributions to the support of their families was available from the majority of the localities studied. This was of interest as indicating the degree of expertness required in the various trades or occupations in which the children were engaged and the opportunities of advancement open to them.

In several of the localities from which some information was obtained in regard to contributions of working children to the family support it appeared that most of the working children 14 and 15 years old handed over their entire earnings to their mothers; in a few localities they gave varying proportions, though many of them gave half or a larger fraction. The average percentage of the total family income derived from the wages of the working children 14 and 15 years old in Allegheny and in Berks Counties, Pa.. in Detroit, in Buffalo, and in Winnipeg and of those 16 and 17 years old in Cincinnati was 26. It varied from 16 per cent in Winnipeg to 30 per cent in Detroit. The percentage for the remaining four localities can not be reported because data were incomplete in regard to the children's earnings, other sources of income, the amount of the allowance, or two or more of these items.

Children neither in school nor at work.

Of the 1,652 children 14 and 15 years old in the families receiving allowances 57 (3 per cent) were neither at work nor in school at the time of the study. Some had employment certificates and were looking for work, some were waiting for their certificates, some were in poor health, some were mentally defective, and for a few no precise information as to the reason was available. Some information was obtained from seven localities as to the results of physical examinations given at the time that applications were made for employment certificates; no data were given, however, as to the number of children who were incapacitated for both school attendance and work.

EDUCATIONAL ACTIVITIES FOR THE MOTHERS

The degree to which mothers receiving aid were encouraged to join clubs and classes of an educational character varied greatly from agency to agency. In some communities the grants were too small to permit the mothers to give their time to anything more than housekeeping and gainful employment. In one or two cities where the grants were reasonably adequate little thought had been given to the matter; in others great stress had been laid upon providing channels to enable the mothers, especially those of foreign birth, to acquire a working knowledge of English and of fundamentals regarding the care of babies and children. In Detroit, for example, the chief concern in the five classes conducted by the board of education and in the two classes conducted by the Merrill-Palmer School for mothers receiving aid was to give something of vital interest and significance which the women could absorb and utilize immediately. The acquisition of English came as a matter of course, but at the beginning the classes almost invariably used an interpreter. These classes became social centers and provided the mothers through class and club organization with a means of self and group expression.

In Chicago all foreign-born mothers were required to have citizenship papers as a requisite to mothers' aid, and those not already citizens were therefore enrolled in citizenship classes. Some workers were very active in connecting the mothers with organized mothers' clubs operating through the settlements and recreation centers. The nutrition classes of the Elizabeth McCormick Memorial Fund in Chicago were attended by the mothers with their children, and group instruction was provided. Mothers also attended the nutrition classes in Buffalo. In Cincinnati they were encouraged to enroll in evening classes in cooking and sewing in the public schools. In Detroit, in Pittsburgh, and in Berks County, Pa., the mothers' aid workers had made special efforts to have foreign-born mothers and their daughters affiliated with the International Institute of the Young Women's Christian Association (a department dealing with foreign-born women and girls and their problems). In Detroit, Seattle, and San Francisco great emphasis was laid upon encouraging the mothers to join the local parent-teacher associations, and several women receiving aid held offices of responsibility in these.

The agency administering the allowances in Berks County, Pa., had organized a home-craft shop, and it was believed that the mothers' work in this shop was a source not only of income and gratification but in some cases of great therapeutic value also.[14]

RECREATION

BUDGET ALLOWANCE FOR RECREATION

The Chicago standard budget,[15] which was used by several agencies, allowed 25 cents a month for recreation for each member of the family not a wage earner. The San Francisco Widows' Pension Bureau allowed 50 cents a month for recreation for children under working age. Often the allowance for incidentals covered recreation also.

Working boys and girls were permitted a more generous allowance by all the agencies, its amount depending somewhat upon their earnings. In Erie County, N. Y., $5 a month for pocket money was allowed a working child under 18 years of age. This was for spending money only and did not include car fare and lunches. In Chicago a working child earning less than $15 a week was allowed 25 cents a week spending money; in San Francisco he was allowed $1 to $2 a month; and in Berks County, Pa., $2 a month was allowed to working children for recreation.

POLICIES OF AGENCIES IN REGARD TO RECREATIONAL ACTIVITIES

Only one agency made no effort to associate its children with recreational activities. Two others made no effort to do this unless a child gave special evidence of need; for example, a difficult child might be encouraged to join the Boy Scouts or the Young Men's

---
[14] After several years' trial this shop was discontinued, as it could not be made self-supporting.
[15] See footnote 6, p. 34.

Christian Association. The policy of the remaining seven agencies was to stimulate and encourage recreational activities; this was carried out with varying degrees of thoroughness, depending upon the time and interest of the individual workers. There was considerable effort to place children in clubs and classes in settlements and community centers, and special attention was given to problem children. Whenever possible the children were encouraged in musical activities and in taking music lessons, especially at settlements where the fees were nominal. Special effort was made to get musical training and musical instruments for handicapped children. Working children were often permitted to purchase musical instruments in order that the whole family might derive pleasure from them.

Comparatively few boys and girls were enrolled in scout troops or similar outdoor organizations. One agency reported that the boys did not have time because they were working out of school hours, and others said they could not afford the dues and incidental expenses. It might be well to consider the value of this combination of outdoor and group activity as a means of preventing juvenile delinquency, especially that of boys and girls whose mothers are away from home part of the time and therefore can not regularly supervise their children's leisure-time activities.

The public library afforded another means for utilizing the leisure time of children, but apparently the agencies had not given much thought to this as yet in their recreational programs. As a rule the children were permitted to attend motion pictures occasionally, but the policy was that they should go with an adult or older child and not oftener than once a week.

In Buffalo a number of members of a men's club acted as "big brothers" to sons of women receiving allowances. They were especially helpful in planning educational opportunities and in securing good jobs for these boys. Nearly all the agencies did a great deal in the way of promoting holiday festivities and summer outings; so far as facilities were available, mothers and children were sent for a week or two to a summer vacation camp; and the workers spent many hours of their leisure time in taking individual children to the circus, theater, zoological garden, parks, and museums. In Pittsburgh a point was made of encouraging mothers to take their children to the parks for a day's outing as often as possible in the summer; and many Chicago families spent happy days on boat trips on Lake Michigan.

In Cincinnati one of the three private relief agencies assisting the agency administering mothers' aid in its supervision of families planned occasional parties and good times for the mothers and children. Refreshments were served; often there would be some form of entertainment, such as a concert.

The majority of the agencies did something at Christmas time to bring cheer to the families. Recognizing the desire of the mothers to be the Santa Claus to their own children, the administrative agency in Berks County, Pa., one year asked a fraternal organization to give directly to the mothers the money it would spend on each family. The organization agreed, and each mother received $10 to spend as she saw fit. After Christmas each mother wrote a letter to the organization telling how the money had been spent. It seems especially important in dealing with dependent families that every means should be used to give to the mother the power of serving her children in ways which they can understand in order that they may preserve to the utmost their confidence in her ability to fulfill their needs.

All the agencies strongly urged that the mother and children join in the good times of their church and take part in its social as well as religious activities, and most of the children under 16 attended Sunday school. In fact, probably the majority of mothers receiving aid secured their educational and social life through their children and their church activities. For many this may have been adequate; others would surely have profited by and expanded under the influence of educational opportunities and a broader social life.

SOME STRONG AND WEAK POINTS IN THE ADMINISTRATION OF MOTHERS' AID

Many of the 10 agencies attempted to do constructive case work and much of it was of a high order. A few agencies did little or no case work. This appeared to be due directly to a lack of understanding of the technique and value of case work (and in one instance to an inadequate administrative staff), and indirectly to the lack of a group of citizens and coworkers who would support an administration based upon the case-work method. The latter agencies were in States where there was State supervision but where the emphasis was placed upon the administrative rather than the educational side of such supervision.

In 5 of the 10 localities studied some form of State supervision was in force. State supervision is greatly needed, especially outside the large cities, to help in the establishment and maintenance of standards of constructive family work. The question of what form of State supervision is best calculated to effect these results deserves careful consideration. Is the most responsible local administration developed under a form of State supervision which is primarily educational in its approach to the local agencies administering the law, or is it best promoted under a form of State supervision which is concerned largely with the direct investigation and visiting of families independently of the local agency administering the law?

In four communities the relation between the agency administering mothers' aid and the private family-relief agencies was one of great friendliness and mutual confidence; two communities had no private family agency; in one the relation was one of indifference; in three there was a lack of harmony that made teamwork impossible. In the communities in which the agencies were cooperating a sympathetic understanding of the peculiar problems of each agency and an exchange of ideas in regard to standards and methods made for highgrade work. In communities where the relations between the mothers' aid agency and the private agency were not satisfactory, and in a less degree in communities where there were no private family agencies, there seemed to be a tendency on the part of the mothers' aid staff not to appreciate that mothers' aid calls for the application of family case work technique and that mothers' aid agencies therefore should take pains to employ workers trained in family case work or should give the workers now employed an opportunity to acquire this training.

The agencies administered through boards or commissions of citizens were protected against political assaults and safeguarded in the maintenance of standards and personnel—provided the members were appointed with reference to their capacity for intelligent and useful service. The boards in Buffalo and Pittsburgh were fortunate in each having one member who was the executive of a private family agency; in Pittsburgh one member was also on the board of directors of a family-welfare society, and a third had been a social worker prior to her marriage; the board in Buffalo had two members who were on district committees of the Charity Organization Society; and one member of the board in Berks County, Pa., had served on the board of the private family society. It was significant that the aid was administered by such unpaid boards in three of the communities where the administrative staff was adequate and in two where the relation between the mothers' aid agency and the private family agencies was good. It was also noteworthy that in Chicago and Cincinnati the juvenile courts had felt the need of such service and had organized advisory committees, which in some measure constituted themselves guardians of the mothers' aid divisions of the courts. The remaining agencies might have profited by the organization of similar committees.

It is often extremely difficult, even when adequate assistance to families is provided, to persuade taxpayers and county and city officials of the importance of adequate personnel, and one of the most serious handicaps in 6 of the 10 agencies was the lack of an adequate administrative staff. In Pittsburgh, in Berks County, Pa., in Chicago, and in Buffalo the case load per worker was from 40 to 60 families and from 1 to 8 new investigations each month. In the remaining six agencies the workers carried from 90 to 250 families, generally in addition to making new investigations. Two of the six employed an investigator whose sole task was to make new investigations. Not only were these workers supervising an excessive number of families, but in two agencies they had to do all their own typing and in a third they did much of it. In one agency where the case load was 60 families per worker one stenographer was employed for the whole department of 24 case workers. As the number of families per worker rises above 50 or 60 the possibilities of intensive case work diminish correspondingly, and case recording is bound to be meagerly and poorly done.

However, it was a truism that even in the communities where all-round intensive social case work was not attempted, the regularity of financial aid and its continuance over a period of years, together with such friendly service as was given and the spirit in which it was administered, fostered an esprit de corps, a sense of security and stability, an appreciation of the spiritual values implicit in the law, and tended to develop and maintain in a large number of families a high degree of personal efficiency and a capacity to organize their own normal activities on a par with those of self-supporting families in their communities.

GENERAL FINDINGS

In the following sections describing the work of each agency and the kind of opportunities afforded to the children who were the beneficiaries of the 10 agencies studied—discussed briefly in the foregoing pages—instances will be found of outstanding service given to children and their mothers, notably in safeguarding their health, both physical and mental. Another especially significant fact brought out by the study is the emphasis being placed in some localities on giving the children educational opportunities that will insure their future success and happiness, and not, as unfortunately is often the case because of inadequate provision for aid, requiring these children prematurely to take up the burden of support—a shortsighted policy, as some of these agencies have recognized.

MOTHERS' ALLOWANCES IN ALLEGHENY COUNTY, PA.[1]

PROVISIONS OF THE LAW

The law creating a mothers' assistance fund was passed in 1913 and amended in 1915. It was repealed and a rewritten act substituted in 1919 and further amended in 1921 and 1923.[2] In this amended form only such mothers were eligible as were widows or wives of men " permanently confined in institutions for the insane." Other conditions of aid were as follows: The mother must be of " proved character and ability "; she must have lived in the State two years and in the county one year prior to her application for aid; she must live with her children in her own home, must be " poor and dependent," and must need aid for the proper maintenance of her children in their own home. The children must be attending school and have a satisfactory record of attendance.

The maximum assistance allowed was $20 a month for the first child and $10 a month for each additional child. An allowance might be given for an unborn child if the mother had one or more children entitled to aid. Aid was permitted for children up to 16 years of age, provided the children were in school with satisfactory school record or were physically unable to earn wages on attaining the age necessary for employment certificates.

The following rulings and policies had been formulated by the State supervisor (see the following section), and some of them had been considered and approved by the attorney general: A mother or children might have an equity in their home of $1,500 and $400 in cash or other assets and still be eligible for aid; aid was not to be granted to a mother who was receiving compensation under the State compensation law for the death of her husband by industrial accident; a mother was not to be permitted to keep men boarders or lodgers other than her brother or father; and she was not eligible if there were relatives legally responsible for the support of the children. The State supervisor recommended that a physical examination be required for all children (and, if possible, for all mothers) as a matter of routine preliminary to the granting of assistance. A

---

[1] The population of this county in 1920 was 1,185,808; of this number, 588,343 lived in Pittsburgh. The native white population was 883,181, the foreign-born white population 248,581, and the negro population 53,517. The nationality of the foreign-born population was as follows, in the order given: Polish, Italian, German, Austrian, Russian, Irish, Czechoslovakian, English, and Hungarian. The child population within the legal age for mothers' aid was 398,156. (Fourteenth Census of the United States, 1920, vol. 3, Population, pp. 857, 859, 883, 885, Washington, 1922.) The chief industries of the county are the great blast furnaces and steel mills, foundries and machine shops, which line the shores of the Allegheny, Monongahela, Ohio, and Youghiogheny Rivers.
[2] Pa., act of Apr. 29, 1913, No. 80, Laws of 1913, p. 118; act of June 18, 1915, No. 439, Laws of 1915, p. 1038; act of July 10, 1919, No. 354, Laws of 1919, p. 893; act of May 27, 1921, No. 433, Laws of 1921, p. 1175; act of May 22, 1923, No. 200, Laws of 1923, p. 307. Appropriations and methods of appropriation have been provided for in the following acts: Act of June 29, 1917, No. 237, Laws of 1917, p. 664; act of July 10, 1919, No. 361, Laws of 1919, p. 907; act of May 27, 1921, No. 438, Laws of 1921, p. 1184; act of May 28, 1923, No. 251, Laws of 1923, p. 459. (See Pa., Stat. 1920, secs. 16717–16734, pp. 1618–1619; Supp. 1924, p. 452.)

manual of mothers' assistance had been issued for the guidance of the boards in the administration of the law, which defined standards of investigation, adequacy of aid, and supervision.

STATE SUPERVISION

The law contains the following provisions in regard to State supervision:

The governor shall appoint a State supervisor, qualified by training and experience, who shall be a woman. The State supervisor shall have general supervision over the boards of trustees of the several counties and shall act as general field organizer. She shall be on the staff of the department of public welfare.

The State supervisor shall formulate and issue to the boards of trustees of the various counties rules of procedure by which they shall be governed, to the end that uniformity of interpretation and practice shall obtain throughout the Commonwealth. She shall visit, at least twice a year, the boards of trustees of each county accepting the provisions of this act. She shall, as general field organizer, visit the county commissioners of those counties which have not availed themselves of the provisions of this act, and shall explain to such commissioners the benefits accruing from the act and the advantages of coming within its provisions, and shall assist such county commissioners in the organization of boards of trustees.

She shall make a report annually to the commissioner of public welfare, reviewing the work done under the provisions of this act by the trustees of the various counties, laying special stress upon educational conditions of the assisted families.

The State supervisor appointed, with the approval of the governor, an assistant State supervisor. The law did not give administrative authority to the supervisor, but provided that the administration of this act within the several counties should be solely in the hands of the board of trustees appointed by the governor—subject, however, to the rules adopted and issued by the State supervisor.

The State office of the mothers' assistance fund acted as a clearing house for the gathering of important facts in relation to mothers' aid in county, State, and Nation, and for redistributing such information to the local boards through circular letters, a manual of mothers' assistance, and other literature. It also outlined certain rulings and policies for the general guidance of the boards. Reprints of papers read at the National Conference of Social Work and of magazine articles, as well as bulletins and reports, were frequently sent to the boards.

The framework for a fairly uniform record system was insured by the fact that the State office provided the boards with forms and blanks, the face card, the school-report blank, the household expense account blank, the physical-examination blank, and an alphabetical card index and application book for filing applications. A standard budget was also furnished to be used as a guide in estimating grants.

The State supervisor passed on all petitions for grants on the basis of the face card and summary for each applicant, which were sent by the local boards to the State office; a monthly pay roll also was sent to the State office, and a State check for half the amount of the grant was mailed by the State supervisor, the other half of the grant being paid by the county treasurer. The State supervisor made a biennial report to the general assembly as provided by law and took the lead in formulating the legislative program as to both the appropriation to be asked and the amendments to be introduced.

Either the supervisor or her assistant visited the county boards twice a year, if possible, working out with them local problems and difficulties. If the trustees were themselves acting as volunteers, doing all the investigating and supervising of families without paid service (as was true in 28 rural counties), or if part-time paid workers were employed (as was true in 6 counties) the supervisor or her assistant, as often as was possible, spent a week or two in the county visiting applicants or families receiving aid with the trustees or worker, showing each in turn how to make an investigation, suggesting constructive steps in treatment, and making clear the responsibility of the trustees in the supervision of the families. This demonstration by doing was the most important single step in the teaching process.

In counties where full-time trained or semitrained workers were employed (22 in all) families were visited with the workers, occasionally also with the trustees, if it seemed advisable; or the survey might consist of a study of records. Families were never visited by the supervisor alone. Her function was not to inspect nor to investigate claims but solely to aid the trustees and workers in acquiring an understanding of case-work methods and point of view.

Intercounty conferences of trustees and workers were held at various points throughout the State as a means of promoting a sense of unity and solidarity, discussing important legislative plans, and gathering and disseminating knowledge as to the best administrative methods in use throughout the State.

ADMINISTRATION OF THE LAW

ADMINISTRATIVE AGENCY

The administration of the law was given to unpaid county boards of seven women trustees appointed by the governor. These boards were under the general supervision of the State supervisor of the mothers' assistance fund. They were allowed traveling expenses incurred in the administration of the law.

The Allegheny County board of trustees of the mothers' assistance fund consisted of women of broad social vision who were identified with the social and philanthropic work of their communities. It included a professional social worker and a woman who prior to her marriage had been a social worker. Two of the trustees, including the president of the board, had served continuously since its organization 10 years before, and two had served for 8 years. The president of the board was also a member of the board of directors of a family-welfare society and of the largest settlement in the city. She had made a practice for years of interviewing every mother during the first month in which aid was given to explain the purpose of the grant and the mother's responsibility not only to her children but to the cause of mothers' aid in the whole State.

The philosophy underlying the relation of the board to the beneficiaries of mothers' aid could be summed up in these words: The State in passing the mothers' assistance law assumed responsibility both financial and social for the welfare and nurture of the dependent, fatherless children who came within the scope of the law and who with their mothers were by this token entitled to all the aids which case work could give in making satisfactory adjustments to their environment and in utilizing the health, educational, recreational, and social resources of the county.

THE STAFF

The board appointed the executive secretary, who in turn, with their approval, selected her staff of 10 field workers and 3 stenographers. The executive secretary had secured her training and several years' experience in private family agencies. Four of the 10 field workers were graduates of the department of social work that was conducted as an undergraduate school of Margaret Morrison College for Women of the Carnegie Institute of Technology in Pittsburgh. All four of these workers had received the field training while juniors in college under the supervision of the Associated Charities and while seniors under the supervision of the mothers' aid staff. They had no other training or experience before their employment as paid workers. Three other field workers were college graduates. One of these had had a year's experience in psychiatric social work under the supervision of a State hospital for mental diseases. Another had done volunteer work for one year with a private family agency and for a second year with a settlement in connection with university undergraduate courses in sociology. The third had had a year's teaching experience and a six weeks' training course with a private family agency prior to her appointment on the mothers' aid staff.

One of the remaining three members of the staff had had three years in college and two years in civilian relief work with the Red Cross; one had had one year of college work and 18 months' experience in a charity organization society; and the third was a high-school graduate who had taken a number of special college courses and a summer course at a school of social work. She had been with the International Institute of the Young Women's Christian Association before joining the mothers' aid staff seven years before the study and was able to speak several languages. The staff were enthusiastic and eager to give the best that was in them to the families under their care.[3]

One automobile was at the service of the staff for county work.

APPROPRIATION AND VOLUME OF WORK

The State legislature at its biennial sessions makes appropriations for the mothers' assistance fund, and the sums appropriated are apportioned to the various counties according to population and need. The State treasurer is required, after deducting the sums designated for the payment of salaries and expenses, to divide the balance of the appropriation into two equal sums and to distribute one of these sums the first of the two fiscal years in the proportions specified to the counties classified by population; the seven classes

---

[3] The members of the staff were given an opportunity for two hours' advanced study each week—one hour for outside courses in social work and the second hour for staff conferences in which a regular course of study of case-work methods was followed.

made on the basis of population and the percentages of the sum to be distributed among them were as follows:[4]

Class of county	Population limits	Percentage of designated sum
First class	More than 1,500,000	24
Second class	1,000,000 to 1,500,000	16
Third class	200,000 to 1,000,000	19
Fourth class	100,000 to 200,000	26
Fifth class	50,000 to 100,000	9
Sixth class	25,000 to 50,000	4¼
Seventh class	Less than 25,000	1¾

No county could receive its allotment of the State appropriation available for any year unless it accepted the provisions of the law in regard to the classification and allotment and placed at the disposal of the trustees a sum equal to the amount available from the State appropriation for that year.[5] Distribution of the sum set aside for the second of the two fiscal years was made in a manner analogous to that described for the first fiscal year of the biennium, surplus funds accruing because any counties did not avail themselves of the provisions of the act being added to the sums available for the second fiscal year in each case. The State appropriation to Allegheny County for the biennial period June 1, 1923, to May 31, 1925, was $276,000. This, when matched by county funds, permitted an annual expenditure of $276,000. Although this was a large increase over the $156,480 a year provided by State and county funds during the previous biennium, it was estimated that an appropriation of $411,000 would be required to meet the entire need on the basis of the maximum grants at that time.

During February, 1924, 477 families, including 1,652 children under 16, received mothers' aid. Each of the 10 visitors supervised 40 to 50 families and made one or two new investigations each month. In addition, each worker had contact with 6 to 8 other families during the month, including families whose grants had been canceled or which required further investigation. There were 425 families on the waiting list.

PROCEDURE IN MAKING ALLOWANCES

Application was made personally at the office by each mother. The applications were investigated and acted upon in chronological order. There was no application blank; the face card was filled out at the dictation of the mother and she made affidavit to it. It contained the following information: The names, addresses, birthplaces, and dates of birth of parents and of children; the date, cause of death, and name of attending physician or hospital if the father was dead; date of commitment and name of hospital if the father was in a hospital for the insane; the father's last occupation, name of last employer, wages, and whether his occupation was in any way responsible for his death or insanity; physical or mental defects of parents and children; grades of children in school, school, and age

---
[4] Pa., act of July 10, 1919, No. 354, sec. 13, Laws of 1919, p. 896, as amended by acts of May 27, 1921, Nos. 433, 438, Laws of 1921, pp. 1175, 1184. (Pa., Stat. 1920, sec. 16729, p. 1619; Supp. 1924, sec. 16729, p. 453.)
[5] Pa., act of July 10, 1919, sec. 14, Laws of 1919, p. 897, as amended by act of May 27, 1921, No. 433, Laws of 1921, p. 1175. (Pa., Stat. 1920, sec. 16730, p. 1619; Supp. 1924, sec. 16730, p. 453.)

at entering; occupations and wages of children at work; previous residences of the family and address of present landlord; employment and wages of mother, and the nationality, citizenship, religion, and length of residence in the United States and in the county of father and mother; the financial conditions at the father's death or commitment to hospital for insane; the present financial situation; facts regarding property, savings, and insurance; names and addresses of relatives, physician, other individuals, and philanthropic agencies interested in or assisting the family; the church; an estimate of the household budget.

Investigation was made as follows: The birth dates of children, residence, marriage, and all statements regarding property, insurance, and savings were verified; the death of the father was also verified, and if he was insane the commitment was verified and a statement obtained from the hospital covering diagnosis, prognosis, and whether the father had venereal disease. The name of the family was registered in the confidential exchange and the agencies registered were consulted. A visit was made to the mother's home, the children's teachers were visited, and generally several relatives were seen in their own homes—if possible, relatives on both mother's and father's side; the minister and the family physician were consulted and sometimes—but not always—the landlord, the employer of the father if he was recently employed, the employer of the mother, and other references.

USE OF A STANDARD BUDGET

The Chicago standard budget [6] was used for all items except food. For this the allowance was that of the budget of the New York Nutrition Council.[7] The budgets were revised at least once in six months and as much oftener as occasion required. The combination budget was as follows:

Rent: As paid, if reasonable.
Food:

Age in years	Boys' cost per month A	Boys' cost per month B	Girls' cost per month A	Girls' cost per month B
Under 2	$5.20	$6.93	$5.20	$6.93
2–3	5.42	7.15	5.20	6.93
3–4	5.63	7.15	5.42	6.93
4–7	5.85	7.37	5.63	6.93
7–8	6.28	7.58	5.85	7.15
8–9	6.72	8.02	6.28	7.37
9–11	7.58	8.67	6.50	7.80
11–12	8.23	9.53	6.93	8.02
12–15	9.20	11.00	7.37	8.45
15–16	9.75	11.92	7.90	8.88
Over 16	10.83	12.78	9.10	9.75

[6] Nesbitt, Florence: The Chicago Standard Budget for Dependent Families. The Chicago Council of Social Agencies, Chicago, 1920.
[7] Good Nutrition and Adequate Food Allowances for the Family. Prepared by the Committee on Economic Standards of the New York Nutrition Council. New York, 1922.

Qualifications for food allowances:
1. Family of 3 or less, B allowance for each member.
2. Nursing mother $13.65 (no extra allowance for baby).
3. Use B allowances where special nourishment required.
4. Deduct one-fourth allowance for adults eating lunches regularly away from home and make special allowance for lunches in budget estimate.
5. For all cases in which B allowance not recommended in above qualifications use A allowance.
6. Allow for the average mother $9.10 per month.

CLOTHING AND TOILET ARTICLES:

	Per month
For a man at ordinary outdoor work	$6.50
(Increase for work involving unusual exposure.)	
For a woman at home	5.00
Working girl or boy	8.15–12.20
(Increase according to standard of dress required by employment.)	
For office work where good standard of appearance is required	10.00–12.00
The requirements for girl or boy in high school are much the same as if the child were at work.	
Children 13 years and up in eighth grade	5.75
Children 10 to 12 years	4.70
Children 5 to 9 years	3.65
Children 2 to 4 years	2.80
Children under 2 years	1.85

In families where there is clothing from older children or parents to be handed down to the younger ones, these figures may be reduced by 10 to 25 per cent for the members of the family receiving such donations.

The larger figure allows $25 a year for "best" clothing.

HOUSEHOLD FURNISHINGS AND SUPPLIES:

Family of 2 members	4.00
Family of 3 or 4 members	4.75
Family of 5 or 6 members	5.50
Family of 7 or 8 members	6.25
Family of 9 or 10 members	7.00

FUEL AND LIGHT:
Four winter months, three-fourths ton per month.
Four spring and autumn months, one-half ton per month.
Four summer months (gas only), $1 to $1.50 per month.
Kindling, $1 to $2 per month.
When families heat by gas, $2 per month per room; $1 per month per room in spring and fall.
Light (gas or kerosene), $1 per month.
Health, 25 cents per month and up for each person.
Car fare as used.
Spending money for earning children, 25 cents to $1 per week.
Insurance as used (if reasonable).
Incidentals, $1.50 to $2 per month per family (when there are no earning children).

The grant was made to fit the need so far as the maximum allowed under the law permitted. The decision as to the amount to be granted was made by the board of trustees on the recommendation of the executive secretary at the regular fortnightly meeting.

The average grants per family and per child in Allegheny County in February, 1924, were $39.10 and $11.20, respectively. The largest grant was $90; the smallest grant was $13. At the time of the study 94 of the 477 families had an income that, with the grant, was inadequate according to the budget.

During the winter of 1924 philanthropic trust funds in the city allowed the mothers' assistance fund $1,000 for gas and coal in addition to the regular grants.

All mothers were required to keep itemized monthly household-expense accounts either on loose slips of paper or on blanks provided by the State office. These were made the basis for suggestions in regard to diet, the proper cooking of foods, marketing, and especially the use of milk, upon which great emphasis was laid. There was no visiting-housekeeper association in the city, so that all instruction had be given by the mothers' aid visitors, one of whom had had special training in dietetics. The monthly accounts under the items of the budget were copied on the yearly household-account summaries. Following are copies of single monthly and yearly account blanks:

ALLEGHENY COUNTY, PA. 37

Commonwealth of Pennsylvania
Department of Welfare
Mothers' Assistance Fund

County_____ No._____
Name_____
Month_____

[Face]
(FOR FOOD' SEE OTHER SIDE)

MONTHLY HOUSEHOLD ACCOUNT

Day of month	Clothing, sewing supplies, shoe mending, toilet articles, etc.		Laundry, house furnishings and supplies, soap, farm supplies		Car fare, lunches	Church, good times, newspapers, magazines, postage, etc.		Doctor, dentist, glasses, medicine, etc.		Fuel, light	Life and fire insurance, lodge dues	Rent, taxes, interest, repairs, etc.		Incidentals	
	For whom	Item	Amt.	Item	Amt.	Amt.	Item	Amt.	For whom	Amt.	Amt.	Amt.	Item	Amt.	Item	Amt.
									Total__							
Total__																

Gifts received during the month—
Clothing, food, fuel. List articles received.

Do not write in this space.

Amount on hand first of month_____
Amount earned by mother_____
Amount earned by children_____(full total)
Name of child   Amt. earned

Amount received from lodgers and boarders_____
Amount received from relatives, lodges, or other sources_____
Amount from Mothers' Assistance Fund_____

Total received during month_____
Total expenses for month_____
Amount on hand at end of month_____

[Reverse]

THE COST OF FOOD FOR THE MONTH

Day of month	Quantity	Article	Cost	Day of month	Quantity	Article	Cost	Day of month	Quantity	Article	Cost
Total carried forward_____		Total carried forward_____		Grand total _____			

MOTHERS ASSISTANCE FUND OF PENNSYLVANIA

Surname _____
Address _____

Children—
___ under 16 years.
___ over 16 years.
___ Total in family.

Average age of children September 1, ____
Average age of children March 1, ____

County _____
Number _____

HOUSEHOLD ACCOUNT SUMMARY ON BASIS OF TWELVE MONTHS

Month	Income							Expenses								Total
	Woman	Children	Lodgers or boarders	Relatives	Mothers' assistance fund	Other money help	Gifts, clothing, supplies	Total	Rent, taxes, interest, etc.	Fuel and light	Food: Milk	Food: Other food	Clothing	Insurance, union dues, etc.	Car fares, lunches	Household furnishings	Health, doctor, dentist	Incidentals	
June																			
July																			
August																			
September																			
October																			
November																			
December																			
January																			
February																			
March																			
April																			
May																			
Total																			

SUPPLEMENTING OF MOTHERS' AID

When the maximum mothers' aid grant was inadequate to cover the family budget it was the policy of the department, as far as was possible, to secure supplementary aid from some family agency or itself to organize relief. The four private family agencies in Pittsburgh all gave supplementary aid both to families receiving mothers' aid and to families on the waiting list. As a rule these agencies granted aid only to families that had been known to them prior to the application for mothers' aid. The understanding on which the family agencies gave supplementary aid was that the maximum grant would be allowed.

The Conference of Catholic Charities gave $627.76 to 14 families receiving mothers' aid and $5,058.71 to 43 families on the waiting list between January 1, 1923, and March 1, 1924. The Pittsburgh Association for the Improvement of the Poor during its fiscal year April 1, 1923, to March 31, 1924, aided 10 families on the waiting list to the amount of $172. No aid was given to families receiving mothers' aid. The Associated Charities of Pittsburgh aided 46 families on the waiting list to the amount of $12,416.89 and two families receiving aid to the amount of $654.77 during 1923. The United Hebrew Relief Association aided 27 families on the waiting list to the amount of $14,460 and 13 families receiving aid to the amount of $4,783 during 1923. The directors of the poor of Allegheny County aided 7 families receiving mothers' assistance to the amount of $235 and 30 families on the waiting list to the amount of $5,319.50 between June 1, 1923, and May 31, 1924.

VISITING

It was the policy of the mothers' aid workers to visit each family at least once a month and oftener if the need was urgent. Families living outside Pittsburgh could not always be visited so frequently, partly because of the condition of the roads and the inaccessibility of the homes and partly because of the time required and the pressure of other work.

HEALTH

PHYSICAL HEALTH

The allowance for health—25 cents per person per month—was that provided by the Chicago standard budget. Allowance was made for special diet and for medical or dental care by increasing the grant if the maximum was not already being allowed.

Physical examinations and general procedure.

In the fall of 1922 a pediatrician in charge of a clinic in one of the large hospitals offered to examine, a few at a time, children under 12 years of age in Pittsburgh for whom aid was being granted if they were not reached by the child-health centers. A physical-health blank was compiled, and as it included a certain amount of personal and family health this history was secured as well as information concerning the health habits of the child. The blank form was as follows:

ALLEGHENY COUNTY, PA. 41

Face
PHYSICAL REPORT OF M. A. F. ALLEGHENY CO.

NAME, _____ AGE, _____ DATE, _____

FAMILY HISTORY

Father, _____. Age, _____. Date of death, _____ Cause of death, _____
Mother, _____. Age, _____. Miscarriage, _____. Child. living, _____ Child dead, _____
Health, _____. Rheum. _____. Tbc., _____. Nerv. dis., _____. Alcohol, _____. Syph., _____

PERSONAL HISTORY

Child born, _____ mo. Labor, _____. Wt. at birth, _____ lbs.
Sat up at _____ mo.   Talked at _____ mo Walked at _____ mo. Teeth at _____ mo
General health and habits:
   Type of house, _____. No. of rooms, _____; outside, _____; inside, _____; ventilation, _____.
   Sleep, _____; amt., _____. No. in room, _____; in bed, _____; bed-wetter, _____; masturbator, _____.
   Bowels, _____; bath, _____; mouth breather, _____.
   Diet, _____; tea, _____; coffee, _____; milk per day, _____; regularity of meals, _____.
   Feeding history, _____; breast, _____; bottle, _____.
Previous diseases:
   Measles, _____. Wh. cg., _____. C. pox, _____. Scarlet, _____. Diphth., _____. Mumps _____.
   G. measles, _____. Rheu., _____. Gastro-enteric, _____. Resp., _____. Ear, _____. Throat, _____.
   Colds, _____. Other diseases, _____

HOSPITAL HISTORY

Where, _____. Date, _____ Cause, _____

MEDICAL EXAMINATION

By _____
Weight, _____ lbs. Height, _____ in. Normal weight for height, _____ lbs.
General condition, _____. Color, _____ Muscles, _____ Mentality, _____
Head:
   Eyes, _____. Nose, _____. Ears, _____.
   Mouth, _____. Teeth, _____. Throat, _____. Tonsil, _____. Adenoid, _____.
Chest:
   Heart, _____. Lungs, _____.
Abdomen:
   Liver, _____. Spleen, _____. Kidneys. _____.
Lymph nodes, _____. Epitrochlears, _____. Genitals, _____.
Skin, _____. Extremities, _____. Feet, _____.
Remarks _____
_____
_____

Reverse

DIAGNOSIS:

PROGNOSIS:

REFERRED TO—

LATER EXAMINATION

Date	Age	Wt.	Ht.	Notes

94535°—28——4

By the end of 1923 this pediatrician had examined 416 children, and 655 were still to be examined. The pediatric clinics of two other hospitals had begun to give their services for the examination of children in their neighborhoods. For the groups of children examined a foundation for good health work was being laid. No coercion had been placed upon the mothers, as nearly all of them were extremely glad to take advantage of the opportunity. During the examination the examining pediatrician gave the mothers advice as to diet, sleep, rest, and other matters of child care; and the examinations were followed up by the mothers' aid visitors, who conferred directly with the doctors. The report of the examination was filed with the social record. As less than half of the initial examinations had been completed no plan had been made for periodic renewal of the examinations, nor had any provision been made for a continuous health record of every child.

The social records usually did not give the family medical history unless there was some striking or unusual malady. In sending a sick child to a clinic the workers generally secured a medical report on the blank used for routine examinations. Sometimes they copied the clinic reports on their medical sheet. The reports were secured through the social-service departments of the hospitals, though the mothers' aid visitors often conferred directly with the examining physicians. Records of treatment were kept up to date through close contacts between the workers and the hospital social-service departments.

Every effort was made to persuade mothers to have the necessary remedial treatment for their children; in extreme cases it was sometimes necessary to threaten withdrawal of aid.

The employment of private physicians was discouraged in the city, since there were excellent clinical facilities, and physicians employed by the city were called only in emergencies. If a private physician of good professional reputation was supervising a family or one of its members and was willing to give his services, this supervision was encouraged.

Follow-up of special types of problems.

Tuberculosis.—Whenever a mother or child had been exposed to tuberculosis it was the policy of the department to refer the patient to one of the State tuberculosis dispensaries in the county and to insist upon regular supervision if there was a predisposition to tuberculosis. The State tuberculosis nurses visited the homes of dispensary patients and advised in regard to health habits. Residence in a sanatorium was insisted upon for active cases of tuberculosis if the doctor recommended it. The State maintained a free sanatorium and preventorium for tuberculosis at Cresson (about 80 miles from Pittsburgh), and tuberculous patients were also cared for at the Pittsburgh Sanatorium, the Tuberculosis League Hospital, and the county hospital. The Tuberculosis League maintained or assisted in maintaining nursing service that covered 22 boroughs or towns in Allegheny County. The Public Health Nursing Association also conducted a tuberculosis clinic.

Venereal disease.—Wassermann tests were given to all members of mothers' aid families who had been exposed to venereal diseases or in whom there was reason to suspect infection, and the necessary treatment was given. There was a venereal clinic at one of the hospitals, and the State department of health furnished salvarsan for treatment.

Orthopedic and cardiac affections.—Great care was exercised in providing expert orthopedic care for all crippled children, and excellent facilities were available at the Children's Hospital and the orthopedic clinics of other hospitals. The Sewickley Fresh Air Home for crippled children received applications through the Allegheny General Hospital. This home provided medical and surgical care and gave a limited vocational training. It also gave free care to cardi c and convalescent cases. The D. E. Watson Home for Crippled Girls provided medical and surgical care and vocational training for girls between 3 and 16 years of age. The Pittsburgh Industrial Home for Crippled Children received white and negro boys and girls from 3 to 16 years of age, the children attending the public schools. Braces and special apparatus were secured through the Rotary Club or the social-service departments of hospitals. There was no bus in the county for transporting crippled children to and from school. Most of the hospitals had cardiac clinics or cardiac specialists in connection with their medical clinics. Two hospital clinics assisted in placing patients in positions suitable to their physical condition.

Eye, ear, nose, and throat affections.—Examinations were made, treatments given, and operations performed at the hospital clinics. The choice of the hospital was determined largely by the locality in which the patient lived.

Dentistry.—The school dental clinics provided free care for school children. The dental school of the University of Pittsburgh gave free treatment also, but it charged for materials. There were dental clinics in several hospitals, and the Public Health Nursing Association in Pittsburgh conducted 15 clinics outside the city. The Tuberculosis League maintained or assisted in maintaining dental clinics in 12 communities outside Pittsburgh.

Health work for infants and preschool children.—The city bureau of child welfare in the department of health had charge of all the municipal child-health work and school medical inspection and nursing. The 14 child-health centers which the bureau maintained cared for children only up to 2 years of age. Mothers receiving aid were encouraged to take their babies to the centers once a week in the summer and once a month in the winter. Milk was furnished to them free or at a reduced price.

The Public Health Nursing Association, in addition to bedside nursing, maintained a variety of services, including 11 weekly baby clinics and 26 weekly health conferences for well babies. All babies under the regular care of the association were examined thoroughly once a month; mothers were asked to attend the conferences weekly, and they were visited monthly by the nurses. One health center was conducted for children between 2 and 6 years of age. The association included in its service Pittsburgh, Braddock, and McKees Rocks, and it supervised the nursing activities in 15 other communities in the county.

Under the Sheppard-Towner Act [8] the preschool division of the bureau of child health of the Pennsylvania Department of Health conducted or cooperated in the maintenance of child-health centers for children up to 6 years of age in 11 communities in the county outside Pittsburgh, and another was soon to be opened.

In Pittsburgh the mothers' aid workers saw that all babies were taken to one of the health centers. The centers furnished the mothers' aid office with reports of the examinations; but after the first connection had been established the follow-up of the babies under the care of the Public Health Nursing Association was left with the association, at its own request. The child-health centers were within fairly easy reach of most homes; the majority of the mothers could walk to one of them and none would have to change cars. Outside Pittsburgh the children of preschool age visited the centers, but there was no periodic follow-up. The medical reports were copied by the workers on the medical blanks used by the mothers' aid department.

School medical inspection.—The State law provided for yearly physical examinations of all school children.[9] In Pittsburgh they were made by the physicians on the staff of the city bureau of child health. The nurses and their assistants connected with the bureau had charge of the follow-up of the physical examinations, which included also dental examination. The nurses inspected the children in each schoolroom once a week. The department of education provided free dental care, X-ray examinations, and eye refractions for needy school children. The State department of health paid for the physical examinations in towns of less than 5,000 inhabitants; in these towns in the year prior to the study examinations had been made of only about half the school children because of lack of adequate funds. The mothers' aid visitors were expected to examine the reports of the school inspectors that were sent to the mothers and to plan with the school nurses for the correction of physical defects.

Malnutrition.—In Pittsburgh the school nurses measured and weighed the school children twice a year. If a child was 15 per cent or more underweight the parents were notified and a midmorning lunch consisting of milk and crackers was suggested. This was provided free or at cost in all schools. The department of education conducted no school nutrition classes; the State college extension department conducted one nutrition class in a public school, and three hospitals conducted classes. Outside Pittsburgh the State college extension department supervised nutrition classes in 11 schools in as many communities; the classes were conducted by the teachers, the children 10 pounds or more underweight being selected for these classes. The Junior Red Cross furnished milk to the children in the nutrition classes, and mothers' meetings were held for the purpose of instruction in proper food and care.

---

[8] See The Promotion of the Welfare and Hygiene of Maternity and Infancy—the administration of the act of Congress of Nov. 23, 1921, for fiscal year ended June 30, 1926 (U. S. Children's Bureau Publication No. 178, Washington, 1927), with text of the act on p. 85.
[9] Pa., School Code, act of May 18, 1911, secs. 1501–1505, Laws of 1911, p. 309, as amended by act of June 20, 1919, No. 253, act of June 23, 1919, No. 271, act of July 17, 1919, No. 394, Laws of 1919, pp. 511, 572, and 997, act of May 20, 1921, No. 329, Laws of 1921, p. 939. (See Pa., Stat. 1920, secs. 5070–5074, pp. 468–469; Supp. 1924, p. 142.)

The mothers' aid visitors were expected to report all cases of undernourished school children coming to their attention through the routine or other examinations to the school nurses for reexamination, midmorning lunches, and extra supervision. If necessary, provision was made for extra diet and for the instruction of the child and mother; and if possible arrangement was made for the admission of the child into one of the few nutrition classes. The mothers' aid visitors, nutrition workers, and infant welfare and school nurses all gave the mothers advice on nutrition as they came in contact with them.

Results of health supervision in two families.

Mrs. H., a widow, had four sons under 12 years of age, a 16-year-old daughter, an 18-year-old son, and an older son who was married. The married son, his wife, and their two children lived with Mrs. H. This family of 11 persons lived in a dilapidated four-room house 1½ miles from the street car and at the top of a steep hill. The 18-year-old son and an 11-year-old son had heart lesions, the former dropping one job after another because of this condition, and both being seriously affected by the long walk from the street car up the hill to their home. The house was dirty and cluttered; Mrs. H. was lackadaisical and indifferent and left the housekeeping largely to her daughter-in-law. As a result of the physical examination made in connection with the granting of an allowance to Mrs. H., the daughter's eyes were treated, and the four younger boys had tonsils and adenoids removed and circumcisions performed. The 18-year-old son was advised to enter a vocational school where he could learn tailoring, and his physical condition and mental attitude both showed marked improvement thereafter. After many weeks of coaxing Mrs. H. submitted reluctantly to a physical examination and accepted the medical and dental care that she needed. She was aided also in finding work. Within the 18 months during which this family had been receiving aid and was under supervision Mrs. H. became a different woman, not only in her improved physical condition but also in her outlook upon life. The family moved to a much better locality, everything was kept spotlessly clean, and all the members of the family were neatly dressed.

When Mrs. M. was granted an allowance her five children, all under 8 years of age, were undernourished and exceedingly timid. The twins, then 7 years old, ran away and hid when the visitor came to the house. They were backward in school, and the teacher stated that they cried on the slightest provocation. The mother appeared dull, though everyone spoke of her as a willing worker and devoted to her children. Physical examinations revealed that the twins were greatly underweight and had serious physical defects. The next younger child was mentally defective and finally was committed to an institution for the feeble-minded. A 4-year-old boy had diseased tonsils, which were removed. The children all came regularly to the clinics and much corrective work was done. The twins were entered in a nutrition class, to which their mother brought them regularly. At first they refused the unaccustomed food, but within a year they were up to their normal weight, owing largely to their mother's cooperation. Part of the treatment consisted of a recreational program. During the holidays and week ends the visitor took the children, their mother, and the grandmother (who lived with the family) to the zoological park and to the department stores to see seasonable exhibits. Summer outings were arranged, and the family went to a vacation camp, which was a great source of happiness. Mrs. M. showed real delight after the worker accustomed her to taking the children several times a week in hot weather to the parks for all-day or half-day picnics. A great change came over the children; their school work improved greatly, and they became friendly, unafraid, and spontaneous. The mother developed also, becoming more resourceful. She took the children to the clinic on her own initiative, and as she could leave the children with her mother she began to look for part-time regular employment instead of doing washing at home.

MENTAL HEALTH

Available facilities.

The Pittsburgh Department of Public Welfare maintained a psychological clinic with a psychiatric social worker on its staff. The mothers' aid department referred to this clinic all mental problems, including psychopathic and behavior cases that were not cared for by the psychological department of the public schools. The mothers' aid visitors followed the clinic's recommendation and reported to the psychiatric worker from time to time on psychopathic and problem cases. The staff of the psychological bureau of the department of education consisted of a psychologist, who was also a physician, and an assistant psychologist, who was a social worker. No child was placed in a special class or removed from one without a mental examination, and routine examinations were made as long as the child remained in the class. The bureau was used principally for this purpose, though the teachers and principals of the public schools might refer to the bureau any school child who presented a mental problem. Schools were encouraged to refer problem and psychopathic children to the bureau for examination. Three of the hospitals had neuropsychological clinics, and the St. Francis Hospital had a ward for the observation of psychopathic cases.

Follow-up of special types of problems.

It was the policy of the mothers' aid department to request psychological examinations for school children who were 3 or more years retarded unless there were obvious physical defects that might account for the retardation. Children under 16 years of age who were truants, who were becoming incorrigible, or who were developing delinquent tendencies were given psychological examinations. Prevailing upon children over 16 to submit to an examination was not always possible. Children whose fathers had been insane or in whose families there had been insanity were not examined as a matter of routine unless they, too, presented symptoms of unbalance. Emphasis was laid upon having a psychiatric examination promptly if evidence of mental difficulty appeared. The proportion of children between 14 and 20 years of age who developed psychopathic symptoms or behavior difficulties was high, especially in Pittsburgh among children of foreign-born parents.

Illustrative case histories.

Antoinette A.'s father was in a hospital for the insane with a diagnosis of dementia præcox. Mrs. A. spoke almost no English, but she kept her one cheerful front room in exquisite condition and thought her 12-year-old daughter Antoinette a model of behavior because she would sit with hands folded in her lap all day. The visitor had the child mentally examined within two weeks of the teacher's report. The psychologist stated that Antoinette was suffering from depression, that she reacted scarcely at all, had no free spontaneous emotional life, and would be almost sure to go the way of her father if something were not done right away to stimulate her mental and emotional nature; she must be made to play and to express herself. The visitor's first task was to tell the mother that she must not let the child sit with folded hands, that that was not "perfect behavior" in Antoinette's case. It was not so easy to persuade her, and a few weeks later the visitor took with her a coworker who could explain in Mrs. A.'s native Italian. A book of fairy tales was left, and the visitor prevailed upon the mother to let Antoinette join a girls' church club. Three months later the report read as follows: "Antoinette is now very interested in reading and gets books regularly from the library. At first she got only fairy tales, then Alice in Wonderland, then the Life of General George Washington, which she liked best of all. The visitor gave her a list of good biographies and autobiographies which she promised to read. Antoinette now belongs to a club connected with the church that she attends and is much interested in its meetings. She goes quite regularly, and her mother never interferes but is encouraging her to go out more." Every means was used to arouse Antoinette's emotions and objective interests. She was in the habit of biting her finger nails very badly; the visitor gave her a manicure set, which appealed to her pride, and now she takes a great deal of care of her nails.

When Mrs. O. was first granted mothers' assistance she was harassed by business troubles in connection with real-estate deals left unsettled by her husband at his death. She was also obsessed by all sorts of imaginary fears; she was afraid to leave the house because it might be dynamited; she was afraid to let the children out of her sight lest they be burned; she was afraid to go out in company lest she say something wrong and the neighbors would molest her; she was afraid to go to a hospital for an examination which she needed or to a dentist to have her decayed teeth extracted; she was afraid of the policeman on the beat and of the health officer. Then she was examined by a psychiatrist who attributed her disturbed state to the unhappiness of her married life and thus helped her somewhat to understand the cause of her fears. He advised her to talk about her past to her friends, thereby relieving her mind.

The first victory over her fears was her consent to have the children examined at a hospital clinic. She finally came to the conclusion that the knives that flashed before her mind's eye and the screams that tortured her ears were imaginary and consented to be examined herself. One of her sons was responsible for the second victory; he had six of his teeth extracted, and his mother decided she could not be less brave than he. The latest triumph up to the time of the study was overcoming her fear of lawyers and courts. The roof leaked, the steps and the railing were falling down, the house needed painting, and other repairs were necessary. She was persuaded by the mothers' aid visitor to borrow money from a building association through the orphans' court and the repairs were made, a kind-hearted lawyer doing the legal work free of charge. Formerly the mother's neurotic condition was reflected in the worried faces and manners of the children, but since she had been able to put her mental house in order their emotional life, too, had become much more stable. She moved from the two rooms on the second floor to the rooms on the first floor of the house which she was buying through a building association. She took great pride in arranging the furnishings and said the children loved to entertain their friends in the "living room" and she "didn't have time now to sit around and worry."

HOUSING

A large section of Pittsburgh is built on the steep bluffs and along the river basins of the Allegheny, Monongahela, and Ohio Rivers, by the side of which stretch the tracks of five different railroad lines and the great blast furnaces and steel mills. The topography in connection with industrial conditions thus induced congestion and in general an unfavorable housing situation.

The exceedingly high cost of living, especially the high rents, and the lack of housing and recreational resources made it difficult for the poorer families, especially those of foreign birth, to maintain proper standards of physical health and family life. Efforts were made to move a family if the neighborhood was morally bad or unusually congested or if the house was insanitary.

Though rents were uniformly high, families in the suburbs were much better cared for than those in the city; a considerable number lived in good frame houses. As a rule in the city a mother and three or four children had a flat of three rooms and sometimes more; there were separate sleeping rooms for boys and girls, and not more than two persons slept in the same bed. A living room was considered essential, though not always attainable, and often it was turned into a sleeping room by night. Sanitary toilets were required, though sometimes two and three families used the same toilet. Few families had the luxury of bathrooms; the majority had running water; nearly all used gas and a few electricity; few had ice boxes. In the city of Pittsburgh it was not possible for many families to grow flowers or vegetables.

The majority of mothers receiving aid paid between $20 and $30 a month rent and some paid as much as $40. Thirty-seven families owned their own homes in whole or in part.

EDUCATION

COOPERATION WITH THE SCHOOLS AND FACILITIES FOR EDUCATION

Contacts with the schools.

It was the plan of the mothers' aid administration that all schools attended by children receiving aid should be visited twice a year. The school reports were not examined as a matter of routine, but special report blanks furnished by the State supervisor were filled out twice a year by the teachers for each child in the families receiving aid. For problem children these reports were sometimes required oftener. The report form used was as follows:

Commonwealth of Pennsylvania
Department of Public Welfare
Mothers' Assistance Fund

SCHOOL STANDING AND ATTENDANCE RECORD.

City,
Name of school, _____ Township, _____
Borough,
Report of _____ Address, _____
Grade, _____ Age, _____ Date, _____
Month
The records of this school for the period of _____ show the following:
Term
Attendance: No. of times tardy, _____ No. of days absent, _____
Reasons for absence or tardiness, _____
Scholarship: Excellent, _____ Good, _____ Fair, _____ Deficient, _____
Deficient branches, _____
Conduct: _____
Remarks in re physical defects, personal appearance, etc., _____
_____
(Signed) _____
Teacher.

Provision for handicapped children.

The physically handicapped child.—The orthopedic ward of the Children's Hospital was supplied with a teacher by the education department. The bureau of rehabilitation in the State department of labor and industry provided tuition for the vocational training of any crippled person and supplied funds for board if the person was crippled as the result of an industrial accident. In the public schools there were five teachers for children with speech defects, but no sight-conservation classes nor classes for the deaf. Provision was made for blind children or those who were partly blind, and also for deaf-and-dumb children through the State institutions for the blind and for the deaf and dumb. A workshop in Pittsburgh gave vocational training to blind residents of the city.

The mentally handicapped child.—There were 11 special classes in the public schools and 5 more were in process of organization at the time of the study.

Provision for children wishing further education.

As has been stated, the policy of the mothers' assistance board was to encourage exceptional children and even those of only normal ability to continue their school work as long as possible. Jewish children in families receiving mothers' aid were eligible to scholarships given by the Irene Kaufman Settlement, the only organized agency administering scholarship funds in Pittsburgh. These were open to boys and girls over 14 years of age for high school, business school, vocational school, college, or musical or art or other training. The high-school scholarships were $15 a month for the 10 months of the school year. For children attending school where tuition was charged the scholarship usually covered two-thirds of the tuition, sometimes all of it. At the time of the study 31 scholarships (amounting to a total of $4,000) were available.

Scholarships in the University of Pittsburgh were available to persons who qualified for them, and it was known that one boy in a mothers' aid family had been granted such a scholarship. Two girls were known to hold scholarships at the time of the study, one to attend high school and another to take a business course.

The following story illustrates the educational advantages of which some children were making good use:

Mrs. R. was a confirmed neurotic. She had living with her her daughter Elizabeth, who was 15 years old, and a son, Frederick, who was 12. Elizabeth was a sensible, wholesome girl and assumed much responsibility in the home. She frequently came to the visitor to talk over her plans and took her counsel in matters of health, diet, and recreation. Frederick also had an excellent school record and was eager to study electrical engineering. Relatives of Mrs. R.'s husband contributed $20 a month and part of the rent and did many kindly acts besides, such as providing summer outings for the family. The home of four rooms and bath had been made more confortable by attractive furnishings given by relatives, and the children could entertain their schoolmates in their own living room. Elizabeth was a senior in high school and had always ranked high in scholarship. She was on the personal column of the school paper and had been elected to the national honor society to which all students ranking in the upper fourth of their class were eligible. She was anxious to become a librarian, but as she would be under 16 when she graduated from high school she would not be eligible for the library course at the Carnegie Library. A plan had been made for her to enter college for one year and then take the library course, or if that was impossible to take a position as page in the library for one year.

The Carnegie Institute of Technology offered extension courses in the evenings and on Saturdays, and many boys who would profit by the work had been entered in these classes. One boy who lived in the surburbs could not ride in the cars on account of car sickness. The visitor arranged for him to drive into town every Saturday morning with a neighbor to attend a class in draftsmanship. When he went to work at 16 he secured an excellent position in the drafting room of a large steel plant. Soon after he entered the mill he won a prize of $25 offered for the best mechanical drawing in connection with work at the plant.

Twenty-four boys and girls over 16 years of age were attending evening classes. One of these was studying English, another drafting, another dressmaking; the remaining 21 were taking secretarial and bookkeeping courses. A company manufacturing electrical equipment conducted a school shop course on the apprenticeship plan, and much effort had been expended to interest boys in the work and to place them in positions. Three or four boys in families receiving mothers' aid were taking the course at the time of the study. Nineteen children were taking music lessons.

SCHOOLING AND WORK OF CHILDREN 14 AND 15 YEARS OLD

The child-labor, compulsory-education, and mothers' aid laws.

According to the child-labor and compulsory-education laws, children could obtain employment certificates at 14 years of age if they had completed the sixth grade and were physically fit.[10] Unemployed children were not excused from school attendance except for mental, physical, or other urgent reasons.[11] Working children 14 and 15 years old were required to attend continuation school eight hours a week.[12]

The mothers' aid law permitted allowances to be granted for children up to 16 years of age provided the children were in school with satisfactory school record or were physically unable to earn wages on attaining the age necessary for an employment certificate.

Children in school and at work.

The board of trustees of the mothers' assistance fund occasionally encouraged a boy or girl over 16 years of age to complete a course of study; this was made possible by continuing for younger brothers or sisters the allowances that would have been withdrawn if the 16-year-old child had gone to work and earned enough to make the grants no longer necessary for the younger members of the family.

There were 203 children (94 boys and 109 girls) 14 and 15 years of age in the families receiving aid; 102 of them were 14 years old and 101 were 15 years old. Of these 203 children 164 were attending school, 32 were working, and 7 were neither attending school nor working.

Children in school.—Among the 164 children 14 and 15 years old attending school were 128 who had completed the sixth grade and therefore were eligible for employment certificates so far as educational requirements were concerned.[13]

The number of boys and girls 14 and 15 years old who were attending school and the grade or type of school attended are shown in the following table:

---

[10] Pa., act of May 18, 1911, sec. 1416, Laws of 1911, p. 309, as amended by act of May 20, 1921, No. 373, sec. 1, Laws of 1921, p. 1034. (Pa., Stat. 1920, sec. 5045, p. 466; Supp. 1924, p. 142.)
[11] Pa., act of May 18, 1911, sec. 1415, Laws of 1911, p. 309. (Pa., Stat. 1920, sec. 5044, p. 465.)
[12] Pa., act of May 13, 1915, No. 177, sec. 3, Laws of 1915, p. 286. (Pa., Stat. 1920, sec. 13287, p. 1308.)
[13] This number was more than four-fifths (83 per cent) of all the children in mothers' aid families who had fulfilled the school-grade requirements for going to work (155).

Number of children 14 and 15 years old who were attending school at the time of the study, by grade or type of school; Allegheny County, Pa.

Grade or type of school	Total	Children 14 and 15 years old attending school				
		Boys			Girls		
		Total	14 years	15 years	Total	14 years	15 years
Total	164	74	40	34	90	50	40
Elementary school:							
Fourth grade	2				2	1	1
Fifth grade	12	7	5	2	5	4	1
Sixth grade	21	15	10	5	6	2	4
Seventh grade	32	13	8	5	19	13	6
Eighth grade	50	22	9	13	28	13	15
High school:							
First year	26	8	6	2	18	11	7
Second year	10	4	1	3	6	3	3
Third year	3	1		1	2	1	1
Fourth year	1				1	1	
Business school	4	1	1		3	1	2
Other and not reported	¹3	3		3			

¹ 1 was attending vocational school and 1 an industrial training school.

In addition to the 4 children in business school 19 of those in other types of school were taking commercial courses. The 15-year-old girl in the third year of high school was taking a teachers' training course. Five children were preparing themselves for special types of work such as drawing, drafting, printing, and electrical wiring.

Occupations and earnings of the working children.—The occupations of the 32 children 14 and 15 years old who were working were as follows:

	Number of children		Number of children
Total	32	Messenger	1
		Worker in poolroom	1
Boys	21	Not reported	2
Laborer	7	Girls	11
Clerk in store	4		
Factory worker	2	Factory worker	3
Elevator boy	2	Houseworker	4
Clerical worker	1	Waitress	1
Errand boy	1	Clerk in store	3

The 32 working children had been enrolled in the following grades when they left school to work: Two in the first year of high school, 9 in the eighth grade, 10 in the seventh grade, 9 in the sixth grade, 1 in the fifth grade, and 1 in the fourth grade.

The monthly earnings of these children were as follows:

	Number of children		Number of children
Total	32	$40, under $50	4
		$50, under $60	3
$15	1	$60, under $70	7
$20, under $30	4	Over $70	2
$30, under $40	9	Not reported	2

Twenty-six of the 30 children whose earnings were reported were giving all their earnings to their mothers. A girl who was earning $22 a month was contributing $17 a month to the support of the family; one who was earning $25 was contributing $20; another who was earning $28 was contributing $24; and the fourth, who was earning $65, was contributing $39.

Children neither in school nor at work.

The seven children 14 and 15 years of age who were neither in school nor working were all girls. The grades in which six of them had been enrolled when they left school to work were from the sixth to the ninth; for one girl no report was given as to grade. Only one of them had left school under 14 years of age. Three of the seven had been employed previously but were out of work at the time of the study; two had not been employed but were planning to enter employment; and two were helping their mothers at home.

EDUCATIONAL ACTIVITIES FOR THE MOTHERS

The Pennsylvania law did not require citizenship for mothers receiving allowances, but the board of trustees encouraged mothers who were not citizens to apply for citizenship; mothers of foreign birth who did not speak English were encouraged to attend citizenship English classes. Five women attended classes conducted by the International Institute of the Young Women's Christian Association, seven attended classes in English or citizenship at the public schools, and eight were enrolled in sewing and cooking classes at the various settlement and neighborhood centers.

RECREATION

The allowance for incidentals covered recreation except for working children, who were allowed about $10 a month for lunches and pocket money. This varied according to individual conditions.

Facilities for recreation were not abundant, and because of the housing shortage it was seldom possible to have families move to be near them. In Pittsburgh the chief sources of recreation were motion pictures, playgrounds, scout troops, the activities of the churches and the International Institute of the Young Women's Christian Association, settlements, parks, free concerts, and summer camps. Nearly all the families were connected with some church, and the mothers' aid workers encouraged participation in church activities by the whole family. Two down-town churches conducted neighborhood activities and the high schools had an educational and recreational program. Children were encouraged to have their good times at the nearest settlement or social center and the workers spent considerable time getting the older children in touch with the neighborhood centers or scout troops. About 150 boys and girls were known to be affiliated with some wholesome recreational activity. A few mothers took the children in summer on weekly picnics to the zoological garden and parks, and about half the mothers and children were sent on summer vacations. Working children were encouraged to purchase inexpensive musical instruments in order that family pleasures might be taken together.

MOTHERS' ALLOWANCES IN BERKS COUNTY, PA.[1]

ADMINISTRATION OF THE LAW [2]

ADMINISTRATIVE AGENCY AND STAFF

The board of trustees of the Berks County Mothers' Assistance Fund consisted of seven women who had been intimately identified with the philanthropic and civic work of the county. Six had served continuously since the organization of the work in 1918 and the seventh had served five years. In the earlier years of the work the trustees had assumed a large responsibility for regular family visiting, and at the time of this study all but one were doing some visiting in the homes. The president in addition to this had carried considerable responsibility for the supervision of the executive work of the office. The vice president had organized and perfected a system for the tabulation of office statistics and of the mothers' household-expense accounts, and another trustee was giving almost full time to the organization of the home-craft shop. (See pp. 55–56.)

The staff consisted of an executive secretary who did some field work, a field worker, and a clerk-stenographer. The executive secretary had had two years of college work; her previous experience had been in the charity-organization, juvenile-court, and hospital social service fields. The case worker had had no previous social-work experience but had been a member of the mothers' aid staff for five years. One automobile was at the service of the staff.

APPROPRIATION [3] AND VOLUME OF WORK

The State appropriation to Berks County for the biennium June 1, 1923, to May 31, 1925, was $65,550. This when matched by county funds permitted a possible annual expenditure of $65,550. The actual expenditure of the county for both grants and administration from June 1, 1923, to May 31, 1924, was $45,989.44. The unexpended surplus may be accounted for in part perhaps by the fact that although Berks County had a population of more than 200,000 but less than

---

[1] The population of Berks County in 1920 was 200,854; 107,784 of this number lived in the city of Reading. The native white population of the county numbered 187,582, the foreign-born white 12,097, and the negroes 1,165. There were 61,897 children within legal age for mothers' aid. The population of foreign birth, listed in the order of their numerical importance, was as follows: Polish, Italian, German, Russian, and Austrian. (Fourteenth Census of the United States, 1920, vol. 3, Population, pp. 857, 859, 883, 885, Washington, 1922.) The chief industries of the county center about the knitting mills, the foundries, and the machine shops. In the country districts there are many large and prosperous farms. The residents are largely descendants of Germans from the Palatinate who came over during the first part of the eighteenth century and the migration of 1848. The people have the characteristic Pennsylvania German traits—thrift, cleanliness, kindliness, love of the soil, a strong sense of family and neighborhood solidarity, the recognition of authority, and the acceptance of traditions of their forefathers.

[2] The provisions of the Pennsylvania law and the extent of State supervision have been discussed in the section of this report dealing with Allegheny County, Pa., pp. 29–31.

[3] Details of the law governing the State appropriations and county apportionments are given in the section of this report dealing with Allegheny County, Pa. (See pp. 32–33.)

53

1,000,000, so that it was one of the five counties designated by law to receive equal parts of a 19 per cent allotment from the sum set aside for apportionment among the counties by the law (see p. 33), the population over 200,000 consisted of only 800 inhabitants.

During February, 1924, mothers' aid was being given to 87 families, including 316 children under 16 years of age. The supervision was fairly evenly divided between the executive and the field assistant.

USE OF A STANDARD BUDGET [4]

The budget of the New York Nutrition Council was used for food, clothing, and sundries and that of the Chicago standard budget for household furnishings and health needs.[5] The budget was as follows:

Rent: Amount paid.
Sundries: $1 a month per person with a maximum of $7 for a family.
Food: Same as Allegheny County budget. (See pp. 34-35.)
Clothing:
    Woman at work _____ $7.50
    Woman at home _____ 5.53
    Older girl at work _____ 7.50
    Older boy at work _____ 7.44
    Girl 10–14 years _____ 4.41
    Boy 10–14 years _____ 4.54
    Child 6–10 years _____ 3.62
    Child 3–6 years _____ 2.67
    Child of 2 or under _____ 2.73
Household furnishings and supplies:
    Family of 2 members _____ 3.00
    Family of 3 or 4 members _____ 3.75
    Family of 5 or 6 members _____ 4.50
    Family of 7 or 8 members _____ 5.25
    Family of 9 or 10 members _____ 6.00
Health: Where public physicians and nurses are used 25 cents per month and up for each person.
Fuel and light:
    $9.50 per month for city families.
    $8 per month for rural families.

It was the policy of the board to make the grant large enough to cover the family budget so far as the maximum allowed under the law permitted. Unfortunately, the maximum of $20 for the first child and $10 for each additional child was not adequate for families in which the mother, because of illness or the care of several young children, could not do any work except her own housework, nor was it sufficient for families of two or three children. The average monthly grant per family and per child for February, 1924, was $39.50 and $11.80, respectively. The largest grant was $90, the smallest $20.

Every mother receiving aid kept, or had the children keep for her, an itemized monthly household-expense account covering all expenses and all income. This was made the basis for constructive suggestions regarding such matters as a balanced diet, the prepara-

---

[4] Procedure in making allowances has been discussed in the section of this report dealing with Allegheny County, Pa. (See pp. 33–34.)
[5] See footnotes 6 and 7, p. 34.

tion of foods, marketing, and planning a household budget. It was explained carefully to each mother that the account was not a form of espionage, but that the trustees acting for the State were anxious that the mothers should receive the full value of their money and that the children should have nutritious food, and, furthermore, that the good management of one mother would prove a source of helpful information to others. (For copies of the forms used see pp. 37–39.)

Literature on proper food and health habits had been distributed to the families. It was the general opinion that the mothers who were ignorant or were careless in the management of their homes had been much helped in improving the dietary and general home standards. The board had voted to employ a trained dietitian to make a home-economics and nutritional survey during the coming summer. The expense accounts afforded invaluable material for this purpose. It was hoped that the survey would lead to a closer correlation of the nutritional work and health work.[6]

The mothers were told that they need not be afraid to report money spent for recreation, as the column heading "Good times" indicated that the families were expected to have pleasure and fun.

When the F. family began keeping the expense account it was intrusted to the 15-year-old son, Thaddeus, who was the sole breadwinner. The visitor explained what each column meant, especially the one headed "Good times." Thaddeus had been working so hard for the family that it seemed best to impress upon him that better times were in store for him. When the visitor inspected the account she found that every day under "Good times" had been entered "milk, 6 cents." When she asked Thaddeus what it meant he explained "Since we have the money I can buy a pint of milk every day at the factory, so that is a 'good time' for me."

SUPPLEMENTING OF MOTHERS' AID

Sources of supplementary relief.

The board refrained from asking for supplementary aid from either a private family agency or the county poor board, as it was understood that the mothers' assistance fund assumed complete responsibility for the families to whom it granted aid. All supplementary relief, therefore, had to be organized through various resources, including private benevolences. Emergencies were often met through personal contributions by members of the board. At the time of the study 27 of the 87 grants were inadequate according to the budget standards.

The home-craft shop.

On request the president of the board of trustees prepared the following statement in regard to the home-craft shop:

After administering the mothers' assistance fund in Berks County for several years the trustees of that fund came to the conclusion that the greatest need

---

[6] The home-economics and nutritional survey proved so valuable that a full-time trained home economist was employed on the Berks County mothers' aid staff from July, 1924, until September, 1926.

of the pensioned mothers was an opportunity to do home work which would be remunerative.

For a mother with two or three children under school age some means must be found to supplement the maximum grant, which is not sufficient for the support of a family. The mother can not leave her children to go out to work, and the only available home work in Berks County is stuffing tobacco, which is insanitary; taping underwear, which is tedious and poorly paid; and laundry work, which is back breaking.

In order to supply this need for home work the trustees of the mothers' assistance fund established a home-craft shop in an old log cabin one-half block from the central square in Reading. A letter was sent to every mother receiving a grant in Berks County asking her these questions: 1. What means she was using to get the extra money in order to live. 2. What work she had done before she was married. 3. What she liked best to do and would do best. The last question was emphasized because the trustees felt that an opportunity should be given the mothers for self-expression so that a certain joy in the work might be achieved. The shop is not yet self-supporting, but the outlook is encouraging, and the quality of production is improving every week. An effort is constantly made to have the mothers enjoy the association with beautiful things and afternoon tea is served whenever there is a group of mothers or purchasers in the log cabin about teatime.[7]

VISITING

All mothers' assistance families in Reading were visited by a member of the staff once a month. More frequent visits were made if necessary. Families living in the country were not visited quite so often because of the condition of the roads. The mothers were expected to call at the office one Saturday morning a month to bring their expense accounts. As has been stated, the trustees also did friendly visiting more or less regularly.

HEALTH

PHYSICAL HEALTH

The allowance for health was that provided by the Chicago standard budget.

Physical examinations.

Before a grant was made a physical examination was required for the mothers and for all children under 16 years of age. The examinations generally were made by the family's regular physician; occasionally they were made at a clinic or at a child-health center. Blanks were supplied to the mother when she applied, and it was the understanding that physicians were to charge, if anything, only a nominal fee. The medical report was filed with the record.

The following are the medical-report forms used for the children and for the mothers:

---

[7] The shop has been abandoned because after several years' trial it was found impossible to run on a self-supporting basis.

BERKS COUNTY, PA.

MOTHERS' ASSISTANCE FUND

PHYSICAL RECORD

Date of examination, _____
Name, _____ Age, _____ Sex, _____ Nationality, _____

Family history (cause of death):   Physical or mental disabilities:
    Father, _____   Father, _____
    Mother, _____   Mother, _____ Miscarriages, _____
    Children, _____   Children, _____

Previous medical history—Birth {Normal, _____ / Instrumental, _____}   Term {9 mos., _____ / Premature, _____}

Feeding {Bottle, _____ / Breast, _____}

Previous illness, including accidents—1. _____ 2. _____. 3. _____
4. _____ 5. _____ 6. _____ 7. _____
Vaccination and special tests—_____ _____ _____

Physical examination:
    Height, _____ Weight (without topcoat and shoes) (child should be
       stripped, _____   General appearance, _____
    Nutrition—Normal, _____ Malnutrition, _____   Mentality, _____
    Scalp, _____   Eyes {Normal, _____ / Glasses, _____}   Nose {Normal, _____ / Obstruction, _____}
    Ears {Normal, _____ / Discharge, _____ / Defective hearing, _____}   Teeth—No. of upper {Regular, _____ / Irregular, _____}
    No. of lower {Regular, _____ / Irregular, _____}   Cavities, _____   Hutchinson's_____   Throat, _____
    Glands, _____ Tonsils, _____ {Normal, _____ / Enlarged, _____ / Diseased, _____ / Removed, _____}   Speech {Normal, _____ / Defective, ____}
    Chest—Shape, _____   Development, _____   Expansion, _____
    Heart (examine before and after exertion). Murmur, _____ Rate, _____
    Lungs, _____ Abdomen—Large, _____ Distended, _____ Tender, _____
    Genitalia {Normal, _____ / Abnormal, _____}   Discharge, _____   Hernia, _____
    Bones and joints, _____   Deformities, _____   Skin, _____
    Nerves, _____ Muscles, _____

Indications for laboratory reports, _____

Recommendations, _____

Signature of examiner—Dr. _____

ADULT HEALTH SHEET

Name, _____ Age, _____ Date of examination, _____
Physical examination, _____ Nutrition, _____
_____
_____
Head:
    Eyes, _____
    Throat, _____
    Neck, _____
Lungs, _____
Heart, _____ Pulse, _____
Abdomen, _____
Menstruation, _____
Extremities, _____
        Signature of doctor, _____

The mothers were uniformly willing to comply with the ruling in regard to the preliminary examination. Its educational value depended largely upon the physician who made the examination and the medical work that followed. Mothers were required to have defects remedied with reasonable promptness, and it was rarely necessary to force the issue by threatening withdrawal of the grant.

Follow-up of special types of problems.

The follow-up of the medical reports was done by the mothers' aid visitors. Defects were corrected at the clinics of the St. Joseph's Hospital and the Reading Hospital. A number of private physicians and specialists gave a great deal of free service, and in special cases patients were taken to Philadelphia hospitals. As a rule the mothers' aid workers did not have a personal conference with the examining physician unless there was a special problem or unless the patient was receiving continuous treatment; in the latter case the physician was consulted and an understanding arrived at as to fees. For the year 1923 the sum of $1,947.81 was spent for medical services by the 95 families receiving mothers' aid. Physicians employed by the city were not called upon; in an emergency the mothers could send for a private physician.

The preliminary physical examinations were not followed up by periodic examinations unless there was obvious need for continued medical supervision. Written diagnoses were generally secured for patients who were referred to clinics and hospitals for specific medical or surgical care, but oral diagnoses were the rule from private physicians. None of the hospitals were equipped with social-service departments.

Entries were made in the running record of all medical work done and of physical defects and ailments as revealed by the statements of the families. With the comparatively small number of families under care it was not difficult to keep track of the health needs. An attempt had been made to compile a continuous health record for each individual in the families under care, but so far a satisfactory blank for keeping this record had not been devised.

Mothers' aid workers, school and infant-welfare nurses, and physicians advised the mothers in regard to health habits, and literature on feeding and on infant and child care had been given to the mothers by the department.

Orthopedic and cardiac affections.—Expert orthopedic treatment was secured for all crippled children. In general, private orthopedists gave their services, and occasionally children were taken to specialists in Philadelphia. Crippled children in two families receiving mothers' aid had been under the supervision of orthopedic surgeons during 1923. Braces and other special appliances were secured through the Rotary Club or were given by members of the board of trustees. Children in two families had received care for cardiac difficulties in 1923. Private physicians gave this medical supervision.

Eye, ear, nose, and throat affections.—A private specialist gave his services in eye, ear, nose, and throat cases, both for the examinations, which he made at his office, and for operations, which he performed at St. Joseph's Hospital. The school department made eye examinations and furnished glasses to school children. A manufacturer in a small town in the county whose sister-in-law at one time had received a grant was so grateful for the oculist's care given by the board for his young nephews and nieces that when he was asked to supply their glasses he offered to donate glasses to any needy child in a family receiving mothers' aid. As the glasses provided by the school department were fitted into inexpensive frames, he made a practice of donating better frames and the lenses also if the school did not furnish them or if the person needing them was not in school. One or more individuals in 37 families had been treated for eye, ear, nose, or throat difficulties during 1923.

Health work for infants and preschool children.—The Reading Visiting Nurse Association, which employed 28 nurses, was commissioned by the city department of health to carry on the child-health work in Reading, the expense being borne in part by the city government. Eleven child-health centers were maintained in school buildings in the city. Ten of these were open three hours once a week and one was open daily; in the summer four conferences were held daily. The centers were within fairly easy reach of all homes, and no mother needed to change cars. Although mothers were encouraged to bring children up to 6 years of age to the centers, the emphasis was laid primarily upon work for children under 2. The board of trustees encouraged mothers with babies to attend the centers, but did not check up on their attendance. In May, 1924, the children under 6 years of age in three families were receiving regular supervision at the centers, and the children in some other families were taken occasionally.

Outside Reading the preschool division of the bureau of child health of the State department of health conducted two centers under the Sheppard-Towner Act [8] in cooperation with other agencies, and the Reading Visiting Nurse Association conducted one center. Although this association did not hold prenatal conferences, it gave prenatal care to such women as came under its observation. All birth registrations were followed up by a visit to the home. Eight women who were beneficiaries of mothers' aid received prenatal care during 1923.

In Reading the school children were given a physical examination (including dental inspection) yearly (see p. 44) by a physician, and later in the year were inspected by a nurse. Eight school nurses and one dental hygienist were employed. School inspections were made when deemed necessary, and visits were made at least once a week. The mothers' aid visitors had not made a practice of examining the school medical reports, but they planned to do so in the future. The form for the school reports of the children in mothers' aid families, which were sent by the teachers to the mothers' aid office, called for a statement in regard to physical defects, and the teachers generally noted any defects brought to light by the school medical inspection.

Malnutrition.—In Reading all school children were weighed and measured as a part of the physical examination twice each year, and among the children in the fourth, fifth, and sixth grades health cap-

---

[8] See footnote 8, p. 44.

tains were chosen, who recorded weight and height once a month. There were no nutrition classes in the city; the nurses gave some individual instruction to undernourished children, and milk was sold to them at a reduced price. Children who could not afford to buy were supplied free through the Reading Sanitarium for Treatment of Tuberculosis (the antituberculosis society).

During 1923 one or more children in five families were diagnosed as undernourished and received treatment and supervision. Milk was given to them to drink at school, and summer vacations were provided at the recreation home of the Reading Nurse Association.

MENTAL HEALTH

An alienist from the State hospital for the insane at Wernersville, Pa. (10 miles from Reading), with the assistance of a psychologist from the State bureau of mental health, conducted a mental clinic in Reading once a month. There was no social-service worker attached to the clinic, and all follow-up was done by the mothers' aid workers. Any adult or child presenting a mental problem might be referred to this clinic. A preliminary physical examination was not required. The school medical inspector examined retarded or subnormal children who were referred to him by the teachers for placement in a special class.

It was the policy of the mothers' assistance board to require that any child in a family receiving mothers' aid who was three or more years retarded in school should be tested at the mental clinic; instructions were followed up by the visitors.

Psychological or psychiatric examinations were not given as a matter of routine even if there was a family history of mental defect or disease; for example, if the father was in a hospital for the insane no examination of the children was made unless mental difficulty was obvious or suspected. If institutional care was recommended application was made to the State school for the feeble-minded at Spring City, Pa., to the training school for feeble-minded children at Elwyn, Pa., or to the colony for feeble-minded women at Laurelton, Pa. All institutions had long waiting lists, and facilities were far from adequate to meet the need.

Up to the time of this study no children in mothers' aid families had been given psychological or psychiatric examinations because of incorrigibility or other delinquency. Only two or three children had given any trouble in this regard. Mothers or children with psychopathic symptoms were observed and given a mental examination if possible.

HOUSING

The majority of families receiving mothers' aid in Reading lived in small, four or five room, semidetached, or row brick houses. There were no tenements. The houses had some space in the rear and at the front, and many of them had bright flower patches. The mothers' aid families lived in clean, well-cared-for homes with sufficient rooms and an abundance of light and sunshine. Families in the city had running water and gas, and they generally had ice in the summer; about one-fourth of the families had electricity. Eighteen of the 87 families had inside toilets, and a few had bathrooms; the rest used outdoor sanitary toilets or closets.

Care was exercised that the houses should be sanitary, but it was not always easy to prevail upon a landlord to make repairs. The women themselves did much papering and repairing. None of the homes were in morally bad neighborhoods. Thirty-three families owned their homes either in whole or in part, and were thus able to live in old, well-established neighborhoods. Some lived with relatives. On applying for aid families were encouraged to retain the ownership of their homes or to invest in a home any savings they possessed up to the limit of $1,500. They were permitted to make monthly payments through a building and loan association, providing these payments and the upkeep did not exceed a reasonable rent.

The 30 rural families living outside Reading occupied single houses with space for vegetable and flower gardens. A few lived on farms. The highest monthly rent paid in the city was $30 and the lowest $6.50; in the country the highest rent was $15 and the lowest $4. There was no limit fixed for rental, but the families were required to keep within a reasonable amount.

Mrs. G. had resourcefulness, good sense, moral strength, and charm. Her husband in a fit of insanity had shot her in the arm and killed himself. Three months after this the maximum grant of $60 for the five children was given. The mother was very ambitious for her children. She wanted to buy a little place in the country where she could have a big garden and where there would be play space and good air. She found what she wanted in a near-by suburb, a cottage with windows on all sides and with plenty of land and fronting open fields. She had so endeared herself to those who knew her that a worker in another social agency put at her disposal the necessary funds to meet the first payments, and the family moved in. They papered and painted the house throughout and they used every available inch of garden space. Mrs. G.'s furniture was not sufficient, but the mothers' aid workers got contributions from their friends. Potted plants were in the windows, the furnishings were old but clean and orderly, and the new furniture was not inharmonious.

EDUCATION

COOPERATION WITH THE SCHOOLS AND FACILITIES FOR EDUCATION

Contacts with the schools.

During the preliminary investigation the school records of the children were always examined. The regular school reports sent to the parents were not examined by the visitors after the grant was made, but reports for each child in school were mailed by the teachers to the mothers' aid office at least twice a year on special blanks furnished by the State office. (See p. 48.) The form of request used was as follows:

STATE BOARD OF EDUCATION,
BERKS COUNTY MOTHERS' ASSISTANCE FUND.
Courthouse, Reading, Pa., ———, 192

——— ———:

The board of trustees of the Berks County Mothers' Assistance Fund is granting aid to the mother of ———.

Under the laws of Pennsylvania the trustees are responsible for the school attendance of all children under their care.

May we have your cooperation by promptly sending us the information asked for on the inclosed blank? Any information or suggestions that you may see fit to give under the head of "remarks" will be greatly appreciated by the board .of trustees.

Should the above-named pupil be transferred or promoted, please state which school building and grade and the name of the teacher or principal.

A stamped envelope is inclosed for reply. Kindly keep this matter strictly confidential.

Very truly yours,

———— ————, *Visitor.*

The mothers' aid visitors kept in close touch with the children and their teachers through frequent visits to the schools. The law laid emphasis upon the educational purpose of the aid, and the boys and girls were taught that the quality of their school work was an important item in the eligibility of the family to assistance.

In order to encourage the children in their school work, the president of the board of trustees had for several years been giving three prizes, one to the boy making the greatest progress in the city public schools, one to the girl making the greatest progress in the public schools, and one to the child making the greatest progress in the parochial schools. The prizes were books chosen according to the tastes of the individual children.

The regular school reports and the frequent conferences with the teachers made it possible for the mothers' aid workers to learn about school difficulties and to apply remedies before the situation became serious. For this reason very few children had given any special trouble. At least once a year the executive secretary reviewed all cases of school difficulties and in this way guarded against the possibility of overlooking any child who might have escaped attention previously.

Provision for handicapped children.

The physically handicapped child.—The educational system made no provision for the treatment of crippled children nor for their transportation to and from school. Expert medical and surgical care was provided for mothers' aid children by the board of trustees. There were one open-air school and one open-window room for undernourished and pretuberculous children, who were supervised and instructed individually by the school nurses. There were no sight-conservation classes. Four teachers gave instruction to small groups of children with speech defects, and one teacher taught lip reading to deaf children.

The mentally handicapped child.—There were in Reading two or three special classes, which were not nearly sufficient. These classes were ungraded, the children being taught in small groups. Rug weaving, chair caning, and brush making were taught. The children were given half manual and half academic work.

Provision for children wishing further education.

No scholarships were available for children who wished to continue their education through high school or college. The John Edgar Thompson Fund, which in addition to maintaining an institution for the care of daughters of railroad men gave aid to such girls in their own homes, gave an allowance for a 16-year-old girl in a family receiving mothers' aid while she completed a business course. As has been stated, the law allowed aid for children up to 16 years of age, and the board encouraged older children to remain in school by continuing aid for younger brothers and sisters.

When mothers' aid was first granted to the Y. family Alice was just 16, Gilbert was 13, and Clara was 5. The family were capable, thrifty, and extraordinarily ambitious. Before Alice graduated from high school she confided to the mothers' aid worker that she wanted to be a physician and had decided to take the two-year premedical course, then the four-year medical course at one of the leading universities. That seemed a stupendous undertaking for a family without any resources but grit. Alice won a scholarship that paid her tuition, and during her spare time she worked in a physician's office and earned enough to pay her year's expenses. At the time of the study she had worked for three summers and was finishing her premedical work. Her school work had been so good that she had been exempt from examinations in several subjects. She was preparing to enter medical school in the fall.

Three girls were taking business courses in evening high school. One of the girls in high school was taking a business course and another girl was attending a commercial college. Only one child was known to be taking music lessons. A textile-machine shop offered a four-year apprenticeship. The wages were 25 cents an hour during the first year, 28 cents during the second, 30 cents during the third, and 33 cents during the fourth. At the end of the fourth year a bonus of $200 was given. Much effort had been expended to place boys in this shop. At the time of the study five or six boys from mothers' aid families were working there.

SCHOOLING AND WORK OF CHILDREN 14 AND 15 YEARS OLD

Although the board of trustees of the mothers' assistance fund was willing to continue a grant to the age of 16 for a child who wished to continue in school, the financial condition of many of the families required that the children contribute to the income of the family as soon as they could get employment certificates.[9] There were 35 children (17 boys and 18 girls) 14 and 15 years old in families receiving aid; 17 of them were 14 years of age and 18 were 15 years of age; 32 of the 35 had completed the sixth grade and therefore were eligible for employment certificates as regards educational requirements.

Ten of the 35 children, 7 of whom had completed the sixth grade, were attending school. One boy was in the fifth grade, a boy and a girl were in the sixth grade, and a girl was in the eighth grade. Six children were in the high school (three girls in the first year and a boy and two girls in the second year).

Twenty-five of the children 14 and 15 years of age—all except 7 of the 32 children who had fulfilled the grade requirement for going to work—were employed. Twenty-one were working in factories, 1 was a cashier, 1 was doing housework, 1 was an errand boy, and 1 was an errand girl. All the 25 had completed at least the sixth grade before leaving school.

---

[9] For a statement of the terms of the compulsory-education, child-labor, and mothers' aid laws in Pennsylvania, see p. 50.

The monthly earnings of these children were as follows:

	Number of children
Total	25
Under $20	2
$20, under $30	7
$30, under $40	11
$40, under $50	4
Over $50	1

Twenty of these 25 children contributed their entire earnings to the support of the family. A girl earning $18 contributed $6.50, a girl earning $22 contributed $13, a girl earning $39 contributed $35, a girl earning $43 contributed $37, and a boy earning $78 contributed $65.

EDUCATIONAL ACTIVITIES FOR THE MOTHERS

Twenty-five mothers of foreign birth, most of whom spoke some English, received aid. Four beneficiaries of mothers' aid attended one of the classes conducted by the International Institute which met in the home of a Polish mother. There was also a Polish mothers' club, to which a number of mothers receiving aid belonged. Foreign-speaking mothers were encouraged to attend classes in citizenship and to join such clubs as were maintained by the International Institute. If they were not already citizens they were encouraged to take out their papers. No classes in sewing, cooking, or home making were conducted for mothers by the board of education or any other agency.

RECREATION

The allowance for recreation was that provided by the Chicago standard budget. Most of the working children up to 16 years of age, sometimes to 18, turned over their entire earnings to their mothers, who gave them what they chose; the arrangements made between the mother and children were not interfered with if they were reasonable. If the mother clothed the child an allowance of 50 cents a week was made for his recreation.

The families of Berks County were closely identified with their churches, and the social and recreational activities of the churches played an important part in the lives of their members. The board of trustees were anxious that the tie between the homes and the church be preserved and that its protection and traditions be passed on to these fatherless children. Each year they sent to the pastors of all families receiving aid a form letter and a blank regarding church and Sunday-school attendance and confirmation, as follows:

BERKS COUNTY MOTHERS' ASSISTANCE FUND,
Courthouse, Reading, Pa.

MY DEAR MR. ―――: We feel that your help and cooperation in regard to this family might be of great assistance to us.
May we ask you to fill out the inclosed slip and return to our office?
Very sincerely,

――― ―――, Executive Secretary.

MOTHERS' ASSISTANCE FUND OF BERKS COUNTY

Telephone No. 2390.
Office hours: Tuesday and Thursday, 10 to 12 o'clock.
Name: _____
Address: _____
Church attendance record { Regularly, _____
                           Occasionally, _____
                           Not at all, _____
Sunday-school attendance record { Regularly, _____
                                  Occasionally, _____
                                  Not at all, _____
Members of family confirmed, _____
Any information or recommendations, _____

_____
(Signature of pastor)

The families had the recreational advantages common to a small city and to the country. There were no settlements, nor were the schools used as social centers. An excellent recreational program, however, was being developed by the city recreational department, and up to the time of the study the chief emphasis had been placed upon athletics, pageants, and outdoor activities. There was a boys' club house in Reading and a number of boys whose families received aid belonged to the club. Only a small number of the children in families receiving aid were connected with the Young Men's Christian Association or the Young Women's Christian Association.

Few children got books from the public library. There were a number of Boy Scout troops in Reading, and there were troops in 13 other towns in the county. A director of the Berks County council of scouts gave his full time to directing activities. Girl Scouts and Camp Fire Girls were organized, but not in so many places. Fourteen children under 16 years of age in mothers' aid families belonged to clubs of one sort or another. Phonographs were in the majority of the homes. There were open-air concerts in summer in the numerous parks. The recreation camp conducted by the Visiting Nurse Association in the summer had been a source of great happiness and physical upbuilding to many mothers with young children. To it were sent for a week or two at a time whole families in need of rest and good food. Recently it had been used only for undernourished and convalescent mothers and children, so that the benefits had been more limited. There were no other summer vacation camps except for Boy Scout troops. The home-craft shop had provided a rich source of social and creative life to the mothers who had been employed. The stimulus which was given them to design and produce on their own initiative was a source of pride and joy, and in one case at least had had a healing and beneficial influence.

Realization of the social needs of the adolescent boy is shown in the following case history:

The V. family lived in a small, one-industry town that did little to stimulate wholesome recreational life for its young folk. Fifteen-year-old James had done well in school and had been allowed to continue in high school. Suddenly it was reported that he was lazy and was deficient in two of his school subjects. At home he was nervous and excitable and wanted more money to spend than could be afforded. The visitor and the high-school principal had a long talk with the boy. The principal promised to coach him in his deficient subjects; and as he greatly desired to become a member of the Young Men's Christian Association, which had an imposing new building near his home, he was given $6 for this purpose. The family grant was also increased in order to provide more nourishing food and better clothing. The last reports for James V. were good.

MOTHERS' ALLOWANCES IN COOK COUNTY, ILL.[1]

PROVISIONS OF THE LAW

The original mothers' aid law in Illinois, called the "funds to parents act," was passed in 1911 and was superseded by an act passed in 1913 granting aid to mothers and children, which was amended further in 1915, 1917, 1919, 1921, and 1923.[2] The law of 1923 provide aid to widows with dependent children, to mothers whose husbands had become permanently incapacitated for work by reason of physical or mental infirmity, and to mothers whose husbands had abandoned their children and could not be apprehended.

Other conditions of eligibility stated in the law were as follows:

1. A mother must have been a resident of the county for three years previous to application.

2. The child or children must be living with the mother.

3. The court must find that it is for the welfare of such child or children to remain at home with the mother.

4. Relief should be granted only when in the absence of such relief the mother would be required to work regularly away from her home and children, or when in the absence of such relief it would be necessary to commit such child or children to a dependent institution and assistance was therefore necessary to save the child or children from neglect.

5. A mother could have, in addition to household goods, an equity or net interest in a home or real estate or personal property not exceeding $1,000.

6. A mother was required to be a citizen of the United States or to have declared her intention of becoming a citizen or to have filed application for citizenship. (A mother not yet a citizen was entitled to assistance only for those of her children born in the United States.)

---

[1] Cook County includes within its borders the cities of Chicago, Evanston, and Oak Park. The population of the county was 3,053,017 in 1920. Of this number, 2,701,705 lived in Chicago. The native white population was 2,045,302; the foreign born, 889,281; the negroes, 115,238. The child population within legal age for mothers' aid was 907,710. The chief foreign nationalities in the order of their numerical importance were as follows: Polish, German, Russian, Italian, and Swedish (Fourteenth Census of the United States, 1920, vol. 3, Population, pp. 252, 261, 270, 271, Washington, 1922). The most important industries are slaughtering and meat packing, the manufacture of men's clothing, the manufacture of foundry and machine-shop products, and printing and publishing.
[2] Ill., act of June 5, 1911, Laws of 1911, p. 126; act of June 30, 1913, Laws of 1913, p. 127; act of June 28, 1915, Laws of 1915, p. 243; act of June 11, 1917, Laws of 1917, p. 220; acts of June 21 and June 30, 1919, Laws of 1919, pp. 780, 781; act of June 29, 1921, Laws of 1921, p. 162; act of June 26, 1923, Laws of 1923, p. 169. See also act of June 30, 1925, Laws of 1925, p. 185. (See Smith-Hurd Rev. Stat. 1925, ch. 23, secs. 322–340, pp. 282–284.)

7. Whenever relief was granted to a mother whose husband was mentally or physically incapacitated and whose presence in the family was a menace to its physical or moral welfare the court might require his removal from the home.

8. Aid might be allowed for children up to 16 years of age. The order granting aid, however, might be modified or vacated in the discretion of the juvenile court, before the child had reached the age of 16 years.

9. In counties having a population of less than 300,000 the allowance to a mother might not exceed $15 a month for one child and $10 a month for each additional child; in counties having a population of more than 300,000, $25 a month was allowed for the first child and $15 a month for each additional child.

10. A mother might not receive aid if there were relatives with sufficient financial means who were obligated by court finding and judgment to support her children.

As the appropriation was insufficient to aid all applicants who were eligible and as the law gave discretionary powers to the judge of the juvenile court, he had ruled that grants would not be made to women who had savings or personal property. The court also ruled that mothers receiving aid would not be permitted to keep men boarders or lodgers and that aid would be granted to a deserted mother only after one year's desertion and after a warrant had been issued for apprehension of the father.

The judge of the juvenile court and the workers of the mothers' pension division heartily approved of the principle of State supervision, but the law made no provision for it.

ADMINISTRATION OF THE LAW

ADMINISTRATIVE AGENCY AND STAFF

The administrative agency was the mothers' pension division of the juvenile court. The staff consisted of the head of the mothers' pension division, 24 investigators and visitors (designated probation officers), and 1 stenographer. The probation officers were appointed by the judge from a list of persons who qualified by a competitive examination outlined by representative citizens and social workers of recognized ability. A high-school education or its equivalent was required of each candidate, and training and experience counted 30 per cent in grading papers. Three probation officers were college graduates, 1 of whom had taken graduate work on social problems at the University of Chicago; 4 had had some college work; 2 (1 of foreign birth and 1 of foreign parentage) had been well educated in Europe; 1 was a graduate nurse who had had 1 year of normal-school work.

The previous social case work training and experience of the staff before coming to the court were as follows: 7 probation officers had worked in case-work agencies and 4 had worked in noncase-work social agencies (it was stated, however, that "some of the work done with other agencies was volunteer work and rather meager"); 8 had had some university training at the University of Chicago School of Social Service Administration or elsewhere; 9 had had no previous training or experience. Most of these nine workers had been on the staff of the court for many years, having been appointed before the training standards had been raised. There was a very small turnover in the personnel of the court. No officer in the mothers' pension division had served less than two years; some officers had worked in several divisions of the court. The salaries of the probation officers and the stenographer were $149 per month.

Each officer supervised about 60 families and in addition made from 8 to 10 new investigations per month. Each probation officer also had to fill out in longhand a number of forms for the court procedure, as a separate application was filed for each child. Some of the probation officers typed their own records, as there was but one stenographer for the entire staff.

The preliminary investigations of the probation officers were checked, and reinvestigations—with reference chiefly to property, insurance, savings, and the financial ability of relatives to assist— were made by representatives of the county agent of Cook County (the officer administering outdoor relief).

A conference committee consisting of the chief probation officer, the supervisor of mothers' aid, a representative of the county agent, and the probation officer who investigated or supervised the family under discussion met each week directly after the regular hearing of mothers' aid cases. This committee passed on all new investigations before they were presented to the judge at the hearing, on all changes of grants, and on questions involving financial policy.

APPROPRIATION AND VOLUME OF WORK

The appropriations for mothers' aid for the fiscal years ended November 30, 1921, 1922, 1923, and 1924 were $450,000, $650,000, $675,000, and $750,000 respectively.[3] All expenses of administration were met by the juvenile court and did not come out of the appropriation for mothers' aid.

On February 1, 1924, the mothers' pension division was granting aid for 3,634 children in 1,207 families. This was not the total number of children eligible for aid in these families; but as some families did not need the maximum grant the children not recipients of relief were excluded from this count. These children received the same treatment as those for whom dependency petitions had been filed. There was a waiting list of 500 to 600 families.

The court set aside one morning a week for mothers' aid hearings. The hearing was conducted as informally as possible, but in the presence of other mothers and children. For this reason it lacked somewhat the privacy that a hearing in chambers would have had. The number of cases to be heard allowed only the most limited discussion. Generally the hearing consisted merely of a roll call of the names of the mother and of each of the children, the address, and the amount

---

[3] The appropriation for 1925 was $760,000 and that for 1926 was $780,000. In 1927 there was an increase of $270,00, the appropriation for that year being $1,050,000.

of the grant for each child. Often the judge spoke some kindly word of admonition or praise, which did much to relieve the tension and provide an atmosphere of kindness and good will.

A representative of the county agent—the officer administering outdoor relief—was always present at the hearing and gave his assent to each grant; a change in the amount of the grant could be made only by means of a rehearing. It was necessary for a mother to bring the children when the rehearing was for the purpose of increasing the pension or continuing the grant for a child 14 years of age.

PROCEDURE IN MAKING ALLOWANCES

Applications were considered in chronological order. An application blank for each child was filed with the court, covering name, place, and date of birth of child; name, birth date, and place of birth of father and of mother; date and place of father's death, date of father's desertion or commitment to hospital or institution for the insane; present address of parents; date and place of marriage of mother and father; facts regarding citizenship, property, wages, and other income; and all available data regarding relatives liable for support of children. This application was made out by the probation officer and was sworn to and signed by the mother. On the signature of the probation officer it became her recommendation that aid be granted, and it was also signed by the judge before the case could be brought to court.

A face card for each family was filled out when aid was granted; this also was sworn to by the mother and became the first sheet of the running record. It called for the following additional information: Housing conditions and landlord's name; mental or physical defects of father, mother, and children; insurance; membership in fraternal organizations; length of residence in county, State, and United States; husband's previous occupation and wages; religion; previous addresses; and names of agencies interested in the family, names of relatives, and references.

The first step in the investigation was the registration of the family in the social-service exchange; form letters of inquiry were sent to all registered agencies. The investigation included a visit to the home and the verification of certain facts, including the marriage of the parents; birth dates of children; citizenship; residence; death, commitment, or desertion of the father; property, savings, and insurance, and the manner of expenditure; wages of mother and of working children. Relatives were regularly consulted, primarily with reference to financial assistance; and if the family was under the care of a physician he was generally interviewed, as was also the minister or priest.

The children's school records were sometimes consulted as part of the investigation, and the references furnished by the mother were sometimes seen. On the day of the court hearing the mother brought all the children to the court, and before the hearing the children were given a physical examination by the court physician.

COOK COUNTY, ILL. 71

USE OF A STANDARD BUDGET

A budget, based on the Chicago standard budget, which was used by family case work agencies in Chicago, was computed for every family. This budget was as follows:

SCHEDULE FOR ESTIMATING A BUDGET FOR A DEPENDENT FAMILY

If family rents and is in satisfactory quarters, count rent as it is paid. If rooms are insanitary, too small, in bad neighborhood, or in any way unsuitable, estimate a rent that will cover suitable housing.

If the house is owned, ascertain taxes, interest on mortgage, or other payments; make a monthly average of expense and add to it an estimate, usually $2 to $5 per month, for upkeep.

FOOD

	Where baking is done at home		Where bread is bought	
	Per week	Per month	Per week	Per month
Man at moderately hard muscular work	$2.70	$11.95	$3.00	$13.00
Man at hard muscular work	3.00	13.00	3.30	14.30
Woman at moderately hard muscular work	2.20	9.55	2.40	10.40
Woman at hard muscular work	2.35	10.20	2.60	11.30
Boy 15 to 18 years	3.05	13.20	3.35	14.50
Girl 15 to 18 years	2.70	11.70	2.85	12.35
Child 12 to 14 years	2.70	11.70	2.85	12.35
Child 6 to 8 years	1.80	7.80	1.96	8.45
Child 6 months to 5 years	1.70	6.40	1.80	7.85
Child under 6 months	1.35	5.85	1.35	5.85
Elderly or incapacitated person not in need of special diet	2.05	8.90	2.25	9.75

Special diet.—Where there is a definite recommendation of special food, calculate its cost.

Add the cost of a quart of milk in tuberculosis where the patient is in good condition and for a child 7 per cent or more underweight.

Add a quart of milk, an egg daily, and an allowance for fresh vegetables of 25 to 50 cents a week in cases of tuberculosis where the patient is in poor condition.

Add the cost of 1 pint of milk daily for a slight tuberculosis infection, such as slightly enlarged glands in children, and for underweight of less than 7 per cent if the general condition is good.

Add the cost of a pint of milk, an egg daily, and an allowance for fresh vegetables; 15 to 30 cents a week for children who have a tuberculous infection and are in poor physical condition and for children extremely underweight and anemic.

Add the allowance of the child under 6 months to that of the woman for the nursing mother and for the expectant mother during the last three months of pregnancy.

Variations with size of family.—For a person living alone add 25 per cent to the food allowance.

If the weekly allowance amounts to less than $4.25 add 15 per cent; if it is between $4.25 and $6, add 10 per cent; if more than $14, deduct 5 per cent.

Clothing and toilet articles

Per month

For a man at ordinary outdoor work (increase for work involving unusual exposure) _____ $6.50
For a woman at home _____ 5.00
Working girl or boy (increase according to standard of dress required by employment) _____ 8.15–[4]10.20

[4] The larger figure allows $25 a year for "best" clothing.

For office work where good standard of appearance is required (the requirements for girl or boy in high school are much the same as if the child were at work) _____ Per month $10.00–$12.00
Children 13 years up in eighth grade _____ 5.75
Children 10 to 12 years _____ 4.70
Children 5 to 9 years _____ 3.65
Children 2 to 4 years _____ 2.80
Children under 2 years _____ 1.85

In families where there is clothing from older children or parents to be handed down to the younger ones these figures may be reduced by 10 to 25 per cent for the members of the family receiving such donations.

Fuel for heat, light, and cooking

4 winter months:
    Where 1 stove is used _____ $12.25–13.25
    Where 2 stoves are used _____ 17.25–18.75
2 spring and autumn months _____ 8.25–9.25
4 summer months _____ 2.50–4.00
Average for year:
    1 stove _____ 7.75–8.75
    2 stoves _____ 9.35–10.35

Household furnishings and supplies

Family of 2 members _____ $4.00
Family of 3 or 4 members _____ 4.75
Family of 5 or 6 members _____ 5.50
Family of 7 or 8 members _____ 6.25
Family of 9 or 10 members _____ 7.00

Car fare

As necessary for work for each member of family. Include necessary trips of housewife to market.

Spending money

For working children who turn their wages into the family income spending money is usually 25 cents to $1 a week. If the custom of the family is reasonable it should be followed in making out the estimated budget for the family. This allowance will take care of expenditures for recreation and education for those members of the family for whom it is estimated; or three weeks' wages of the working child may be counted as family income, allowing the remainder to cover his clothing, car fare, and spending money, which are omitted from the family budget. This plan should not be used until the child's weekly wage exceeds the minimum estimate for his clothing, car fare, and spending money.

Care of health

Where public physicians and nurses are used, 25 cents a month and up for each person.

Education

Family education expenses (newspaper, magazine, etc.), per month ___ $1.00 up
School supplies, per pupil _____ .15

Insurance

Insurance premiums, lodge dues, etc., as paid (if reasonable).

Recreation

For members of the family not provided with money for recreation under "spending money," 25 cents per month and up.

Incidentals

Education, care of health, and recreation may be lumped under incidentals. An average of $1 for each member of the family will cover these items in most cases.

The amount granted equaled the estimate of the family's expenses minus the earnings of the family, provided this was within the maximum allowed by law. At the time of the study the income of 209 families was at least $5 a month less than that called for in the budget, even including such supplementary assistance as was rendered by other agencies. It was very difficult to secure supplementary aid outside Chicago, Evanston, and Oak Park. The budget was brought up to date at least every six months and the grant revised in accordance with changing conditions. Uniformity of computation was insured by having one probation officer in charge of the budget work for the entire mothers' pension division.

When the maximum grant was not adequate on the basis of the budget requirements, it was the policy of the court to secure supplementary relief from one of the private family agencies which were generous in this respect. For February, 1924, the average grant per family was $50.31. The largest grant per family for that month was $130; the smallest was between $5 and $10. The average grant per child under 16 years of age was not ascertained. The mothers called for their checks twice a month at the office of the county agent.

Each mother receiving aid was required to keep on prescribed forms an itemized account of her household expenses covering a two-week period. Food expenditures were classified under cereals, proteins, fats, sweets, fruits and vegetables, and accessories. The form had been prepared by a trained dietitian who at one time had been on the staff of the mothers' pension division of the court and had supervised this part of the work. She had visited the homes of the mothers and had given much personal instruction in food values, marketing, and diet for young children. Her work had been of great educational value. It had been some years since a dietitian had been attached to the staff, but the forms were still in use. The probation officers made them the basis of recommendations and suggestions.

A copy of such an expense account is as follows:

[Face]

MOTHERS' PENSION DIVISION, JUVENILE COURT OF COOK COUNTY, JUVENILE COURT BUILDING, ROOSEVELT ROAD AND OGDEN AVENUE, CHICAGO

Phone, Seeley 8400   Probation officer, _____

SEMIMONTHLY STATEMENT OF FAMILY INCOME AND EXPENSE FOR THE PERIOD BEGINNING MARCH 13, 1924, AND ENDING MARCH 26, 1924

Pension funds granted by the order of the juvenile court are paid on the 8th and 23d of each month through the office of the county agent. This account sheet will cover the period between those dates. A new sheet will be given to the mother with her check for funds each half month.

Accounts are to be carefully kept showing each item of expenditure and each item of income. This statement is intended not only to account for all money spent but also to show the mother for what things the money is spent in order that there may be the most intelligent use of the funds.

These sheets will be called for by the juvenile-court probation officer each month.

The summary statement for the period should balance. The probation officer will assist mothers with their accounts if desired.

I certify that the accounts following represent the total family income and its expenditure:

Name of mother, _____. Address, _____.

| | March 13 ||| March 14 |||
Item	Quantity	Article	Price	Quantity	Article	Price
Cereal products (flour, bakery, cereals, macaroni, etc.)						
High-protein foods (meat, fish, eggs, cheese, milk, nuts, dried peas and beans)						
Fats (butter, lard, oil, etc.)						
Sweets						
Fruits and vegetables						
Accessories (coffee, tea, yeast, salt, spices, etc.)						
Lunch money						
Total for food						

NOTE.—Similar columns for the following days to Mar. 20 on remaining face of this blank form.

[Reverse]

[Upper part of form contains columns for Mar. 21 to 26 similar to those on the face of this form. Lower part only is reproduced]

Expenditures of the period in addition to food (which is listed daily)

Quantity	Household supplies: Soap, linen, furniture, etc.	Price	Quantity	Fuel and light	Price	Clothing. Specify article and for whom bought	Price	Car fares	Price	Miscellaneous expenses, including rent, medical and dental bills, spending money for children, etc.	Price

Summary statement

Money on hand at beginning of period_____ _____
Money received:
   1. From mother's work_____ _____
   2. From children's work_____ _____
      From children's work_____ _____
      From children's work_____ _____
   3. Pension_____ _____
   4. Other sources_____ _____

      Total_____ _____
Amount spent during period_____ _____
Amount on hand at end of period_____ _____

SUPPLEMENTING OF MOTHERS' AID

The outdoor-relief department of the county did not supplement mothers' aid, but it aided families on the waiting list. The United Charities of Chicago spent in the year ended September 30, 1923, $51,747.50, divided as follows: $43,922.95 on behalf of 345 families awaiting aid and $8,824.55 as supplementary aid to 168 families already receiving mothers' aid.[5] The Jewish Social Service Bureau supplemented mothers' aid to Jewish families when it was not adequate and helped Jewish families on the waiting list. In the year ended December 31, 1923, it spent $6,026.08 in relief to 18 families receiving allowances and $4,452.99 in relief to 5 families on the waiting list. The Bureau of Catholic Charities likewise assisted Catholic families, but the exact amount given during the last fiscal year of the organization was not available.

VISITING

It was the policy of the court to have each family visited at least once a month; many families were visited oftener, as often as once a week if necessary. The relationship between the visitors and the families under their care was one of mutual respect and genuine friendship.

HEALTH

PHYSICAL HEALTH

The budget allowed 25 cents a month for health needs for each member of the family. In addition special diet and medicine were allowed whenever necessary.

Physical examinations.

On the day of the hearing of the families' applications for aid all children received a physical examination, which was made by the court physician and included examination of eyes, ears, nose, throat and teeth, heart, lungs, and genitals (of the boys). A regular form was not used in reporting the results of the examinations, but the mothers' pension division was notified of defects, and the nurse who assisted the physician made appointments with hospitals and clinics immediately after the examinations for the correction of defects or for treatment. At intervals the nurse checked her records with those of the probation officers to make sure that the necessary medical attention had been given. The probation officers were responsible for attending to all medical work, and the services which the nurse rendered were by courtesy.

---

[5] The expenditure of the United Charities of Chicago for families receiving or eligible for mothers' allowances during the three years ended October 1, 1922, fluctuated in almost exactly inverse proportion to the expenditures made by the juvenile court for the pensions. For example, a considerable increase in the amount expended by the court for allowances in October, 1919, was paralleled by an approximately equivalent decrease in the amount expended by the United Charities of Chicago for families on the waiting list. By February, 1920, the monthly expenditure of the court had risen to $38,000 through the amendment to the law extending the eligibility requirements and authorizing a larger appropriation (which became available that month), although by November, 1921, it had decreased to $34,000. As the juvenile court rose to this plane of $34,000 to $38,000 a month the United Charities of Chicago spent a correspondingly smaller sum because of the transfer of families from its lists to those of the court. By March, 1922, the juvenile court had increased its expenditures (from $34,000 in December, 1921) to $60,000 in pursuance of the amendments of 1921—which increased the allowances authorized from $15 a month for the oldest child in the family to $25 a month and from $10 a month for each other child to $15 for each other child, and also permitted grants to parents having an equity of $1,000 on a homestead. Increase in both the number of pensions and the amount granted caused the court to be confronted by a deficit in April, 1922, and retrenchment was begun. At once the United Charities' expenditures, which previously had decreased, began to increase on account of the necessity of aiding families waiting for allowances. Supplementary aid was not granted to families unless the maximum amount was already being given by the court.

The following is a copy of the report blank for recommendations by the court physician:

Form 62 A

Probation officer, S----------------------

JUVENILE COURT OF COOK COUNTY, 2246 ROOSEVELT ROAD, CHICAGO

REPORT OF PHYSICAL EXAMINATION

Name, ---------------------- No. ------
Is suffering from ----------------------
The following treatment is recommended, --------------------
Date, ----------------------

Juvenile court physician.

My consent to above treatment is hereby given {Parent. / Guardian.

These examinations did not aim to be exhaustive. They did, however, uncover an enormous number and variety of physical defects and pointed the way toward a health program for these children. The mothers were always present and the physicians frequently gave them friendly advice as to health habits as well as physical conditions calling for corrections. No medical history either of the child or of the family was taken, neither were the records complete in this regard. Height and weight measurements were not taken, but if there were signs of undernourishment the physician commented upon them. Frequently the mother was questioned and advised as to the child's diet, habits, etc. If a child was found to have a serious defect his mother was required to have it remedied, but the policy of persuasion was adhered to so far as was consistent with the child's well-being.

Although the examination by the juvenile-court physician was brief and hurried, it was obvious that the mothers were impressed with the value of having their children looked over; some of them were visibly grateful for his service and advice. He seldom saw the child a second time; his function was to direct the children to the proper medical agency. Periodic physical examinations after the preliminary examination were not the established rule except for the children receiving attention from the Elizabeth McCormick Memorial Fund (see p. 80) or under the regular supervision of a municipal, tuberculosis, or hospital clinic.

The mothers either were examined by the court physician or when it seemed advisable were sent to a clinic. The examinations might be in the course of investigation of the application for aid or at any time while aid was being granted. A urinalysis was made and a pelvic examination if the woman complained of symptoms indicating that such would be desirable. No Wassermann test was taken, but if it seemed necessary she was referred to a clinic for more intensive examination and treatment. The court physician sent to the mothers' pension division a report of the symptoms, diagnosis, and recommendations for treatment, and a statement as to the amount of work the woman was able to do. The following is a copy of such a report:

COOK COUNTY, ILL.

CHICAGO, ———.

Mr. ——— ———
Chief Probation Officer, Juvenile Court, Chicago.
Re: Mrs. S ———, ———, 34 yrs.—5 children, 11, 10, 8, 6, and 2 yrs.

MY DEAR MR. ———: Examination shows a healthy-looking woman. Weight, 120 pounds. She was operated on in March, 1923, at Wesley Hospital, when hysterectomy, appendectomy, and perineorrhaphy were performed. She complains of pelvic pains for the past six months. These occur every two or three weeks and last two or three hours. She has defective vision and needs to have her eyes refracted for glasses. Pelvic examination does not show any cause for the pains she complains of. Physical examination is otherwise negative.

She is not physically able to do any laborious work but could do light work, such as sewing, at home.

Very truly yours,

——— ———,
Juvenile Court Physician.

A health blank was included in each record. The date of the examination, the name of the physician who made the examination, the diagnosis and recommendations were given for the mother and each of the children. Space was left to enter the date and character of treatment for each person. The following is a sample:

HEALTH RECORD

Surname: *W.* ———. Father, *Frank* ———. Mother, *Mary* ———.
Name: *Mary* (mother) ———.
Date:
    3/2/23. Ex. by Dr. *X* ———.[6] Received gynecological treatment (report attached).
    3/21/23. Under treatment at Central Free Dispensary.
    5/7/23. Operation for uterine tumor at Presbyterian Hospital.
Name: *Mary* ———.
Date: 3/2/23. Apparently O. K.
Name: *George* ———.
Date:
    4/5/23. Examined at board of education—undernour.; immature (report attached).
    10/8/23. Examination at board of education O. K.
Name: *John* ———.
    4/5/23. Examination at board of education—undernour.; tons. removed.
    5/5/23. Tons. at Michael Reese Dispensary.
    9/7/23. Entered nutrition clinic at Northwestern Settlement.
Name: *Charles* ———.
Date:
    4/26/23. Examined by Dr. ———. Circumcision recommended.
    5/1/23. Circumcised.
Name: *Philip* ———.
Date: 4/26/23. Examined by Dr. ———. O. K.
Name: *Annie* ———.
Date:
    4/26/23. Examined by Dr. ———. Received examination at Municipal Tuberculosis Sanatorium.
    4/15/23. Examined at Municipal Tuberculosis Sanatorium. Glandular observation.
    8/15/23. Sent to Ridge Farm.

The various health agencies to which the court referred families receiving mothers' aid generally sent a written statement if they were reporting on a first examination; but sometimes an oral report was made. The social-service departments of the hospitals reported the diagnosis and recommendations as to treatment. The visitors

---
[6] Dr. X was the physician on the staff of the juvenile court.

were responsible for keeping the medical records up to date and for follow-up in cooperation with the nurse employed by the juvenile court, the school and infant-welfare nurses, and the social-service departments of hospitals. The visitors often conferred directly with the physicians who examined the patients. This was always the case when the examination was made by the juvenile-court physician or at one of the nutrition clinics of the Elizabeth McCormick Memorial Fund.

Except in cases of emergency and of some acute illnesses the free service of hospitals and clinics was utilized. Physicians employed by the county could be secured in an emergency on the order of the county agent. Mothers were not expected to employ private physicians unless such physicians gave their services free; an abundance of free medical service was available, and almost all families made use of it.

Follow-up of special types of problems.

There were numerous clinics at the hospitals; the municipal tuberculosis dispensaries and the Social Hygiene Association also maintained clinics. The court used whichever clinic happened to be most accessible to a family.

Tuberculosis.—It was the policy of the court that all mothers and children who had been in any way exposed to tuberculosis should be examined, and if there were signs of infection they were placed under the care of one of the municipal tuberculosis dispensaries. Sanatorium care was insisted upon for all active cases, and facilities for care were said to be adequate at the Municipal Tuberculosis Sanatorium. A few mothers with incipient tuberculosis were given home treatment on the advice of the dispensary. Both the nurses connected with the tuberculosis dispensaries and the probation officer followed up the cases.

The tuberculosis nurses were intrusted with the nursing supervision of the children in the fresh-air classes of the public schools, including nutrition work for them; they also took these children to the clinics regularly for examination.

Venereal disease.—It was the policy of the court to have Wassermann tests made for all mothers and children when there was reason to suspect venereal disease.

Orthopedic affections.—There were numerous facilities for the care and treatment of crippled children. The agencies used most extensively by the court were the Crippled Children's Home and Hospital (which provided both institutional and out-patient care with educational and vocational instruction), St. Luke's Hospital and Orthopedic Clinic, and the Children's Memorial Hospital and Clinic.

No child was permitted to go without needed orthopedic advice and care, though patience sometimes was required before foreign-speaking mothers could be persuaded that an orthopedic operation would really help the child. Braces and special shoes were sometimes provided through the hospitals or the jurors' fund.[7]

Cardiac affections.—Most of the large hospitals had cardiac clinics. The court used especially the Michael Reese Hospital and clinic.

---

[7] A small fund consisting of fees returned by any jurors who served in the court on dependency cases. This emergency fund could be used for any cases of need coming into court.

Children having cardiac trouble were admitted to the Crippled Children's Home and Hospital either as institutional or as day pupils. The hospital nurses and social-service departments cooperated with the probation officers in the follow-up work.

Eye, ear, nose, and throat affections.—The Illinois Charitable Eye and Ear Infirmary and the hospital clinics cared for eye, ear, nose, and throat operations and treatment. The probation officers, court nurse, and school nurses attended to the follow-up.

Convalescent care.—Ridge Farm was a free preventorium for girls of grammar-school age; Arden Shore was a privately financed home for recuperating boys and girls of grammar-school age who had been refused employment certificates because they were undernourished. Admission to both these homes was through the board of education, and hundreds of children were sent to them for building up. Convalescent mothers were sometimes sent to Grove House in Evanston, Ill., or to the Home for Convalescents for Women and Children, or to Rest Haven. There was also a convalescent home for crippled children.

Health work for infants and preschool children.—The Chicago Department of Health operated 22 child-health centers, 6 of which did prenatal work. The mothers were encouraged to bring babies under 3 months of age every week, those 3 to 6 months old every two weeks, and those 6 months to 2 years old once a month. These centers did not aim to work with children over 2 years of age. The Infant Welfare Society maintained 27 centers, in 13 of which nutrition clinics were conducted for children 2 to 6 years of age. The work for children in their other centers was primarily for those under 2 years of age. The mothers were encouraged to bring the children to the nutrition clinics once a month. The society employed 46 nurses, 7 dietitians, 1 supervising dietitian, and 3 supervising nurses. The department of health and the Infant Welfare Society selected the districts for their centers in such a way that there was no overlapping of work. Most mothers could walk to the centers in their neighborhoods, and the few who had to ride could reach a center without changing cars. The department of health service of Cook County, which employed 5 nurses and a supervisor for work outside Chicago, Evanston, and Oak Park, stimulated and in part supervised 4 child-health centers for children of preschool age and 16 summer centers for children of preschool age in the county schools. Though it was the policy of the court to encourage mothers receiving aid to attend the centers their actual attendance depended upon the individual probation officers and mothers.

School medical inspection.—Every school child in Chicago was examined as a matter of routine by a physician about once in three years. There were 110 school nurses for a school population of 600,000. The nurses often took mothers' aid children to the dental clinics maintained by the health department.

Nurses of the county department of health service made yearly inspections of children in the schools outside Chicago, Evanston, and Oak Park. Height and weight measurements were taken. There were no nutrition classes, but individual instruction was given to undernourished children. The nurses frequently arranged for the correction of physical defects for mothers' aid children. They were usually in rather close touch with the families and often communicated directly with the probation officers in regard to the children.

Free dental clinics were available for all school children in Chicago. The three dental colleges—of Northwestern University, the University of Chicago, and the University of Illinois—operated free dental clinics, charging only for the cost of materials.[8] The facilities for free dental care for mothers and older working children were not adequate, however.

The reports of the physical inspections of the school children were not consulted, as a rule, nor followed up by the probation officers.

Malnutrition.—Through the Elizabeth McCormick Memorial Fund 1,254 children under the supervision of 10 of the probation officers had been at least weighed and measured. The valuable cooperation of this organization with the mothers' pension division had been developed gradually as one probation officer after another had expressed her interest in having its health supervision extended to the children in her care. At the time of the study 8 of these 10 probation officers were using its nutrition classes, the remaining 2 having health inventories made for mothers' aid children not living in districts where the fund conducted classes. The children of the first group (those under the supervision of the eight probation officers) were first weighed and measured; those who were underweight or seemed in need of medical care were given complete physical examinations by the pediatrician who did the medical and diagnostic work for the fund, and if he recommended it they were entered in a nutrition class. The pediatrician not only made a thorough and careful examination but was sympathetic in his approach to both mother and child; he took pains to use language intelligible to them and to make them see the reasons for his advice and the advantages to be gained by following it. From September 1, 1923, to May 29, 1924, there were enrolled in these nutrition classes of the Elizabeth McCormick Memorial Fund 131 children who were members of mothers' aid families. (Children under 6 years of age were not enrolled in these classes if they lived in districts having health centers for preschool children.) The mothers attended the classes in which their children were enrolled and seemed to enjoy them and to be eager for help. The nutrition classes thus served the purpose of diagnostic clinics and offered a solid and constructive basis for a program of child health. Not only was expert diagnosis provided but also continuous instruction of the child or his mother until he could be discharged as well.

For the children under the supervision of the two probation officers in districts where no classes were conducted the pediatrician made a survey (1) to learn how many of these children needed intensive nutrition work, (2) to collect data on the relation of the height-weight index to other signs of malnutrition, and (3) to obtain information that would be of value to the probation officers in their handling of the mothers' aid families concerned. The nutritionist on the staff of the Elizabeth McCormick Memorial Fund who weighed

---

[8] The facilities for dental care have been much improved through the new clinic at the Cook County Hospital, which cares for children up to 14 years of age. No charge is made, even for materials. The county board supports the clinic, and the Chicago Dental Society selects the dentists.

and measured the two groups of children gave individual instruction on diet and other health habits to the children and their mothers, and also usually gave a talk to the entire group on one or two points that needed emphasis. The children found to be underweight or apparently in need of medical care were given physical examinations at a hospital clinic and referred to that hospital's nutrition class.

The Michael Reese Hospital and the central free dispensary of the Presbyterian Hospital conducted nutrition clinics, and other hospitals did some nutrition work.

Illustrative case histories.—Nutrition classes were the means of opening the eyes of more than one mother. The following case history may serve as an illustration:

Mrs. S., who had six children under 12 years of age, had been a hard drinker, as her husband had been. They had taken men lodgers and the neighbors had complained of boisterous drinking parties. When aid was granted to Mrs. S. upon her husband's death an attempt was made to win her cooperation in caring for her children, whose physical condition was deplorable, all being badly undernourished and two having glandular tuberculosis as well as other defects. The United Charities of Chicago supplemented the maximum allowance ($55), bringing the total up to $90 a month. The children were examined at a nutrition clinic, and when Mrs. S. saw a rosy child and looked at her own pale brood she exclaimed, " I got eyes; I can see! I bring them every week."

The following case history shows the long-continued and painstaking care that is necessary to help the children or the mothers to overcome physical handicaps or chronic diseases:

Mrs. E. had three children, 8-year-old Helen, 6-year-old Ruth, and 4-year-old Frank. Her husband had died of tuberculosis after a life of intemperance. When aid was granted in 1914 Mrs. E. had incipient tuberculosis and was anemic and undernourished. Helen was much underweight, and one of her legs was crippled from infantile paralysis. Ruth and Frank were both undernourished and suffering from glandular tuberculosis. The family was placed under the care of the municipal dispensary, where they continued to report regularly until the last one was discharged in 1922. On the advice of the dispensary, Mrs. E. was given home treatment; and as she was an intelligent woman this worked very well. Helen was taken to an orthopedic hospital, where an operation was performed in 1916, and braces and a special shoe secured for her. One of the visiting nurses took her once a week to the clinic for treatment, and she received expert care during the entire period of supervision. Special diet was provided, and the grant was continued for her until she was 16 in order that she might secure a fair education. She attended a commercial high school near her home where she could get a free hot lunch. After she passed her sixteenth birthday a scholarship of $15 a month was secured to enable her to finish her course. In October, 1923, she took a job as stenographer. A position was found for Mrs. E. as matron in a telephone exchange, and her physical improvement was no doubt due to some extent to the feeling of partial independence which her position gave her. In February, 1924, she wrote to the judge offering to relinquish her grant.

MENTAL HEALTH

Available facilities.

The department of child study of the Chicago Board of Education examined retarded and deficient children recommended by school principals for placement in the special classes; it also examined and made recommendations for children who presented behavior problems or physical defect. For example, a six-year-old deaf child in a family receiving mothers' aid, who was referred to the department by the probation officer, was placed in a school for the deaf with excellent results. There were no social case workers on the staff of the department, and all follow-up work was done by the teachers, nurses, or social workers in touch with the child.

The Institute of Juvenile Research was maintained jointly by the Cook County juvenile court and the State department of public welfare. It had on its staff psychologists, psychiatrists, and psychiatric social workers. The court referred problem children to this institute for examination and advice. As an agency designed primarily for research the institute aimed to do very intensive work with a few children, but gladly gave examinations and advice to all children referred to it. If the child presented a problem of sufficient interest or importance the institute might do the follow-up through one of its own staff. Otherwise, the agency reporting the child did the follow-up work. The institute made detailed recommendations in regard to treatment, and if there was any uncertainty as to diagnosis it requested that the child be returned for reexamination in six months. Social agencies, courts, schools, and private citizens throughout the State referred to this institute any children presenting problems in the field of mental hygiene.

The Psychopathic Hospital provided hospital care for psychopathic patients while under observation. It was infrequently used by the mothers' pension division, however, and only for mothers about to be committed to a hospital for the insane. The University of Illinois maintained a psychological clinic which was used for the examination of adults.

Follow-up of special types of problems.

The procedure with reference to mental problems varied considerably with the different workers. Some probation officers laid great stress upon early examination, diagnosis, and treatment. Psychological examinations might or might not be arranged for by the probation officers for children two or three years retarded in school, as it was generally assumed that the teachers took care of this type of problem through the child-study department and that children were placed in the special classes whenever necessary.

For children so defective as to require institutional care application was made for commitment to the Lincoln State School and Colony for the Feeble-Minded. This institution was crowded and there was a waiting list.

If the family history of the child showed mental disease, as in the case of a child whose father was insane, the child was not given an examination unless he also showed symptoms of mental unbalance. If mental difficulty was suspected the child was examined by the Institute of Juvenile Research. The treatment of behavior problems also varied considerably. It was the desire of the court that all the light which psychiatry could throw on conduct and the treatment of delinquency should be brought to bear on difficulties of behavior.

HOUSING

It was not easy for mothers' aid families to find an adequate number of rooms in desirable neighborhoods at reasonable rentals. Considering the difficulties to be overcome, it seemed remarkable that these families were on the whole so well cared for. Very few families were living in tenements; many of the families dwelt in the rear rooms of cottage houses occupied by two families or in rooms in two-story houses occupied by four families. There was usually an inside toilet for each two families, though the court workers preferred that each family should have a separate toilet. Every room had a window opening on the outside, and the houses were not insanitary. Most of the families had access to some kind of front or back yard, but very few had a vegetable or even a flower garden.

The average number of rooms for a mother and three children was four. A living room was considered essential, though it was frequently used for sleeping purposes, too. All families had inside running water and a few had bathrooms. Most houses were equipped with gas for lighting and cooking, but only a few had electricity. It was reported that about two-thirds of the families had ice boxes.

Good homes at reasonable rents were so scarce that it was impossible to give as much consideration as would have been desirable to play space and accessibility of playgrounds. Great emphasis was laid upon having families live in sanitary houses and in decent neighborhoods.

There was no precise limit as to the amount of rent, each family being considered separately. Generally rents were from $25 to $35 a month. As the law had permitted aid to a mother who had an equity of $1,000 in her home only since 1921 the number of families who owned or partly owned their homes was small.

The homes of the families were generally furnished with the necessaries for decent and wholesome living. There was an adequate number of beds, and with few exceptions the families appeared to have enough dishes and chairs so that the whole family could sit at the table together. Most of the houses visited had a homelike atmosphere, and even those that were sparsely furnished conveyed a sense of orderliness, security, and comfort. The probation officers had done much toward making the homes comfortable by enlisting help for making repairs or finishing partly built houses. One family was made happy by having their house painted, the work being done by the Boy Scouts.

EDUCATION

COOPERATION WITH THE SCHOOLS AND FACILITIES FOR EDUCATION

Contacts with the schools.

Reports on special blanks were obtained for each school child every two or three months and reports for difficult children were obtained every month. The following is a copy of such a report blank:

[Form 9]

SCHOOL STANDING AND ATTENDANCE BLANK

_____ School,
Chicago, _____, 192—.

CHIEF PROBATION OFFICER,
 Juvenile Court Building, 2246 Roosevelt Road, Chicago:
 Attention of probation officer_____
 In the matter of _____ Room No. ____
 Address_____
 The records of this school for the month of _____, 192—, show the following:
  (1) Grade _____
  (2) Scholarship _____
  (3) Deportment _____
  (4) Neatness _____
  (5) Attendance {Absences excused _____
           {Absences unexcused _____
 Remarks: _____
                                    (Signed)   _____ _____,
                                              Principal or Teacher.
MOTHERS' PENSION DIVISION,
 Juvenile Court of Cook County.

It was the policy of the court to have the probation officer visit the teacher of each child at least once a year. Some probation officers visited the schools regularly; others did not. The regular school reports sent to the parents were not followed up. Summarized yearly school reports detailed by months were incorporated in the records of the mothers' aid families. These reports were left with the teachers to fill out month by month, or the probation officers copied the reports received on the special blanks furnished by the court. A copy of one of these yearly summary blanks is as follows:

Name of child, _____
School, _____   Room _____

Year	1923					1924					
	Sept.	Oct.	Nov	Dec.	Jan.	Feb.	Mar	Apr.	May	June
(1) Grade										
(2) Scholarship										
(3) Deportment										
(4) Personal appearance										
(5) {Absences excused										
{Absences unexcused										
(6) Difficult studies										

Remarks: _____

Provision for handicapped children.

The physically handicapped child.—The Chicago school system gave unusual consideration to the handicapped child. There were five schools for crippled children and children with cardiac affections. Each child in these schools was placed under the supervision of an orthopedic or cardiac specialist and was taken to clinics for correction work and supplied with braces and necessary apparatus. A school bus provided transportation. There were 3 classes for epileptic children, 2 classes for the blind and 9 sight-conservation classes, and 5 schools for the deaf and semideaf. There were 66 open-air rooms for anemic and pretuberculous children, and 12 peripatetic teachers gave individual speech instruction to pupils having speech defects. Blind, epileptic, and deaf children were allowed 50 cents a day for the services of an attendant, generally another child, to guide them to and from school. In addition to providing medical and surgical care the court gave extra attention to the provision of educational opportunities and also to the placement of physically handicapped children in suitable positions.

The mentally handicapped child.—There were 110 special classes for subnormal children in 100 schools. No child with an intelligence quotient under 50 was admitted to the regular classes in the public schools. It was expected that the children in the special classes would be reexamined mentally on leaving school. A vocational counselor from the vocational-guidance bureau of the Chicago public schools was assigned to special classes. For retarded pupils 14 to 21 years old there were five prevocational schools. The intelligence quotients of the pupils in these schools ranged from 75 to 90, and admission was made on the recommendation of school principals. The pupils were given mental group tests but not as a preliminary to entrance.

Provision for children wishing further education.

Scholarships were obtainable through the Vocational Supervision League and the Scholarship Association for Jewish Children, private organizations which were given office room in the quarters of the vocational-guidance bureau of the Chicago public schools.[9] These two agencies imposed practically the same qualifications for scholarship grants. The child must be between 14 and 16 years of age and doing good work in school. Physical examinations were given by the medical examiners of the bureau and mental tests by the Institute of Juvenile Research. The administration of the scholarships was in the hands of vocational advisers who were trained social workers. They visited the homes of the children and studied the social and economic needs of the family. The amount of the scholarship was then determined on the basis of the Chicago standard budget. The average amount granted was $15 and the maximum $20 (for 10 months in the year). Usually this was not for a definite period, the grant being continued until the child had completed the course or had dropped out of school because the sum granted was inadequate for his own or his family's needs, or because of some other carefully considered reason. At the time of the study 20 children 14 and 15 years old in families receiving aid were receiving scholarships from the Vocational Supervision League, 11 were re-

---

[9] The Vocational Supervision League is one of the two agencies through which the great majority of Chicago school children receiving grants of money to cover all or part of their living expenses while attending school receive such scholarships. The other is the Scholarship Association for Jewish Children. Both these organizations are given free office room in the quarters of the vocational-guidance bureau of the Chicago public schools. The cost of the scholarships as well as of the workers for these organizations is provided for from private funds, but the work is conducted as if it were a function of the vocational-guidance bureau. See Vocational Guidance and Junior Placement, pp. 155, 176 (U. S. Children's Bureau Publication No. 149 and U. S. Employment Service Publication A, Washington, 1925).

ceiving them from the Scholarship Association for Jewish Children, and 11 were receiving them from some other agency.

The following information was given in regard to assistance to children 16 years of age or older who wished to continue in school: Nine children 16 years old and two children 17 years old were attending school, five of them being members of families that received private supplementary aid. Three had scholarships from the Scholarship Association for Jewish Children and also aid from the Jewish Social Service Bureau; one had a scholarship from the Vocational Supervision League; and one received help from the Chicago United Charities. Two were working also, no supplementary aid being received by their families. One who was physically handicapped and one who was a problem child were receiving special training. Six of these nine children were in the high school (four in the first year, one in the third year, one in the fourth year) and one was in the eighth grade.

Working children under 16 who had not completed high school were required to attend daytime continuation school and consequently were not found in evening classes. Very few children over 16 in families receiving allowances were attending evening school. Apparently not many children in these families were learning trades. The Chicago typothetae school admitted boys on the basis of half-time school instruction and half-time actual work, and one boy in a family receiving aid was in this school. Opportunity for musical instruction at nominal fees was given at the settlement houses.

The following case stories illustrate the opportunities placed in the way of promising children:

Mrs. V. was granted aid when her older daughter, Edith, was 11 years old and the younger one, Celia, was 9 years old. Edith had exceptional ability, and as soon as she reached her fourteenth birthday a scholarship was secured for her from the Vocational Supervision League in order that she might continue through high school. By going to summer school every year she graduated from high school in three years and in September, 1919, entered the university. The Vocational Supervision League helped her to secure a university scholarship which paid her tuition and allowed her $20 a month besides. At the time of the study Edith had graduated from the university and had taught school for one year. She was helping Celia to finish her high-school course.

Mrs. Z. had a 15-year-old daughter, Adeline, a 13-year-old daughter, Lily, and a 9-year-old son, Elmer. Her husband was blind. The family lived in a shabby but respectable flat in a run-down section of the city. Adeline was in the third year of high school on a scholarship. Both Adeline and Lily were enrolled in classes in rhythmic dancing and dramatics at a near-by settlement. All three children had musical ability. Through the help of the settlement they were receiving violin lessons from one of the good musicians of the city.

Fifteen-year-old Barbara was in her second year of high school on a scholarship, and for two summers she had attended summer school in order to make faster progress. She wished to take a normal course and expected to support her mother and three younger brothers as soon as she could become a teacher. She was absorbed in books.

COOK COUNTY, ILL. 87

SCHOOLING AND WORK OF CHILDREN 14 AND 15 YEARS OLD

The child-labor, compulsory-education, and mothers' aid laws.

The child-labor law permitted children to work between 14 and 15 years of age if they had completed the sixth grade, had attended school 130 days during the preceding year, and were physically qualified for employment.[10] They were required to submit to physical examination by a physician on the staff of the vocational-guidance bureau's employment-certificate division [11] and to obtain employment certificates. Those who had not completed a four-year course of instruction in high school were required to attend continuation school not less than eight hours a week.[12]

The mothers' aid law allowed aid to be granted to the age of 16.

Children in school and at work.

It was the policy of the juvenile court to require children to go to work at 14 if they were eligible for employment certificates unless they were physically handicapped or unless they were up to their normal grades, had attained during their last school year an average of B in scholarship (the same conditions as those required by the Vocational Supervision League for the granting of its scholarships), and wished to continue in school.

There were 521 children 14 and 15 years of age in the families receiving aid; the number of boys and girls among them was not reported, nor the number who were 14 years old and the number who were 15. Of these 521 children 347 were attending school, and 172 were working; in regard to 2 the information was not complete, although it was known that they were not in actual attendance at school.

Children in school.—Among the 347 children 14 and 15 years old attending school were 162 who were eligible for employment certificates.[13] The school attendance of 136 of these 162 children was approved by the court. The remaining 26 were attending school against the court's advice; 6 were working outside school hours and earning $5 or more a week, but the potential earning capacity of the 20 who were not working was estimated as part of the family income, and deduction was made accordingly from the amount of allowance granted.

The grade or type of school attended by the 347 children 14 and 15 years old who were attending school and the number eligible and

---

[10] Ill., act of June 26, 1917, Laws of 1917, p. 511, as amended by act of July 13, 1921, Laws of 1921, p. 435. (Smith-Hurd Rev. Stat. 1925, ch. 48, secs. 17–31, pp. 1236–1240.)
[11] The vocational-guidance bureau of the Chicago public schools had in 1924 among its six principal divisions an employment-certificate division and a placement office. See Vocational Guidance and Junior Placement, pp. 155–189 (U. S. Children's Bureau Publication No. 149 and U. S. Employment Service Publication A, Washington, 1925).
[12] Ill., act of June 28, 1919, Laws of 1919, p. 919, as amended by the act of June 28, 1921, Laws of 1921, p. 816. (Smith-Hurd Rev. Stat. 1925, ch. 122, sec. 639, p. 2403.)
[13] These 162 children were eligible not only so far as age and grade completion were concerned but in all particulars. They constituted nearly half (49 per cent) of the total number of 14 and 15 year old children (334) in the mothers' aid families who were eligible for employment certificates.

ineligible for employment certificates are shown in the following table:

Number of children 14 and 15 years old who were attending school at the time of the study, by grade or type of school attended; Cook County, Ill.

Grade or type of school	Total	Not eligible for employment certificates	Eligible for employment certificates but attending school— With approval of the court	Eligible for employment certificates but attending school— Against advice of the court
Total	347	185	136	[1] 26
Elementary school:				
Fourth grade	6	6		
Fifth grade	21	21		
Sixth grade	60	60		
Seventh grade	54	33	5	16
Eighth grade	81	34	44	3
High school:				
First year	69	20	42	7
Second year	34	6	28	
Third year	8	1	7	
Fourth year	1		1	
Commercial school	9	2	7	
Other	[2] 4	2	2	

[1] 6 were working outside school hours.
[2] 1 was taking a prevocational course, another a filing course, and 2 were in a special class.

The sources through which the 136 children attending school with the approval of the court were able to postpone the necessity of working to contribute to the family income were as follows:

```
                                                                Number of
                                                                 children
    Total _____ 136
                                                                 ———
      Mothers' allowances continued_____  52
      Scholarships (from Vocational Supervision League, Scholar-
        ship Association for Jewish Children, or other agency)____  42
      Family's income up to budget, allowance discontinued_____  40
      Assistance from relatives_____   2
```

Six months before a child reached his fourteenth birthday he was sent to the employment-certificate division of the vocational-guidance bureau for a physical examination in order that any defects might be corrected by the time he was eligible for an employment certificate. (Children frequently were sent to Arden Shore; see p. 79.) The reports of the employment-certificate division for the year ended June 30, 1923, showed that 45 per cent of the children in families receiving aid who applied for employment certificates in 1923 were ineligible because of physical defects.

Children at work.—It was reported that 172 of the 521 children 14 or 15 years of age in the mothers' aid families were working but no information in regard to their occupations or their earnings was obtained.

EDUCATIONAL ACTIVITIES FOR THE MOTHERS

As the mothers' aid law required that a mother be a citizen, or at least that she should have made her declaration of intention to become a citizen of the United States, the judge allowed a temporary grant to a woman who had filed her declaration of intention. The grant was allowed only for the two years which must elapse between the declaration of intention and the application for citizenship; if the mother failed to pass her examination the grant was canceled unless there was some special reason for continuing it a few months. It required considerable time on the part of the probation officers to make sure that all the women were enrolled in the citizenship classes conducted by the board of education and were equipped to pass the examinations at the end of the two-year period. The classes were conducted in schoolhouses, settlements, and neighborhood houses whenever an enrollment of 20 was guaranteed. Attempts were made to include some social diversion in connection with these classes. There was often 15 minutes of singing, occasionally tea was served, and often a party was the climax of successful examinations. Arrangements were sometimes made for the care of young children during the class time. Two classes were conducted exclusively for mothers receiving aid. A few mothers became quite interested and continued to attend the advanced classes after they had secured their citizenship papers.

The number of mothers attending classes or clubs was not known. The citizenship classes and the nutrition classes were the group activities in which the largest numbers of the mothers were interested. As has been stated, all mothers were expected to attend the nutrition classes regularly if they had children enrolled, and a few mothers attended classes in cooking and sewing at the settlements. Some of the probation officers were encouraging mothers to join the mothers' clubs conducted in the neighborhood recreation centers. One probation officer's weekly schedule of clubs and classes for mothers under her supervision was as follows:

1. Four citizenship classes with an enrollment of 16 in each class.
2. Three mothers' clubs.
3. Two nutrition clinics conducted by the Elizabeth McCormick Memorial Fund; one nutrition clinic conducted by the Municipal Tuberculosis Dispensary; and one nutrition clinic conducted by Michael Reese Hospital. (There was a total enrollment of 25 families in the four clinics.)
4. One monthly weighing and health inventory at a settlement house by the Elizabeth McCormick Memorial Fund.

A yearly round-up of children receiving aid for the health inventory by the Elizabeth McCormick Memorial Fund.

RECREATION

The budget allowed 25 cents a month for recreation for each member of the family except the working children. If a working child earned less than $15 a week, four weeks' earnings were counted in estimating the family's monthly income and an allowance was made in the budget for his clothing, car fare, lunches, recreation, etc., and 25 cents a week was allowed him for spending money; if he earned more than $15 a week, two and two-thirds weeks' earnings were counted and one and one-third weeks' earnings were allowed him for spending money, car fare, and clothing.

The city afforded many facilities in the way of gymnasium and athletic facilities, boys' clubs, girls' clubs, settlement-house and neighborhood-house activities. Several municipal agencies conducted recreation centers which in addition to providing playgrounds and both indoor and outdoor athletics afforded women's club activities and boys' and girls' club work. One worker had just succeeded in persuading 12 Polish mothers to attend one of these mothers' clubs. The babies and little children were entertained by trained kindergartners, the club leaders played simple games with the women (this was only the second or third meeting), and the women sang one or two of their national songs. Later tea and cake were served to the mothers and milk and crackers to the children. One of the mothers was elected president and another secretary.

Some of the boys and girls had cards and used the libraries, though no special encouragement was given to children to use the public library.

The settlements provided opportunities for such activities as dramatics, music, painting, pottery and homecrafts, and dancing. Children presenting behavior problems were especially encouraged to join a club at one of the settlements, and the workers sometimes promised children in the nutrition classes that if they tried to reach normal weight they would be entered in a settlement class or club. The court encouraged mothers and children to attend their own churches and Sunday schools and to identify themselves closely with them. The Young Women's Christian Association and the Young Men's Christian Association were considered too expensive for the children to join. It was not known how many children were in scout troops. Some families had a piano or a phonograph; the purchase of either was encouraged only under special conditions, as when a working child assumed full responsibility. At least two-thirds of the families were in the habit of attending motion pictures. The probation officers received for distribution many tickets to theaters and the circus, and these gave great delight. One worker was using the $50 given her by an anonymous donor to take children on picnics to the parks or to the Field Museum or the art gallery.

As far as possible the mothers and children were given summer outings at vacation camps. One favorite form of amusement in the summer was the all-day boat excursions.

Probably all families had access to several of these sources of recreation. The degree to which families were definitely encouraged to join clubs and classes depended upon the individual probation officers, some of whom were very active. The records were full of stories of good times given children by individual visitors.

MOTHERS' ALLOWANCES IN ERIE COUNTY, N. Y.[1]

PROVISIONS OF THE LAW

The New York mothers' aid law was passed in 1915 and amended in 1916, 1917, 1919, 1920, 1922, and 1923. In its amended form aid was provided to four groups of mothers with dependent minor children: Those whose husbands were dead, inmates of State institutions for the insane, confined under a sentence of five years or more in a State prison, or permanently incapacitated or confined in an institution for the care of their particular ailment.[2]

The following conditions were imposed:

1. The allowance was to be made only on condition that if such aid were not granted the child or children would have to be cared for in an institutional home.

2. The mother was required, in the judgment of the county board of child welfare, to be a "proper person, mentally, morally, and physically, to care for and bring up the child or children."

3. The mother or relative must have been for at least two years prior to application a resident of the State and legally entitled to relief within the county or city in which she resided and in which she made application; and, further, she must have been (1) a citizen of the United States; or (2) the mother of a child or children born in the United States whose father had been a resident of the State for a period of two years immediately preceding his decease or commitment and had declared his intention to become a citizen of the United States within a period of five years immediately preceding his decease or commitment; or (3) the mother of a child or children born in the United States if she had resided in this country for a period of at least five years prior to making application for the allowance and had declared her intention to become a citizen of the United States.

---

[1] Erie County had in 1920 a population of 634,688, 506,775 of whom lived in Buffalo. The number of foreign born was 147,309, or 23.2 per cent of the total. The negroes numbered 4,954. The child population under 16 years, the legal age for mothers' aid, was 193,112. The foreign population in the order of numerical importance was as follows: Polish, German, Italian, Canadian, and Irish. (Fourteenth Census of the United States, 1920, vol. 3, Population, pp. 685, 690, 701, Washington, 1922.) The chief industries center about the flour and grist mills, slaughtering and meat-packing establishments, and the foundries and machine shops.

[2] N. Y., act of Apr. 7, 1915, ch. 228, Laws of 1915, p. 690, adding Art. 7-A to Consolidated Laws 1909; ch. 24 (Gen. Municipal Law), p. 1399, as amended by act of May 10, 1916, ch. 504, Laws of 1916, p. 1348; act of May 18, 1917, ch. 551, Laws of 1917, p. 1592; act of May 5, 1919, ch. 373, Laws of 1919, p. 1089; acts of May 11 and May 13, 1920, chs. 700, 759, Laws of 1920, pp. 1744, 1856; act of May 24, 1923, chs. 730, 731, 733, Laws of 1923, pp. 1294–1295, 1304; and act of Apr. 10, 1922, ch. 546, Laws of 1922, p. 1252, adding Art. 7-B to Consolidated Laws 1909, ch. 24 (Gen. Municipal Law), p. 1399, as amended by act of May 24, 1923, chs. 730, 733, Laws of 1923, pp. 1294, 1304. (See Cahill's Consolidated Laws 1923, ch. 26, secs. 148 to 159–a, pp. 839–844.) Further amendments were made by act of April 25, 1924, ch. 458, Laws of 1924, p. 856. (See Cahill's Supp. 1925, ch. 26, secs. 153, 157, p. 123.)

4. The allowance might not exceed the amount necessary to pay for the care of such child or children in an institution.

5. An allowance might not be made for a longer continuous period than six months without renewal but might be continued from time to time at the discretion of the local board.

6. A full and complete record was required of every case coming either directly or indirectly within the jurisdiction of the board, and reports must be filed at least quarterly.

7. Aid might be granted for a child or children up to the age of 16 years.

8. In case of the mother's death the aid might be granted for a dependent child to a " relative within the second degree of the father or mother."

According to rulings and policies adopted by the county board, a mother was permitted to have $300 in savings and to own her home if the upkeep did not exceed a reasonable rental in satisfactory quarters. Though each case was decided on its own merits, no mother receiving aid had more than $2,500 invested in a home.

STATE SUPERVISION

The law provided that the county board of child welfare should " be subject to the general supervision of the State board of charities and make such reports as the State board of charities may require." It further provided that the State board of charities, on the complaint that aid was being given in violation of the law, might make investigation and revoke the allowance or " make such order as it may deem just and equitable, and such order shall be complied with by the local board of child welfare."

A State supervisor and an assistant State supervisor of the boards of child welfare served on the staff of the New York State Board of Charities. The State supervisor in New York, as in Pennsylvania, was a standard bearer rather than an inspector. Unlike Pennsylvania, however, the State of New York provided no funds for the administration of the law. Consequently, grants were not approved by the State supervisor, nor were there kept on file at the State office any records of families receiving assistance. State supervision in New York was thus more unequivocally and exclusively educational than in any other State having State supervision. The State supervisor acted as a clearing house of information on all subjects touching mothers' aid. She prepared forms which were furnished to all the boards and which insured uniformity of record keeping. She kept in touch with the boards through frequent circular letters, sent them literature from time to time, recommended a standard budget, and kept them informed of important steps in the whole mothers' aid field in State and Nation. The State supervisor or her assistant visited each board at least once a year, studying the county work and making suggestions for its improvement. Regional conferences were held under her auspices in different parts of the State about once a year. They were attended largely and were very helpful. The

State supervisor interpreted her function as that of teacher and advisor, and her attitude was always one of encouragement to local initiative and autonomy.

ADMINISTRATION OF THE LAW

ADMINISTRATIVE AGENCY

The administration of the law was lodged in an unpaid county board of child welfare, consisting of seven members, of which the county superintendent of the poor was a member ex officio. As in other counties in which there was more than one superintendent of the poor, the county judge designated which superintendent was to serve, and he also appointed the other six members of the board for six-year terms, the term of one member expiring each year. Three of the members were women. Two of the women members and one of the men had served since the organization of the board in 1915. One member was the executive of an important family agency, two members were on district committees of the Buffalo Charity Organization Society, and all but one of the members were closely affiliated in one way or another with the social and philanthropic work of the city.

The board established rules and regulations for the conduct of its business and provided through the appointment of the executive secretary and her staff for the careful investigation of applicants and the adequate supervision of all persons receiving allowances.

THE STAFF

The staff of the Erie County Board of Child Welfare consisted of an executive secretary, a domestic educator, five field workers, one clerk, and two stenographers. No member of the staff had had less than a high-school education. The secretary had received her training in the Buffalo Charity Organization Society, having been a member of its staff for some years before her appointment as secretary of the board of child welfare. She had directed the mothers' aid department since its organization in 1915. The domestic educator had taken the course in household arts at the State normal school in Buffalo and had been on the staff of the board six years. Of the five other field workers one was a college graduate who had received one year's training in the Charity Organization Society before coming to the board of child welfare; one had been well educated in Europe, had had three and a half years' experience in the Charity Organization Society, and also had experience in the Young Women's Christian Association and Red Cross; one had taken short training courses in home service and in Americanization, and had had three years' experience in Red Cross work; one was a trained nurse with one year's experience in the Charity Organization Society; and one had been with the International Institute of the Young Women's Christian Association for three years before her appointment on the mothers' aid staff. The salary range for the field visitors was $1,200 to $1,400. The domestic educator received $1,600 per year. The entire staff were appointed under civil service and were intelligent, enthusiastic workers.

Two automobiles were furnished by the county, and automobile maintenance was allowed for three visitors who owned their cars.

APPROPRIATION AND VOLUME OF WORK

The county board of supervisors appropriated the funds for administering the law, and to them were submitted estimates of the sums necessary to carry on the work. The appropriation for 1922 was $245,439.85; for 1923, $250,000; and for 1924, $245,103.89. In 1922, $15,439.85, and in 1924, $19,103.89 was spent for administrative purposes. There was no waiting list, but the director estimated that at the time of the study 84 families were receiving inadequate grants.

On October 1, 1923, 354 families were receiving assistance, including 1,163 children under 16. The domestic educator was conducting three nutrition clinics and supervising 40 families, doing all the case work for these families. The five visitors were thus carrying between 60 and 65 families in addition to making new investigations—about 5 a month for each.

PROCEDURE IN MAKING ALLOWANCES

Applications were accepted and investigated in strict chronological order. A standard application blank was in use which had been prepared by the New York State Board of Charities. It was the most comprehensive and well-correlated form of its kind found in use in the course of the study. The following points were covered: Names, addresses, ages, birthplaces, residence in State and United States, citizenship, and marriage of parents; names, ages, and birthplaces of children; names and addresses of relatives, employers, three references, family physician, landlord, and pastor; facts regarding property, savings, wages, debts, insurance, income, and assistance rendered to the family; facts regarding the father's last illness or commitment to an institution; the health of the family; schools and grades of children or, if they were working, occupations, hours of work, employers, and wages. The application blank was filled out by the visitor and sworn to by the mother. The board of child welfare was authorized to verify statements as to property and bank accounts, and permission was to be secured from the mother for physical examinations of the children.

The first step in investigation was an inquiry at the social-service exchange as to what other agencies had been in touch with the family, and consultation with them. Verification of data was required, i. e., as to marriage, father's death or commitment, property, savings, insurance, wages, citizenship, residence, birth dates of children, and employment and wages of mother and children. The investigation also included, besides a visit to the home, visits to relatives, to the children's teachers, sometimes to the family's pastor, and to two references. Mother and children were always given a physical examination before the grant was made.

USE OF A STANDARD BUDGET

The allowances were based on the standard budget compiled by the Westchester County (N. Y.) Department of Child Welfare. The following is a copy of the budget used:

Food budget—Erie County Board of Child Welfare, June, 1923

	Per cent	Per month
Man, 17 years and up	100	$13.35
Woman, 16 years and up	80	10.68
Boy, 14–16 years	90	12.02
Boy, 12–13 years	80	10.68
Boy, 10–11 years	60	8.01
Girl, 14–16 years	70	9.35
Girl, 10–13 years	60	8.01
Child, 6–9 years	50	6.68
Child, 2–5 years	40	5.34
Under 2 years	35	4.67

Clothing cost—Erie County Board of Child Welfare

	Per month
Child, 1–3	$2.00
Child, 4–6	3.00
Child, 7–14	4.00
Woman at home or day work	4.00
Boy or girl or woman at work in store, factory, or shop, about one week's wages	6.00 or 8.00
Girl at housework	4.00

Fuel, $5.50 from November; $3.50 before November.
Light, $1.
No allowance for insurance.
Sundries, $1 for each of first three members and 50 cents for each of the others.
Pocket money, $5 per month for each working child under 18.

All mothers receiving assistance were required to keep itemized expense accounts in books furnished by the department. These books were examined by the visitors, and furnished the basis for suggestions as to diet, food values, health habits, economy in expenditures, and other matters. Each mother was required also to send to the board a monthly summary of her expenditures for rent, food, fuel, light, clothing, insurance, and sundries. Following is a copy of such a report:

ERIE COUNTY BOARD OF CHILD WELFARE

Date, _____

Name: *Mrs. D.*
Address, _____

Give your monthly expenditures here:

Rent	*$4.17*
Food	*16.39*
Fuel	*4.00*
Light	*.90*
Clothing	*16.67*
Insurance	-----
Sundries	*4.01*
Total	*46.14*

Allowance, *$59*.
Other income _____

_____
Remarks: *All are well except having colds.*
　　　　　　　　　　　　　　　(Signature)　　Mrs. D.

These monthly reports were summarized by the workers on a yearly sheet, on which was tabulated also the standard budget, so that it was possible to know how nearly the budget conformed to actual living expenses. The following is one of these yearly summaries:

Index: 5 [61].   Name: Mrs. _____   Address: _____

1923	Estimate of needs	Jan.	Feb.	Mar.	Apr.	May	June	July	Aug.	Sept.	Oct.	Nov.	Dec.	Special needs
EXPENSES														
Rent	$9.00	$9.00	$9.00	$9.00	$9.00	$9.00	$9.00	$9.00	$9.00	$9.00	$9.00	$9.00		
Food	45.42	53.91	52.99	54.13	51.99	59.99	53.45	59.97	59.81	64.40	65.99	64.98		
Fuel	5.50	13.25	13.25		13.25		9.25		13.00					
Light	1.60	.89	.77	.93	.69	.79	.77	.77	.78	.76	.76	.91		
Clothing	20.00	1.75	1.75	6.69	6.00	6.75	9.08	9.00	11.75	8.53				
Insurance		2.00	2.00	2.00	2.00	2.00	2.00	2.00	2.00	2.00	2.00	2.00		
Sundries	4.00	2.25	1.98	1.75	1.75	6.69	6.00	6.75	9.08	9.00	11.75	8.53		
Total	84.92	83.05	82.97	82.04	80.80	107.13	104.93	110.48	99.63	99.42	99.42	98.18		
INCOME														
Allowance	79.00	79.00	79.00	79.00	79.00	64.98	64.98	54.00	54.00	54.00	54.00	54.00		Lessons.
Woman to supply deficiency		4.00		4.00	3.00	1.75	3.00		5.50	5.50	5.50	4.15		
Ella's earnings							40.00	40.00	40.00	40.00	40.00	40.00		
Total	79.00	83.00	83.00	82.00	80.75	107.98	104.98	100.38	99.50	99.50	99.50	98.15		

REMARKS.—Allowance reduced in May, as Ella became 16 years of age, and was no longer entitled to the allowance. Allowance reduced in August, as family's income was over the budget.

The maximum amount of mothers' aid in Erie County was $5 a week per child. This was considered adequate except for families with one or two children and in these instances private charities were sometimes asked to supplement. The grants were paid to the mothers monthly by check. For October, 1923, the largest grant to any family was $134 a month, the smallest was $15.70, and the average was $51.81. The average grant per child was $15.73.

SUPPLEMENTING OF MOTHERS' AID

The bureau of public welfare disbursed public outdoor relief in the city of Buffalo and the county superintendent of the poor disbursed it in the county outside Buffalo. Neither of these public agencies made a practice of supplementing mothers' aid even though the maximum aid might be insufficient. However, occasional exceptions had been made. During the fiscal year ended June 30, 1923, the bureau of public welfare had given $66 for one family receiving mothers' aid, and during the calendar year 1923 the county superintendent of the poor had given $396 in supplementary aid to another family. During 1923 the Buffalo Charity Organization Society had given $472.18 in supplementary relief to four families.

VISITING

All mothers who were physically able were required to call at the office once in two months for their checks and visits were made to the homes in alternate months. In this way every mother was seen once a month and if difficulties arose more frequent visits were made. Some families were seen as often as once or even twice a week.

HEALTH

PHYSICAL HEALTH

The standard budget made no separate allowance for medical or dental care. City or county physicians could always be secured in an emergency. In cases of undernourishment, underweight, and suspected tuberculosis 10 per cent was added to the food allowance, or the higher " B " allowance, provided in the standard budget, was used.

Physical examinations.

All mothers and children were given a physical examination before a grant was made and at least once a year thereafter; in Buffalo the examinations were made at one of the seven dispensaries maintained by the city department of health. If there was need of a more thorough examination and of treatment the mothers were sent to the general diagnostic clinic at the Buffalo City Hospital; this hospital, with its clinics, was the one most generally used for mothers and adults in families receiving aid. Its social-service department was in charge of the district nurses' association, which undertook the follow-up of families in cooperation with the mothers' aid visitors. Children who were found by the preliminary examinations to be in need of further examinations and of treatment were referred to the diagnostic clinic of the Children's Hospital. The interested specialists and the hospital social-service workers cooperated with the visitors in making plans for the children. In the country examinations were made either by the county physicians or by the family's own physician, if they preferred, provided he was in good standing and would make no charge.

The examinations were considered to be of direct educational value to mothers and children in promoting a better understanding of preventive health measures. Mothers were always willing to have the children examined and usually were willing to carry out the recommendations.

The following are copies of medical reports required by the county board of child welfare:

MEDICAL-EXAMINATION REQUEST, ERIE COUNTY BOARD OF CHILD WELFARE OF BUFFALO

HEALTH CENTER No. 8:
 Please examine person described in this request and report your findings to the undersigned:
Name of patient: *Mrs. M.*
Address: _____
Persons dependent upon applicant for support or assistance: *Four children.*
Usual occupation: *Laundress.*
Physical complaint as described by patient to visitor, or as suspected by visitor:
_____ General examination required at least once a year.
Special points desired by visitor in report from dispensary:
 Name of visitor referring: *B. S.*
 District: *Domestic educator.*
 Telephone number: _____
  Respectfully,
      ERIE COUNTY BOARD OF CHILD WELFARE,
           ———— ————, *Secretary.*

MEDICAL-EXAMINATION REPORT, DISPENSARY FOR CHILDREN, FILE NO. _____
(CHILDREN'S DIAGNOSTIC CLINIC)

BUFFALO, N. Y., _____.

To ERIE COUNTY BOARD OF CHILD WELFARE:

Complying with your request of _____, the examination of James B. _____; address, _____; age 9 years, discloses the following disease or condition:

Pulse, 88; temp., 98–6; resp., 22; weight, 58 lbs.; height, 51½ inches; 10 per cent underweight for age; heart and lungs normal; abdomen negative; no orthopedic defects; vision normal.

_____ physical disability is _____, the probable duration of which will be _____.

Recommendations: (As made by examiners.)

Throat in good condition; posterior and anterior cervical glands enlarged; teeth in fair condition; coagulation time, 4 minutes; urinalysis negative; Wassermann negative; secondary anemia; nutrition advised; return to this dispensary for observation.

Respectfully,

[Signature] _____, M. D.

MEDICAL-EXAMINATION REPORT, DISPENSARY NO. _____, FILE NO. _____, DIAGNOSTIC
CLINIC (ADULTS)

BUFFALO, N. Y., _____.

Attention of _____

To ERIE COUNTY BOARD OF CHILD WELFARE:

Complying with your request of _____, the examination of Mrs. _____ discloses the following disease or condition: Dental caries, error in refraction, chronic pharyngitis, deviated septum; hyp. turbinates—left side, enlarged liver and gall bladder, visceroptosis.

Disability of 50 per cent, the probable duration of which will be three months. Anacidity; secondary anemia; external hemorrhoids; varicose veins; possible gall-bladder trouble; moderate-sized cystocele; lacerated cervix for which operation is advised; neurasthenia.

Recommendations: (As made by examiners.)

We have advised patient to return to the Buffalo City Hospital, 462 Grider Street, on Tuesday at 1 o'clock for eye, nose, and throat, gastrointestinal, and surgical clinics.

Dental care at health center No. 7, Saturday morning at 9 o'clock.

Respectfully,

[Signature] _____, M. D.,
City Physician.

The hospital clinic took the responsibility for making the yearly report of all mothers and children under its care; the yearly examinations in all other cases were made at the diagnostic clinics. The reports of the physical examinations were not filed with the social record, but so far as possible were copied on the medical-report sheet, which aimed to give a continuous picture of the health and medical treatment received by every individual under the care of the board. The following is a copy of such a medical-report sheet:

[Face]

MEDICAL-REPORT SHEET

Index: 4.　　　　　　　Name: _____　　　Address: _____

MOTHER (Mrs. Elizabeth) _____

Age	Date of examination	Examined by—	General condition	Recommendations	Follow-up work
------	5/19/18	Dr. B., U. B.	Suffering from nervous, mental, and physical strain.	Requires 1 or 2 whole days' rest from work each week.	
------	7/19/21	----------------	See attached letter of Dr. K., psychiatrist.	----------------------	Woman returns to Dr. K. frequently for physical examination and advice.

CHILDREN

Name and age	Date of examination	Examined by—	General condition	Recommendations	Follow-up work
Stanley, 14	5/7/18	Dr. L. W.	Adenoids; stunted in growth; otherwise normal.	Remove adenoids	5/23/18, adenoids removed.
James, 3	5/7/18	---do---	Well	All children need attention of dentist.	
Alice, 12	5/7/18	---do---	Stunted in growth; otherwise normal.	They should have more sleep and play and less work.	6/27/18, children had teeth cared for at U. B. dental dispensary.
Marie, 9	5/7/18	---do---	Well	----------------------	
Marie	3/9/20	Dr. R.	No disease	----------------------	
Stanley	3/9/20	---do---	---do---	----------------------	
James	3/9/20	---do---	Hypertrophied tonsils.	Operation	
Alice	3/9/20	---do---	No disease	----------------------	
Stanley	5/20	Dr. K.	See report filed	----------------------	
James	5/20	---do---	---do---	----------------------	
Alice	6/2/20	---do---	---do---	----------------------	
Marie	7/7/20	---do---	---do---	----------------------	

[Reverse]

MEDICAL-REPORT SHEET

Index: 4. Name: _____ Address: _____

MOTHER

Age	Date of examination	Examined by—	General condition	Recommendations	Follow-up work
------	1922	Dr. K------	Rheumatic condition..	W. to give up all outside work.	Recommendation carried out, with exception 1 day every 2 weeks, when W. does light work for family she has known for years and who are very helpful to her in many ways.

CHILDREN

Name and age	Date of examination	Examined by—	General condition	Recommendations	Follow up work
Alice--------	7/15/21	Dr. C------	Adenoma of thyroid. Dental caries, oral sepsis, negative neurology.	Does not require treatment at present. Report at H.C.No. 8 any Saturday morning at 9 a. m. for dental care.	
Marie--------	7/15/21	---do-----	Comparatively negative adenoma of thyroid. Dental caries, oral sepsis.	Thyroid needs no treatment. Dental care at H. C. No. 8 any Saturday at 9 a. m.	
Alice--------	7/27/22	Dr. K------	See report attached---	--------------------	Later report: Improved and gained in weight.
Do------	9/23	---do------	Slightly run down—not accustomed to her work yet, which is quite hard.	Tonic given----------	
Marie--------		---do------	Good condition at present.	To continue school work this year.	

The family visitors were responsible for securing up-to-date reports and for incorporating them in the medical-report sheet. The health agencies were careful to send written statements of diagnosis and treatment. A medical blank was always sent with the patient both when he made his first visit and when he went to the hospital or dispensary for the yearly examination. This blank was to be filled out and returned. None of the reports required very much family history, nor was the record full in this regard.

Follow-up of special types of problems.

Tuberculosis.—The city department of health maintained tuberculosis clinics. All mothers and children who had been exposed were examined and were followed up for periodic examination both by the nurses connected with the department and by the visitor in charge of the family. Sanatorium care was insisted upon for all active cases and if the mothers did not agree to this willingly the withdrawal of aid was threatened.

Venereal disease.—It was the policy of the board to have Wassermann tests taken of all members of a family when there was a history of venereal disease or reason to suspect it. Medical care needed for children was secured through the clinics of the Children's Hospital and for adults at the clinics of the City Hospital.

Orthopedic and cardiac affections.—The Children's Hospital maintained an orthopedic clinic as well as an orthopedic ward. The Crippled Children's Guild maintained a well-conducted institutional home, which gave both vocational and school instruction. Braces and all necessary apparatus were provided by the city and county departments of charities or by the Rotary Club. The Children's Hospital had a cardiac clinic and provided hospital care if necessary. At the time of the visit the Goodyear Convalescent Home was having an addition built exclusively for children with cardiac affections.

Mrs. A.'s daughter, Bertha, was badly crippled and Mrs. A. finally was told that only an operation would enable the child to walk. She was reluctant to have this done, and, though urged by physicians and mothers' aid visitors, she put off the operation from month to month, waiting a year before she finally consented. The operation was so successful that she told the surgeon to 'send her anyone who was hesitating to have such an operation performed and she would show what it had done for her child.

Mrs. H., after the death of her husband, struggled to raise her five children on the stony farm which had been her only legacy. The oldest son, Robert, 16 years of age, had been particularly opposed to his mother's applying for aid, though he was walking 5 miles twice a day to attend a business college. She made application chiefly for the sake of her crippled 13-year-old son, Ralph, who had been born with clubfeet and had spent much of his life in hospitals. Finally one leg was amputated below the knee, and as soon as possible thereafter he began attending high school, though he was sensitive and shy because he was retarded on account of continued absence. At the suggestion of the mothers' aid visitor, the family moved from the farm to a small apartment in town so that the children could be nearer school. The Rotary Club furnished a good artificial limb for Ralph and advanced his tuition at a business college in order that he might become self-supporting. As soon as Robert started to work he began to pay off the many debts which the family had been forced to contract before they began to receive mothers' aid. All the debts had been paid at the time of the visit to this home in October, 1923, and the family was moving from the small and crowded apartment to a house with bath where they would have room for the old square piano they had had to leave behind when they went away from the farm. The visitor picked up a library book which Mrs. H. said Robert was reading; it was Lamb's Essays of Elia.

Eye, ear, nose, and throat affections.—Examinations of the eyes were made at the health centers. Other treatment and operative work for affections of the ear, nose, and throat were done at the Children's Hospital.

Convalescent care.—Mothers needing convalescent care were sent to private homes in the country through the convalescent fund which was raised by private subscription. The children needing such care were sent to the Josephine Goodyear Convalescent Home, which provided excellent medical and physical care.

Health work for infants and preschool children.—Seven child-health centers for children up to 6 years of age were conducted by the city department of health under the nursing supervision of the district nurses' association. The board insisted that all mothers receiving aid take their babies regularly to the centers, but less emphasis was put on taking children over 2 years old. If mothers with young babies failed to attend, the child-health centers reported their nonattendance to the executive secretary of the county board of child welfare. Most of the mothers in the city could walk to the centers, and none needed to change cars. For the mothers living beyond the city limits no such centers were available.

School medical inspection.—School children were given physical examinations, including dental inspection, once a year. Five dental clinics were available for children and adults at the child-health centers. Twenty-four school nurses arranged for the correction of physical defects. The quarterly school report sent to the board of child welfare called for the "result of the last physical examination and the need of follow-up work" and asked whether the child seemed tired or ill nourished (see p. 105). If this report indicated that medical care was necessary the visitor arranged for it; otherwise the school reports of medical inspections were not followed up.

Malnutrition.—Height and weight measurements of school children were taken by the teachers or by a member of the physical-education staff, and nutrition classes were conducted by school nurses for children 10 per cent or more underweight in 20 schools. These children were weighed weekly. It was not known how many mothers' aid children attended the nutrition classes in the schools.

A domestic educator had been on the staff of the board of child welfare for six years. As a part of her regular duties she supervised three weekly nutrition classes each having an enrollment of about 20 children. These were in neighborhoods not covered by the nutrition classes in the schools. Two classes were held in an Italian and one in a Polish community. They were conducted by six senior students in the household-arts department of the Buffalo State Normal School. In addition to the class work the supervision of one family was assigned to each student, who was required to visit the family once a week and to submit a monthly written report.

The doctor's report following the periodic examinations of the children at the health center was used as a basis of selection for these nutrition classes. The children were weighed and measured every other week, and weight charts were made showing their actual and normal weight and the curves up or down. Health habits were inculcated by means of games, songs, lantern slides, and plays. Most of the children reached their normal weight. The mothers were urged to attend the Saturday morning classes with the children and the average attendance of mothers was about 14.

When there were cases of malnutrition in families who lived too far from the city to attend the classes instruction was given in the homes. The children were given copies of the health rules and stories and were weighed every two weeks. The charts were drawn and weights recorded. One child who was reported by the examining physician as weighing 57 pounds and being 12 per cent underweight was given home instruction and weighed every other week. The mother was very cooperative, and in three months the child gained the amount required to bring her up to normal weight. In another case it was the mother whom the doctor reported as being underweight to the point of emaciation; he recommended close supervision, good diet, and plenty of fresh air. The mother followed the plans faithfully and gained 14 pounds in the course of a year in spite of a severe attack of grippe.

Supervision of selected families.—The domestic educator supervised about 40 families selected because of malnutrition, improper diet, poor management, or untidy and dirty housekeeping. She was responsible for handling all the problems in these homes. Each family kept an account book of daily expenditures. Where there were improper diet and malnutrition the families were given a dietary to follow, which was designed to remedy these ills and at the same time to keep them within the allowance provided in the budget for food. Keeping within the clothing allowance was a problem; it was often possible to teach the women how to use patterns and to make over garments. Few could attend the night-school sewing classes, as they had no one with whom to leave the children. As a rule they were very grateful for this help, though it required in some instances a number of purely friendly visits before the problems could even be broached. The following story illustrates the education of such a mother by the domestic educator:

Mrs. D.'s family, who were transferred to the supervision of the regular mothers' aid visitor in October, 1923, had been visited first by the domestic educator in September, 1919. At that time Mrs. D. and her six children under 12 years of age were living on the insurance left by Mr. D. at his death. Mrs. D. owned her little frame cottage, but it was badly in need of repair. There was only one bed in the house; those of the family who could not sleep in the bed slept on a mattress on the floor or on the floor without a mattress. Yet Mrs. D. had just invested her last $50 in a rug. A grant of $80 a month was allowed, and the domestic educator sought to inculcate some appreciation of thrift in Mrs. D. She called once a week; and as she often brought with her a bargain she had picked up, Mrs. D. began giving her a few dollars ahead to apply on household necessities when she saw bargains. Thus were purchased beds, mattresses, and blankets, a stove, sewing machine, sideboard, and rug. Repairs were made on the house also, and the domestic educator gave much instruction and help in making clothes for the children.

This progress was not without difficulties, and once or twice Mrs. D. reverted to her former habit of getting into debt or buying on installments; but as she learned how much she saved by the thriftier method of "pay as you go" she became entirely converted eventually. When the visitor called it was not unusual to find Mrs. D. varnishing the woodwork, painting the old beds, or papering the kitchen. Together with the transformation in Mrs. D. there came about a great improvement in the children. The school reports, which formerly had been discouraging, stated, "The children do well in school and are a credit to your department." By October, 1923, the family had been transferred to one of the regular mothers' aid visitors. Mrs. D. gave the domestic educator a cordial welcome when she returned for a friendly chat.

MENTAL HEALTH

Available facilities.

Mental clinics were conducted at the Jewish Community House and the Children's Hospital by a psychiatrist from the Buffalo State Hospital for the Insane. No social worker was connected with the clinics, but case workers connected with other agencies did the follow-up work under the direction of the psychiatrist. There was no psychopathic institute nor any opportunity for observing the psychopathic child under hospital care. The City Hospital maintained a psychopathic ward for adults only.

The psychological department of the board of education was chiefly concerned with mental testing as a basis for placement in the special classes and in the opportunity school. This department also examined children from the court.

Follow-up of special types of problems.

The visitors did not ordinarily ask to have a child examined for retardation alone, but it was the policy of the board to have children examined if the recent family history showed mental defect or disease. Members of mothers' aid families who showed symptoms of mental defect were examined at the mental clinic of the Children's Hospital, and those needing institutional care were placed in the Syracuse Custodial Institution or in the State custodial school at Rome, N. Y. Children who appeared to be psychopathic or who presented behavior problems were likewise examined at the mental clinic, and the family visitors attempted to carry out the instructions of the psychiatrist. The help of the child's mother, teacher, and minister was enlisted, and frequently an effort was made to interest the child in clubs or to secure a "big brother." The court was appealed to only as a last resort.

HOUSING

Buffalo had not been affected quite so seriously by the housing shortage as had some cities like Cincinnati, Chicago, Detroit, and Pittsburgh, and it had been possible to define and live up to certain housing standards. The board preferred single houses, and much emphasis was laid upon rearing the children in good neighborhoods. The families were encouraged to cultivate a small garden, if possible; if the house was not situated on a lot large enough for cultivation, vacant lots could be secured through the department of public welfare, which also provided seed. Nearly all the 66 country families lived in single cottages in good neighborhoods. They were sanitary and had abundant room and yard space and small flower and vegetable gardens. Most of them were provided with outdoor closets and had running water inside the house. These families used the cellar for cooling and had neither gas nor electricity. Many of the other families lived in cottages on the outskirts of the city. It was the policy of the board to have all families move away from the congested tenement district, and only one family was living in a downtown tenement, the mother not yet having been persuaded to leave her friends and neighbors for sunshine and fresh air. All city families had running water; the majority had gas and some had electricity; most families had adequate facilities for keeping food cool though not always in an ice box.

Three rooms were the minimum requirement for a mother and three children—the average number of children per family. A living room was considered essential, especially where there were growing children, though it might be used as a sleeping room. The board insisted that there should be a bed for every two people and that adolescent girls and boys should have separate sleeping rooms. No

dark rooms were allowed. The board preferred that each family should have its own toilet, though two families sometimes used the same toilet. A considerable number of the city families had bathrooms.
There was no absolute limit as to rent; generally rents were not more than $20 or $25, though a few families paid $30 or $35 per month. Home ownership was encouraged, providing the upkeep did not exceed a reasonable rental. Sixty-five mothers owned or partly owned their homes. The efforts of the board of child welfare to have good homes for mothers' aid families may be inferred from the following case story:

In one of the good residence sections of Buffalo was an attractive six-room cottage which had been the home of the B. family for more than a generation, and in which Mrs. B. and her five children had been born. With the idea of reducing her living expenses, Mrs. B. sold the house. She regretted this step almost immediately when she realized that the rent for another house as good was quite beyond the family's reach. The children were under the supervision of a tuberculosis clinic and had been making good use of the flower-filled garden that surrounded this old home. A member of the board of child welfare, realizing the importance to the family of the life in their old home, succeeded in buying back the place—after many tedious parleys with the new owners—for $500 more than the price for which it had been sold. The good effects of the return to the familiar surroundings and the renewed contacts with old acquaintances was plainly shown by the family.

EDUCATION

COOPERATION WITH THE SCHOOLS AND FACILITIES FOR EDUCATION

Contacts with the schools.

The mothers' aid workers watched over the school progress of the children under their care. The schools were visited whenever special need arose, and confidential school reports covering attendance, deportment, aptitude, punctuality, scholarship, disposition, and health were mailed quarterly by the teachers to the mothers' aid office on forms furnished by the State board of charities.
The following is a copy of such a school report:

ERIE COUNTY BOARD OF CHILD WELFARE

CONFIDENTIAL SCHOOL REPORT—ISSUED QUARTERLY

School: _____Date: _____
Name of child: *James B.* Age: *12.* Grade: *7th.*
Address: _____
Attendance: *Perfect.* Punctuality: *Good.* Deportment: *Excellent.* Scholarship: *Excellent.*
Special aptitude: *Music.* Is child cheerful? *Yes.* Is he cooperative? *Yes.* Is he quarrelsome? *No.* Does he make friends easily? *Yes.* Does he seem tired? *No.* Does he seem well nourished? *Yes.* Does he appear well cared for. *Yes.*
Remarks: *It is a pleasure to teach the B. children.*
Results of physical examination and need of follow-up work, if any_____
(Signed) _____
Teacher.

Less detailed reports were received monthly for each school child, all children in one family being listed on one sheet. This report covered only attendance, grades, and progress. The following is such a monthly report:

ERIE COUNTY BOARD OF CHILD WELFARE

SCHOOL-ATTENDANCE BLANK

School: _____
School records of: _____   Address: _____

Names	Grade	Present	Absent
Annie Z_____	Sixth_____	40 days_____	
Bessie Z_____	Fifth_____	____do_____	
Caroline Z_____	Third_____	39 days_____	1 day.

Progress: Annie and Caroline have average standings of *Excellent* (90 to 100). Bessie has *Good* (80 to 90).
            (Signed) _____
                                                       Principal.

Provision for handicapped children.

The physically handicapped child.—The department of education conducted two sight-conservation classes, four open-air classes, and one class for the deaf; one teacher was employed for the children having speech defects. The department also supplied a kindergarten and grade teacher to the Crippled Children's Guild, a home for crippled children, where besides expert medical care vocational training was given, such as manual work, sewing, music, business training, or special education suited to individual needs. No teacher was assigned to the orthopedic ward of the Children's Hospital. No bus was provided for transportation. No mothers' aid children were in any of these classes.

The mentally handicapped child.—There were 25 special classes for subnormal children and also an opportunity school for mentally defective boys 13 to 16 years of age. Instruction was given in shoe, rug, and broom making, in chair caning, and in carpentry. Two boys in families receiving mothers' aid were in this school. The number of mothers' aid children attending special classes was not known.

Provision for children wishing further education.

Very few scholarships were available, and none for work below college grade. The University of Buffalo offered freshman scholarships based upon academic work in high school, and a woman's club had helped several girls in families receiving mothers' aid. The mothers' aid workers expended much energy in ascertaining the special aptitudes of children approaching working age and in providing opportunities for short intensive courses, such as business courses. Psychological tests were made if it seemed advisable to have them as a basis for determining the kind of training necessary. Tuition for such courses was not given from the mothers' aid fund, but a loan was generally forthcoming to be repaid when the child secured work or an interested member of a men's club was appealed to or a relative or the church.

Few children were attending night school, though one 15-year-old boy was attending high school both in the daytime and in the evening in order to spend as much time as he could on chemistry, in which he was greatly interested. One boy was taking a correspondence course in bookkeeping and was doing well; another was apprenticed to a tinsmith and was making fine progress in learning the trade. A small number of children were taking music lessons at settlements, a few of which provided free music lessons or made only a nominal charge. The budget did not allow for any special items of an educational nature. Most families took a daily paper and some a magazine.

The following case story illustrates the work done in securing opportunity for children capable of further education than had seemed to be within their reach:

<blockquote>
Margaret L. had been an honor student all through high school. Her father had been a locomotive engineer up to the time of his sudden death, and there had been no reason to think that she would not have the college education upon which she had set her heart. But there were two children younger than Margaret, and the mother was suffering from goiter. The maximum grant of $52 a month was allowed, and Mrs. L. was able to take a half-time clerical position. Margaret worked in the summer and on Saturday and Sunday as a telephone operator. She won a $200 scholarship at the university, which tided her over the first year, and the second year she was able to borrow from the university loan fund the money for her college fees. The board of child welfare secured still another small scholarship for her from a club.
</blockquote>

SCHOOLING AND WORK OF CHILDREN 14 AND 15 YEARS OF AGE

The compulsory-education, child-labor, and mothers' aid laws.

The compulsory-education law required that children should not leave school to work full time until they were 14 years old. Children 14 years old might obtain employment certificates if certain school-attendance requirements had been met and they had graduated from a public elementary school or its equivalent; children 15 years old might obtain employment certificates if school-attendance requirements had been met and they had completed the sixth grade; children 16 years old were required to have certificates after September 1, 1925, and might obtain them irrespective of school attendance or educational requirements. Certificates of physical fitness were required for all children between 14 and 17 years of age before they could obtain employment certificates. Attendance at continuation school was required to the age of 17 years [3] where such schools had been established (as in Buffalo).[4]

The mothers' aid law permitted allowances to be granted for children up to the age of 16.

Children in school and at work.

The board encouraged children to obtain as much education as possible, and when they were of normal intelligence and the mother could be persuaded to consent they were kept in school until 16 years of age. If a child had unusual ability or especially desired to stay in school beyond the age of 16 years some plan was made whereby he might

---

[3] After September, 1928, to 18 years.
[4] N. Y., Cahill's Consolidated Laws, 1923, ch. 15, secs. 601, 621, 626, 630, pp. 461, 466, 467, 468. (Cahill's Consolidated Supp. 1923, ch. 15, sec. 601, p. 76.) This was further amended by act of May 1, 1924, ch. 524, Laws of 1924, p. 943.

continue even though it was necessary to discontinue the allowance for his support when he reached this age.

There were 160 children (76 boys and 84 girls) 14 and 15 years of age in the families receiving aid; 77 of them were 14 years old and 83 were 15 years old. Of these 160 children, 139 (87 per cent) were attending school, 14 were working, and 7 were neither attending school nor working.

Children in school.—Among the 139 children 14 and 15 years old attending school were 81 who were eligible for employment certificates so far as educational requirements were concerned.[5]

The number of boys and girls 14 and 15 years old who were attending school and the grade or type of school attended are shown in the following table:

Number of children 14 and 15 years old attending school at the time of the study, by grade or type of school; Erie County, N. Y.

Grade or type of school	Children 14 and 15 years old attending school						
	Total	Boys			Girls		
		Total	14 years	15 years	Total	14 years	15 years
Total	139	62	37	25	77	37	40
Elementary school:							
Third grade	1	1	1				
Fifth grade	3	2	2		1	1	
Sixth grade	11	6	5	1	5	4	1
Seventh grade	32	19	12	7	13	8	5
Eighth grade	31	12	9	3	19	8	11
High school:							
First year	29	[1]9	3	6	20	8	12
Second year	11	1		1	10	6	4
Third year	6	1		1	5		5
Vocational school	7	7	4	3			
Business school	4	1			3	1	2
Special class	2	1	1		1	1	
Other and not reported	2	2		[2]2			

[1] 1 in parochial college (first year). [2] 1 in agricultural training school; 1 not reported.

The 14-year-old boy in the third grade was a moron, but was not attending a special class because none was available in the district school. Twenty-seven of the children in high school or vocational school were studying commercial subjects or preparing themselves for special kinds of work, such as cabinet making, drafting, electrical work, household arts, and painting and finishing. Eleven children were working after school, helping to pay their expenses in this way.

Occupations and earnings of the working children.—All the 14 working children had started to work when they were 15 years old except a girl who had left school at 14 years of age when she was in the eighth grade. Of these 14 children 1 had left school in the fifth grade, 3 in the sixth, 2 in the seventh, 4 in the eighth, 3 in the first year of high school, and 1 in vocational school. The occupa-

[5] This number was 85 per cent of all the children in mothers' aid families who had fulfilled the school-grade requirement for going to work (95).

tions of these children were as follows: Two boys were cabinetmakers, two girls were factory workers, and two were housemaids. One boy was employed in each of the following occupations: Shopwork, machine operating, driving delivery wagon, working for furniture company, working in department store, and acting as errand boy. One girl was kitchen worker in an institution and one was a bundle girl. Ten of the 14 were earning $30 to $39 a month, 1 was earning $43, 1 was earning $52, 1 was earning $60, and 1 was earning $61. Only two families had no income except the children's earnings and the mothers' allowances. All the children except one contributed their entire earnings to the family support.

Children neither in school nor at work.

Six boys and one girl had left school and were not working. Three of the boys were looking for work at the time of the study, however, and the girl was helping her mother with the housework. The three remaining children were mentally unstable or inferior, one being in an institution for epileptics and another on the waiting list for admission to an institution for the feeble-minded.

EDUCATIONAL ACTIVITIES FOR THE MOTHERS

The county board of child welfare encouraged the foreign-born mothers under its supervision to attend citizenship and English classes and about 15 were enrolled. A number attended classes conducted by the International Institute of the Young Women's Christian Association. Five were members of sewing classes. One who was interpreter in a broker's office in a Polish neighborhood was attending an evening real-estate class in a high school. Home making, cooking, sewing, food values, marketing, and proper expenditure of money were taught by the domestic educator on the administrative staff and also by the county home bureau.[6]

RECREATION

The budget allowed $5 a month to working children under 18 years of age for spending money. This was not expected to cover lunches, car fare, nor clothing. When the boy or girl became 18 years old a satisfactory plan was generally worked out with the mother or reasonable board was paid.

The recreation available to most of the city families included the social activities of the churches, the nine settlements, playgrounds, Boy Scout troops, the Young Men's Christian Association, and the Young Women's Christian Association. Much stress was laid on a close church connection, and in the country, especially, the mothers' aid families found their good times in the church and neighborhood gatherings. Many children had library cards. A few children belonged to the Young Men's Christian Association and the Young Women's Christian Association, but in general it was felt that the fees were prohibitive except for those boys in whom members of the

---

[6] The county home bureau had organized about 30 women's clubs with a membership of some 700, acting under the Smith-Lever law (the act of Congress of May 8, 1914 (38 Stat. 372), providing for cooperative agricultural extension work between certain agricultural colleges and the U. S. Department of Agriculture).

Kiwanis Club had become interested. The children in many of the families were in touch with the settlements, which provided opportunities for much wholesome fun; but not many mothers had learned as yet to use them. A number of families owned pianos or phonographs, and the board encouraged the purchase of inexpensive instruments by working children as a means of home entertainment.

Many children, but few of the mothers, were able to get away for a two weeks' outing at one of the summer-vacation camps operated by the settlements or the fresh-air mission. Members of the Kiwanis Club were interested in 10 boys in families receiving mothers' aid. Each man thus interested visited the home of the boy assigned to him, followed his school work, opened a bank account for him, depositing $5 to his credit, encouraged him to join a Boy Scout troup, provided for a two weeks' summer outing, and planned for educational or employment opportunities. Two brothers under the care of one club member visited him every week, were taken on Sunday motor rides, and were advised as to books and reading.

MOTHERS' ALLOWANCES IN HAMILTON COUNTY, OHIO [1]

PROVISIONS OF THE LAW

The Ohio mothers' aid law, passed in 1913 and amended in 1915, 1919, and 1921,[2] provided for allowances to four classes of mothers with dependent minor children: Widows, mothers whose husbands were permanently disabled by reason of physical or mental infirmity or were prisoners or had deserted, provided such desertion had continued for a period of three years. Two years' legal residence in the county granting assistance was required, and the following other conditions were imposed by the law:

1. The child or children must be living with the mother.
2. The allowance was to be made only when in the absence of such allowance the mother would be required to work regularly away from home and children.
3. The mother must, in the judgment of the court, be a proper person morally, physically, and mentally, for the bringing up of her children, and it must appear to be for the benefit of the children to remain with the mother.
4. Such allowance must, in the judgment of the court, be necessary to save the children from neglect and avoid the breaking up of the home.
5. Aid might be allowed up to the age when a child was eligible for a work certificate.

An important amendment to the law, which increased the maximum tax levy for mothers' aid from one-tenth of a mill to two-tenths on the dollar valuation of taxable property in the county, became effective in 1920. Another increased the maximum allowance to $35 a month for the first child and $10 a month for each of the other children.

The law provided that the order making the allowance to a mother should not be effective for a period longer than six months, but might be extended at the end of that time at the discretion of the judge. It also provided that the homes of the pensioners should be visited from time to time by a probation officer or other trained person, the report of such visits to be considered by the court in making the allowance.

---

[1] The population of Hamilton County in 1920 was 493,678, of whom 401,247 lived in Cincinnati. The native white inhabitants numbered 411,199; the foreign born, 48,658; and the negro, 33,747. The inhabitants of foreign birth were as follows, in the order of their numerical importance: German, Russian, Irish, Hungarian, and Italian. The child population within the legal age for mothers' aid was 124,811. (Fourteenth Census of the United States, 1920, vol. 3, Population, pp. 778, 784, 793, 794, Washington, 1922.) The chief industries center around slaughtering and meat packing, foundries and machine shops, and the manufacture of men's clothing, boots, and shoes.

[2] Ohio, act of May 9, 1913, Laws of 1913, p. 877, as amended by act of June 2, 1915, Laws of 1915, p. 436; act of June 5, 1919, Laws of 1919, p. 624; act of Apr. 8, 1921, Laws of 1921, p. 70. (See Page's Annotated Gen. Code, secs. 1683-2 to 1683-10, pp. 898-900.)

The law did not designate the amount of property and savings a mother might have, but stipulated simply that she be "poor." If a family was paying for its home at the time the mother applied for aid the juvenile court (which was the administrative agency) encouraged her to keep up the payments, provided they did not exceed a reasonable rental, the house was a good investment, and the mortgage did not exceed $3,000 or $4,000. The average value of the homes owned was about $3,500. A mother was allowed to have cash savings amounting to $200, but there was no formal ruling on this subject. A mother was not permitted by the court to keep men roomers or lodgers.

ADMINISTRATION OF THE LAW

ADMINISTRATIVE AGENCY AND STAFF

The administration of the mothers' aid law in Hamilton County, Ohio, was lodged in the department of mothers' pensions and dependency of the juvenile court. The judge of the juvenile court had appointed a committee of five persons (including representatives from local private relief agencies) to consider each application for an allowance and make recommendation to him.

The staff of the department consisted of the supervisor and two field workers, all of whom were probation officers appointed by the judge under civil-service regulation. The supervisor gave part time to the mothers' aid work, and the two field workers usually gave most of their time to this work (though at the time of the study one of them had been giving half time to mothers' aid work and half time to the dependency work). The supervisor was a college graduate, also a graduate of the New York School of Social Work, and she had had considerable experience in case work, both in courts and elsewhere. One field worker had had three and one-half years of college work, had taken training courses in social work, and had been on the staff of the juvenile court for six years; the other had had no case-work experience before she was appointed probation officer three years previously.

As the juvenile court had not the funds to employ a staff sufficiently large to supervise all the families to whom allowances were granted, three private family agencies in Cincinnati gave assistance in the supervisory work. These were the Cincinnati Associated Charities, the Bureau of Catholic Charities, and the United Jewish Social Agencies.

The advisory mothers' pension committee consisting of five citizens appointed by the judge of the juvenile court considered each application for an allowance and made a recommendation to the judge, who generally acted in accordance with it. This committee did not meet except to consider applications, and it had held no meeting for a year, as the small size of the appropriations had precluded any grants during that time.

APPROPRIATION AND VOLUME OF WORK

The amount spent for mothers' aid in 1922 was $187,012 and in 1923 was $183,404. There was a waiting list of about 500 families.

The September payment to mothers' aid families was $14,649. All administrative expenses were met by the court from its general budget. The average monthly grant was $30.71 per family and $11.40 per child.

The total number of families receiving allowances in October, 1923, was 470, including 1,285 children under 16 years of age. The juvenile court was supervising 238 of these families. In general it retained under its supervision those families whose need was primarily economic and whose plans could be made with a little friendly guidance, as the limited staff did not permit intensive visiting to many families. The court also supervised all the mothers' aid families living outside the city of Cincinnati. The average number of mothers' aid families supervised by each of the court workers was 119, not including the work of the supervisor, who as a rule did not do actual case work. The three private relief agencies assisting the court supervised the remaining families as follows: The Cincinnati Associated Charities, 132; the Bureau of Catholic Charities, 86; and the United Jewish Social Agencies, 14. (The first two of these private agencies assumed responsibility only for the families receiving aid who had been known to them previously; the third supervised all the Jewish families to whom allowances were granted.)

PROCEDURE IN MAKING ALLOWANCES

Application was made in person at the mothers' aid office in the juvenile-court building. An application form was filled out with the information given by the mother on date of birth, birthplace, citizenship, residence, and religion of both parents; facts regarding the father (whether dead, imprisoned, disabled, or deserting); names, ages, schools, and grades (or, if working, employers and wages) of children; the mother's occupation, earnings, and hours away from home; sources of income, insurance, debts, property, and weekly expenses; housing conditions; health; names of relatives; names of pastor, physician, and other references; and the date of juvenile-court record if any of the children had been before the court.

The name of the family was registered in the confidential exchange and the interested agencies were consulted. Marriage, citizenship, facts regarding the father's death, incapacity, desertion, imprisonment, or insanity, and facts regarding property were verified. A visit to the home was made, and several references (usually four or five) such as a relative, landlady, physician, and friends were consulted. A written statement covering school attendance and scholarship for each child in the family was obtained from the children's teachers. Although in the past the private relief agencies had assisted in the work of investigation, it was the policy of the court at the time of the study to make its own first investigations. The families selected for assistance were those in which the mothers seemed most able to make good homes for their children.

USE OF A STANDARD BUDGET

A budget following a schedule prepared by the dietitian of the Cincinnati Associated Charities and used by all the local case-work agencies had been adopted. Rent was allowed as paid, and no allowance was made for insurance. A copy of the budget is as follows:

Weekly budget for families of specified sizes

Number of units[1]	Food	Clothing	Light and fuel	Miscellaneous	Number of units[1]	Food	Clothing	Light and fuel	Miscellaneous
1.0	$3.18	$1.00	$0.80	$1.00	4.1	$11.74	$3.46	$1.87	$3.46
1.5	5.25	1.55	.84	1.55	4.2	12.02	3.52	1.91	3.52
1.6	5.55	1.63	.87	1.63	4.3	12.30	3.58	1.94	3.58
1.7	5.84	1.70	.91	1.70	4.4	12.59	3.65	1.97	3.65
1.8	6.13	1.78	.95	1.78	4.5	12.88	3.71	2.01	3.71
1.9	6.41	1.89	1.01	1.89	4.6	13.17	3.78	2.03	3.78
2.0	6.68	1.98	1.07	1.98	4.7	13.45	3.85	2.07	3.85
2.1	6.95	2.06	1.12	2.06	4.8	13.76	3.92	2.12	3.92
2.2	7.21	2.15	1.18	2.15	4.9	14.02	3.98	2.15	3.98
2.3	7.47	2.23	1.22	2.23	5.0	14.31	4.04	2.18	4.04
2.4	7.72	2.32	1.28	2.32	5.1	14.44	4.09	2.21	4.09
2.5	7.99	2.41	1.33	2.41	5.2	14.72	4.15	2.25	4.15
2.6	8.29	2.49	1.37	2.49	5.3	15.01	4.21	2.29	4.21
2.7	8.59	2.57	1.43	2.57	5.4	15.12	4.26	2.31	4.26
2.8	8.89	2.66	1.46	2.66	5.5	15.41	4.32	2.34	4.32
2.9	9.19	2.75	1.50	2.75	5.6	15.59	4.37	2.35	4.37
3.0	9.48	2.84	1.53	2.84	5.7	15.77	4.43	2.39	4.43
3.1	9.76	2.90	1.56	2.90	5.8	16.05	4.49	2.43	4.49
3.2	9.98	2.95	1.59	2.95	5.9	16.33	4.55	2.46	4.55
3.3	10.18	3.01	1.62	3.01	6.0	16.41	4.62	2.50	4.62
3.4	10.39	3.06	1.65	3.06	6.1	16.68	4.68	2.54	4.68
3.5	10.58	3.12	1.67	3.12	6.2	16.96	4.74	2.57	4.74
3.6	10.77	3.17	1.71	3.17	6.3	17.02	4.80	2.60	4.80
3.7	10.96	3.23	1.73	3.23	6.4	17.30	4.87	2.63	4.87
3.8	11.13	3.28	1.76	3.28	6.5	18.57	4.95	2.67	4.95
3.9	11.29	3.34	1.80	3.34	6.7	18.10	5.02	2.70	5.02
4.0	11.45	3.39	1.83	3.39	7.0	18.92	5.09	2.73	5.09

[1] The family needs were calculated by using the needs of an adult man as a base and computing for a family living together the needs of the mother and of children of different ages as percentages of this, as follows:

Adult man 1.0
Adult woman, boy 13–14, girl 15–16 8
Boy 15–16 9
Boy 12, girl 13–14 7
Boy 10–11, girl 10–12 6
Child 6–9 4
Child under 2 3

No special effort was made through the use of expense accounts or family menus to ascertain the diet of the families receiving allowances, and only in individual cases was an attempt made to regulate food purchases or to give the mothers instruction in regard to foods.

SUPPLEMENTING OF MOTHERS' AID

Although the maximum aid allowed by law was liberal and it was intended that the grants should cover the deficit in the family budget, a reduction in the appropriation had seriously handicapped the department of mothers' pensions during the year in which the study was made, and many families in Cincinnati would have suffered if the private agencies had not generously supplemented their allowances. Information as to how the families outside Cincinnati had maintained themselves was not available.

In 1922 the Cincinnati Associated Charities spent $6,000 in behalf of the mothers' aid families under its supervision. This did not include the aid given to families on the waiting list (the amount of which was not ascertained). At the time of the study supplementary aid on a large scale had ceased because of lack of funds, and was confined to milk for five families and material relief for one; but a considerable number of families on the waiting list were still being aided.

The Bureau of Catholic Charities spent in 1923 the sum of $7,104.75 for supplementary relief to mothers' aid families. In addition, medical service was rendered by its clinics, and relief was being given to families on the waiting list. During approximately the same time (in the fiscal year ended February 28, 1923) the United Jewish Social Agencies gave $4,686.65 in supplementary relief to the 16 Jewish families that received mothers' aid during the year and $3,050.76 to 4 Jewish families on the waiting list.

VISITING

As the court did not have a staff sufficiently large to permit frequent visits to all the families under its supervision, some of those outside the city of Cincinnati could be visited only once or twice a year by the probation officers. However, the nurses employed by the county department of health gave much friendly service and were in touch with these families; and the policy of the private agencies assisting in supervision required a visit at least once a month, and oftener if necessary.

HEALTH

PHYSICAL HEALTH

No allowance was made in the budget for medical care, dentistry, or other expenses incident to health. Special diet was generally procurable through relief societies or the Babies' Milk Fund Association.

Physical examinations.

The foundation of the health work lay in the physical examinations of mothers and children required before or just after the grants were made. The majority of the city families were examined at the Cincinnati General Hospital. The Jewish families were examined at the general or specialized medical clinics maintained by the United Jewish Social Agencies at their community center. No special forms were used, and the reports were incorporated in the family medical record, which was not a part of the social record.

The children living outside Cincinnati, Norwood, and St. Bernard were examined at the county clinics conducted by the district board of health.

Follow-up of physical examinations and special types of problems.

Families under the care of the United Jewish Social Agencies attended its diagnostic and corrective clinics and the follow-up work was done by nurses under medical supervision. This agency was the only one of the three assisting the court that had the children under its supervision examined annually; but the mothers were examined only when specific need was indicated. Most of the Catholic families were cared for through the clinics maintained by the Bureau of Catholic Charities and were followed up by the nurses connected with that bureau. The diagnosis and medical treatment advised for these families were incorporated in the medical but not in the social record.

Families examined by the Cincinnati General Hospital were referred for corrective work to a specialized clinic as the need indicated. This clinic was generally at the hospital and follow-up work was done by medical social workers at the hospital. A written statement was sent to the court, which incorporated it in the column on the medical sheet headed "Treatment given." The treatment given was indicated also on the case record and long-continued follow-up work was done by the hospital social-service department or by the family visitor. Mothers and children living in the country were brought to the city hospitals and clinics by the district nurses, who attended to all the health needs of the families. The follow-up of families by medical agencies often continued for years, and the records showed that it might be close even though the case-work agency did not always keep in touch with them.

Dental work for adults was provided free by the dental clinic of the Cincinnati General Hospital. Physical defects were generally corrected promptly; mothers were induced to give their consent through threatened withdrawal of the grant if necessary, though persuasion nearly always produced the desired results. The mothers were for the most part very willing to have the preliminary examinations made, and the supervisor was of the opinion that they were of direct educational value. A few mothers consulted their own private physicians, and this was not interfered with if no fee or only a nominal one was charged. City physicians could be secured in an emergency, but they were not generally used.

Tuberculosis.—Tuberculous patients were referred to a health center conducted by the city board of health and were followed up by the nurses connected with the department. In the country there were no clinics, but the district board of health nurses visited the patients and attempted to secure medical care for them. All mothers' aid families who had been exposed to tuberculosis were referred to the clinic, and it was the policy of all the family agencies to keep undernourished and pretuberculous families under their regular supervision.

Venereal disease.—Whenever there was reason to suspect venereal disease Wassermann tests were taken of all members of the family. Treatment could be obtained at venereal clinics at the health center and the general hospital.

Eye, ear, nose, and throat affections.—There were numerous clinics for eye examinations and for affections of the eye, ear, nose, and throat.

Orthopedic and cardiac affections.—Orthopedic cases were referred to the orthopedic clinic of the Cincinnati General Hospital and were followed up by the hospital school if treatment was needed. Occasionally a child was committed to the State department of welfare, which would secure the necessary care and charge the bill to the county. The Rotary Club in the county paid for braces and special apparatus. Children suffering from cardiac affections were given medical care at the cardiac clinic of the Cincinnati General Hospital.

Two girls for whom aid was being granted were receiving treatment. One who was 13 years old had had infantile paralysis at 7 months of age and her 15-year-old sister had tuberculosis of the hip. Both were receiving massage, muscle training, posture work, and other forms of physiotherapy.

Health work for infants and preschool children.—In the city the children under 6 years of age were referred to the six child-health centers maintained by the Babies' Milk Fund Association or to one of the three centers conducted by the board of health. The children were followed up by the nurses connected with the centers. In the summer months the board of health maintained four additional centers. In Cincinnati at least half the mothers lived near enough to a center to walk to it, and none needed to change cars nor to ride more than half an hour.

In the county outside Cincinnati the district board of health maintained 15 child-health centers. Conferences for infants and preschool children were held at these once a month, and clinics were held for school children 10 per cent or more underweight and for the care of postoperative cases. Five nurses were employed. The average distance from the home of the children to the schoolhouse where a center was maintained was about 2 miles.

It was the policy of the court and the private agencies assisting to advise the mothers to attend the centers; but no method of insuring the attendance of infants and children of preschool age had been developed, and the workers were not sure how many were in actual attendance.

School medical work.—All school children in Cincinnati were weighed and measured by the nurses three times a year. If they were found to be 10 per cent or more underweight they were examined by physicians. All children in the first three grades were given a yearly examination by a physician. In the county outside Cincinnati the five nurses under the district board of health inspected all school children once a year, and the children found to be 10 per cent or more underweight and others thought to be in need of a thorough physical examination were examined by a physician.

When the children who had attended the child-health centers entered school their health records were transferred to the school. This provided a continuous health record through infancy and the school period. Though no formal follow-up work was done by the case workers in charge of the families, the school nurses were in such close touch with the court and the social agencies that presumably much of the necessary corrective work was attended to by them. The school nurses followed up the nutrition defects, and eighth-grade girls acted as "big sisters" to undernourished children, the nurses supervising them. Three times a year the nurses gave the eighth-grade girls special instruction in diet and health.

Dentistry.—The child-health center and three dental clinics provided free dental work for school children. Dental examinations were made in the country schools, but the only corrective work provided was through the city health center, which opened its dental clinic to country children for one month in the year. The Babies' Milk Fund Association also did some dental work for country children, but the facilities were not adequate.

Malnutrition.—In the county outside Cincinnati there were no nutrition classes. Nurses gave individual instruction to underweight children at the child-health centers, and instruction was given to mothers in diet and hygiene once a year, if possible, through mothers' clubs and similar groups. In Cincinnati the Babies' Milk Fund Association nurses gave instruction to mothers in nutrition individually or in groups at its child-health centers. The association planned also to conduct a nutrition class of 20 children whose mothers were to be brought into the group. A clinician was to direct the class and students in the department of home economics of the University of Cincinnati were to do the field work. The United Jewish Social Agencies employed a nutrition worker who followed up all underweight Jewish children in mothers' aid families, but there was no regular method of reporting underweight children to the court nor to the family agencies. When extra diet was recommended the nurses communicated with the agency in charge of the family. Undernourished families, those lacking sufficient income, and those managing poorly were put under the supervision of the dietitian employed by the Cincinnati Associated Charities.

There was a camp for undernourished children, where they could remain for the entire summer, and the United Jewish Social Agencies operated a convalescent home for Jewish children requiring any type of care.

MENTAL HEALTH

Available facilities.

Cincinnati has a number of facilities for the study or care of persons having mental defect or disease. Most of these were used for the mothers' aid families, in accordance with the affiliations with hospitals and clinics obtaining among the four agencies giving supervision. The psychological laboratory of the vocation bureau of the Cincinnati Board of Education [3] served all these agencies as well as the schools. It gave examinations to children recommended for special classes. Assignment of children to these classes, also to observation classes, opportunity classes, disciplinary classes, and college-preparatory classes, and recommendations for scholarships all were based upon the tests made by this laboratory.

The juvenile court employed a psychologist who was available for consultation in regard to any problem involving mothers' aid families. The Council of Social Agencies conducted a central clinic; it employed a psychiatric social worker and served as a general clearing house for all cases of mental defect or disease. The United Jewish Social Agencies conducted a neuropsychiatric clinic in connection with its medical clinic. The psychopathic institute of the Jewish Hospital employed a psychiatric social worker and provided temporary institutional care while the patient was under observation. The Ohio Bureau of Juvenile Research at Columbus, Ohio, provided institutional care for psychopathic patients under observation; usually a physical examination was given also.

The treatment of children with psychopathic or behavior problems varied somewhat among the four agencies supervising mothers' aid families, but if the difficulty was pronounced, the need of expert

---

[3] See Vocational Guidance and Junior Placement, pp. 191–197 (U. S. Children's Bureau Publication No. 149, U. S. Employment Service Publication A, Washington, 1925).

psychological advice was generally recognized. Jewish children were examined at the neuropsychiatric clinic of the United Jewish Social Agencies and sometimes given observation at its psychopathic institute. Non-Jewish children were examined by the court psychologist, who referred them, if continued treatment was necessary, to the central clinic of the Council of Social Agencies, to the psychopathic institute of the Jewish Hospital, or more rarely to the Ohio Bureau of Juvenile Research at Columbus. The follow-up work was done either by the agency's family visitors or by its nurses. The United Jewish Social Agencies had taken advantage of the services of the National Committee for Mental Hygiene in its survey of Cincinnati in November, 1921, and had thorough examinations made of a number of children in the families receiving mothers' aid.

Although it was the ideal of the agencies supervising mothers' aid families to give special consideration to children with mental difficulties, it seemed doubtful whether all the workers were familiar with the services available for psychological examinations, and they may have neglected to refer to the clinics mothers and children who needed such help. Probably the policies and practice varied among agencies giving supervision. It was pointed out that relatively few behavior problems arose in mothers' aid families, as the selection of families to receive grants was based upon the character of the family.

Follow-up of special types of problems.

Teachers, social workers, neighbors, and parents referred school children who were retarded or whom they suspected of mental defect to the psychological laboratory of the board of education's vocation bureau, for examination and recommendation as to placement. If institutional care was required application was made to the Ohio State Institution for the Feeble-Minded at Columbus. Children in whose families there had been a history of mental defect or disease were not given a psychological examination unless they had symptoms of mental difficulty.

Illustrative case histories.

The following case histories show what may be achieved when the results of psychological examination are coordinated closely with physical care and adequate social activities:

Nine-year-old Elsie was examined by the court psychologist because of psychopathic symptoms, and her mother was advised to place her for observation in the Psychopathic Institute. This she refused to do, but two years later she brought Elsie for reexamination, after the little girl had packed her clothes, taken some money, and with her 4-year-old sister started for another city where she had relatives. She was then studied for several weeks at the Psychopathic Institute. She had a history of impudence, untruthfulness, extreme nervousness, poor school work (due partly to absence), and desire for much attention. The report of the court psychologist stated that she carried exaggeration, imagination, and dream states so far that it verged on pathological lying. It was thought that Elsie's conduct was based on "some unfortunate sex experience or at least on some emotional experience, causative of mental conflict." After eight months of careful follow-up and of reeducation of the mother and of the child it was reported that Elsie had improved wonderfully in every way, and that there was a marked improvement in her school work, though it was not yet up to standard.

Mrs. N., who was in a nervous and physically upset condition, was examined in the general medical clinic of the United Jewish Social Agencies five weeks after the death of her husband. She continued under the supervision of this clinic for a period of several years. Her eyes were tested, she was treated for chronic skin disease, and she was fitted with special shoes. Two of her four children were given psychological examinations, John at 8 years of age and Henry at 7 years of age. The entire family had been examined in 1921 during the survey made by the National Committee for Mental Hygiene. It was reported that Henry had little initiative and much suggestibility and that John had "an inadequate personality." Extra nourishment was provided, tonsil operations were performed, and treatment was given for positive endocrine disturbances. Both boys were under observation at the Psychopathic Institute. All the children were brought in touch with recreational and social activities at the community center and the recommendations of the institute were followed in every detail by the family visitor; one of the recommendations called for "big brothers," who were accordingly secured. John and Henry reported regularly to the neuropsychopathic clinic of the United Jewish Social Agencies, and the last report the psychiatrist had given indicated that both were improving mentally and physically and that they had good school records.

HOUSING

The standards which the agencies would have liked to enforce in regard to housing and the actual conditions with which they were confronted were often at variance. In Cincinnati, for example, though all the workers agreed that a single house was highly desirable, scarcely anything save tenements was available. It was said that a large majority of the families receiving mothers' aid in the city lived in two-room or at best in three-room tenements—a combined kitchen and living room and one bedroom. The rooms, however, were of fair size, they were generally light and well aired, and the streets and even the alleys were kept clean. The dark hallways were very objectionable. The toilet was usually in the hall and was shared by another family; some families had outside toilets.

Among the families supervised by the United Jewish Social Agencies the housing conditions were markedly superior, as that agency supplemented the mothers' aid to insure good conditions. One family lived in an old well-established residential section on a wide boulevard, with substantial and even elegant homes in the immediate neighborhood. The house had been intended originally for one family, but later was made over to accommodate two families. The rent was $55 a month. Another family lived in an almost equally good neighborhood in a second-floor apartment, with abundance of room, sunshine, and air. The standard of the agency allowed for at least three rooms, including the living room and generally a bathroom.

All the agencies insisted upon separate sleeping rooms for adolescent boys and girls. A living room was considered essential, though some families had to use a fair-sized kitchen for the living room. In one such combined kitchen and living room was a much-used piano, but the room was so neat, cozy, and homelike that the children had no hesitancy about bringing their friends in for an evening's fun. It was significant that this family voluntarily gave up the grant before they considered moving to a more roomy abode. A number of families had to use the living room as a sleeping room. The families living in the city had running water, but this was not always true in the country.

The majority of city homes had gas and about half had electricity. Most families had some provision for keeping ice in summer. The court placed much stress upon the sanitary conditions of the homes and the character of the neighborhoods in which the families lived, and as far as possible consideration was given to play space and accessibility to playgrounds. The homes visited were in good or fair condition. There was no fixed maximum rental, but the rents were generally less than $30 a month. Sixty-seven families owned or were paying for their own homes. More country than city families owned or partly owned their homes, and in these cases housing conditions were good. There were yard space, flower and vegetable gardens, and more rooms in the houses.

Mrs. C.'s husband committed suicide in a fit of temporary insanity. At the time application was made for aid her children had been suffering for several years from lack of adequate nourishing food, and tuberculosis was feared. This family was moved from poor rooms in a badly congested neighborhood to bright, sunny rooms in a good suburban locality, where the physical conditions would be better. The entire family was placed under the care of the health center and reported every month. Mrs. C. became a member of a domestic-science class, and the three children were entered in a dramatic class.

Mrs. W. had three children under 5 years of age. Her husband had died of tuberculosis of the hip. This family was moved from a crowded, dark down-town tenement to a cozy little cottage in the country, where the children could almost live out of doors. This was the more necessary because the youngest child had rickets. This child was under the care of the Cincinnati General Hospital.

EDUCATION

COOPERATION WITH THE SCHOOLS AND FACILITIES FOR EDUCATION

Contact with the schools.

The Cincinnati Associated Charities twice each year sent the following form letter to all schools attended by children receiving mothers' aid:

[Date.]
[Name.] [Address.]

The ——— PUBLIC SCHOOL,
Cincinnati, Ohio.

GENTLEMEN: Will you kindly forward us a report relative to the health, attendance, deportment, cleanliness, and grades of the above-mentioned children, in whom we are very much interested? This is a requirement of the mothers' pension department, juvenile court, each year, of the children whose mother receives a mothers' pension.

Thanking you in advance, we are,
Very truly yours, THE ASSOCIATED CHARITIES,

———————,
Supervisor, Mothers' Pensions.

The visitors of the United Jewish Social Agencies visited the children's school-teachers twice each year. The visitors of the Bureau of Catholic Charities and the juvenile court examined the school reports and had occasional conferences with the teachers.

Provision for handicapped children.

The physically handicapped child.—The Cincinnati public schools provided two classes for the blind and six classes for children with defective vision. The oral school had seven classes for the deaf and semideaf. Open-air classes cared for anemic and tuberculous children. The Cincinnati General Hospital had an excellently equipped school for both hospital patients and out-patients. The latter were brought to the hospital every day in the school bus. Needlework, woodwork, and cabinetwork were taught. Trousseaus had been made by the girls, and their work was for sale. The teachers made special effort to know each child individually and to help him overcome the timidity and feeling of inferiority that frequently develop among crippled children. Music lessons were given them as a means to this end, and their families were helped to get musical instruments for them if they had none.

One child in a mothers' aid family was attending one of the sight-conservation classes, one was attending a class for the deaf, and four were in open-air classes.

The mentally handicapped child.—A special school had 16 classes, and in addition there were 13 special classes in various schools in different parts of the city. There was one observation class, to which children who could not succeed in the first and second grades but whose intelligence quotients did not indicate mental defect were admitted, the aim being to return these children to the regular school as soon as possible. Opportunity classes were reported for six of the schools.

Provision for children wishing further education.

Cincinnati had a variety and number of scholarships provided to help needy children to secure an education. The Schmidlapp Bureau of Cincinnati, a private memorial fund devoted to promoting the educational interests of girls and young women, gave scholarships ranging from approximately $20 a month for the 10 months of the school year to $700 a year. The vocation bureau of the board of education, through contributions from the community chest, the Council of Social Agencies, and other organizations granted high-school scholarships to children of legal working age who were financially unable to remain in school but were of superior scholarship or were specially granted the scholarship for some other reason approved by the scholarship committee. Psychological and physical examinations were given as seemed necessary. The board of education was also authorized to grant relief in order to enable a child to attend school.[4] This so-called scholarship was usually in groceries and in amounts of $5 per week, but it might take the form of clothing, shoes, or car fare. The Council of Jewish Women gave scholarships to Jewish children who showed merit and were ready for university or special training. The amounts varied from $20 a month (for 10 months) to high-school pupils to $30 a month in addition to college fees, books, and other necessary university expenses. The United Jewish Social Agencies gave scholarships to children in families under its care if thereby they were aided in rehabilitating themselves. Some high-school and university scholarships were competitive, and there were single scholarships, such as the Helen T. Woolley scholarship of the Women's City Club for the first year in the university. The workers in all the case-work agencies had been alert and active in planning for higher educational opportunities for

---

[4] Ohio, Gen. Code 1910, sec. 7777, p. 1646, as amended by act of Apr. 9, 1921, Laws of 1921, p. 376. (Page's Annotated Gen. Code 1926, sec. 7777, p. 2876.)

children under their care and securing through scholarships the means for their attainment, though it seemed that not all of them were fully aware of the advantage of referring the children under their supervision to the vocation bureau of the board of education so that they might have the advantage of its services.

At the time of the study 16 children in families receiving mothers' aid were receiving scholarships as follows: One from the Schmidlapp Bureau for a course in the University of Cincinnati, seven from the board of education for courses in commercial high schools, one from the board of education for an academic high-school course, and six from private sources for courses in commercial high school. One boy had won a competitive scholarship for a high-school course.

Carolyn V. was a Jewish girl 16 years old whose father had died of tuberculosis. Her mother was of low mentality, as were also an older brother and sister, and another sister was subnormal. The family had been under the continuous care of the United Jewish Social Agencies since before the father's death, and at one time aid was withdrawn in order to persuade Mrs. V. to allow physical examinations to be made of the children. The whole family had received the most thorough and painstaking social treatment, including medical care, psychological examinations, and follow-up. Special effort had been made on behalf of the oldest daughter, who could not hold a job and for whom much careful vocational work was done. Carolyn, however, was of superior intelligence (having an intelligence quotient of 110), and at the request of the United Jewish Social Agencies the vocation bureau granted to her a scholarship of $20 per month. At the age of 16 she had already finished her second year in commercial high school, had an average of 85 to 90 per cent in all subjects, and had been excused from examinations.

Thirteen boys 16 and 17 years old in families receiving mothers' aid who were working full time were attending night school. Four were in high school, three were taking business courses, and one was taking a premedical course at the University of Cincinnati. Each of the remaining five was taking one of the following courses: Show-card writing, salesmanship, commercial art, electricity, and pattern making. In the vocational school and the university engineering school the students could arrange to attend school four weeks and then work four weeks in plants providing field work that supplemented the school work. A number of children in mothers' aid families were securing their education in this way. Some junior high-school children were able to take commercial courses on a similar basis.

Much effort had been expended, especially by the workers in the Cincinnati Associated Charities, upon securing pianos for children and encouraging them to take lessons at the Union Bethel Settlement, where only a very small charge was made. Piano stores had been generous in donating used pianos for this purpose, particularly to crippled children or those physically handicapped otherwise. The Women's City Club conducted classes in dramatics and the family visitors had entered about 25 children from mothers' aid families in these classes.

While calling upon Mrs. Z. one day the mothers' aid visitor was told that Dick was to take part in a school entertainment, and at the mother's suggestion he sang his part for her. The visitor noticed the fine quality of his voice and set about securing free lessons for him in voice culture. During the visit of the Paulist Choir to Cincinnati Dick entered a vocal contest, successfully passed the test, and was selected as a prospective choir member. He was taken to New York and for two years received excellent vocal training. Then his voice began to deepen, and he was sent home to wait until his voice had changed. He was to reenter the choir if the tone quality was not impaired.

When Mrs. F. applied for mothers' aid in June, 1918, her husband had just died. The family had high standards and a fine sense of solidarity. There were two children 15 years of age or over and three under 15. Sarah, the oldest girl, was a senior in high school and worked in a private family for her board and $5 a week. The oldest boy, 15-year-old Jonas, was in his second year at high school and earned $2 a week carrying papers. Sarah was awarded a scholarship from the Schmidlapp Bureau to enable her to take a nurses' training course at the Cincinnati General Hospital, from which she graduated in June, 1923. She had since repaid the loan. Out of her earnings of $85 a month and board at the hospital, where she was still employed, she gave her mother $40 a month and in addition put away $5 a month toward a building fund for a home for the family. She also bought a used piano and was paying for music lessons for her 11-year-old sister. At the time of the study Jonas was taking an engineering course at the University of Cincinnati on the co-operative plan, according to which he worked four weeks and studied four weeks.

The family lived in four rooms on the second floor of a cottage in the outskirts of the city, facing the hills and open fields. They were a little crowded with a combined kitchen and dining room, but that was the alternative they chose in order that the children might have every possible advantage.

In October, 1923, Mrs. F. voluntarily gave up her grant, saying the children had talked it over and had decided that they could take care of the family.

Thirteen-year-old Lucy T., bent on a university degree, was granted a scholarship of $5 a week by the board of education, beginning in September, 1922. She was at the time of the study (October, 1923) in her second year in high school. It was reported that during the previous school year she had not missed a single day's attendance; she passed with high marks and was at the head of her class in Latin. Through the encouragement of the mothers' aid visitor, Lucy had been a member for three years of the dramatic class conducted by the Women's City Club, and she had taken many leading parts. Her mother, who had had a very unhappy life, had started to work at 12 years of age and could hardly read or write. Mrs. T. had become interested in making Lucy's costumes and in going to the rehearsals with her. She told the visitor that when her daughter first began to tell her of Dickens and Shakespeare and what they were reading in the English class at school she was bored, but after a set of Dickens had been given her and many passages had been read out loud she grew more and more interested. The mother's personality, too, was unfolding.

William P., who was 17 years old, had graduated from high school in June preceding the study. His intelligence quotient was 116. He had received a scholarship of $5 a week from the board of education throughout his high-school course. In addition he had been employed at the office of the department of education in the evenings and on Saturday afternoons. He wished to become a physician. It was necessary that he make a contribution to the family support, as there were two younger children and his mother was not strong. The mothers' aid worker secured a clerical position for him at the university and he was taking French and German in the university evening classes. In addition to the stimulating contact of the vocation bureau and his association with a "big brother" he also joined the Young Men's Christian Association and had been able to spend some vacation time at its summer camp.

SCHOOLING AND WORK OF CHILDREN 16 AND 17 YEARS OLD

The child-labor, compulsory-education, and mothers' aid laws.
A minor between 16 and 18 years of age was of compulsory school age under the Ohio law, and if not employed under an age and schooling certificate or determined to be incapable of profiting substantially by further instruction was required to attend a public, private, or parochial school. An age and schooling certificate could be issued to a minor over 16 years of age who had completed the

seventh grade (with certain exceptions).[5] Attendance at a continuation school was required for minors between 16 and 18 where such schools were established.[6] Boys and girls who had not completed the required grade were considered individually to determine whether they should be granted employment certificates on the ground that they were not mentally able to complete the required academic work. If necessary, these children were tested in the psychological laboratory of the board of education's vocation bureau. The mothers' aid law allowed a grant to be made for a child until he was eligible for an employment certificate.

Children in school and at work.

The juvenile court encouraged children to remain in school and continued the grant for younger children to enable the older boys and girls in the family to go through high school or the university or to receive special training. The fact that all children were in school to the age of 16 years enabled many to get an excellent start. There were 167 children (85 boys and 82 girls) 16 or 17 years of age in the families receiving mothers' aid. Of these 167 children, 40 were attending school, 114 were working, and 13 were neither in school nor working.

Children in school.—Among the 40 children 16 and 17 years old attending school were 38 who had completed the seventh grade and thus were eligible for employment certificates so far as educational requirements were concerned.[7]

The number of boys and girls 16 and 17 years old attending school and the grade or type of school attended are shown in the following table:

Number of children 16 and 17 years old who were attending school at the time of the study, by grade or type of school; Hamilton County, Ohio

Grade or type of school	Total	Children 16 and 17 years old attending school					
		Boys			Girls		
		Total	16 years	17 years	Total	16 years	17 years
Total	a 40	21	15	6	19	18	1
Elementary school:							
Seventh grade	1	--------	--------	--------	1	1	--------
Eighth grade	6	3	3	--------	3	3	--------
High school:							
First year	5	5	4	1	--------	--------	--------
Second year	11	5	3	2	6	5	1
Third year	3	2	1	1	1	1	--------
Fourth year	2	2	1	1	--------	--------	--------
Business school	8	2	2	--------	6	6	--------
Other	4	2	1	b 1	2	c 2	--------

a 8 of these children were working outside school hours.
b In the third year of a seminary preparing for the priesthood.
c 1 was taking a commercial course in a hospital school for cripples; the other was learning sewing in a special school (not for mental defectives).

[5] Ohio, Gen. Code 1910, sec. 7766, p. 1644, as amended by act of May 9, 1913, Laws of 1913, p. 864, act of Feb. 17, 1914, Laws of 1914, p. 129, act of Apr. 29, 1921, Laws of 1921, p. 376. (See Page's Annotated Gen. Code 1926, secs. 7762, 7762–6, and 7766, pp. 2865, 2866, 2870.)
[6] Ibid., sec. 7762–5, added by act of Apr. 29, 1921, Laws of 1921, p. 376; sec. 7767, p. 1644, as amended by act of May 9, 1913, Laws of 1913, p. 864, act of Apr. 29, 1921, Laws of 1921, p. 376. (This was amended further by act of Mar. 27, 1925, Laws of 1925, p. 63.) (See Page's Annotated Gen. Code 1926, secs. 7762–5, 7766, 7767, pp. 2866, 2870, 2873.)
[7] The 38 children in school who had fulfilled the grade requirement for employment certificates were 17 per cent of all the children in families receiving aid who could satisfy this requirement (164).

Occupations and earnings of working children.—Of the 167 children 16 and 17 years of age 114 (more than two-thirds) were working. Their occupations were as follows:

	Number of children		Number of children
Total	114	Tinner's helper	2
		Odd jobs	2
Boys	61	Other	[8] 13
Factory worker	11	Girls	53
Clerical worker	8		
Clerk in store	7	Clerical worker	17
Stock boy	5	Factory worker	[9] 11
Printer's helper	4	Clerk in store	[9] 6
Errand or messenger boy	3	Cashier	[9] 4
Automobile mechanic	2	Bundle wrapper	4
Worker in shipping department in store	2	Telephone operator	3
		Seamstress	3
Bell boy	2	Other	[10] 5

Of the 61 boys who were working 24 had been in high school when they left school to go to work (11 in the first year, 12 in the second, 1 in the fourth), and 26 had been in the eighth grade. Four had been in the seventh grade and 5 in the sixth, and for 2 the grade was not reported. Of the 53 girls who were working 28 had been in high school when they left school to go to work (12 in the first year, 15 in the second, and 1 in the fourth), and 18 had been in the eighth grade. Four had been in the seventh grade and 2 in the sixth, and 1 was attending continuation school.

The earnings of the 114 children who were working and of the 8 school children who were working outside school hours were as follows:

	Number of children		Number of children
Total	122	$60, under $70	26
		$70, under $80	6
Under $20	3	$80, under $90	5
$20, under $30	3	$90, under $100	2
$30, under $40	19	$100, under $110	2
$40, under $50	28	No earnings	1
$50, under $60	26	Not reported	1

There were three cases in which two children in the same family were earning money. One brother and sister were earning a total of $146 a month; but as the boy was paying back money he had borrowed the only contribution to the family was $43 of the $81 which the girl earned. Two brothers were earning $68 and $83 a month, respectively; they contributed a total of $121 a month to the family's support, and $31 a month was the allowance granted to the family. A brother and a sister who were earning $43 a month apiece were contributing all their earnings to the family's support. A girl who was earning $108 a month was working in another city and making no contribution to the family's support. All but one of the children working after school or on Saturdays contributed something, though their earnings were small. About 40 per cent of the children gave

---

[8] Includes one who was reported for each of the following: Parcel-post clerk, helper in bakery, helper in laboratory, machinist's helper, electrician, locksmith, butcher, clothing cutter, driver on ice wagon, assistant on truck, cobbler, laborer, and helper in drug store.
[9] 1 of these was reported as mentally defective or feeble-minded.
[10] Includes 1 laundry operator, 1 waitress, 1 employed at housework, 1 model in an art school, and 1 who was doing embroidery and crocheting at home.

their mothers all their earnings. One of these was a boy earning $108 a month. The next largest amount contributed was $91 a month.

Children neither in school nor at work.

Among the 13 children 16 and 17 years of age who were neither attending school nor working were 3 boys who were temporarily out of work, 4 girls who were assisting in housework (or farm work) at home, 4 girls who were married, and 1 girl who was in an institution for the feeble-minded. Five of these children had completed the grade requirements for employment certificates, 2 were still in the seventh grade, and for the remaining 5 (excluding the feeble-minded child) the grade was not reported.

EDUCATIONAL ACTIVITIES FOR THE MOTHERS

The mothers were encouraged to attend cooking and sewing classes in the public schools. The board of education conducted evening-school classes for adults in domestic science, including cooking, dressmaking, and millinery in nine school centers. A class was organized whenever 20 women were enrolled (at a fee of $2 a year). Five mothers receiving aid from the group supervised by the Cincinnati Associated Charities had attended such a class during the winter preceding the study and the teacher reported that they were the most eager and responsive members of the class. It was expected that 25 mothers from among those under the care of the Cincinnati Associated Charities would attend during the coming winter.

Foreign-speaking mothers, of whom there were very few, were encouraged but not required to attend English or citizenship classes. The Jewish Community House and the American House conducted classes in English, and mothers receiving aid had attended classes in both centers.

Mrs. R., who had been married at the age of 17, was left a widow with four young children. She was hysterical, untrained, and spoiled, and in the first days of supervision was wont to throw shoes at the visitor over the fence when reprimanded for her constant visiting among her neighbors. She could neither read nor write and knew nothing of sewing or of housekeeping.

Finally, after much fruitless effort the agency offered her a prize if she would keep her house clean. She responded with enthusiasm to this suggestion and the prize turned out to be a refurnishing of the entire house. This was the turning point for Mrs. R. The friendly visitor started to teach her to read and write, to cook, to keep house, and to sew.

In the fall of 1923, seven years later, the family was living in an apartment of four comfortable rooms in a good residential section, for which they were paying $55 a month. Elizabeth, 19 years old, was receiving a scholarship of $20 a month to enable her to continue her nurse's training. Katherine at 18 years of age was a telephone operator earning $20 a week. She was taking special work in dramatics and lessons in singing and dancing and frequently appeared in recitals. Estelle had just left high school in her third year and gone into the telephone exchange. She had been taking piano lessons. Ferdinand was doing well in his second year of high school and was bent on becoming a doctor.

RECREATION

The small item for sundries in the budget included recreation as well as health, education, and household supplies. The allowance was of course only nominal, as, for example, $3.71 was allowed for sundries for a family consisting of the mother and five children.

As a rule working children were expected to give two-thirds of their earnings to the upkeep of the home and to buy their clothing and provide themselves with car fare, lunches, and recreation out of the remaining third. Some boys and girls over 18 years of age contributed a definite amount for board; and some working children gave their mothers all their wages and the mothers purchased clothing and gave them spending money.

Cincinnati was well supplied with recreational resources. The public schools were used as social and community centers and were within access of most city families. The following types of recreation were available through the school centers, the six church centers, and the three settlements, one of which was the Jewish Community Center: Mothers' clubs, girls' and boys' clubs, athletic and gymnasium facilities, dramatics, music, dancing, scout activities for both boys and girls, and classes in cooking, sewing, and home economics.

One or more of these forms of recreation was easily available to the children in mothers' aid families, and, as has been shown, much effort had been expended in connecting children with educational and semirecreational activities. Mothers, too, were encouraged to take advantage of opportunities afforded in a social way. Not so much stress had been laid upon their membership in mothers' clubs.

An interesting experiment was being tried by the worker of the Cincinnati Associated Charities in charge of mothers' aid families in an attempt to bring good cheer and social intercourse to the mothers under her care. Since October, 1919, informal monthly gatherings of mothers had been held at which refreshments were served. Sometimes there was a program of music, motion pictures, or a talk on cooking or home economics. Sometimes there was no program, and simple games were played. The attendance had varied from 20 to 200. These meetings had been very happy occasions, and on October 12, 1923, an organization was effected and a president elected from the group of mothers for the purpose of encouraging them to initiate activities of their own and to develop self-confidence and self-expression.

MOTHERS' ALLOWANCES IN KING COUNTY, WASH.[1]

PROVISIONS OF THE LAW

The Washington mothers' aid law was passed originally in 1913, rewritten in 1915, and amended in 1919.[2] It provided for aid to a mother with dependent children under 15 years of age, regardless of her marital status. The allowance might not exceed $15 a month for the first child and $5 a month for each additional child. Aid was granted on the following conditions:

If a mother had been a resident of the State for three years and of the county for one year; if her children were living with her; if she was a "proper person, morally, physically, or mentally, for the upbringing of her children," she was eligible for a pension. In the absence of any specification in the law as to the amount of property or savings a woman might have, the juvenile court of King County as a rule did not grant aid to a woman who had an equity of more than $3,000 in her home and more than $300 in savings. The court had also ruled as follows: In a case of desertion a woman was required to swear out a warrant; aid would not be given if the father had been gone less than six months; if the father was apprehended the grant was revoked and the father was sentenced to the stockade for a six-month period. In that case his earnings of $1.50 a day were turned over to his wife. Some men who had been apprehended had been ordered by the court to return in monthly installments the entire amount of aid given to the family. Mothers' aid was not granted to divorced women if alimony had been allowed. Mothers were not allowed to keep men roomers or lodgers other than a father or brother unless there were two or more.

ADMINISTRATION OF THE LAW

ADMINISTRATIVE AGENCY AND STAFF

The administrative agency was the mothers' pension department of the juvenile court. The staff of the department was appointed by the judge and included a commissioner of mothers' pensions, an investigator, two visitors, and a stenographer. The commissioner had been a member of the staff for a number of years prior to her appointment as commissioner. She had a background of professional social work training and experience. The visitors and the investi-

---

[1] The population of King County in 1920 was 389,273, of whom 315,312 lived in Seattle. The native white population was 281,694, the foreign-born population, 91,207. The population of foreign birth was as follows in the order of numerical importance: Canadian, Swedish, Norwegian, English, and German. (Fourteenth Census of the United States, vol. 3, Population, pp. 1086, 1088, 1093, Washington, 1922.) The child population within legal age for mothers' aid (under 15 years) was 91,083 (unpublished figures furnished by the U. S. Bureau of the Census). The chief industries of Seattle center around the flour mills, meat packing, foundry and machine shops, lumbering, shipbuilding, and various types of manufacturing. In rural sections farming and dairying are leading industries.
[2] Wash., act of Mar. 24, 1913, ch. 179, Laws of 1913, p. 644; act of Mar. 17, 1915, ch. 135, Laws of 1915, p. 364; act of Mar. 13, 1919, ch. 103, Laws of 1919, p. 254. (See Remington's Comp. Stat. 1922, secs. 9993–9998, pp. 2680–2681.)

gator were all high-school graduates; one of them had had some college work and had been a church visitor, one had had a number of years of business experience, and all three had received their professional training in the mothers' pension department. The spirit of the department was informal and cooperative, and there seemed to be great friendliness and confidence between the workers and the families. The salaries of the field staff ranged from $1,500 to $1,800 a year. There was no State supervision of any kind.

APPROPRIATION AND VOLUME OF WORK

The appropriation for mothers' aid was fixed at the beginning of each current year, but the department was permitted to overdraw and the deficit was covered by a superior-court order. There was no waiting list. The expenditures had been steadily increasing, as follows: 1920, $59,983.71; 1921, $77,996.87; 1922, $99,494.32; 1923, $108,147.50.

In December, 1923, 453 families, including nearly 1,000 children, were receiving assistance. Supervision of these was divided between the two family visitors, each of whom supervised about 225 families. The investigator made all the investigations of applications for aid—between 25 and 35 a month—out of which an average of 10 to 18 were given assistance. The visitors and the investigator did most of their own typing.

PROCEDURE IN MAKING ALLOWANCES

Application was made by the mothers in person at the office of the mothers' pension department in the juvenile-court building. The application was taken by the commissioner and the mother signed a petition under oath. The petition included the following: Name, age, place of birth, address, former addresses, and length of residence in State and county of the man and woman; whether they were citizens and whether the father had served in the United States Army or Navy; facts regarding organizations, societies, churches, and Sunday schools to which the parents or children belonged; facts regarding property, savings, income, previous support, rent, debts, and relief from other sources; facts regarding the father's death, commitment, desertion, or divorce; facts regarding employment, wages, insurance, and boarders; names, places of birth, ages, school grades, and health of children; employment and wages of working children; names and addresses of relatives and of five references.

Investigations were made by the investigator in the order in which the applications were received. The first step was consultation of the social-service exchange and communication with agencies that had known the family. Verifications were made of the marriage of the parents; the death, desertion, or commitment of the father or the divorce of the parents; residence; dates of birth of the children; insurance, property, savings; and all legal data. A visit was always made at the home. The schools attended by the children were visited, also the family physician or lawyer, and at least three of the references whose names were furnished by the mother. Relatives, ministers, and employers were not visited as a matter of routine, unless there was reason to doubt the mother's statement.

A summary of the investigation and the important facts was submitted to the judge at a private hearing. One day a month was devoted to these hearings, which were in the nature of conferences between the judge and the mothers' aid staff. The mothers were not obliged to attend unless there was some matter of special importance in regard to which the judge desired a personal interview.

DETERMINATION OF ALLOWANCES

No standard budget was used. The judge determined the amount of the grant on the basis of the mother's statement of all income, debts, and rent. The average grant per family was $20 a month; the highest grant was $40 a month, the lowest, $7.50. Payment was made by check once a month at the office of the county auditor where the women called for their checks.

The "spirit fund" (consisting of cash donations from friends of the court, amounting to $200 to $300 a year) was used for emergencies such as tiding a family over an illness, extras such as a dentist's bill, providing special shoes, or repairing a phonograph for a family in the country. The 1922 report showed that the greater part of this fund was used for groceries, clothing, and fuel.

Every mother at some time kept an expense account for a period of at least a month; if she was a poor manager she might be required to keep it regularly. About 100 mothers were keeping such accounts at any one time. The itemized accounts were written on loose slips of paper and the total summarized monthly on a blank form under the headings rent, food, light and fuel, clothing, car fare, lunches, debts, installments, and insurance. A copy of such report follows:

Financial statement

Name: _____ | Date: Jan. 2, 1920.

RESOURCES	OBLIGATIONS
Property value, _____ Equity, _____	Debts, about $57.85.
Savings, _____	Installments, 2 firms.
Other sources, _____	Premium on ins., _____
Total, _____	Total, _____
MONTHLY INCOME	NECESSITIES
Mother's earnings, about $40.	Rent, $28. Carfare, _____
Roomers, _____	Food, $50. Lunches, _____
Boarders, _____	Light and fuel, $1.50 and $11–$12.50.
Older children: Two boys gave $42.	Clothing, _____
Other sources: Pension, $25.	
Total, $127.	Total, $90.50.

SUPPLEMENTING OF MOTHERS' AID

The county public-welfare department gave emergency aid, consisting of fuel, groceries, rent, and shoes, when asked to do so. Its workers made no investigation. During the year before the study the department had given assistance amounting to about $100 to 20 families receiving mothers' aid. Four private societies had given emergency aid to a total of 22 families.

Because of the straightened economic conditions in two families, the court was allowing them to live at the Theodora Home, which was operated by the Volunteers of America and was located on the extreme outskirts of the city. This institution provided a home for families and also cared for babies and children while the mothers worked. A mother and children generally were given two rooms for their own use. One mothers' aid family which had been at the home more than a year had just moved with the help of the institution to a near-by cottage on the grounds.

VISITING

The visitors were able to visit the families under their supervision about once in six weeks, and the commissioner made occasional visits to their homes. The mothers came frequently to the office to consult the visitors or the commissioner. The relation of the judge, the commissioner, and the visitors to the families was exceedingly friendly. Occasionally the judge visited the homes in which the father was incapacitated.

HEALTH

PHYSICAL HEALTH

General procedure.
The court had formerly required all mothers, before aid was given, to have a physical examination made (including a blood test) at the City Hospital dispensary. This practice had been discontinued, however, as satisfactory results had not been obtained. At the time of the study no physical examinations were required of the mothers or the children at any time, unless there was obvious need or unless there was a question of the mother's ability to work. In Seattle the mothers and children were sent for examination, diagnosis, and treatment—if this could be supplied through the clinic—to the City Hospital dispensary, which was operated by the board of health. A steering blank was used, which was returned with the report of the examination in writing. A copy of such a report is as follows:

CITY HOSPITAL DISPENSARY

Diagnosis for mothers' pension department, juvenile court:
    Date: _____
    Name: _____
    Address: _____
    Prev. diag.: _____
    Made by _____, M. D.
    Dept.: _____
    Race: _____ S. M. W. Sep.
    Age, _____ Ht., _____ Wt., _____
    Final diag., _____
    Confirmed by _____ M. D.
    History: _____
    Transferred or referred, _____
    Taken by _____
    Date: _____

There was no hospital nor medical social service in the city. All follow-up work except that resulting from the school health work was done by the mothers' aid visitors. Whenever it seemed necessary the visitors conferred directly with the examining physicians. In addition to the services of the City Hospital dispensary the court secured much free service from private physicians and specialists.

Hospital care was provided by the City Hospital, the King County Hospital, and the Children's Orthopedic Hospital, and occasionally a free bed in a private hospital was available.

In Seattle the Junior Red Cross clinic served all children in the public schools whose parents could not afford necessary medical care, and it did both diagnostic and corrective work. Though intended primarily for the use of the schools, it was at the disposal of the social agencies, which used it freely.

Physicians employed by the city or county could be called upon by mothers' aid families in cases of acute illness anywhere in the county, but they were rarely used except in emergency.

The families outside Seattle were under the care of private physicians and the county health department. When the families were under the care of private physicians the mothers' aid visitors consulted with them in regard to the family, and if there were no working children the physicians frequently gave their services. Often the investigator or the visitor was able to have a doctor's bill canceled. However, if older children could do so, they were encouraged to pay a small fee. The services of a specialist in the city were sometimes secured for a country family when the case required expert care.

It was seldom necessary to threaten withdrawal of the grant in order to persuade mothers to have necessary treatment given. Instruction in food values and health habits was often given incidentally in the course of the visit by the workers. No attempt was made to give a continuous or complete record of the health history of each individual in the family.

Follow-up of special types of problems.

Tuberculosis.—It was the policy of the court to have all contact cases examined; adequate sanatorium care was insisted upon for active cases. The city department of health maintained a tuberculosis clinic, and the Firland Sanatorium took care of both city and county patients. Children with incipient tuberculosis or with a family history of tuberculosis were placed under the care of the tuberculosis clinic and the nurses kept in touch with them. Two tuberculosis nurses employed by the county department of health had charge of the home visiting in the county outside Seattle.

Venereal disease.—The city department of health conducted venereal clinics. Wassermann tests were made for all mothers and children if there was reason to suspect venereal disease.

Orthopedic and cardiac affections.—The Children's Orthopedic Hospital treated orthopedic, cardiac, and other pediatric cases. It conducted orthopedic clinics and often provided braces, shoes, and special apparatus. Braces were purchased through the previously mentioned spirit fund. The visitors arranged for treatment for all children that needed it.

Eye, ear, nose, and throat affections.—Children's eye, ear, nose, and throat work was done at the Red Cross clinics and the Children's Orthopedic Hospital and free of charge by specialists. Adults' cases were treated at the City Hospital clinics.

Medical welfare work for infants and preschool children.—The child-welfare division of the city department of health conducted eight district child-health centers. Two of these were at the central office of the department. A nurse was assigned to each center and did the follow-up work in the district. Mothers were encouraged to bring their children under 6 years of age at least once a month, and the nurse visited at least once the home of every child who had visited a center. It was estimated that a third of the mothers receiving aid lived near enough to a center to walk to it and that the majority of them would not need to change cars. They were encouraged to attend the centers, but no special stress was laid upon their doing so, as it was necessary for the majority of them to contribute to the family income by working for wages outside or within their own homes. There were no child-health centers in the county outside Seattle.

The Visiting Nurse Association conducted three prenatal clinics under the sponsorship of the Red Cross.

School medical inspection.—The school children in Seattle were inspected once a year by the school nurses. This inspection included height and weight measurements and a dental survey. There were 12 nurses, and each nurse supervised 4,000 children, visiting the schools in her district at least once a week. The nurses took children to the Red Cross clinic for the correction of physical defects. In the schools outside Seattle there were no school nurses, but examinations of some children were made by physicians.

The school physical inspection reports were not followed up regularly by the mothers' aid visitors. School reports were sent to the parents about twice a year, and at the same time a report of the child's school record was sent to the court on a special blank furnished by the mothers' pension department. This report blank did not request a health report, but if there were special health needs the teacher often mentioned them. The visitor examined the school report or consulted the teacher in regard to a child's health if there appeared to be special need. Each visitor made a practice of calling on the principals of the schools in the country districts where children from mothers' aid families were enrolled whenever she was in the neighborhood, and she discussed with them any school problems, including the child's health.

Malnutrition.—No nutrition classes were conducted by the school department, but the antituberculosis league maintained seven centers for undernourished children in Seattle and five in the county outside Seattle. These centers were conducted for the children whom the school nurses had examined and found to be 10 per cent underweight. All the children were given a thorough examination by a pediatrician and were weighed and measured each week. The mothers were encouraged to attend the centers, but as few of them could arrange to do so the dietitian and her assistants gave individual and group instruction and demonstrations in the homes of the mothers. The school department of Seattle operated 50 milk stations in the public schools, and the children were encouraged to buy milk regularly. It was furnished free if they were not able to pay for it. In the country the league encouraged the school-teachers to conduct nutrition classes under its supervision. The league also furnished speakers to give health talks illustrated with slides.

In the summer of 1922, 14 children receiving mothers' aid attended a summer camp for undernourished children; a smaller number were at the camp in 1923. The court referred few children to the nutrition classes, nor was there close and regular follow-up of the children by the mothers' aid visitors. If extra diet was needed the Fruit and Flower Mission was often asked to provide it.

MENTAL HEALTH

Available facilities.

The child-study laboratory or clinic of the public schools gave psychological examinations to school children referred to it by principals, teachers, and other school officials, the juvenile court, and other social agencies. Its staff included a psychologist and three assistants and had the part-time services of two nurses and a physician. All first-grade pupils were given a group test, all the pupils were given another test at least once during their years in school, and individual tests were given for the purpose of assigning children to special classes, making other classroom adjustment, recommending double promotion, and determining whether a child might be allowed to go to work because he could make no further progress in school. Children suspected to be defective or psychopathic were referred to this clinic, also children having behavior problems. Problem children were put into an observation class at the clinic one to seven days before permanent adjustment was made. Reports on home conditions were obtained by a nurse, and physical examinations were given if this seemed necessary. All pupils in the special classes for defectives were retested each year.

The psychological clinic of the Bailey and Babette Gatzert Foundation, conducted under the auspices of the University of Washington, gave examinations to a number of children, especially those referred to it because of physical or nervous disorders. Some psychiatric work was done in connection with the mental and physical measurements. No social worker was employed, the case work being done largely by students. The court used this clinic for the examination of patients who were likely to require long-continued observation.

There was no psychopathic hospital or ward in the county for the observation of psychopathic cases. The court frequently consulted private psychiatrists, who gave their services.

Follow-up of special types of problems.

The mothers' aid workers did not ask for psychological examinations of children who were retarded, as the child-study laboratory of the public schools handled this problem. The children in a family having a history of mental defect or disease were not examined as a matter of routine unless there were symptoms of mental trouble. If there was obvious or suspected mental defect a psychological examination was arranged for at the child-study laboratory or at the psychological clinic of the Bailey and Babette Gatzert Foundation, and application was made if necessary for admission to the State custodial school at Medical Lake. Any patient presenting a psychopathic difficulty was taken to a private psychiatrist. The staff visitors attempted to solve any behavior problem through conferring with the child and getting a clear understanding of the underlying factors of the misbehavior. Sometimes the child was brought to court and a conference arranged with the judge; and if the occasion seemed serious enough to warrant it he was sent to the parental school maintained by the board of education. If, in the judgment of the worker or the commissioner, a psychiatric examination was desirable the child was taken to a psychiatrist. All follow-up work was done by the mothers' aid workers.

HOUSING

In general the families receiving mothers' aid occupied comfortable bungalow cottages in good neighborhoods with an abundance of sunshine and air and ample play and garden space. The judge had ruled that families must live a reasonable distance away from the down-town district, beyond the railroad, cheap rooming house, factory, and water-front section. A family was told to move if the neighborhood was morally undesirable or if the house was in bad repair or insanitary; sometimes also if a mother had had neighborhood difficulties, if it was thought best for the mother to live among people of her own nationality, or if a change of schools was desirable for the children.

The court saw to it that flower and garden seeds were available. A number of families lived in attractive little bungalows among the young firs and spruces in the uncleared or partly cleared woods across Lake Washington where the natural landscape was of great beauty. A mother and three children generally occupied not less than four rooms. There was always a living room, which was sometimes used also as a sleeping room with a folding bed or couch, but this was not often necessary. There were always separate sleeping rooms for adolescent boys and girls. Nearly all houses had electricity and running water; in the city all houses were required to have sanitary toilets. Few households used gas; wood or coal was used for cooking; and there was no need of ice.

Rents were seldom more than $20 a month. A few mothers paid from $25 to $50, but these sublet or rented rooms. Half the women owned or partly owned their own homes. Much resourcefulness and thought had been expended in helping mothers to build or buy cottages, real homes to live in. For example, the mothers' aid worker had succeeded in having a carpenters' union send its members to finish out of working hours a partly built house for one family. The worker, too, had been able to have the lumber donated, and herself had cooked 20 dinners for the men while at work. For a family of eight, who had been moved by the Theodora Home to a large seven-room house on the grounds of this home in the open country, the worker had solicited wall paper for five rooms, a gallon of ivory enamel, a gallon of white paint, and 20 pounds of calcimine. The mother and children did the renovating and the Volunteers of America the much-needed repair work.

<small>Mrs. O. came to Washington from England by way of Canada. On the death of her husband, who had been' insane, she was left with four children to provide for. She had $425, which she said she would like to put into a home. The judge persuaded a woman who owned some property on the outskirts of the city to donate 50 square feet of ground on which Mrs. O. could</small>

build a five-room cottage; a lumber company furnished lumber and a hardware store gave locks, screws, and all necessary hardware. The paper and paint also were donated. The building was erected by neighbors at a minimum cost. Two years later the judge prevailed upon a liberal-minded friend to install a bathroom.

The house was colorful with plants and flowers and was well kept. In the summer Mrs. O. had cultivated a garden for which she had won a neighborhood prize. She was thrifty and she always had something for a neighbor needier than herself; she mentioned mending and washing clothing that her children had outgrown for a family a few doors down the street. Her only extravagance had been the enlarging to photograph size of an old daguerreotype of her husband to keep on the parlor table so that the children might not forget "that their father was as good as he looked."

EDUCATION

COOPERATION WITH THE SCHOOLS AND FACILITIES FOR EDUCATION

Contacts with the schools.

The most important contact with the schools was by means of personal visits, particularly in the country where the workers consulted the principals and teachers on their regular bimonthly rounds. The school reports sent to the parents were not consulted, but special reports on a form provided by the court were mailed by the teachers to the mothers' pension department once or twice a year. A copy of such a report is as follows:

SCHOOL RECORD

Date: _____

To the MOTHERS' PENSION DEPARTMENT,
 Juvenile Court, 200 Broadway, Seattle, Wash.
Name of child: _____ Address: _____
Name of school: _____ Grade: _____ Age: ____
 The records of this school for the period of _____ show the following:
  Attendance: No. of times tardy, _____ No. of days absent, _____.
  Scholarship: Excellent, _____; good, _____; poor, _____.
    Deficient branches: _____
    Conduct, _____ Parental care, _____.

  (Signed) _____
                                                                  Principal.

Provision for handicapped children.

The physically handicapped child.—In the Seattle schools there were three classes for blind children or those having defective vision, six classes for deaf and semideaf children, and three classes for children having speech defects. Three teachers (one giving half time only) gave instruction to children individually in the Orthopedic Hospital.

The mentally handicapped child.—There were four special classes of primary grade and four special-class centers or schools (each occupying an entire building) for children of various ages with intelligence quotients of 50 to 70. Eight children in families receiving mothers' aid were attending special classes.

Provision for children wishing further education.

Much interest was shown by the court in the ambitious boy or girl who was eager to continue education. No scholarships were available except those provided by Jewish organizations for Jewish children.

Two Jewish children were receiving scholarships of $20 a month each to enable them to go through high school. Aside from the academic high-school work 27 children were receiving special training. Eight were attending college or normal school, 10 were in business school, and 4 were in an electrical school; 4 were learning banking, and 1 was studying pharmacy.

The following case histories illustrate the educational advantages that the court aided promising boys and girls to obtain:

> Laura had had one year in the high-school art course; as she was compelled by family need to go to work, the mothers' aid visitor secured a position for her at the School of Fine Arts and introduced her to a commercial artist. She did tinting very well and the artist gave her some of his overflow work, such as coloring cards and pictures, at which she was very successful. She got a position later in the art section of a department store and attended art school at night. Her work was frequently exhibited in art shops and music stores. Finally the visitor learned that Laura had a well-to-do uncle in another State, and he was written to and told of Laura's ambition to go to art school. He became interested in his bright young niece and promised to send her in the fall for a two or three year course at an art school.

> Agnes B., the oldest daughter in a family receiving aid, had worked her way through normal school. During the entire last year of her course her mother sent her but $3.45. At the time of the study she had been teaching four years and was earning $135 a month. She had put her younger sister through business college and provided so well for the home that her mother could stop work. She was attending the university summer school and expected to get her degree.

> Irene, the oldest daughter of a crippled mother, graduated from a city high school and was salutatorian in a class of 350 students. She paid her expenses by working afternoons and Saturdays during the entire four years. Her ambition was to be a lawyer. She had learned stenography and had worked for a year, but she was planning to enter a law school and work half time in the office of a prominent lawyer.

SCHOOLING AND WORK OF CHILDREN 14 AND 15 YEARS OLD

The child-labor, compulsory-education, and mothers' aid laws.
All children not high-school graduates were required to attend school up to the age of 18 years, with the following exceptions: A child 14 years old who had completed the eighth grade or who, in the judgment of the superintendent of schools, could not profitably pursue regular school work might obtain an employment certificate, provided the need of the family or the welfare of the child required it; and a child 15 years old might obtain an employment certificate, regardless of school-grade attainment, if the need of the family or the welfare of the child required it. All children under 18 years of age were required to obtain employment certificates and to attend part-time school four hours a week unless excused according to the provisions of the law, which permitted exemption to high-school graduates, to children who could not profitably pursue further study, and to those for whom attendance would be injurious to health.[3] The mothers' aid law permitted allowances to be granted to children under 15 years of age.

---

[3] Wash., act of Mar. 18, 1919, ch. 151, Laws of 1919, p. 420. (Remington's Comp. Stat. 1922, secs. 4907–4909, 4912, pp. 764–765.)

Children in school and at work.

Although aid could not be granted to children who had passed their fifteenth birthday, the court allowed aid for the younger children in a family in order that an ambitious boy or girl might continue in school, if this enabled the family to get along without the wages the children 15 years old could have earned. The mothers' pension department also found for a considerable number of boys and girls homes in which they earned their board and were permitted to go to school. This practice, of course, required careful supervision to guard against any exploitation of the children and to insure good moral surroundings. As the high school was on the two-session basis, it was possible for pupils to go to school half time and work half time.

There were 154 children (78 boys and 76 girls) 14 and 15 years old in the families receiving mothers' aid; 108 were 14 years old and 46 were 15 years old. Of these 154 children 144 (69 boys and 75 girls) were attending school, 8 were working, and 2 were neither in school nor at work.

Children in school.—Among the 144 children 14 and 15 years old attending school were 74 who were eligible for employment certificates so far as educational requirements were concerned.[4]

The number of boys and girls 14 and 15 years of age attending school and the grade or type of school attended are shown in the following table:

Number of children 14 and 15 years old who were attending school at the time of the study, by grade and type of school; King County, Wash.

Grade or type of school	Children 14 and 15 years old attending school					
	Total	Boys			Girls		
		Total	14 years	15 years	Total	14 years	15 years
Total	144	69	55	14	75	52	23
Elementary school:							
Sixth grade	1				1	1	
Seventh grade	15	8	7	1	7	7	
Eighth grade	59	30	26	4	29	24	5
High school:							
First year	43	19	16	3	24	17	7
Second year	16	5	2	3	11	2	9
Third year	2	1		1	1		1
Special class	8	6	4	2	2	1	1

Twenty-four of these 144 children were working outside school hours, earning from $2 or $3 for work on Saturday only to $5 to $12 a week for work on both week days and Saturdays. Five were delivering newspapers, 4 were delivery or messenger boys, 3 were clerking in stores 3 were doing housework, and 2 were doing janitor work. One child was engaged in each of the following: Newspaper work, electrical work on school plant, milking cows and serving on milk

---

[4] This number was 95 per cent of all the children in mothers' aid families who had fulfilled the school-grade requirement for going to work (78).

route, ushering in theater, and doing odd jobs. The kind of work was not reported for two children.

Occupations and earnings of working children.—Three of the 8 children 14 and 15 years old who were working were messenger boys, 1 boy and 1 girl were working in stores, 1 boy was working in a garage, 1 on a milk route, and 1 in a factory. Six of the eight were attending vocational school part time, and one was taking a business course at night school and intended to return to school the following year.

Three boys were earning $43 a month, 1 was earning $56, 1 was earning $57, and 2 boys were earning $65. The earnings of one boy were not reported. The boy who was earning $56 and a boy who was earning $65 were contributing their entire earnings, and a boy who was earning $43 was contributing $22 to the family support. No information was obtained as to the contribution of the remaining four boys. The one girl who was working contributed to the support of her family, but the amount was not reported.

Children neither in school nor at work.

Two boys 15 years of age were neither attending school nor working at the time of the study. One was ill at home, the other was a cripple, who helped in garden work at home.

EDUCATIONAL ACTIVITIES FOR THE MOTHERS

The mothers who did not speak English were encouraged when possible to attend an Americanization center, three of which were conducted by one of the down-town churches. The Woman's Christian Temperance Union operated a housekeeping center where classes were conducted in cooking and sewing. The Hebrew Benevolent Society employed visiting housekeepers who visited in the homes of Jewish families receiving mothers' aid whenever necessary. Fourteen mothers were attending various classes in citizenship, housekeeping, and home nursing.

RECREATION

The court made no ruling as to the amount which working children must turn over to the mother, but it was the expectation of the court that "a good mother would get all the money the children earned up to the age of 16 years." She was allowed to make her own arrangement with the children as to spending money. Lunches were carried from home. Children over 16 paid their board, amounting to at least half of their earnings.

Twenty city playgrounds provided recreation for young children, and there were community dance halls supervised by matrons appointed by the chief of police. The schools conducted some special activities with a "mothers' night," "dads' night," "open house," and "community sings," but were not generally used as social centers. The parent-teacher association was very active, and membership in it was encouraged by the court. Weekly or biweekly meetings were held in nearly all the schools. Two mothers receiving aid were presidents of parent-teacher associations, and one mother had organized a group in the school attended by her children.

Children were encouraged to attend the story-telling hour at the public library, and mothers' aid visitors were expected to see that the children had library cards. Attendance at church and Sunday school and participation in the social activities of the church were also encouraged. One of the down-town churches conducted a neighborhood center and had a strong juvenile department in connection with its Sunday school. This furnished the children all kinds of sports and opportunities to join classes in wood carving and cabinetwork, sewing, and cooking (attendance at church and Sunday school was required of children who wished to participate in the social activities). Two other churches conducted vacation Bible schools where children were provided with play space. Membership in the Young Men's Christian Association and the Young Women's Christian Association was precluded by the cost. Boys and girls were encouraged to join the scout troops if they could afford it, but few of them had time or money for these forms of recreation. Factories and stores conducted recreation camps for their employees and their families, who occupied small cottages and used a common meeting hall. Thirty mothers and their children were given vacations in this way by one company that employed the mothers as elevator operators or janitresses. The Lions' Club gave to 65 girls 14 to 18 years old in families receiving mothers' aid a week's vacation at a summer camp, the wives of the members acting as chaperons. At Christmas time they gave to the same group of girls a banquet, theater party, and Christmas tree. Children were not expected to attend motion pictures oftener than once a week. Families were encouraged to own or buy a cheap phonograph or piano.

MOTHERS' ALLOWANCES IN NEW BEDFORD, MASS.[1]

PROVISIONS OF THE LAW

The Massachusetts mothers' aid law, applying to all mothers with dependent children of specified ages, was passed in 1913 and remained unchanged except for an amendment in 1922 which raised the age limit to conform with the compulsory education law.[2] The conditions of eligibility were as follows:

1. A mother must have resided within the State for not less than three years immediately prior to her application for aid. There was no citizenship requirement nor legal-settlement requirement. The amount of State reimbursement in a given case depended, however, upon whether the mother aided had a legal settlement; that is, a claim for support upon a particular city or town within the State. If she had, the city or town granting the aid sent a bill to the State department of public welfare and was reimbursed by the State for one-third the amount granted. If she had no settlement, the State reimbursed the city or town for the total amount. If she had a legal settlement in another town, two-thirds of the amount of the aid given might be recovered from that town and one-third from the State.

2. The mother must be " fit to bring up her children " and the other members of the household and the surroundings of the home must be such " as to make for good character."

3. Aid must be necessary to enable the mother to " bring up her children properly."

4. Aid was allowed up to the age of 14 years " or between the ages of 14 and 16 if and during the time when such children are required * * * to attend a public day school."

5. No maximum grant per child was specified. The law provided that " the aid furnished shall be sufficient to enable them [the mothers] to bring up their children properly in their own homes."

---

[1] The population of New Bedford, Mass., in 1920 was 121,217. The native white population was 67,453. the foreign-born population 48,689; and there were 4,998 negroes. The population of foreign birth in the order of numerical importance was as follows: French-Canadian, natives of Atlantic islands (including the Azores), English, and Portuguese. The child population within the legal age for mothers' allowances was 33,448. (Fourteenth Census of the United States, 1920, vol. 3, Population, pp. 446, 467, Washington, 1922.) The chief industries are the manufacture of cotton yarns, cotton and silk goods, twist drills and machine tools, fine cut glassware, and lubricating oils.
[2] Massachusetts, act of June 12, 1913, ch. 763, Acts and Resolves of 1913, p. 726 (Gen. Laws 1921, ch. 118, secs. 1–6, pp. 1172–1173), as amended by act of May 2, 1922, ch. 376, Acts and Resolves of 1922, p. 393. (This was amended further by the act of Apr. 14, 1926, ch. 241, Acts and Resolves of 1926, p. 236, dealing with reimbursement of the counties, cities, and towns by the State.)

The department of public welfare had established rules and policies as follows:

Aid might be granted to widows; to women whose husbands were totally incapacitated by reason of chronic illness or insanity; to women whose husbands were serving a prison sentence of more than one year; to women who were divorced or legally separated from their husbands under certain conditions; and to women whose husbands had deserted, provided they had been gone more than a year and an application had been made for the issuance of a warrant for nonsupport in accordance with the law. The applicant was not debarred from consideration if the court refused to issue the warrant. Aid might not be granted to a mother of illegitimate children except with the approval of the department of public welfare.

Aid might not be granted to a mother who had savings or easily liquidated assets in excess of $200, or equity in a house in which the family resided in excess of $500, the assessed value of which did not exceed $2,500. The total assets of the mother, including equity in her home and savings, might not exceed $500. No mother who received aid was permitted to have any men lodgers other than her father or brother. It was recommended that every member of the families aided under the law receive a medical examination. Aid was granted by check (except as to fuel, shoes, and medical care, which were furnished by the local overseers of the poor) and the women called for their checks once a week at the mothers' aid office.

STATE SUPERVISION

The State department of public welfare was required to—

supervise the work done and the measures taken by the overseers of the several towns in respect to [mothers' aid] families subject to this chapter; and for this purpose may make such rules relative to notice as it deems necessary and may visit and inspect any or all families so aided, and shall have access to any records and other data kept by the overseers or their representatives relating to such aid; and the department shall include in its annual report a statement of the work done by its own agents and by the overseers of the poor in respect to such families, any of whose members are without legal settlement in the commonwealth; and a separate statement of the work done by the overseers of the poor in respect to such families in which all the members have a legal settlement in the commonwealth.

In interpreting the function of the department of public welfare so far as it related to the supervision of mothers' aid under the section of the law quoted in the preceding paragraph the director of the division of aid and relief, which was responsible for the supervision of mothers' aid, stated: " It has always been the opinion of the department of public welfare that unless each family was investigated by our own agents we would not have sufficient knowledge to formulate proper policies for the guidance of the overseers and would not be able to act properly upon claims for reimbursement."

The department of public welfare formulated policies for the guidance of the local overseers and established forms for applications, notices, and quarterly statements. It also recommended as a guide certain budget figures.

The State supervisor and the 10 visitors under her supervision were appointed under civil-service rules and formed a subdivision of mothers' aid in the division of aid and relief of the department of public welfare. The State mothers' aid visitors investigated all families in whose behalf the local overseers sent notices to the department of public welfare requesting State reimbursement. No reimbursements were made for any part of the administrative expense. The State agents visited all families receiving mothers' aid at least once in six months and reported any conditions needing attention to the State supervisor who on the basis of these reports made recommendations to the overseers. The contacts between the State agents and the overseers offered many opportunities for helpful suggestions.

One of the State workers spent one day each week in New Bedford. She was in close touch with the overseer's office and made many constructive recommendations, especially in regard to medical care. The records showed that increases in aid were not infrequently recommended and that the overseers generally complied but often did not increase the grant to the total recommended. The visits which the State mothers' aid visitor made to families receiving aid were independent of those made by the local mothers' aid visitor, though sometimes they visited together.

ADMINISTRATION OF THE LAW

ADMINISTRATIVE AGENCY AND STAFF

The law gave the administration of mothers' aid to the town or city boards of public welfare (the department administering outdoor relief).[3] In New Bedford the board of public welfare consisted of two men and one woman appointed by the mayor for a period of three years, one vacancy occurring each year. Their appointments were confirmed by the city council, and either the mayor or the city council could remove them at any time. Each member received $500 a year. This board employed a paid executive secretary, who might or might not be a member of the board, and who administered both mothers' aid and outdoor relief.

One visitor investigated applications and supervised families receiving mothers' aid. She worked under the general direction of the board, which at its regular weekly meeting discussed mothers' aid families and determined upon the grants. This worker was appointed by the board of public welfare under civil-service regulations. She had had practical experience in home making and had established friendly contacts with the mothers and children under her care.

APPROPRIATION AND VOLUME OF WORK

The expenditures for mothers' aid were $68,673.38 in 1922 and $69,014.99 in 1923. The grants averaged $10 to $15 a week. The average grant in money during 1922 was $43 per month. The smallest weekly grant was $4, the largest was $20. Fuel (about one-half ton a month), shoes, medical attendance (at home or in the hospital) and medicine, and some merchandise were provided in addition. In March, 1924, 96 families, including 377 children under 16 years of age, where receiving allowances. The one mothers' aid worker was

---
[3] Formerly called overseers of the poor. The change of name was authorized by act of Feb. 20, 1923, ch. 26, Acts and Resolves of 1923, p. 12.

responsible for investigating and supervising all the families receiving allowances, and she also saw the mothers each week when they called for their checks. She did her own typewriting.

PROCEDURE IN MAKING ALLOWANCES

The mothers applied in person at the mothers' aid office and the visitor filled out at the mother's dictation an application blank, which she signed. The following information was called for: The names, addresses, and places and dates of birth of mother, father, and children; the place and date of marriage, and name of person by whom the parents were married; the date of the father's death, commitment, or desertion, or of the decree of divorce or separation; the school and grade of children in school, and the wages and places of employment of working children; the names and addresses of relatives and their ability to aid; the length of residence in Massachusetts and places of residence; facts as to savings, property, insurance, income, debts, and installments; health; the families' religious preference and the church attended; a weekly estimate of the family expenses and income.

The investigation by the New Bedford mothers' aid worker included a verification of legal data and an especially careful inquiry as to settlement. A visit was always made at the home and the amounts of the mother's and children's wages were verified. The mother and the children were examined by one of the physicians employed by the board of public welfare.

USE OF A STANDARD BUDGET

The State department of public welfare recommended as a guide certain budget figures which had been prepared very carefully by the mothers' aid department in consultation with dietetic experts. Budget systems already in use elsewhere, the reports of the Massachusetts special commissioner on the necessaries of life, and the recommendations of dietitians and hospital social workers were used in preparing this budget, which was as follows:

[Budget is figured on a weekly basis]

I. Food:
 Mother (according to amount of work) _____ $2.45–$2.80
 Older boys (over 14 years) _____ 3.30
 Older girls (over 12 years) _____ 2.75
 Children, both sexes, 6 to 12 years _____ 2.00
 Children, both sexes, under 6 years _____ 1.55
 NOTE.—Food for incapacitated father at home _____ 2.45
 Food for mother's adult brother (if a boarder in her home) _____ 3.40
 Food for adult woman boarder _____ 2.75
 Food for elderly parent _____ 2.20

II. Clothing:
 Mother (according to whether she works out or stays at home) _____ 1.10–2.00
 Children over 16 years _____ 2.00
 Children 12 to 16 years _____ 1.25
 Children 6 to 12 years _____ .85
 Children under 6 years _____ .60
 NOTE.—Clothing for elderly parent _____ 1.10
 Clothing for incapacitated father _____ 1.10

III. Fuel and light:
  Summer months _____ $1.10
  Spring months _____ 2.50
  Fall months _____ 2.50
  Winter months _____ 3.90
  NOTE.—Average for whole year _____ 2.50
IV. Rent: As charged.
V. Sundries:
  Allow for the first 3 members _____each_ .40
  Allow for all other members _____do__ .20

NOTE.—Food costs equal 43 per cent of the entire cost if sundries are included in the total, or 46 per cent if sundries are not included in the total.

The board of public welfare of New Bedford, however, did not base its grants upon a budget estimate of household expenses,[4] and the mothers were not required to keep household-expense accounts. The board kept at its offices a supply of shoes, and it occasionally furnished such merchandise as sheets, towels, or bedding. Milk was furnished to families in which the children were delicate. Few mothers receiving aid did work outside their homes; about one-half earned a little through laundry work in their own homes; a few did day's work. No children were in day nurseries.

As the mothers' aid law permitted adequate relief, the private agencies as a rule did not give supplementary aid, although they occasionally furnished milk for a delicate child.

VISITING

The mothers' aid law required that the board or its duly appointed agent should visit each mother and her dependent children in her own home at least once in three months and after each visit should make to the State department of public welfare a detailed statement (on a form furnished) as to the condition of the home and family and all other data which might assist in determining the wisdom of the measures taken and the advisability of their continuance. (At least once a year the reconsideration of each grant was required.) The visitor went to the homes more frequently than once in three months if she felt that circumstances required it. As has been stated, the State visitor also visited each family at least once in six months.

HEALTH

PHYSICAL HEALTH

Physical examinations and general procedure.

All applicants for mothers' aid and their dependent children under 16 years of age were given physical examinations before aid was granted. These examinations were given by one of the five city physicians employed by the board of public welfare, and written reports of the diagnosis and recommendations were made on blanks furnished by the board. The board provided medical care and all

---

[4] The use of a budget for determining the amount of the grants was begun after the period of the study.

medicines prescribed by the city physicians. These reports were filed with the record. The following is such a report form:

No. 1.

Date :_____

City of New Bedford

BOARD OF PUBLIC WELFARE

Physician's Diagnosis

Name of patient : _____
Address : _____
Diagnosis : _____
Recommendation : _____
_____

Doctor's signature : _____

The examination did not include any recorded individual or family medical history, nor was the weight indicated. The mothers' aid visitor followed up the examinations. She saw the physicians personally or conferred with them by telephone. The necessary treatment was generally given by the physician who made the examination. If an operation requiring hospital care was needed the board of public welfare paid for surgical and hospital care at the rate of $15 per week.

The preliminary examinations were not followed by further examinations except in individual cases where special need was indicated. Continuous health records of each individual in the families assisted were not kept systematically. Physicians employed by the city generally were used except for hospital care and specialized treatment; the mothers' aid visitor endeavored to follow up their medical advice and treatment. If a specialist's advice was necessary the patient might be referred to a clinic at St. Luke's Hospital. Service at the clinics was free, but none was extensively used for mothers' aid families except the orthopedic clinics and the tuberculosis clinics of the department of health. The follow-up work had generally been attended to by the hospital social service department or by the nurses attached to the clinic.

Mothers were given advice in regard to food and health habits by the mothers' aid visitors, the nurses, the doctor, or the social-service departments of hospitals.

As free medical care was provided for the families receiving aid, the services of private physicians were not requested. Mothers who consulted these did so at their own expense and entirely on their own initiative.

Follow-up of special types of problems.

Tuberculosis.—If a mother or children had been exposed to tuberculosis or if there was any reason to suspect that they had tuberculosis it was the policy to advise them to attend the tuberculosis clinic of the board of health. It was the expectation of the worker that the clinic would attend to the follow-up work, which, however, had not been very close; nor had regular examinations and treatment been required. This seemed especially important in view of the fact that from a study of 20 records selected at random it was found that three fathers had died of tuberculosis and that in three other families the mothers had been in a hospital for tuberculosis. Both the supervisor of public-health nurses, who directed the three tuberculosis nurses attached to the clinic, and the mothers' aid worker were planning for a close follow-up of all tuberculosis cases. Care for active tuberculosis cases at a sanatorium at Sassaquin, about 10 miles from New Bedford, was generally insisted upon. This hospital, operated by the antituberculosis association, was used by the city for tuberculosis patients and had ample facilities for both adults and children.

Venereal disease.—It was the policy of the department to have Wassermann tests taken if there was reason to suspect venereal disease. Patients were examined and treated at the venereal clinic operated by the board of health, which required a patient to attend regularly if the disease was found to be active. A nurse from the clinic was in close touch with all patients and visited in the homes.

Orthopedic and cardiac affections.—Children who were crippled or who had cardiac trouble were referred to St. Luke's Hospital, which operated both orthopedic and cardiac clinics. A new building was being erected for a children's orthopedic hospital which would have better facilities. The Massachusetts Hospital School at Canton, Mass., provided medical and surgical care and educational and vocational training for deformed and crippled children. Special shoes and all necessary appliances were paid for by the board of public welfare.

Eye, ear, nose, and throat affections.—All cases of eye, ear, nose, and throat affections were treated by the specialist employed by the board of public welfare or at one of the hospital clinics.

Medical welfare work for infants and preschool children.—The board of health maintained five child-health centers under the supervision of eight nurses. All birth registrations were followed up. Mothers with babies under 1 year of age were encouraged to bring them to a center every week; nurses supervised all the babies under 1 year of age and any undernourished babies up to 2 years of age. No work was being done for children between 2 and 6 years of age. Most of the centers were within walking distance from the homes, and none of the mothers who were farther away needed to change cars.

The board encouraged the mothers to attend the child-health centers, but it was not known how many attended regularly. Often they went directly from the mothers' aid office in the city hall, where they called for their weekly checks, to the center at the central office of the board of health, which was in the same building.

School medical inspection.—Physicians employed by the board of health examined all children in the public and in the parochial schools at the beginning of the first term of school and again at the beginning of the second term. The mothers' aid visitor had not made a practice of examining the children's school medical reports, but she planned to do so in the future. There were seven school nurses, one of whom was attached to the mental clinic; each school was inspected every day. The nurses gave health instruction at least three times a year. Through the continuation schools the nurses were in touch with all working children 14 and 15 years of age.

Dentistry.—Three dental clinics were maintained; seven dental hygienists made inspections and cleaned the children's teeth twice yearly. They also gave instruction on the care of the teeth.

Malnutrition.—Height and weight records were taken for all school children twice a year by the teachers. If children were underweight, they were weighed every month. The schools in poor neighborhoods furnished milk at 3½ cents a half pint, and undernourished children were encouraged to buy mid-morning lunches of bread, butter, and milk. It was reported by the health department that there was not a large number of underweight children. There were no nutrition classes, but the school nurses gave individual instruction whenever necessary. There was no arrangement whereby the teachers or the nurses notified the mothers' aid visitor in regard to underweight children. The principals of the school gave reports to the overseers when requested, but the overseers hesitated to make known the fact that the children were being aided.

MENTAL HEALTH

Available facilities.

Two psychiatrists and a psychometrist from the Taunton State Hospital for the Insane, assisted by two social workers from the same institution, conducted a mental clinic one afternoon a week in the clinic rooms of the New Bedford Board of Health. Psychopathic and behavior problems were given careful attention, and patients returned to the clinic regularly for advice and treatment.

A traveling clinic conducted by a physician and a psychologist from the State training school for the feeble-minded at Waverley, Mass., visited New Bedford for periods of 1, 2, or 3 weeks about three times a year. They examined retarded children whom the teachers in the public schools recommended for examination. The director of special classes in the schools obtained full social histories of these children. The visiting physician first made a physical examination of the children selected, then the psychologist gave a psychological examination and determined their mental ages. Only the children for whom this clinic recommended enrollment in a special class (usually those whose intelligence quotient was 40 to 70) were put in the special classes of the schools. No child who could return to the grades was placed in such a class.

The director of special classes in the public schools tested any 15-year-old children who had not completed the sixth grade and who made application for employment certificates. She also gave individual mental tests occasionally to children markedly deficient.

Follow-up of special types of problems.

Children whose families had a history of mental defect or disease were not given special examinations unless mental trouble was apparent. Those obviously defective were referred to the traveling clinic previously mentioned, and if institutional care was recommended an application was made for their admission to the Wrentham State School or the State school for the feeble-minded at Waverley.

One child with a psychopathic difficulty had been referred to the weekly clinic conducted by the psychiatrists and psychometrist from the State hospital for the insane, but at the time of the study no child in a mothers' aid family had had behavior difficulty sufficiently serious to make reference to this clinic seem advisable.

HOUSING

The families receiving mothers' aid that were visited in New Bedford lived in clean homes, comfortably furnished, and in decent neighborhoods; the city was well known for its clean and orderly streets. The majority of families receiving aid lived in four-room or five-room flats in tenement houses containing two, three, four, or more tenements. The rooms were all outside, well aired and lighted and good sized. All the flats were equipped with running water and gas and about half of them had electricity. Most families had ice boxes, and many had bathrooms, though the latter were not considered a necessity. The law required that all houses should have inside toilets,[5] though in the large tenement houses one toilet was shared by two families. A mother with three children generally had a flat consisting of kitchen, two bedrooms, and parlor. The parlor was seldom used for sleeping purposes.

The tenement usually had a small rear yard space shared by all the families in the house; but this seldom was sufficient for individual family garden plots. Many families had small flower beds, and some families—especially the Portuguese—raised vegetables even if there were only a few feet of available space.

Families were required to move if they were living in too congested quarters, if the neighborhood was undesirable from a moral standpoint, or if the tenements were in poor repair or below standard. Only five or six families lived in cottage houses and only three families owned or partly owned their own homes. The average rent was $5 a week and the maximum rent allowed was $7 a week.

EDUCATION

COOPERATION WITH THE SCHOOLS AND FACILITIES FOR EDUCATION

Contacts with the schools.

The mothers' aid worker visited the schools only when special problems or questions required personal contact. She frequently examined the reports that the children brought to their parents, but no regular supervision of the school progress had been undertaken. The department was planning, however, to supply to the schools blank report forms to be filled out and returned at regular intervals.

Provision for handicapped children.

The physically handicapped child.—The public schools supplied a teacher for the crippled children in St. Luke's Hospital, but no arrangement had been made for the transportation of crippled children to and from school. There were two sight-conservation classes, one for the primary grades and one for the intermediate grades, and

---
[5] Mass., Gen. Laws 1921, ch. 144, sec. 32, p. 1487; sec. 35, p. 1488.

two open-air classes. Children who had serious physical handicaps were encouraged to learn trades at the vocational school. The school nurses referred underweight and undernourished children to the tuberculosis clinic.

The mentally handicapped child.—There were eight special classes.[6] There were also opportunity classes to which teachers recommended children, and "helping teachers" gave special assistance.

Provision for children wishing further education.

No scholarships seemed to be available. Children in mothers' aid families were expected to go to work as soon as they could get employment certificates, regardless of ability or desire for further education. However, there were an excellent night vocational school and numerous classes in vocational subjects at the community centers, the city mission, and the church centers.

SCHOOLING AND WORK OF CHILDREN 14 AND 15 YEARS OLD

The compulsory-education, child-labor, and mothers' aid laws.

The compulsory education law required that children between 7 and 14 years of age and children between 14 and 16 without employment certificates or special permits authorizing them to work at home should attend school or receive instruction equivalent to that provided in the public schools. Exemptions were made as to school attendance of children "whose physical or mental condition was such as to make attendance inexpedient or impracticable."[7] Children over 14 and under 16 years of age were eligible for employment certificates if they had completed the sixth grade and were physically fit, provided they had attended school 130 days after becoming 13 years of age.[8] Working children of these ages were required to attend continuation school four hours a week.[9] The mothers' aid law permitted allowances to be granted to children up to the age of 14 years, or between 14 and 16 during the time they were required to attend public day school.[10]

Children in school and at work.

The clear intent of the law was that children in families receiving aid should go to work as soon as they were eligible for employment certificates, and the policy of the State department of public welfare and of the board of public welfare in New Bedford was in accordance with this.

There were 26 children (15 boys and 11 girls) 14 and 15 years of age in the families receiving aid; 16 of them were 14 years old and 10 were 15 years old. Of these 26 children 14 were attending school, 10 were working, and 2 were neither attending school nor working.

---

[6] The establishment of special classes was required in all towns where 10 or more children were retarded three years or more (Mass., Gen. Laws 1921, ch. 71, sec. 46, as amended by act of Mar. 31, 1922, ch. 231, Acts and Resolves of 1922, p. 253).

[7] Mass., Gen. Laws 1921, ch. 76, sec. 1, p. 731, as amended by act of May 27, 1927, ch. 463, Acts and Resolves of 1921, p. 552. Children might also be excused for "necessary absence" (not exceeding seven days in six months).

[8] Ibid., ch. 149, sec. 87, p. 1570; sec. 88, p. 1572, as amended by act of Feb. 19, 1925, ch. 47, Acts and Resolves of 1925, p. 26. Provision was made permitting the sixth-grade requirement to be waived under specified conditions.

[9] Ibid., ch. 71, sec. 22, p. 706.

[10] It frequently happened, especially in the textile towns, that during an industrial depression children eligible for employment certificates could not find work. These children were then obliged to attend day school, and the department of public welfare had ruled that aid might continue in such cases.

Children in school.—Among the 14 children 14 and 15 years old attending school were 8 boys and 6 girls; 8 of them had completed the sixth grade and thus were eligible for employment certificates so far as educational requirements were concerned.[11] Four of these 14 children were in the fifth grade, 2 were in the sixth, 2 were in the seventh, 5 were in the eighth, and 1 was in the high school (year not reported).

Occupations and earnings of the working children.—Among the 10 children 14 and 15 years old who were working were six 15-year-old boys employed in the textile mills and two 14-year-old girls working in these mills as learners and not receiving any pay. One girl 15 years old and one boy 14 years old were clerks in stores. Three of these 10 children had left school in the sixth grade, 2 in the seventh, 3 in the eighth, and 2 in the first year of high school.

The monthly earnings of the 8 children being paid for their work were as follows: 1 boy was earning $22, 2 were earning $39, 1 was earning $43, 1 was earning $48, 1 was earning $49, and 1 was earning $52. One girl was earning $35. All these children contributed their entire earnings to the support of the family.

Children neither in school nor at work.

Two girls, one 14 years old, the other 15 years old, were neither attending school nor working. Both were reported to be mentally defective.

EDUCATIONAL ACTIVITIES FOR THE MOTHERS

Mothers of foreign birth were encouraged to learn English and to get citizenship papers. Many classes were available, and three mothers receiving aid had attended Americanization classes. About 12 of the mothers were enrolled in sewing, cooking, millinery, and basketry classes in the evening.

RECREATION

Children up to 18 years of age turned over their entire wages to their mothers, who bought their clothing and allowed them $1.50 to $2 a month for spending money.

The recreational facilities provided by the public and private agencies were excellent and varied. The library was well equipped to serve young and old, and there were children's story hours. The seven community centers in the public schools were under the direction of a full-time supervisor attached to the board of education. The activities were patterned somewhat on the Detroit model; boys', girls', and women's clubs formed the nuclei for the various athletic, educational, and social activities. In two centers forums were conducted. Scout troops were organized as part of the boys' and girls' work. It was estimated by the director that every home was within walking distance of a community center. In addition to the community centers in the public schools there were two centers conducted by churches; and the city mission, a settlement house, had health, educational, recreational, and social activities. An extensive program of sports, handicraft, and dramatic activities was promoted

---

[11] There were thus 20 children eligible for employment certificates among the 26 mothers' aid children 14 and 15 years of age.

during the summer on the playgrounds under the direction of the department of parks.

The tie between the families and their churches seemed close. Several churches had established a variety of neighborhood activities, which met many of the social and recreational needs of their people. Scout troops also were organized in the churches, both Protestant and Catholic. It was not known how many mothers' aid children were members.

The Young Men's Christian Association and the Young Women's Christian Association offered opportunities for amusement and social life, and the International Institute of the Young Women's Christian Association organized clubs and classes among foreign-born women and girls. The Boy Scouts had a summer vacation camp of their own, and the Rotary and Kiwanis Clubs financed boys' vacation camps. The Country Week Association provided a two weeks' vacation on farms in the summer to sick or undernourished mothers and children. However, few members of families receiving mothers' aid were offered these opportunities. Occasionally the theaters gave tickets, especially at Christmas time, and fraternal organizations arranged summer picnics and outings to which families receiving mothers' aid were invited.

Every family had abundant sources of wholesome recreation almost at its very threshold, and doubtless many boys and girls, and possibly mothers, were taking advantage of them. The mothers' aid department had not assumed any responsibility in directing recreation.

MOTHERS' ALLOWANCES IN SAN FRANCISCO, CALIF.[1]

PROVISIONS OF THE LAW

In 1913 the California Legislature defined the general provisions of its constitution (ratified in 1879) relating to half orphans so as to embody them into what became known as the half-orphan aid law, and these provisions were further amended in 1917, 1919, 1921, and 1923.[2] If the child for whom application was made for aid had not been born in the State, residence in the State for two years preceding the application was required. A mother entitled to aid for her child or children could receive it anywhere in the State, regardless of her county residence. The amount of the grant was not to exceed $120 per child per year. It was provided also that in addition to the amount paid by the State the county, city and county, city, or town might pay an amount equal to the sum paid by the State. (As the law did not require that the county match every State expenditure for aid, it frequently happened that State aid was all that was given to a family; if the family need was met sufficiently by the State's maximum allowance the administrative agency would draw the entire allowance from State funds and use no county funds.)

Abandoned children and the children of permanently incapacitated or tuberculous fathers were eligible for aid, as well as orphans and half orphans. Allowances could be given to children under 16 years of age. The local administration, though not specifically mentioned, was obviously the responsibility of the county, city and county, city, or town maintaining the children. Applicants denied grants by the local authorities might appeal to the State board of control.

STATE SUPERVISION

The State board of control had defined a half orphan as a child whose parent was dead, had been committed to a State hospital for the insane or to a State or Federal prison, or had deserted for a period of seven years (affidavit to this effect by five disinterested persons being required). The State exercised supervision through the State department of finance.[3] This department had a bureau

---

[1] The population of the city of San Francisco (which was coterminous with the county of San Francisco) in 1920 was 506,676. Of these, 349,822 were native white, 140,200 were foreign born, and 2,414 were negroes. The inhabitants of foreign birth were as follows, in the order of their numerical importance: Italian, German, Irish, English, French, and Canadian. The child population within legal age for mothers' allowances was 103,296. (Fourteenth Census of the United States, 1920, vol. 3, Population, pp. 115, 123, 124, Washington, 1922.) The chief industries are shipbuilding, slaughtering and meat packing, coffee and spice roasting and grinding, and automobile manufacturing.
[2] Calif., act of May 26, 1913, ch. 323, Stat. 1913, p. 629; act of May 15, 1917, ch. 472, Stat. 1917, p. 560; act of May 9, 1919, ch. 292, Stat. 1919, p. 473; act of June 3, 1921, ch. 890, Stat. 1921, p. 1687; act of May 2, 1923, ch. 77, Stat. 1923, p. 148. (See Deering's Political Code, 123, secs. 2283–2289, pp. 674–678.)
[3] A State department of finance, created by the legislature of 1921, succeeded to the duties, powers, and responsibilities of the State board of control, the latter constituting the governing body of the department of finance. (Calif., act of May 31, 1921, ch. 603, Laws of 1921, p. 1027.) (See Deering's Political Code, 1923, secs. 360–360g, pp. 92–95.)

of children's aid, which maintained offices in Sacramento, San Francisco, and Los Angeles. The bureau, whose staff included a chief children's agent and six field agents, was authorized to inquire into the management of any institution or agency caring for children who were recipients of State aid, to visit such institutions and agencies, and to visit the homes of children receiving State aid. It issued rules of procedure by which the agencies administering mothers' aid (generally called half-orphan aid) should be governed, furnished forms for the use of the agencies, and approved the grants and annual renewals of grants. If there was any doubt as to the proper course of procedure it made independent investigations of families on its own initiative, at the request of a local agency, or at the request of a mother applying for aid. Possibly the bureau assumed that investigation was incumbent upon it in view of the fact that State aid was nearly always in excess of county aid and the maximum State aid was drawn upon before any aid was demanded of the county. As a considerable part of the time of its agents was spent in administration and the making of investigations, the bureau's functions were administrative as well as supervisory.

The law permitted the State board of control to appoint advisory county committees to act in cooperation with the agents of the bureau of children's aid, but no such boards had been appointed at the time of the study.

Among the rulings and policies of the State department of finance were the following: A mother was allowed to possess property free from debt the assessed value of which did not exceed $2,500, or she might have an equity of $2,500 in the home if the upkeep did not exceed a reasonable rental. She was permitted to have money in the bank or other assets amounting to $1,000, but if she had real property the other assets might not exceed $500. As a general policy men roomers and boarders were not permitted. In order that the mother might remain at home, unless there was some other caretaker, a full allowance of State and county aid was recommended when there were young children or when the family was large. Payments for insurance on children were not allowed. When the father was incapacitated on account of tuberculosis, mothers' aid was conditional upon his treatment in a sanatorium involving separation from his family. The mother was required to live with her children and to be able to maintain a good home for them if aid were granted.

ADMINISTRATION OF THE LAW

ADMINISTRATIVE AGENCIES

After the earthquake and fire in 1906 provision had been made for the care of dependent children in the home through the dependency department of the juvenile court in San Francisco. This had been accomplished by interpreting the early provision of the constitution in regard to half-orphan children—that those in institutions should be paid for at the rate of $100 a year until they were 14 years old—as permitting direct payment to the mother by substituting her for the institution. The court committed the children to the children's agency of the San Francisco Associated Charities, the Eureka Benevolent Society (which later became the family-welfare department of the Federated Jewish Charities), or to the Catholic Humane Bureau (which later became the Little Children's Aid Society). These three social organizations supervised the children in their own homes, in foster homes, and in institutions. In 1913, a few months after the half-orphan aid act was passed, the juvenile court separated its cases of widows with children from those of other dependent families under its care and protection, and the board of county supervisors established the Widows' Pension Bureau of San Francisco.

Mothers who were not widows but whose husbands had deserted, were tuberculous, incapacitated, or in a State or Federal prison continued to make application to the juvenile court for their allowances. If the court granted their applications they were committed to the supervision of one of the three private agencies previously mentioned and a dependency order was made upon the county.

The widows' pension bureau granted the allowances to needy mothers who were widows. This bureau was directly responsible to the finance committee of the county board of supervisors, which nominally passed upon all grants and whose chairman signed the monthly pay roll, though in actual practice the entire administration was left to the bureau's director.[4] The administration of the widows' pension bureau only is discussed in this report.

The State payment of $10 a month for each child was given to the county, regardless of which agency acted as the unit of administration.

STAFF OF THE WIDOWS' PENSION BUREAU

The staff of the widows' pension bureau consisted of a director, an assistant director, two visitors, and a secretary-bookkeeper. The director was a university graduate who had had 7½ years' experience as worker and director of a settlement and 10 years' experience as visitor and then director for the widows' pension bureau. The assistant director was a physician who had had previous experience in hospital, immigration, and housing work and had been with the widows' pension bureau since 1916. One of the visitors was a university graduate who had had experience in settlement work and in volunteer work with the widows' pension bureau before joining its staff in 1919. The other visitor had worked for short periods with two private family-relief agencies, a juvenile court, and a national relief organization before her appointment to the staff in 1921. The salaries of the field workers were $1,800 to $1,920 a year.

AMOUNT OF ALLOWANCES AND VOLUME OF WORK

The distribution of State and county aid administered by the widows' pension bureau for the fiscal year ended June 30, 1923, was as follows: 10 per cent of the families receiving allowances had State aid only, 25 per cent had maximum State aid and part county aid, and 65 per cent were receiving State and county aid. San Francisco County allowed $7.50 a month for each child as a maximum supple-

---

[4] In addition to its administration of mothers' aid the widows' pension bureau also administered the county pensions to blind persons, 75 to 100 of whom were receiving assistance at any one time.

ment to the State's allowance of $10. The average monthly grant for the year ended June 30, 1923, was $37.41 per family and $15.32 per child. The largest monthly grant per family was $122.50 and the smallest $10. The director of the bureau estimated that about $6,000 a year more would have been granted to mothers if the county had permitted $10 per child a month to match the $10 allowed by the State, instead of only $7.50; and this difference would have provided reasonably adequate aid to all families.[5]

As before the establishment of the widows' pension bureau the court had had the assistance of the three social agencies mentioned, the custom of giving the mothers their checks through these agencies had not been changed to conform with altered conditions. The Jewish mothers who received allowances were permitted to call for their monthly checks at the office of the Eureka Benevolent Society, the Catholic mothers at the office of the Little Children's Aid Society, and the remaining mothers at the office of the San Francisco Associated Charities. These agencies were then reimbursed by the county. (According to a recent understanding with the bureau, however, these agencies were not to supervise widows' families unless they had been known to the agencies before the granting of the allowances or had been granted a dependency order by the court.)

In January, 1924, the widows' pension bureau was granting aid to 473 families, including 1,139 children under 16. Each of the two family visitors therefore supervised about 236 families, and in addition they typed all their records. The visitors did not work with the same families continuously.

PROCEDURE IN MAKING ALLOWANCES

Application was made in person by the mother at the office of the widows' pension bureau in the city hall. A preliminary investigation by the secretary-bookkeeper at this time brought out any clear cause for disqualification, such as lack of evidence bearing on residence, marriage, death of husband, age of children, or property or income above the limit set. The application blank called for the following information: Names, addresses, places and dates of birth, and state of health of child's parents and their marital condition; date, place, and cause of the father's death; residence in State and county; names of fraternal organizations of which father or mother was a member; name and address of father's last employer; names, addresses, places and dates of birth of all children; if in school, grade and health; if over school age, occupation, employer, and wages; and if married, the number of children, date and place of marriage; religion, facts regarding property, insurance, savings, lodgers; names, addresses, and occupations of relatives; names and addresses of teacher and of three references; an itemized estimate of the family income and the necessary expenses. Legal data were to be verified and a brief summary to be made under the heads of finance, health, moral standards, and habits of sobriety; housing; relatives and their ability to assist; references and their recommenda-

---

[5] Since the date of this study the county supervisors of San Francisco County have granted $10 per month for each child.

tions. The worker who filled out the application blank was required to state whether she had visited the home and to give her own recommendations and plans for the family.

When filled in the application blank thus recorded the important legal and social facts concerning the family, gave to the State bureau of children's aid a picture of the whole family situation, and guaranteed that adequate investigation had been made. Before the application was forwarded to the bureau of children's aid the affidavit of the mother and the written approval of the county board of supervisors were required. (Procedure for renewals required the filing of a new application blank containing up-to-date information.)

One of the two visitors on the staff was in charge of visiting and investigating for all new applications, verifying legal data, and filling out the State and county blanks. On the first of the month following receipt of the application she visited the widow's home and verified such items as dates and places of children's birth, marriage of parents, death of father, residence, facts regarding property, insurance, lodge benefits, savings, and wages of mother and children. One or two relatives and the three persons whom the mother gave as references were asked to call at the office. The children's school-teacher, the family physician, and sometimes the minister were consulted; and an attempt was made to see working children. The names of families were not registered in the social-service exchange, but the San Francisco Associated Charities records were consulted.

If the information obtained through this investigation indicated that the need was primarily economic and that with financial assistance the applicant would have little or no difficulty in making her own adjustments she and her family were retained under the supervision of the widows' pension bureau after the allowance had been granted. The assistant director, assisted by the second visitor on the staff, was in charge of the revisiting and the renewal of allowances. These workers promoted friendly relations between the widow and the pension bureau's office and helped her to use the allowance wisely and to adjust it to the changing needs of her family. The assistant director (a physician, as has been stated) made note of obvious physical defects in the families visited; and the physical condition and the general welfare of the family were looked after to such extent as the case load of the bureau's staff permitted. If, however, it appeared that the mother would need careful supervision in order to guarantee adequate home life for her children, or if she was given aid on probation, she was turned over to the juvenile court, which granted a dependency order and committed the children for supervision to one of the three child-caring agencies that were cooperating with the court.

USE OF A STANDARD BUDGET

The estimate of the cost of food for a given family was based on the Jaffa budget.[6] The bureau of children's aid had formulated and recommended the allowance that was made for clothing and in-

---

[a] Formulated by Professor Jaffa, of the University of California.

cidentals. The budgets used were revised twice a year at the time of renewal of allowances. Following is a copy of the budget:

	Amount allowed		Amount allowed
Woman doing light work	$11.83	Child 9 to 13 years	$10.36
Man doing light work	15.78	Child 6 to 9 years	9.89
Man doing hard work	17.75	Child 2 to 6 years	7.40
Boy over 13 years	15.78	Child under 2 years	5.07
Girl over 13 years	11.83		

To this family budget 20 per cent was added where there was a history of tuberculosis or where the family had been exposed to tuberculosis and was below par. Where working members bought lunch one-third was deducted from the food budget and $7.80 allowed for lunches.

For rent the mother's statement was taken providing the sum was not in excess of the average rental required to cover cost of living in a normal house. Five dollars a month per person was allowed for shoes and clothing, except where wage earners must meet the public, and then $10 per person was allowed. The mother's figures as to the allowance for insurance were taken, provided the insurance was not excessive and did not partake of the nature of saving. For working members of families who were under 21 years of age the sum of $1.50 was allowed for amusement, and for members not employed 50 cents a month. Working sons and daughters over 21 years of age were required to pay a reasonable board and provide their own amusement and incidental expenses. The sum of $1.50 per person was allowed for sundries, and 50 cents a month per person was allowed for medicine.

There was no allowance for extensive medical care, as the mothers and children could obtain very satisfactory care at the clinics and the San Francisco Hospital. The numerous health centers established throughout the city under the board of health had offered their cooperation in making health surveys for the mothers' pension work.

SUPPLEMENTING OF MOTHERS' AID

Supplementary aid was given to families under the care of the widows' pension bureau only in emergencies, when the maximum grant of the State and the county was inadequate, as the bureau did not wish its beneficiaries to receive aid from other sources. The amount of supplementary aid contributed annually by the three private relief agencies to the families under the care of the bureau was estimated to be approximately as follows:

From the children's agency of the San Francisco Associated Charities, $1,800; from the Eureka Benevolent Society, $1,200; and from the Little Children's Aid Society, $600. (All these agencies also gave supplementary aid to the mothers committed to them by the juvenile court and under their immediate supervision.)

VISITING

The policy of the widows' pension bureau was to have each family visited about four times a year unless some required more frequent visits. The relation of the workers in the bureau to the families receiving aid was one of constant and uniform friendliness. The mothers retained under the bureau's supervision were those who seemed capable enough to make their own plans. Doubtless they would have profited by further guidance in regard to health, education, recreation, and employment; but the bureau held that for the sake of preserving individual liberty and initiative, eligibility to aid having once been established, the mothers should be free to manage their households in their own way without close follow-up, however friendly. According to this interpretation, as long as the mothers conformed to the regulations, any case work would be an impertinence unless the mothers expressed a desire for it. Unfortunately, the staff was not large enough to enable the bureau to do intensive case work except occasionally nor to demonstrate to the families and to the community its worth in terms of helpful service.

On the occasion of the semiannual renewal of her allowance the mother visited the office and had a conference with the director, who covered at length all matters relating to health, education, work of mother and children, and income. These visits were made the special occasion of explaining to the mothers their relation and obligation to the State and county. This loyalty to a cause was stressed as an incentive to good conduct. An effort was also made to bring home to the mothers the fact that the officers of the bureau were there as public servants to express to them the good will and protection of the State, and to administer a law which in their capacity as citizens the beneficiaries sanctioned and upheld and the provisions of which were entirely in their interest.

HEALTH

PHYSICAL HEALTH

General procedure.

The mothers were required to give the height and weight of each child at the time of application, and these were recorded on the application blank. On her first visit to the home the physician who was assistant director observed the general appearance of the family, especially in regard to nutrition and nervousness, and gave the mothers advice as to health habits and food. No blanks were used, nor was any attempt made to get a medical history of the individual children or of the family nor to embody in the record a continuous medical history of each child. No comment was made in the records or application blank regarding the physical condition unless there were obvious defects.

If the investigator or the visitors in the course of treatment or the director at the semiannual renewal of allowance suspected physical defects the mother was given information in regard to one of the hospital clinics—generally those of the University of California or Leland Stanford University—where examination and treatment could be secured. A steering card was given to the mother and this was returned, giving the name of the clinic and physician to whom she had been referred. Generally if the bureau had referred the patient a written report was returned to it covering diagnosis and treatment prescribed. This report was filed with the record.

Following is the form of steering card used in referring to the University of California medical department:

[Face]

Referred from the Widows' Pension Bureau, Room 462, City Hall.
Park 8500; Local 403

Date: _____

Name: _____
Address: _____
Nativity: _____ Married_____

[Reverse]

University of California Medical Department, Second and Parnassus Avenues

(Take Hayes Street car No. 6 on Market Street and get off at Second Avenue)

Referred to_____ Clinic.
Especially referred to_____
To report (date)_____
Remarks: _____
_____

The policy of the bureau was to encourage the mothers to have the necessary medical care for themselves and for their children. It directed them to clinics, but it did not actually insist upon care unless the children were a menace to the other children in the family or to the community. In keeping with this policy, the examinations and treatment of patients at clinics or under the care of private physicians were not closely followed up as a matter of general practice, the bureau staff believing that no pressure should be exerted in such matters and that the initiative of the mother should be preserved.

Mothers were permitted to employ private physicians, who were expected to reduce their fees at the request either of the mothers or of the bureau. Physicians employed by the city could be secured in an emergency. Families were encouraged, however, to secure medical care through the hospital clinics.

The guaranties of physical well-being were those afforded by the initial observation of the staff workers, the general appearance of the family, their failure to complain of specific ailment, and the close inquiries made by the director at the time of renewal of allowance. The bureau recommended to all the mothers semiannual examinations of children of preschool age at a child-health center.

On the whole the policy of the bureau in regard to health supervision was to recommend medical care when advice was asked but not to follow up these cases. This practice was attributable in part to the desire to encourage the mother to take the initiative in the care of her children and in part to the lack of an adequate staff; and also possibly to the fact that the need for such follow-up did not seem pressing inasmuch as the general health was reported as excellent and housing conditions were good.

Follow-up of special types of problems.

Tuberculosis.—It was the policy of the bureau to ask for examinations of all contact cases. Active cases were cared for in sanatoriums or boarding homes. Incipient cases or pretuberculous patients were advised to report regularly at the tuberculosis clinics conducted by the department of health. The bureau would not use coercion in regard to a tuberculous child or mother but " would expect to get the cooperation of the mother," and the pension has sometimes been held up pending the receipt of a promised medical report.

Venereal disease.—Wassermann tests were given whenever there was reason to suspect venereal disease. The bureau encouraged infected patients to take treatment at one of the hospital clinics.

Orthopedic and cardiac affections.—Orthopedic clinics were available at the University of California Hospital, the Leland Stanford University Hospital, and the Children's Hospital; and orthopedic examinations and treatment were advised for children in need of them. Braces and special apparatus were secured through one of the family agencies, the Fruit and Flower Mission, or an organization called the " Doctors' Daughters." Cardiac cases were treated by the hospitals or in their homes in accordance with the advice of the clinic. There was a convalescent home, but it was used very seldom for this purpose.

Eye, ear, nose, and throat affections.—The San Francisco (city) Hospital and clinics were used for examination, operations, and treatment of diseases of the eyes, ears, nose, and throat.

Medical supervision of infants and preschool children.—The newly organized division of child welfare of the San Francisco Board of Health was to have as its function the direction of school medical work, including infant-welfare work and the nutritional supervision of undernourished children. It conducted eight child-health centers, including one child-health conference held three days each week at the largest department store in the city. Babies under 1 year of age were brought once a month. The mothers were encouraged to bring children up to 6 years of age, but particular attention was given to the care of babies under 2 years of age. Two health centers were maintained by neighborhood houses. It was stated that all mothers who could not walk to the neighborhood centers could reach the conference held at the down-town store without a change of cars, as many car lines converged at the shopping district. The widows' pension bureau workers did not place great emphasis upon regular attendance at the centers by mothers with babies.

A form letter was given to mothers of children of preschool age recommending a semiannual examination at one of the child-health centers. It was not known how many children had been examined as no follow-up work was attempted. Following is a copy of the form used:

CITY AND COUNTY OF SAN FRANCISCO

Widows' Pension Bureau
Room 462, City Hall
Telephone Park 8500, Local 403
Refer to No. _____

DEAR MADAM: The widows' pension bureau of this county and the children's bureau at Sacramento are interested in promoting and safeguarding the health of the families on the widows' pension bureau list. Your cooperation is therefore requested. It has been suggested that it might be well as a preventive measure to request reports twice a year on the health of the children from one of the following health centers or clinics.

HEALTH CENTERS

The Emporium—Monday and Thursday, 9 to 12; Friday, 2 to 4 p. m.
Quesada and Railroad Aves.—Tuesday, 9 to 12 o'clock.
Bernal Heights, 300 Bennington—Friday, 9 to 12 o'clock.
Visitacion Valley, 66 Raymond Ave.—Wednesday, 9 to 12 o'clock.
Telegraph Hill Neighborhood House, 1736 Stockton St.—Tuesday, 9 to 12; Wednesday, 1 to 4 p. m.
South of Market St., 228 Harriet St.—2d and last Saturday of month, 9 to 12 o'clock.
Precita Ave. and Harrison St.—Monday, 1 to 4 p. m.
Association of University Women, 953 Haight St.—Wednesday, 1 to 4 p. m.

CLINICS

Children's Hospital, California and Maple Sts.—every day, 9 to 11 a. m.
Lane Hospital, Sacramento and Webster Sts.—every day, 8.30 to 10.30 a. m.; 1.30 to 2.30 p. m.
Mary's Help Clinic, 14th and Guerrero Sts.—every day, 9 to 11 a. m.
Mount Zion Hospital clinic, Post and Scott Sts.—every day, 8.30 to 9.30 a. m.
St. Luke's Clinic, 27th and Valencia Sts.—every day, 9 to 12 o'clock.
St. Mary's Hospital clinic, Hayes and Stanyan Sts.—Children: Tuesday, Thursday, Saturday, 9 to 11 a. m. Women: Monday, Wednesday, Friday, 9 to 11 a. m.
San Francisco Hospital Chest clinic, 23d and Potrero—every day except Wednesday and Saturday, 8.30 to 10 a. m.; Wednesday evening, 6.30 to 8 p. m. for adults; Saturday, 8.30 to 10 a. m. for children.
San Francisco Polyclinic, 1535 Jackson St.—every day, 9 to 12 o'clock.
University of California clinic, 2d and Parnassus Aves.—every day, 8.30 to 10.30 a. m.

You are not to understand that any coercion is to be used. Your cooperation is simply asked and desired. Should you think well of the plan kindly have the suggested examination made and request the people in charge of the health center or the clinic to mail this office a report on the condition of the person examined.

Very sincerely yours,

------------------------------,
Director Widows' Pension Bureau.

The division of child welfare did prenatal work on behalf of the women (about 40 a month) who registered at the San Francisco Hospital for free confinement. There were no prenatal clinics except at the hospitals.

School medical inspection.—School children were examined by physicians four times during the elementary-school course. Examinations were made of all children entering the first grade and all children in the last semester of the eighth grade, and examinations were made twice between the first and eighth grades. Twenty-nine school nurses made classroom inspections four times a year, each nurse supervising a school population of about 2,500. Free dental care was provided by the four school dental clinics and a municipal dental clinic. The school medical records of children receiving mothers' aid were not consulted by the visitors.

In the preschool health drive held every summer the division of child welfare of the San Francisco Board of Health aimed to have all children who were going to enter school in the fall examined at a health center, and the board of health dodgers were mailed by the widows' pension bureau to all mothers under its care having children who would enter school the following year.

Malnutrition.—At the beginning of each school year the school nurses weighed and measured all children, and those 10 per cent or more underweight were weighed every other week and were given instruction individually or in small group conferences by teachers, nutrition workers, or nurses. All underweight children were examined by the school physician, and visits to the homes were made for follow-up of remediable physical defects. The nutrition work was under the supervision of the division of child welfare of the San Francisco Board of Health. A director of nutrition work and two dietitians worked in 5 schools; in 33 others the teachers did some nutrition work, under the supervision of the director, for which they were paid $10 a month by the Tuberculosis Association. Three school nurses also were doing nutrition work, one of whom was engaged in placing a health-education program in the schools. Lunches of milk and crackers were served in all schools and were supplied to needy children without cost.

The nutrition workers who visited the homes of underweight children in mothers' aid families reported cases to the widows' pension bureau only if there were special problems. The bureau did not attempt to keep in touch with the nutrition workers or nurses who were working with undernourished children nor to place children found to be undernourished at the time of the semiannual renewal of allowances under the supervision of the nutrition division.

MENTAL HEALTH
Available facilities.

There were ample facilities in the county for psychological and psychiatric examination and for treatment. The neuropsychological clinic of the University of California Hospital conducted examinations for the juvenile court and was at the service of the public schools for special problems which might be referred by the teachers, the director of the special schools, or the parents. This clinic was also at the service of the social agencies and the general public. The majority of children receiving mothers' aid whom the workers judged to be in need of such service were referred to this clinic. Generally a careful physical examination was required preliminary to or accompanying the psychological examination; the follow-up might be done by a social worker or student connected with the clinic, by the physician on the staff of the widows' pension bureau, or by the visitor in charge of the family.

The Leland Stanford University Hospital maintained a phychological clinic and the San Francisco Hospital had recently installed a ward for the observation of psychopathic patients.

The school psychologist was the supervisor of special classes; he examined children referred by the teachers and principals on account of retardation, mental defect, behavior problems, and psychopathic difficulties. Some children were placed in special classes for several weeks' observation. Physical examinations were not made as a routine preliminary to the psychological examinations but might be given if need was indicated. Children whose intelligence quotient was below 70 were assigned to the special classes. The follow-up work was done by the teachers or nurses.

Follow-up of special types of problems.

It was the policy of the widows' pension bureau to have children under its supervision given a special examination if they presented serious problems of retardation or if the father was in a hospital for the insane or if there was a family history of mental defect or disease and the children also gave evidence of mental difficulties.

The procedure in regard to children who presented behavior problems varied somewhat according to the individual situation. The usual plan, however, was for the visitor or the director of the widows' pension bureau to endeavor to win the cooperation of the child and the mother by a conference with them and with the teacher. Sometimes the child was asked to report at the office twice a month, bringing from the teacher a statement in regard to his conduct. If this method failed the child probably would be given an examination.

Illustrative case history.

The following case history shows the result of efforts made to improve the mental attitude of a child in a mothers' aid family:

> Life for 12-year-old Walter C. consisted of school, which he hated, and odd jobs in the sordid neighborhood in which his widowed mother lived. Eight months before the mothers' aid visitor went to the home he was reported as a hopeless truant. An interview was had with him at the widows' pension bureau, and it was made plain to him that he must attend school regularly. He was told that it was his job to get an education and that he would have to attend to his school duties regularly whether he wanted to or not. The cooperation of the teachers and of the principal of the school was asked and gladly given. The boy was told to call at the mothers' pension office with his report every two weeks. At the end of the first two weeks the report showed that Walter had attended school every day and had not been tardy, his conduct left nothing to be desired, and his scholarship was good. This report was duplicated every two weeks. It had become apparent to the visitor that Walter was a great lover of beauty, and arrangements were made for him to take a trip to Berkeley, where he visited the State university and was much impressed by the natural beauties of the place. He was also taken to Golden Gate Park for the first time in his life, though he had always lived in San Francisco. The museum and the aquarium were of great interest to him, and he could not believe that all these opportunities were offered the public gratis. He felt that he must take his mother as soon as possible and show her what he had seen. What he needed more than anything else was normal healthful association with boys of his own age, and at the time of the study an effort was being made to place him with the Boy Scouts. He gave promise, and there was no doubt that he had some special gifts. It was the visitor's plan to watch for these and develop them if possible.

HOUSING

Fully half the families receiving mothers' aid lived in single houses, most of the others lived in flats, and only a very few lived in rooms. All houses and many flats had yard space and a number of mothers had flower gardens. A mother with three children occupied at least four rooms, including a living room, which was rarely used as a bedroom. All rooms were outside rooms and there was abundance of air and sunshine. As a rule each family had its own sanitary toilet. A bathroom was not considered essential if the children were very young. All families had running water and gas and nearly all had electricity. Most of the houses were equipped with coolers; ice was not used.

Emphasis was laid upon the importance of bringing up the children in good neighborhoods, and families were advised to move if the locality was morally undesirable or if the house was in poor repair or below standard. Consideration was given also to play space and accessibility to playgrounds and sources of education and recreation. The average rent per family was about $22 a month and no family paid more than $40 a month. The State ruling allowing a mother to have an equity of $2,500 in her home permitted families possessed of homes to live in good neighborhoods amid surroundings congenial to them. Many bore testimony to the fruitful savings and sacrifices of the parents in their early married lives and were a constant incentive to the maintenance of the same high standards of comfort and order. Twenty-eight per cent of the families owned or partly owned their own homes; about one-half of these owned them clear and one-half mortgaged.

EDUCATION

COOPERATION WITH THE SCHOOLS AND FACILITIES FOR EDUCATION

The budget contained no provision for items that were educational in character. The allowance for sundries covered any expense for papers or magazines. All the families took a daily paper. Families were encouraged to incur moderate expenses for educational purposes, such as music and radio.

Contacts with the schools.

The visitors of the widows' pension bureau communicated with the teachers or visited the schools only when they felt there was some special need. The teachers did not make reports to the visitors, nor were the school reports examined periodically. If children were in difficulty at school a plan was worked out whereby a child might be said to be on probation. Some boys and girls reported at the bureau at regular intervals with their reports on attendance and scholarship. It was stated that whenever such an effort to encourage the children had been made, an improvement resulted in both school work and general behavior.

Provision for handicapped children.

The physically handicapped child.—There were in the public schools a sight-conservation class, an oral school for deaf children, a class for children having speech defects in every elementary and high school, and three open-air schools. A teacher was assigned to each of the three children's orthopedic wards in the hospitals. No busses were provided for transportation of crippled children to and from school. The widows' pension bureau made an effort to assist physically handicapped children in obtaining their education and in adjusting themselves in industry.

The mentally handicapped child.—There were 21 special classes throughout the city, also an ungraded school of 5 classes. One of the teachers in the ungraded school helped the children of subnormal mentality in their efforts to find suitable employment.

Provision for children wishing further education.

No scholarships were available, but, when possible, encouragement was given to children desirous of continuing in school both by allowing aid up to the age of 16 and also by continuing aid for younger brothers and sisters if the older child was over 16. A few boys were taking electrical courses in the technical high school and a few girls were taking courses in home economics. Some were taking university extension courses, but none were in college. A few boys and girls were taking business or vocational courses at night, or were taking art courses at the art institute affiliated with the University of California. Possibly 100 children were receiving piano or other music lessons. Some of them were given free instruction and others were paying a nominal charge at a settlement house or were using the recreation allowance for this purpose.

The R. family had lived for years on so inadequate an income that when the daughter Harriet became 15 years of age there seemed to be no alternative but for her to go to work, much as she desired to continue her education. To her great happiness, the San Francisco Associated Charities arranged with a business college for her to take a course in the college and pay for her course after she began to earn. At the time of the study she had been working for a year and her salary had been increased 50 per cent. Her education had proved to be worth while.

SCHOOLING AND WORK OF CHILDREN 14 AND 15 YEARS OLD AND WORK OF CHILDREN OVER 16

The compulsory-education, child-labor, and half orphan aid laws.

The compulsory education law required children between 8 and 16 years of age to attend school unless they were 14 years old and had employment certificates. A child was permitted to obtain an employment certificate at 14 years of age if he had completed the eighth grade and was physically fit and the family was in need. At 15 he could obtain an employment certificate, regardless of family need, if he had completed the seventh grade and was physically fit for work. At 16 he could work without regard to school grade completed. All working children not graduates of high school were required to attend continuation school four hours a week until they were 18 years of age.[7]

The half orphan aid law permitted aid to be granted for children up to the age of 16.

Children in school and at work.

Although the law provided that 14-year-old children could obtain employment certificates if they had completed the eighth grade and the family needed their earnings, the widows' pension bureau encouraged children to remain in school to the age of 16 unless the lack of their wages entailed too great a hardship on the rest of the family. Aid was continued for younger children to enable a child 16 years old or over to remain in school if he was especially anxious to continue or showed promise.

There were 187 children 14 and 15 years of age in the families under supervision; 181 of these were in school and 6 were working. All except one of the working children were 15 years of age. About 75 per cent of these children were in high school or vocational school. The majority of those in high school were attending the commercial high school; the next largest group were in the polytechnic high school. It was also reported that 35 children 16 years of age or

---

[7] Calif., Deering's General Laws, 1923, act 7487, secs. 1 (5) and 3a, pp. 3033, 3034; act 7496, sec. 3, p. 3054. Children disqualified for attendance because of physical or mental condition or living more than a specified distance from school were exempted from attendance at regular day and continuation school.

over were still in school, most of them attending public or private business schools.

The occupations and earnings of the six children (all boys) 14 and 15 years of age who were working were not reported. For this reason the occupations of the 188 boys and girls 16 years of age or over, which were reported, are shown in the following list in order to indicate to some extent the character of the employment entered by children in families receiving allowances under the supervision of the widows' pension bureau:

	Number of children		Number of children
Total	188	Girls	73
Boys	115	Clerical workers	24
		Factory workers	16
Clerical workers	37	Stenographers	16
Errand boys	21	Telephone operators	7
Factory workers	17	Bookkeepers	4
Paper carriers (after school)	12	Saleswomen	3
Apprentices	9	Comptometer operators	3
Truck drivers	7		
Jitney drivers	4		
Cabin boys	2		
Draftsmen	2		
Salesmen	2		
Musicians	2		

The wages of working children under 21 years ranged from $43 to $100 a month. The average was about $80.

EDUCATIONAL ACTIVITIES FOR THE MOTHERS

The few foreign-speaking mothers were not required to take courses in English or citizenship, but the bureau encouraged their doing so. Six evening schools conducted Americanization classes, but so far as the bureau knew only two mothers receiving allowances were enrolled in these classes. The settlements conducted classes in sewing, cooking, and child care, but no mothers who received aid were attending these classes.

RECREATION

The budget allowance for recreation was $1 to $2 a month apiece for working children and 50 cents a month for children under working age. Working children under 21 years of age gave their mothers all their earnings and were allowed $1 to $2 a month for spending money and $10 a month for clothing if their occupation required them to dress well. After they reached their twenty-first birthday they were expected to pay a generous board.

Families were allowed to attend motion pictures once a week. Playgrounds were used considerably by the younger children. A few boys and girls belonged to the Young Men's and Young Women's Christian Associations and to scout troops, though no effort was made to link children with these agencies except for special reasons. Nor was any effort made to get children to use the libraries and settlements, though some boys and girls were connected with the settlements and community centers. The parent-teacher association used the schools for plays, games, and motion pictures. The recreation centers conducted athletic activities. The families availed themselves of these forms of recreation according to their own inclination. Many families owned or were paying for pianos or phonographs. There were free concerts at the civic auditorium, and a few of the families visited the parks and the museums. A daily paper operated a summer vacation camp which provided outings for some children, but no provision was made for summer outings for mothers. Some families had relatives in the country whom they visited. A number of the mothers belonged to mothers' clubs or parent-teacher organizations, and membership in these was encouraged by the widows' pension bureau.

MOTHERS' ALLOWANCES IN WAYNE COUNTY, MICH.[1]

PROVISIONS OF THE LAW

The Michigan law provided aid to the following classes of mothers with dependent children: Widowed, deserted, divorced, or unmarried; mothers whose husbands were insane, feeble-minded, epileptic, paralytic, or blind, and confined in State hospitals or other State institutions; mothers whose husbands were inmates of State penal institutions or mothers whose husbands were suffering from tuberculosis in such a stage that they could not pursue a gainful occupation. Aid was allowed for a dependent child under the age of 17 years; the mother must be " poor and unable to properly care and provide for said child, but otherwise a proper guardian," and it must be " for the welfare of such child to remain in the custody of its mother "; the amount of aid should not exceed $10 per week nor be less than $2 a week for the first child with an allowance of $2 per week for each additional child. The law did not provide for State supervision in any form.[2]

The judge of the Wayne County juvenile court had ruled that in cases of desertion a mother must have been deserted for two years and the whereabouts of the father must have been unknown during that period; in cases of divorce a year must have elapsed from the date on which the divorce was granted before the mother was considered eligible for mothers' aid. In case the father was ill with tuberculosis he was required to live in a sanatorium before aid was granted. Mothers receiving aid were not permitted to have men lodgers or roomers. A mother was permitted to have $500 in savings and an equity in her home of $3,500. The mother must have had a residence of two years in the State and one year in the county directly preceding aid.

ADMINISTRATION OF THE LAW

ADMINISTRATIVE AGENCY AND STAFF

The administrative agency was the mothers' pension department of the county juvenile court. The juvenile-court procedure was set forth in the law dealing with dependent children and needy mothers.[3]

---

[1] Wayne County contains the cities Detroit, Hamtramck, and Highland Park. Though the latter two are within the geographical limits of Detroit, they have their own city administration and are entirely distinct political units. The population of the county in 1920 was 1,177,645, of which number 993,678 lived in Detroit. The native white population numbered 788,297, the foreign born 344,725, and the negroes 43,720. The population of foreign birth, in the order of numerical importance, was as follows: Polish, Canadian, German, Russian, English, Italian, and Hungarian. The child population within legal age for mothers' aid (under 16, as interpreted by the juvenile court, which was the administrative agency) was 344,420. (Fourteenth Census of the United States, 1920, vol. 3. Population, pp. 487, 488, 493, 494, Washington, 1922.) The chief industries center about the manufacture of motor cars and automobile bodies, and foundry and machine-shop products are next in importance, the great bulk of industry in Detroit calling for unskilled labor.

[2] Mich., Comp. Laws 1915, sec. 2017, p. 890, as amended by act of Apr. 28, 1921, No. 92, Public Acts of 1921, p. 199, act of June 15, 1921. No. 16 (first extra session), Public Acts of 1921, p. 785, and act of May 25, 1923, No. 294, Public Acts of 1923, p. 467.

[3] Mich., Comp. Laws 1915, secs. 2012, 2015, 2016, pp. 885, 887, as amended by acts of June 15, 1921, Nos. 16 and 24 (first extra session). Public Acts of 1921, pp. 785 and 797, and act of May 2, 1923, No. 105, Public Acts of 1923, p. 143.

The mothers' pension department in Wayne County was under the general direction of the chief probation officer for women and girls, who was also referee of the court and who heard all mothers' aid cases except so-called "trouble cases," which were heard by the judge of the juvenile court.

The workers in the mothers' pension department were probation officers of the juvenile court. They were appointed by the judge on the recommendation of the chief probation officer for women and girls. At the time of the study there were a supervisor, nine field workers, and two stenographers; the department had also the services of a Slavic interpreter and of a psychiatric social worker for one-third time. In addition one volunteer, a college graduate, gave full-time service. Several workers used their own automobiles, for which they were allowed upkeep. The supervisor was a college graduate who had been on the staff of the Detroit Associated Charities for three years, both as a volunteer and as a paid worker. Four of the nine field workers were college graduates, one having specialized in sociology and another having taken graduate work at the school of social service administration of the University of Chicago. One of the other five (a physician) had had experience in a correctional institution for children, one had had experience in medical social service, one had had a year's social-service training in a religious training school and experience in church social work, one had been executive secretary in a city charity organization society, and one was a normal-school graduate with special training in domestic science.

APPROPRIATION AND VOLUME OF WORK

The appropriation for the fiscal year December 1, 1922, to November 30, 1923, was $650,000. This was more than adequate to meet the needs on the basis of the maximum aid allowed by the law. The appropriation for the following fiscal year ended November 30, 1924, was $625,000. Though a definite appropriation was made, the expenditures for mothers' aid were not limited to the amount provided, and any deficit incurred one year was made up in the appropriation for the following year. The entire appropriation was for relief. The administrative expenses of the mothers' pension department were borne by the court.

During October, 1923, the court aided 999 families, including about 2,990 children under 16 years of age. Each of the nine field workers had under her supervision from 100 to 130 families. One county worker had 92 families. In addition each worker made an average of 7 new investigations a month.

PROCEDURE IN MAKING ALLOWANCES

Mothers were required to make personal applications, to which they made affidavit. Social and legal data were recorded on a face sheet which called for the following specific information: Names, addresses, birthplaces and birth dates of man, woman, and children; date and cause of man's death, date of his commitment or desertion or date of divorce; school grades, occupations, and wages of children; mental and physical defects, relatives, church, citizenship, time in county, court records; charitable agencies interested; housing conditions; facts regarding property, insurance, debts, and income, and an estimate of the budget.

It was the policy of the court to verify all data such as dates of birth, marriage, date of man's death, commitment, or desertion, divorce of couple, residence, and facts regarding property, insurance, savings, and wages of working children. Inquiry was made of the social-service exchange, and all registered agencies were consulted through a form blank or by personal interview. School reports, including medical reports, were secured for the children attending school.

A visit was always made to the home. It was customary to visit one or more relatives, the minister, and the family physician, and generally one or more references.

The juvenile court devoted one morning each week to the hearing of mothers' aid cases. The hearing was conducted in a small private room by the chief probation officer for girls, who as referee heard all but "trouble cases," as has been stated. No one was present but the mother and children, the supervisor, and the clerk who took stenographic notes. The hearing was informal and an atmosphere of friendliness prevailed. The purpose of the aid and the necessity for following the orders of her pension officer were explained to the mother as well as the advisability of adequate medical attention.

USE OF A STANDARD BUDGET

A standard household budget prepared by the Visiting Housekeeper Association and revised quarterly was used as a guide in estimating the budget for each family. It included food, fuel and light, clothing and toilet articles, rent, household furnishings and sundries, and extras. The actual expenses of the family for rent, insurance, payments on property, gas, and electricity were allowed, however, if they were reasonable. Following is the standard budget:

Visiting Housekeeper Association (Detroit) scale for estimating minimum budgets for dependent families

(including man)

SEPTEMBER 1, 1923.

Food:
The amount of food per person varies according to age, size of person, and occupation. The average cost per day per person is:

Calories needed	Per day	Per month
3,600 for man	$0.49	$14.70
2,800 for woman	.38	11.40
3,450 for boy 14–17 years	.47	14.10
2,950 for girl 14–17 years	.40	12.00
2,825 for boy 11–14 years	.38	11.40
2,500 for girl 11–14 years	.34	10.20
2,200 for boy 9–11 years	.30	9.00
2,075 for girl 9–11 years	.28	8.40
1,875 for boy 7–9 years	.25	7.50
1,750 for girl 7–9 years	.24	7.20
1,580 for child 5–7 years	.21	6.30
1,460 for child 3–5 years	.20	6.00
1,380 for child under 3 years	.19	5.70

In families of 5–7 people reduce grocery bill 8 per cent.
In families of 7–9 people reduce grocery bill 10 per cent.
In special-diet cases add 10 per cent.
If man carries lunch add 10 per cent to his food allowance.

Fuel and light:
  This is figured out for the entire year, and it is expected that money will be set aside in summer for winter months.

  Light—   Per month
    Kerosene, at $0.18 per gallon_____ $0.77
    Gas, at $0.79_____ 1.00
    Electricity_____ 1.10
  Fuel—
    Cook stove—
      6 tons soft coal, at $10.75_____   5.38
      ½ cord of wood for summer, at $21_____   .88
                                                                        ─────
        Coal and wood_____   6.20
      Gas for cooking, at $0.79_____   2.11
    Heating—
      2 tons hard coal (when coal is used for cooking), at $16.25__   2.71
      5 tons hard coal (when gas is used for cooking), at $16.25__   6.77
      5 tons soft coal (when gas is used for cooking), at $10.75__   4.48
      7 tons soft coal (for furnace), at $10.75_____   6.27

Clothing and toilet articles:
  Clothing for man_____ 9.33
  Clothing for woman_____ 7.18
  Clothing for boy 12–14 years_____ 6.02
  Clothing for girl 10–12 years_____ 6.61
  Clothing for child 5–10 years _____ 4.85
  Clothing for child 3–5 years _____ 3.99
  Clothing for child under 3 years _____ 3.49
    If some clothing is made at home reduce allowance 7 per cent.
    For dependent families reduce allowance 8 per cent.
    Deduct 20 per cent if part of the clothing is bought secondhand.

Rents:
  Unheated—
    Three rooms_____ 25.50
    Four rooms_____ 36.00
    Five rooms _____ 45.00
    Six rooms _____ 50.00
  Heated—
    Three rooms_____ 56.25
    Four rooms_____ 62.00
    Five rooms _____ 67.00

Household furnishings and household sundries (household furnishings include cleaning and laundry supplies, repair and replacement of furnishings; sundries include thread, darning cotton, pins, needles, etc.):
  Family of two _____ 6.24
  Family of three_____ 7.17
  Family of four_____ 8.10
  Family of five _____ 9.02
    If secondhand furniture is bought reduce this item 36 per cent.

Extras (this includes recreation, education, car fare, etc.):
  Family of two, including man who works_____ 5.00
  Family of three, including man who works _____ 5.67
  Family of four, including man who works _____ 6.34
  Family of five, including man who works _____ 7.01
    Sixty-seven cents per month is added for each additional member.
  Family of two, not including man who works _____ 3.02
  Family of three, not including man who works _____ 3.69
  Family of four, not including man who works_____ 4.36
  Family of five, not including man who works _____ 5.03
    Sixty-seven cents per month is added for each additional member.
    If children are under school age reduce the extras 14 per cent.

New applicants were required to keep summarized daily expense accounts from the time of their application to the time of the worker's visit to their homes. After the first two weeks or more the families were required to keep accounts only when there seemed to be bad management and the court wished to learn where the difficulty lay. The following is a copy of an expense account:

JUVENILE COURT, DETROIT, MICH., MOTHERS' PENSION DEPARTMENT

Name: _____

Expenses for two weeks ending February 21, 1923

	Thursday	Friday	Saturday	Sunday	Monday	Tuesday	Wednesday
Rent				$25.00			
Groceries	$4.00	$3.12	$1.40	1.74	$2.86	$0.84	$1.77
Meat							
Hard coal							
Soft coal	.50	.50	1.00		.50	.50	.75
Gas	3.47						
Car fare	.24	.12	.12		.12	.12	.12
Electric light	3.80						
Medicine	.20	.25					.50
Taxes							
Water							
Insurance				.30			
Clothing	.60	.45	.95				
Debts					3.00		

A representative of the court will call on you within two weeks. Please have ready contract of house, tax receipts, bills, and all receipted bills, birth certificates, pay envelopes, or badge numbers of all members of family who work.

The grants conformed to the family's need, as shown by the budgets, as far as the maximum under the law permitted. The average monthly grant per family for the year 1923 was $42.45, or $14.17 per child. The largest monthly grant to a family was $104 and the smallest was $8.66. The mothers were required to call at the office twice a month for their checks unless excused because they lived at a considerable distance or had young children.

SUPPLEMENTING OF MOTHERS' AID

The Detroit Department of Public Welfare had a liberal policy in regard to supplementing mothers' aid when the maximum grant was inadequate, and it furnished temporary, emergency, or continued aid on the recommendation of the court without further investigation. During the winter of 1924 this department gave supplementary assistance to 166 families receiving mothers' aid. It made no contact with the families, all supervision being left with the court, which made a monthly report to the department. Relief took the form of milk and coal principally, though monthly grocery orders were allowed. Outside the city there were township overseers of the poor who disbursed outdoor relief. They were not so willing as the Detroit Department of Public Welfare to supplement the allowances, and sometimes it was extremely difficult to secure additional relief from them.

There was no private relief agency in Wayne County.

VISITING

It was the aim of the department to have the probation officers visit the home every other month and to see the mothers at the office at least every month on one of their semimonthly calls for their checks. The probation officers were able to visit the families under their care only once in two or three months unless some special problem arose. The 18 families under the care of the psychiatric worker were sometimes visited as often twice a week, but they had been turned over to her for intensive supervision because they presented serious problems.

HEALTH

PHYSICAL HEALTH

No special allowance was made in the budget under health, but an extra 10 per cent was added to the food allowance for children who were suffering from tuberculosis or malnutrition. Special effort was made to see that the income reached the budget needs; and, if necessary, extra help was secured from the city department of public welfare. Practically all medical service could be secured free.

Physical examinations.

It was the policy of the court to require as a part of the investigation a physical examination of all children of preschool age whose families lived in Detroit and of mothers who gave evidence of need or who had been exposed to tuberculosis. These examinations were given usually at the Harper Hospital clinics, but sometimes children were examined at the children's clinics of the city board of health and women at the clinics of the Women's Hospital. Following is a copy of the form used in referring to Harper Hospital:

COOPERATION BLANK

Ref. by Miss W., of Mothers' Pension, Juvenile Court, to Harper Hospital, 2/4/24.
   (Worker)   (Organization)

Name of patient: Adeline D.
Address: _____
Date of birth: _____
Kind of work: _____
Hours employed: _____
Household (names and ages):
    Father: _____
    Mother: Adeline D., 30.
    Children—
        Linda D., 8.
        Jergus D., 4.
    Boarders: 1.
Health record of patient:
    Dr. J. M. B. states woman is suffering from pelvic inflammation, which may need surgical treatment.
Previous medical treatment, places and dates: _____
Significant facts in family history, social and medical: _____
Financial situation: Woman receives mothers' pension of $20.58 per month. This is supplemented by $47.33 paid by boarder and $10.83 which woman earns.
Reason for referring: General examination.

REPLY TO REFERRING AGENCY

Name: Adeline D. Age, 30. Date: 2–9–24.
Medical agency reporting: Harper out-patient department to mothers' pension department.
Name of social worker: C. J. M.
Examined by: Drs. L. and K.

Significant medical facts brought out: Wassermann, neg.; urine, negative; lacerated infected cervix.
Diagnosis: _____
Explanation of: _____
Prognosis: Recovery.
Probable length of time under treatment: _____
Probable outcome if treatment faithfully continues: _____
Character of treatment: _____
Days to report: _____ How often: _____
Ways in which agency can cooperate in doctors' plan: _____
To enter hospital for operation 2–12–24.

For children in school a copy of the last school report, including the report of the physical examination, was secured before the grant was made. The following is a copy of such a report:

MOTHERS' PENSION DEPARTMENT, SCHOOL RECORD FOR JUVENILE COURT, WAYNE COUNTY, MICH.

Please state if medical record shows any physical defects.

School: _____

Below is the record of attendance, conduct, etc., of _____;
(Name)
_____, from new semester, _____, 1924, to date:
(Address)

Month	Days present	Days absent	Conduct	Month	Days present	Days absent	Conduct
February							
March							
April							

Total days present, _____   Total days absent, _____
Average conduct, _____   Effort, _____
Grade, _____   Date of Birth, _____
Remarks: Hearing, _____
         Tonsils, _____
         Teeth, _____

_____
Principal.

A court worker was at the Harper Hospital out-patient department four mornings a week to steer mothers through the clinics, to make direct contacts with the doctors and the social-service department, and to secure detailed statements as to diagnosis and treatment.

Preliminary examinations were seldom made by private physicians, but mothers were permitted to call upon their own doctors in case of sickness if the latter gave their services. No medical history was taken for the child or family unless something unusual presented itself and the physician called for it, nor was there provision for a continuous medical record of each member of the family. The probation officers were responsible for keeping up to date the record of all examinations and medical care received by families under their supervision. The follow-up work was done by the probation officer if the examinations were conducted by the board of health clinics, and by both the probation officers and the social-service department if they were conducted by the hospital clinics. There were no periodic examinations except when treatment was required and in the case of tuberculosis suspects. The mothers were required to have serious physical defects of children attended to with reasonable promptness. Only occasionally was it necessary to threaten the withdrawal of the grant. As a rule the mothers were quite willing to permit the examinations, and some had an appreciation of their value.

Follow-up of special types of problems.

Tuberculosis.—Tuberculosis clinics were conducted in Detroit by the city board of health, which also operated one sanatorium for incipient tuberculosis cases and two sanatoriums for advanced cases. A new preventorium had just been completed for children. Sanatorium facilities were adequate. In the country the Red Cross nurses visited contact cases and brought them to the city clinics for examination. In families receiving mothers' aid all mothers and children who had been exposed to tuberculosis were placed under the care of the clinics, which advised whether sanatorium care was necessary, the court acting on the basis of the clinic's advice. It was the policy of the court to require sanatorium care for active tuberculosis cases, and if the father was ill with the disease he was always required to accept sanatorium care.

Venereal disease.—When there was a history of venereal disease or reason to suspect it the court had Wassermann tests taken for the mother and the children. The city board of health and Harper Hospital both maintained clinics for venereal diseases.

Orthopedic and cardiac affections.—Expert surgical and medical care was obtained for all crippled children. The Children's Hospital and the Harper Hospital provided all necessary hospital treatment. Most of the orthopedic work for children (not requiring hospitalization) in the city and county was done by the Sigma Gamma orthopedic clinic, which was excellently equipped and free. Two social workers were employed in its medical social-service department. Two physiotherapists and a nurse were assigned to the Leland Day School for Crippled Children, operated by the board of education, and all children attending it were under the medical supervision of the Sigma Gamma clinic. Braces, shoes, and special apparatus for mothers' aid children were generally paid for by the city department of public welfare at the request of the court.

Children with cardiac trouble were cared for at the clinics at the Harper Hospital or the Children's Hospital and were placed in the open-air rooms of the public schools.

Eye, ear, nose, and throat affections.—The Harper Hospital and its clinics were used by the court for treatment for most cases of eye, ear, nose, and throat affections. Operations were paid for through a special fund known as the Coyle Fund.

Medical welfare work for infants and preschool children.—The Detroit Board of Health conducted in various parts of the city 13 health centers for babies and children of preschool age (8 of these clinics did prenatal work also); they were used occasionally by the court. Though not within walking distance of many homes, they were accessible to most mothers without change of cars. Nurses and court workers did the follow-up work. There was but one child-health center outside the city. The court had no fixed rule in regard to the attendance at centers of mothers with children under 6 years of age. This was left to the discretion of the individual workers, who as a rule did not lay great emphasis on routine supervision of well babies.

School medical inspection.—At the beginning of each year the nurses in the schools in Detroit inspected all children except those in the first and fifth grades. Height and weight measurements were a part of the yearly physical inspection. The children found to be 15 per cent underweight were referred to the physicians, who examined these as well as the children in the first and fifth grades. As an experiment in some schools, the nurses were making preliminary inspections of all the children. Those whom they suspected of having physical defects were then examined by the physicians. The court expected each visitor to review quarterly the school medical reports for all school children under her care in order that she might work with the nurses in the correction of defects. In the rural districts medical inspection in the schools was not uniformly provided. However, a health educator, supported by a group of health agencies, public and private, was engaged in a health-education training program in the schools of the county. The Red Cross provided nursing service. The teachers referred children having obvious physical defects to the nurses, who took them to a clinic in one of the larger towns or in Detroit. The nurses were in close touch with the mothers' aid visitors and did much follow-up work for the health of the children under their supervision.

The dental bureau made yearly examination of the children's teeth, and the 12 free dental-school clinics provided ample dental facilities in Detroit. School nurses did the follow-up work for both physical and dental examinations.

Malnutrition.—Much nutrition work was being done in the schools. Forty-five nutrition classes were conducted weekly for 12 weeks by the school nurses. Children found to be 15 per cent or more underweight, who had been examined by the school physicians, as has been stated, were classified in A and B groups, according to whether they had defects that could be corrected. It was required that such defects be corrected and that the parents' consent be obtained before children were enrolled in a nutrition class. The mothers did not attend these classes, but the nurses instructed these mothers in their visit to the homes. The milk for undernourished children was furnished by women's clubs. The quarterly inspection of the school medical reports was a means of checking the children who were in nutrition classes or who were underweight and undernourished. It was estimated that about 40 children in mothers' aid families were attending nutrition classes.

The Harper Hospital conducted a nutrition department and sent dietitians into the homes of patients for instruction in cases where diet was involved. If the patient was a member of a family receiving mothers' aid diet lists were sent to the court and its cooperation enlisted.

The Merrill-Palmer School was conducting two nutrition classes for the benefit of Italian women who were receiving mothers' aid. One of the school dietitians gave the instruction and a worker from the

International Institute interpreted. The classes met once a week for one and one-half hours, and once a month there was a cooking lesson. The subjects taught included besides nutrition such subjects as child care, discipline, psychology, and habit forming. The women appeared to be greatly interested and to consider their attendance at the classes a real privilege. As a part of their field work two student dietitians gave home supervision to mothers receiving aid. The Visiting Housekeeper Association included nutrition among the subjects taught to families referred to it for supervision.

MENTAL HEALTH
Available facilities.

At the request of teachers, social agencies, or parents, the psychological clinic of the department of education gave individual psychological examinations to school children who presented behavior problems or who were emotionally unstable.

Every child entering school was given a psychological test, as were over-age children and the so-called repeaters. Children whose intelligence quotient was found to be below 75 were enrolled in the special classes, and all children in the special classes were examined again before leaving school. Psychological tests were given also to children with sensory defects who were recommended for tests by the teachers, and to children entering the Leland Day School for Crippled Children. The medical department of the psychological clinic made physical examinations at the time of the psychological examinations. The examinations of this department were followed up by the social workers on the clinic staff, though they might secure the cooperation of the court workers for mothers' aid families.

The juvenile court and the domestic-relations court had a court clinic, employing a psychiatrist and case workers. The juvenile court had four psychiatric case workers, one of whom gave about a third of her time to families receiving mothers' aid. The case workers referred all mental problems to the court clinic. Physical examinations did not invariably precede the psychiatrist's examinations, but that procedure was preferred. He determined for each case separately whether the follow-up should be done by the psychiatric worker or by one of the family visitors.

Follow-up of special types of problems.

The probation officers rarely asked for a test because of retardation, as it was understood that these examinations were attended to by the school department as a matter of routine. A child whose father was or had been insane or in whose family there had been a history of mental difficulty was not examined unless he, too, exhibited unfavorable mental symptoms. Obvious or suspected cases of mental defect were examined at the court psychiatric clinic or at the psychological clinic of the department of education. If institutional placement of a child was required an attempt was made first to persuade the mother to apply for commitment to the Michigan Home and Training School at Lapeer; if she refused to do this and the case was urgent proceedings might be instituted through the probate court.

Problems of behavior or mental instability, whether exhibited by the mothers or their children, were referred for advice to the psychiatric clinic of the juvenile court as a matter of routine. The women most frequently referred were those whose burden had been extremely heavy and who manifested symptoms of instability, often coupled with bad management and shiftless housekeeping. Much of the work with the mothers was done by a psychiatric worker, but in some cases a few conferences between the psychiatrist and the mothers sufficed. To the psychiatric worker were assigned for intensive supervision mothers who were bad managers, erratic, or unresponsive for divers reasons. The standards of aid in the families turned over to this worker were somewhat higher than those for the usual mothers' aid families, and she was given great freedom in the plans she made for them. These mothers were not expected to work outside their homes; the children sometimes were allowed to continue in school for a longer period; and such families were often referred to the Visiting Housekeeper Association, whose workers gave friendly instruction in home management.

Illustrative case histories.

The following case histories illustrate situations in which improvement resulted from the efforts of the psychiatrist and the psychiatric worker:

Mrs. J. and her five children under 7 years of age lived in a four-room house which she owned in the village. Her husband had been committed to a hospital for the insane several years before, and disorder and confusion evidently prevailed in the management of the household. A worker from the Visiting Housekeeper Association helped to plan a weekly budget and showed the mother how to cook nutritious food. Mrs. J. was responsive and evidently eager to learn. Finally she stated that her youngest child, Ethel, had violent fits of crying about once a month, and one Sunday while in church suddenly began to scream and to bite her mother. Ethel was taken to the juvenile-court psychiatrist, who said that her tantrums were the result of bad habit formation. Mrs. J. had several talks with the psychiatrist and followed explicitly her directions in good habit training. Ethel improved wonderfully, the psychiatrist reporting that she had never been consulted by a mother who tried more carefully to follow instructions.

Mrs. W. never exhibited a real psychosis, but she was crushed and broken by abuse and the misery of her life with her husband. For years he had been in and out of jail for forging checks, breaking contracts, stealing, and other crimes. When he was not in jail warrants generally were out for his arrest. Both the mother and her children appeared undernourished and in need of medical supervision. With the strain of her husband's constant misdeeds and the lack of income it is not astonishing that Mrs. W. became nervously exhausted, emotionally unstable, and easily discouraged. She had accepted alms so long that she needed to learn the lessons of self-restraint and discipline, and even to build some ideals afresh; but in the course of three years this family, accustomed to living in cheap rooming houses, had acquired a neat, seven-room cottage in an excellent suburban neighborhood, with furnishings of their own. The children made rapid progress in school when their health improved, and at the time of the visit all were up to grade and in school regularly. Previously some of them were absent as often as three and one-half days a week. The 16-year-old daughter was taking a business course at the intermediate high school and was planning to go to work in a few months. Mrs. W. became a good housekeeper, took great pride in her family, and joined the parent-teacher association of the school attended by her children. The assurance of a grant of $78, the security of an allowance of alimony, and the very good case work of a psychiatric worker had enabled her to reconstruct her life.

Mrs. Q. was diagnosed as a "psychopath of the turbulent type." She at first refused to cooperate with the court or the social workers. Her five children were undernourished, but she would not take them to the clinics, though the grant was increased to the maximum and the department of public welfare was supplementing it. The family lived on sausage, canned milk, and delicatessen food. Mrs. Q. swore at the worker from the Visiting Housekeeper Association and abused the nurse. The record, unfortunately, did not show by what process the results were obtained, but the first visible sign of this woman's regeneration was her voluntary enrollment for an English class composed of Polish women receiving mothers' aid. The Visiting Housekeeper Association's worker was welcomed, and after some months she reported that Mrs. Q. was capable of managing her own work, that her house was clean, the children better dressed, and the food satisfactory.

HOUSING

Most of the families receiving mothers' aid in Detroit lived in small houses; those of foreign birth usually were in houses which had been made over into flats. In the down-town section old homes had been utilized for apartments, one apartment to each floor, or sometimes two on a floor. There were few families living in tenements. No outside toilets were allowed in the city limits. Families living on the outskirts of the city often had yard space for a small vegetable garden or flower plot. A mother and three children generally occupied at least three rooms, one of which might be used as a living room. There were no dark rooms; a number of houses had bathrooms, but that was not the rule. The majority had inside running water and gas; few had electricity or ice boxes.

The court workers made every effort to move families out of disreputable neighborhoods or insanitary houses, and were very desirous that they have an adequate number of rooms, especially separate sleeping rooms for boys and girls. The housing bureau of the Community Union cooperated in finding suitable homes and in having the sanitary laws enforced. Rents for good homes were extremely high. According to an old ruling which could not be enforced strictly on account of the housing shortage a mother might not pay a rental of more than $35 a month if heat was supplied and $30 a month without heat. A few families paid $50, but these took lodgers, thereby reducing their own rent. The court had ruled that a mother might have an equity of $3,500 in her own home, and about 430 of the families receiving aid (43 per cent) owned or partly owned their homes.

The following stories illustrate the efforts of the visitors to obtain fit homes for the families under their supervision:

The father of the three little R.'s had been sentenced to prison for deserting his family, and Mrs. R. was granted a divorce on the ground of desertion and extreme cruelty. The mothers' aid visitor found the family living on a dark alley in what had once been a shed, one part of it still being used for that purpose. The house could be reached by a narrow alley or by going through a saloon in front. There was no floor and the roof leaked. The only toilet accessible was that in the basement of the saloon, which was used by the saloon patrons. For this dwelling place Mrs. R. had paid $17 a month in pre-war days. The court worker moved the family into four light, sanitary rooms in a good neighborhood.

Mrs. B.'s husband had become insane from chronic alcoholism and was committed to a hospital for mental diseases. He previously had saved $2,400 and had invested it in eight lots, which he mortgaged for $2,800. With this sum he built a comfortable, two-family house on one of the lots. Mrs. B. was ignorant of financial affairs, and when mothers' aid was granted the house was about to be sold for taxes and special improvements, which amounted to more than $2,000. The court worker determined to save the home by selling the lots, which had increased greatly in value. A special dispensation had to be given by the orphans' court for the sale of the property, as it was in the father's name. The worker displayed perseverance and tact in preventing a forced sale of the house. When everything was settled Mrs. B. owned the house clear, the taxes were paid, and some very necessary repairs had been made. Besides there was a balance of $900 in the bank, on which the mother received a court order of $50 a month for the support of her children.

EDUCATION

COOPERATION WITH THE SCHOOLS AND FACILITIES FOR EDUCATION

Contacts with the schools.

The court workers kept in touch with the school progress of the children principally by means of the individual school-record blanks which were mailed by the teachers to the court every quarter. These reports covered attendance, conduct, effort, and grade. Following is a copy of such a report:

SCHOOL RECORD FOR JUVENILE COURT, WAYNE COUNTY, MICH.

Miss _____. School: _____

_____

Below is the record of attendance, conduct, etc., of name: *Elizabeth W.;* address, _____ from Sept. 6, 1921, to date.

Month	Days present	Days absent	Conduct	Month	Days present	Days absent	Conduct
1921				1922			
September____	13½	4½	2	January_____	15	2	2
October_____	15	4½	2	February_____	18	2	2
November____	15	3	2	March_____	14	6	2
December_____	16½	2½	2				

Total days present, 107½. Total days absent, 24½. Average conduct, Good (2); effort, Good (2). Grade, B-7th. Date of birth, 9-16-08.
Remarks: Elizabeth was absent the week of March 13 on account of her father's illness and death.

_____,
Principal.

The court workers visited the schools at intervals and whenever any special need arose in connection with some child. They were expected to examine also the children's quarterly reports, including the reports of the physical examination.

Provision for handicapped children.

The physically handicapped child.—The department of education conducted the Leland Day School for Crippled Children for children 5 to 18 years of age; both academic and vocational instruction was given. It operated also a day school for deaf children, a class for blind children, and 12 sight-conservation classes. Lessons in typing and piano lessons were given to the blind children in addition to regular school work. There were 180 classes in 60 school centers for children having speech defects, and there were 9 open-air classes. School busses were provided for transportation to and from school for all children who required such assistance. The Community

Union operated a bureau for the handicapped, which was of service in finding employment for the children.

The mentally handicapped child.—The department of education conducted 63 special A classes for subnormal children under 13½ years of age and 19 special B classes for children 13½ to 16 years of age; a few older children were also enrolled. This work was primarily vocational in character.

Provision for children wishing further education.

Twenty-three children 14 and 15 years old were in high school and a few boys and girls over 16 were in school full time or part time. Seven children had scholarships and were taking commercial courses in the high schools. These scholarships generally amounted to $15 or $20 per month; six of them were given by the council of Protestant churches and one by the public-welfare department of Hamtramck. A few children (the exact number was not known) were taking business or other vocational courses at night school. Twenty-seven boys in mothers' aid families were enrolled in a school maintained by a local automobile company that combined school and trade training but conformed to the board of education's curriculum. As the boys worked one week and attended classes the alternate week this afforded opportunity for trade training. Boys between the ages of 12 and 15 could enroll provided they were up to the school grade for their ages. They were paid $1 a day from the start, attended the school until they were 18, then were given work in the factory.

Comparatively few children in the mothers' aid families were known to be receiving musical instruction, and no special effort was expended in this direction, although instruction could be had at a nominal charge at various settlements. Free vocal lessons had been secured from the conservatory of music for two children, however.

SCHOOLING AND WORK OF CHILDREN 14 AND 15 YEARS OLD

The child-labor, compulsory-education, and mothers' aid laws.

Children were required to attend school from 7 to 16 years of age with the following exceptions: If the child had completed the eighth grade, provided he had an employment certificate and was employed or had an excuse for work for which an employment certificate was not required; if he was physically unable to attend school; if he was 14 and had completed the sixth grade and his work was essential to the support of his parents, in which case he might be excused by the county or city superintendent of schools, at his discretion.[4] Employment certificates were granted to children 15 years old but under 16 who had completed the sixth grade if it was demonstrable that their wages were necessary to the support of their families, each case being considered individually. Children 16 years old were subject to the same requirements except that certification that their wages were essential to the support of their families was not required. The requirement of a physical examination was optional with the officer issuing employment certificates. Working children under 17 years of age who had not completed the second year of high school

---

[4] Mich., Comp. Laws 1915, Cahill's Annotated Supp. 1922, sec. 5979, p. 650; sec. 5331, p. 523, as amended by act of May 17, 1923, No. 206, Public Acts of 1923, p. 319. (This was amended further by act of May 26, 1925, No. 312, Public Acts of 1925, p. 469.)

were required to attend continuation school unless they were physically unable to do so or unless such attendance would deprive them of wages essential to their support and that of their families.[5]

The mothers' aid law permitted allowances to be granted to children under 17 years of age.

Regular employment certificates were granted in 1923 to only 277 children between 14 and 15 years of age in Detroit, although there were about 24,000 children of these ages in the city.[6]

Children in school and at work.

The court had ruled that with certain exceptions allowances could be granted to children only until they were eligible for employment certificates. If a child was frail or physically handicapped, or if he was finishing a unit of education such as a commercial course, the allowance might be continued until he was 16 years of age.

There were 255 children (137 boys and 118 girls) 14 and 15 years of age in the families receiving aid; 141 of them were 14 years old and 114 were 15 years old. Of these 255 children 198 were attending school, 29 were working, and 28 were neither attending school nor working.

Children in school.—Among the 198 children 14 and 15 years of age attending school were 36 who were eligible for regular employment certificates so far as age and completion of school grade were concerned; that is, they were 15 years old and had completed the sixth grade.[7]

The number of boys and girls 14 and 15 years old attending school and the grade or type of school attended are shown in the following table:

Number of children 14 and 15 years old in school at the time of the study, by grade and type of school; Wayne County, Mich.

Grade or type of school	Total	Children 14 and 15 years old attending school					
		Boys			Girls		
		Total	14 years	15 years	Total	14 years	15 years
Total	198	105	66	39	93	67	26
Elementary school:							
Third grade	1				1	1	
Fourth grade	5	3	3		2	1	1
Fifth grade	17	11	6	5	6	4	2
Sixth grade	44	19	10	9	25	22	3
Seventh grade	49	27	20	7	22	17	5
Eighth grade	29	12	11	1	17	11	6
High school:							
First year	14	5	4	1	9	7	2
Second year	8	3		3	5	2	3
Third year	1				1		1
Trade school	15	15	8	7			
Special class	15	10	4	6	5	2	3

[5] Mich. Comp. Laws 1915, sec. 5988 (1), (2), pp. 653-654.
[6] See Trend of Child Labor in 34 Cities in the United States, 1922 to 1923, Monthly Labor Review (U. S. Bureau of Labor Statistics), vol. 18, no. 5 (May, 1924), p. 114, and Fourteenth Census of the United States, 1920, vol. 2, Population, p. 293 (U. S. Bureau of the Census, Washington, 1923).
[7] This number was nearly half (47 per cent) of the whole number of 15-year-old children in mothers' aid families who had fulfilled the school-grade requirement for employment certificates (76).

Occupations and earnings of working children.—All the 29 children 14 and 15 years of age in families receiving aid who were working were 15 years old, and only 2 had started working before they had become 15. One of these 2 was a girl who became inspector in a department store; the other was a boy who had run away when he was 14 years and 6 months old and had enlisted in the Army. The occupations of the 29 children were as follows:

	Number of children		Number of children
Total	29	Girls	14
Boys	15	Factory worker	5
		Clerk in store	3
Messenger	4	Waitress	2
Clerical worker	2	Inspector in store	1
Factory worker	2	Cashier	1
Laborer	2	Messenger	1
Delivery boy	2	Kitchen helper	1
Stock-room helper	1		
Worker in bakery	1		
In United States Army	1		

None of these children had left school before reaching the sixth grade; 6 had been in that grade when they left school; 9 had been in the seventh, 9 in the eighth, and 5 in the high school (3 in the first year, 2 in the second).

The monthly earnings of the 29 children (all of whom contributed their entire earnings to the support of the family) were as follows:

	Number of children
Total	29
$30, under $40	3
$40, under $50	4
$50, under $60	10
$60, under $70	7
Over $70	[8] 3
Other and not reported	[9] 2

Children neither in school nor at work.

Twenty children 14 and 15 years old in families receiving allowances were neither attending school nor working. Eight were looking for work, 1 was waiting for an employment certificate to be issued, 1 was about to take a business course and work half time, and 2 were getting some trade instruction. Two had been employed (1 having run away from trade school and worked at odd jobs before returning home), and 3 were married (only 1 of these 3 girls was at home). A tuberculous child was in a sanatorium, a mentally defective cripple was in the school for crippled children, and a feeble-minded child was at home.

Eight children were in institutions (5 delinquent, 2 feeble-minded, and 1 epileptic).

EDUCATIONAL ACTIVITIES FOR THE MOTHERS

A remarkable program of group instruction had been developed among the mothers who did not speak English. These classes had

---
[8] One was earning $87, one was earning $108, one was earning $121.
[9] Includes a boy receiving Army pay and subsistence and a girl whose earnings were not reported.

gradually furnished the nuclei for social activities and seemed to offer a real outlet for group expression. There were seven classes organized for instruction in English and civics, homemaking, nutrition, and child care.

The first group was organized in the winter of 1920. It consisted of Sicilian mothers who not only had not learned English but were also illiterate in their own tongue. They were brought together by the International Institute of the Young Women's Christian Association at the suggestion of the mothers' pension department. They seemed helpless, inferior, and without ambition. The class began with instruction in their own language as to the care of babies and the home. The second year the department of education supplied a teacher and it was made an English class; the teacher used the direct method without an interpreter, and once a month a nurse from the board of health conducted the lesson. The class had continued to meet each year and had gathered momentum, awakened new interests, and stimulated new ideals. It was meeting twice weekly for 2-hour sessions at a public school. On the day of the visit the mothers appeared alert and clearly interested in the world and life around them. Some had taken out citizenship papers or were preparing to do so. They had just organized into a club with officers of their own choosing and were planning social activities.

A number of Italian mothers were enrolled in a class which had been meeting for six months. This class was not made up entirely of mothers who were receiving aid. A teacher from the department of education was giving instruction in nutrition, homemaking, child care, and English. They, too, met twice weekly for two hours. The Widows' Club of St. Anne's consisted of 22 Polish mothers receiving aid who met at St. Anne's Community House in Hamtramck once a week. Their first class work had been the Red Cross course in home nursing, from which they had been proud to receive diplomas. The club had held many socials and parties. They were given instruction in sewing during the winters of 1923 and 1924 and were looking forward to having a Christmas sale. Six of these mothers attended an English class besides, with the hope of taking out citizenship papers. Another Polish group was just being organized by the Polish Aid Society under the auspices of the League of Catholic Women, 50 women having responded to the invitation. English and domestic science were being taught. A group of Hungarian mothers were studying English, civics, and child care in the combination course prepared by the city departments of education and of health. This was the instruction generally given to any new group. The Merrill-Palmer School conducted two classes for Italian mothers receiving aid. These included instruction as to child care, habit forming, nutrition, and discipline.

Individual instruction in household management and cooking was given to mothers by the Visiting Housekeeper Association. Itemized expense accounts were kept by these mothers as a basis for helpful advice. When a family was assigned to its care its workers sometimes did all the case work, with the collaboration of the court worker. At the housekeeping center was a model flat, which was occupied by a whole family for three weeks at a time and used for demonstration and teaching purposes. About 30 mothers' aid families were under the supervision of the association.

RECREATION

The budget allowance for extras covered such items as recreation, education, health, car fare, and church contributions. For a family of a mother and three children $6.34 per month was allowed for extras. If it was deemed advisable a special item such as car fare to a gymnasium was included in the budget, or a scout outfit might be secured through a special contribution. Working boys and girls were expected to turn most of their wages into the home. The family were permitted to make their own adjustment, and if it was reasonable it was not interfered with. Special difficulties were solved case by case. A boy or girl 18 or over was expected to pay a reasonable amount for board—a boy at least $10 a week and a girl $7 or $8 a week.

There were many recreational facilities in Detroit. The department of recreation used 60 or 70 school buildings for recreational activities, 30 of which were utilized full time. It also operated a large, well-equipped community house and several smaller neighborhood centers. An all-round development program for women and girls designed to promote physical and mental poise and self-expression was being successfully carried out. The physical education included gymnastics and athletics, games, hikes, swimming, gardening, and dancing; the manual education included handicrafts, modeling, painting, interior decoration, and designing of theater costumes and scenes; the mental education included dramatics, pageantry, chorus work, story-telling, and study courses. All the work was presented through organized clubs. The eight settlements of the city were utilized freely, and the mothers' pension department endeavored to have the families under its supervision make use of the nearest neighborhood center. The court encouraged regular church and Sunday-school attendance, and many churches conducted clubs and social and recreational activities. Though the housing shortage made it impossible to move families in order to make more recreation facilities available, the workers believed that the variety of activities afforded by churches, settlements, playgrounds, and school centers enabled every family to have access to one or more of these sources of social life.

The court laid great emphasis upon membership by the mothers in the parent-teacher associations. All the visitors were asked to have every mother join the association in the school attended by her children. The purchase of cheap phonographs was encouraged as a means of promoting family unity, and payments on pianos were not forbidden if they were already nearly paid for. Some children belonged to scout troops, and the court encouraged this recreational activity. About one-third of the city mothers with their boys under 10 and girls under 11 years of age were sent for a two weeks' vacation each summer to Bay Court, a summer-vacation camp operated by the Community Union. The seven classes for foreign-born women mentioned in the preceding section were of social as well as educational value.

MOTHERS' ALLOWANCES IN MANITOBA, CANADA [1]

PROVISIONS OF THE LAW

The Manitoba law "to provide allowances for mothers" with "neglected or dependent children" was passed by the Provincial Parliament in 1916.[2] It provided for aid to widows, to mothers whose husbands were inmates of penal institutions or insane asylums or who because of physical disability were unable to support their families, provided the mother was without means to care properly for her children and their welfare and best interests would be served by permitting them to remain in her custody. Rules as to residence, citizenship, property, and amount of aid were left to a provincial commission appointed to administer the law subject to the approval of the lieutenant governor in council.[3]

The following regulations as to eligibility were in force:

1. Applications were considered only from mothers who were widows or whose husbands were confined in a hospital for mental diseases, provided there were two or more children.

2. The husband of an applicant must have been a Canadian citizen.

3. An applicant must have resided in the Province with her husband and family for two consecutive years (with certain exceptions) prior to his death or admission to a hospital for mental diseases. There was no municipal residence qualification.

4. Applicants were allowed to retain $200 in cash for emergency use. Any additional sums which the family had were turned over to the commission and the interest applied toward the beneficiary's allowance. The principal to the amount of $1,000 was returned when an allowance was discontinued.

5. Ownership of real estate was allowed up to the amount of $2,000, if the family actually resided in the home and the taxes, the insurance, and the interest on the mortgage did not exceed what would otherwise have to be paid for rent.

6. Mothers receiving allowances were not permitted to keep boarders or roomers, a mother's brother or father only being excepted.

---

[1] The population of Manitoba, Canada, was 610,118 in 1921. Of this number 179,087 lived in Winnipeg, the capital and only large city. There were 222,372 inhabitants of foreign birth, of whom 113,114 were British born. The main racial sources of the population were as follows, in order of their numerical importance: English, Scotch, Irish, French, Austrian, Ukrainian, and Dutch. (Sixth Census of Canada, vol. 1, Population, pp. 221, 245, 357, Ottawa, 1924.) The area of the Province is 231,926 square miles, or more than five times the area of the State of Pennsylvania. The chief industries are farming, fishing, dairying, trapping, and mining.
[2] Manitoba, act of Mar. 10, 1916, ch. 69, Stat. 1916, p. 221. (See Stat. of Manitoba, Consolidated Amendments 1924, ch. 30, secs 19–28, pp. 156–158, as amended by act of Apr. 23, 1926, ch. 4, Stat. 1926, p. 11.)
[3] The act of Apr. 23, 1926, made a citizenship qualification.

ADMINISTRATION OF THE LAW

ADMINISTRATIVE AGENCY

Manitoba is nearly as large as the State of Texas, and traveling over its entire area is impossible part of the year because of the lack of railroad facilities, the snow, and the extreme cold. Still the Parliament of Manitoba clearly intended that the law should be administered directly by the provincial government; no provision was made in the act for local administrative groups of any kind, and their development was due to necessity. The central provincial agency ultimately delegated a considerable share of administration to local groups and became itself both administrative and supervisory in character. A mothers' allowances commission of five members (three men and two women) was appointed by the lieutenant governor in council to administer the law. This unpaid provincial commission met at least once a month, generally twice a month, and acted upon all cases requiring a financial decision.

On the recommendation of the mothers' allowances commission the lieutenant governor in council ratified, on March 16, 1917, a ruling that provided for the appointment by every municipality of a committee of not less than three members whose duty it was to " receive applications for allowances, investigate all applications received, forward a complete record of all investigations to the commission, and supervise all families receiving allowances." Often the secretary-treasurer of the municipality was secretary-treasurer of the committee. The committee members were supplied with forms and budget estimates by the commission. They received no salary nor any compensation for traveling expenses, and no money passed through their hands.

THE STAFF

The commission's staff consisted of an executive secretary and three field workers (two for Greater Winnipeg, one for the territory outside the city). Originally the area outside Greater Winnipeg had been divided between two field workers; but as the northern part of Manitoba was inaccessible in winter and many sections of it were difficult of access at any time, a man probation officer residing there was supervising the 150 mothers' aid families in that part of the Province at the time of the study. The executive secretary was experienced in administrative work. Two field workers were college graduates and one was a trained nurse; two had had previous training in social case work; one had been a teacher and also had received two months' training in an agency administering mothers' aid in a city in the United States. One car was at the disposal of the secretary and staff.

THE FRIENDLY VISITORS

In addition to the officially designated administrators of the law there were in the Province about 350 so-called friendly visitors, who might or might not be members of local municipal committees.

Nearly every local community, at least in the southern half of the Province, had one or more of these volunteer workers. They visited families once a month, secured school reports, assisted in providing medical care, helped the family to weather emergencies, and gave counsel. The friendly visitors were expected to send in monthly reports on prescribed forms, and they were extremely conscientious about it. At least one such visitor had not missed a monthly report in five years, and many were rendering excellent service. The following is a form for a friendly visitor's report:

Visitors' monthly report of family under allowance

Name of family, L.
Name of visitor, (Mrs.) J. D. E.

Address,
Date of visits, Jan. 20, 1923

Municipality of D.
During month of January

Names of all children	School record	Name of school _____ Signature of principal _____			Work record of children over 15 years of age		Health record		
	Days absent	Cause	Times late	Grade	Prog-ress	Wages last month	Employer's name and address	Good	Fair	Poor
Jane_____	1	Not well__	{ 0 / 1 }	Sr. II	Fair___			Good		
George____			0		Fair___			Good		
Elsie_____								Good		
James_____								Good		

Income from mother's work, None.
Income from relatives, None.
Income from roomers, None.
Income from any other source except allowance, None.

Write G, F, or B for good, fair, or bad.
Housing, F. Children's clothes, G.
Mother's appearance, G. Cleanliness, F.
Signature of visitor: J. D. E.

Total, _____

Give any further interesting or important details in writing on reverse side of this report, and return before the 15th day of the month to 302 Parliament Building, Winnipeg.

The only organization of these friendly visitors was in Winnipeg, where the 120 visitors were banded into a ladies' auxiliary that, in addition to friendly visiting, took care of the Christmas work, sent mothers and children to a fresh-air camp each summer, made garments, and furnished a medium for publicity. The auxiliary met every month in the Parliament Building for a discussion of some problem of child welfare. Its prime object was to aid the mothers' allowances commission, and it had rendered great service in disseminating information and in maintaining adequate aid during the government economy drive.

A member of the mothers' aid staff was organizing the Winnipeg friendly visitors into groups of 30 for purposes of case training and discussion. They met monthly for class instruction. The following is a copy of the monthly report sent to the commission by the friendly visitors of the auxiliary:

LADIES' AUXILIARY

All allowances are adjusted as conditions change and until family can become self-supporting

FRIENDLY VISITOR MONTHLY PROGRESS REPORT

Name of family visited: *I.*   Address: _____   Date of visits: Jan. 15, 1924.
(important)
Housing conditions: *Warm and comfortable.*
Names of children seen: *Two girls, one 7 and one 9.*
Health: *Mrs. I has not been well since having teeth extracted.*
Cleanliness: _____
Schooling: *All children attending regularly.*
Clothing: *Mother has remade some clothing given her and has the children and herself looking very tidy.*
Can suitable work be planned for mother without neglecting children? *Mother can do dressmaking.*
What is mother's disposition toward your cooperation? *Kindly.*
Remarks: *I hope the commission may be able to make some allowance for Mrs. I. until she is well enough to do dressmaking again.*

(Signed)   Mrs. L. B. R.

THE PUBLIC-HEALTH NURSES

A further help in the administration of mothers' aid was the service provided through the 32 public-health nurses who covered 19 rural municipalities and 11 suburbs of Winnipeg. They were expected to have general oversight of families receiving aid and to report at least once a year on prescribed forms like the following:

CONFIDENTIAL REPORT FROM DEPARTMENT OF PUBLIC HEALTH FOR MOTHERS' ALLOWANCES COMMISSION

No. 836.   Name of family: *Mrs. J. C.*   Date: *July 26, 1922.*
Municipality: _____   Nurse: *Miss A. M.*

Names of children	Age	School	Remarks
Bessie	9 yrs	Graysville	The 3 younger children have bad throats. Opinion is the tonsils and adenoids require removing at once, especially _____ and _____. Should like to bring these children to the hospital right away, as the throats are urgent.
June	8 yrs		
Ralph	4 yrs		
George	2 yrs		

House new and clean, provided by elderly grandparent. Mother seems healthy and family fairly happy.

NOTE.—Please report as to health of mother and children, any necessary medical treatment needed, and physical or mental defects; also any outstanding features, re-housing, food, clothing, care of house and children, etc., using other side.

APPROPRIATION AND VOLUME OF WORK

The entire appropriation was made by the Provincial Parliament each year. The Government levied at large on all the municipalities of the Province for half the total appropriation, irrespective of the expenditures for any one locality. The other half was met from Provincial funds.

For the fiscal year ended August 31, 1923, $450,000 was appropriated for mothers' allowances. The administration the following year reduced the appropriation to $425,000. The deficit was met by reducing administrative expense, by utilizing various resources (such as private benevolences), by requiring mothers having two or three children, all of whom were in school, to contribute to the family income, and by requiring children of legal working age to secure employment.

On the basis of the appropriation Manitoba obligated itself for mothers' aid more heavily than any State in the United States in proportion to its population, the per capita expense for mothers' aid in 1922–23 being 74 cents. In November, 1923, 611 families, including 2,146 dependent children, were receiving mothers' aid. The average monthly grant for that month was $57.40 per family and $16.40 per child.

PROCEDURE IN MAKING ALLOWANCES

In Winnipeg applications were made to the social-welfare commission, which was the public outdoor-relief agency; it investigated and reported its findings to the mothers' allowances commission, which received the recommendations and forwarded them to the provincial commission, as has been stated. The other municipal committees made both the preliminary investigations and the recommendations. The application blank (furnished by the commission) called for the following information: Date, place, and cause of husband's death or commitment to institution; date and place of birth, nationality, and religion of the father and mother; dates and places of birth of all children, their health, grades, and schools, or occupations and wages; if they were not in school, the grades at which they left school and began work; employers' names and addresses; facts regarding property, insurance, savings, and assets or liabilities; and an estimate of the monthly budget and income. The application had to be sworn to by the mother and the recommendation for the grant signed by three members of the local committee.

The following items were verified: Marriage, death, or commitment of father, naturalization, residence, birth of children, ownership of property or savings. A visit was made to the home of the applicant and references were consulted. Generally in the rural communities the families were known to the members of the committee. A statement accompanied the application blank covering the family history before and after death or commitment of the father, financial status, housing, health, relatives, references, and plans for the future.

USE OF A STANDARD BUDGET

The law set no maximum to the amount which might be given per child and per family, and it was the intention of the commission that the allowance should be sufficient to maintain health and to provide the essentials necessary to wholesome living. The grants were computed on the basis of a budget that the dietitian employed by the public welfare commission had prepared in consultation with the staff of the mothers' allowances commission and the ladies' auxiliary, using also the Chicago standard budget for suggestions and general standards. The following is a copy of the budget used:

Schedule of allowances, September, 1924

Actual rent, or interest, taxes, and insurance.

MAXIMUM RENT, OR INTEREST, TAXES, AND INSURANCE

Two or more children living at home_____ $20.00
Three or 4 children at home_____ 25.00
Five or more children at home_____ 30.00

	Operating heat	Winter fuel		
		October	November to March	April
6–7-roomed house_____	$4.00	$9.00	$18.00	$9.00
4–5-roomed house_____	4.00	8.00	16.00	8.00
2–3-roomed house_____	4.00	6.00	12.00	6.00
2–3 unheated rooms_____	3.00	4.50	9.00	4.50

	Food	Clothing	Total
Adult_____	$10.50	$4.50	$15.00
Child 1–3_____	3.25	2.25	5.50
4–7_____	4.25	3.25	7.50
8–11_____	5.00	4.00	9.00
12–15_____	6.50	4.50	11.00
15 up_____	11.00	_____	11.00

	Cleaning	Recreation	Light
Families of 2 or 3 children_____	$1.00	$1.25	$0.75
Families of 4 or 5 children_____	1.50	1.75	.75
Families of 6 or over_____	2.00	2.25	.75

	Winnipeg	St. Boniface
Water, 4-roomed house_____	$0.56	$0.67
Water, 5-roomed house_____	.70	.80
Water, 6-roomed house_____	.82	.93
Water, 7-roomed house_____	.93	1.07

MAXIMUM ALLOWANCE EXCLUDING WINTER FUEL

Two dependent children_____ $65.00
Three dependent children_____ 80.00
Four dependent children_____ 90.00
Five dependent children_____ 95.00
Six or more dependent children_____ 100.00

INCOME

In estimating the amount required to care for a family the above schedule of allowances is applied and income from all sources deducted from total of such schedule.

The assumption is that the cost of living can be reduced in the larger families:
- Mother and 5 children 3 per cent off food and clothing.
- Mother and 6 children 4 per cent off food and clothing.
- Add 1 per cent for each additional child.

Estimated cost of living for earning child:
```
Food_____ $11.00
Clothing _____  12.00
Sundries _____   5.00
                                                    _____
                                                     28.00
```

Income over and above cost of living expenses for earning child must be paid into the home on following basis:
- Until 18 years of age, 100 per cent.
- Until 20 years of age, 80 per cent.
- 21 years and over, 70 per cent.

If a child of earning age, single or married, is not earning or is not supporting his or her mother, but is deemed able to earn and support his or her mother in whole or in part, and if a mother who is a beneficiary is not earning but is deemed able to earn and support her family, in whole or in part, the total allowance may be reduced by potential earnings of such child or mother, and discontinued as soon as family can be self-supporting.

Note.—When earning children are unemployed for any reason other than sickness one-third of their average monthly wage may be taken as income, the minimum reduction to be $11.

Income from roomers:
- Furnished rooms, 75 per cent of rental.
- Unfurnished rooms, 100 per cent of rental.
- Income from mother with 2 children: $5 as each child attains school age.
- Income from mother with 3 children: $5 when two children attain school age.
- In cases of families where there are two or three children: Not until mother's earnings are over $15 and $10, respectively, will the total allowance be subject to a further deduction of 75 per cent of such earnings.

In the case of an applicant owning an equity of $2,000 or over in her home or other real estate and other moneys in the form of cash or securities that may be readily liquidated, such other moneys shall be handed over to the commission and returned to the applicant in the form of a monthly allowance, excepting $200, which may be retained by the applicant for emergency purposes.

Note.—Exemption from above general rulings in cases due to illness or other exceptional conditions will be considered by the commission.

In addition to the grant the commission allowed coal, an extra allowance for winter clothing in a lump sum of $10 to $20, and emergency help, such as money for doctors or dentists. Fifty dollars was allowed for funeral expenses. No provision was made for insurance.

The mothers were not required to keep itemized expense accounts except in some cases as a check on their veracity. Once a year in the fall all mothers receiving aid were required to file with the commission a statement on a prescribed form having special reference to the financial status of the family and calling for data regarding all income and expenditures on a monthly basis, together with the present assets (such as property) and liabilities. The statement also included the names of the children; their ages and grades if in school; and if working, wages, names of employers, and contributions to the family. If the family lived on a farm an exhaustive questionnaire was to be filled out giving the names and value of farm implements, number of livestock, amount and kinds of crops harvested, amount of sales of crops, and value of farm products consumed.

SUPPLEMENTING OF MOTHERS' AID

Inasmuch as the commission was authorized by law to grant sufficient aid to each family to meet its needs as shown by the budget the need of help on a large scale from other agencies did not arise. However, the reduction of $25,000 in the appropriation had necessitated supplementary aid, especially for clothing, and this was provided by the ladies' auxiliary and the friendly visitors.

VISITING

The staff visitor assigned to the territory outside Greater Winnipeg could not make visits oftener than once or twice a year, depending upon the locality in which the families were; but in the southern part of the Province, which contained more than three-fourths of the mothers' aid families, a friendly visitor was assigned to every family and visited every month.[4] The two case workers assigned to Greater Winnipeg were expected to visit the families under their care once a month, oftener if necessary; and a friendly visitor, who likewise visited monthly, was also assigned to every family. The following case story shows the results attained in one family through the joint effort of the staff visitor and a friendly visitor:

Mrs. P., to whom an allowance was granted in August, 1918, for her three children aged 11, 8, and 2, was thoughtless and untruthful, did not manage well on the grant, and was continually in debt. The children were not regular in school attendance and often were late. As an aid in helping to keep the expenditures within the income part of the grant was placed as an order in one of the department stores which included a grocery division; the store furnished a list of expenditures to the visitor each month. There were lengthy discussions after the monthly bill was received and careful instruction as to the kinds of food which were suitable for young children and how these foods should be prepared. At first it was not uncommon for Mrs. P. to say that she was quite clear of debt, though when the staff worker returned to the office she would find that some creditor was demanding a settlement. On being questioned the following day Mrs. P. would merely look surprised and say she had forgotten to mention it but would see that it was attended to. This happened so often that a new strategy was adopted. When an irate merchant complained thereafter the visitor made an appointment to meet him at Mrs. P.'s home, and there an agreement would be written and signed in regard to monthly payments, with no credit allowed. These disciplinary interviews were followed the next day by a friendly call on the part of the visitor, who expounded the advantages of a pay-as-you-go policy, especially for the sake of the children. In the course of time Mrs. P. improved so much that she was permitted to keep her own list of expenditures and was given her full allowance in cash. The same tactics were used as to school attendance until there was no reason for complaint. The oldest child was apt with her needle and a few hints as to how she could beautify the home were all that were needed. The friendly visitor gave partly used clothing to the family and Mrs. P. learned to make over clothes so as to keep the children more neatly dressed. After four years of patient service on the part of the two visitors and of positive striving on the part of Mrs. P. the new habits became well established and the old attitude of fear and self-defense gave way to candor and self-confidence.

HEALTH

PHYSICAL HEALTH

No allowance was made in the budget for health needs, nor did the commission pay physicians' fees. Allowances were made, however, for eyeglasses, teeth, special diet, and other health items.

---

[4] The distribution of the mothers' aid families was as follows: In the northern part of the Province, about 150; in the southern part (not including Greater Winnipeg), about 150; in Winnipeg, 150; in the suburbs of Winnipeg, 160.

General procedure.

No physical examinations were made preliminary to the granting of aid nor periodically after aid was granted. The records of families receiving allowances did not generally include family medical histories, and no attempt was made to keep a continuous record of the physical condition of each member of the family. The families were assumed to be well unless they complained of ill health or there were obvious signs of disease.

Families in Winnipeg and near-by towns could obtain excellent clinical services at the Winnipeg General Hospital, which was supported in part by provincial funds, and at the Children's Hospital; private physicians also gave generous service. Both these hospitals had social-service departments, and the family visitors were responsible for keeping in touch with them in regard to patients who required long-continued treatment. The visitors also had frequent consultations with the examining physicians. The Winnipeg General Hospital conducted 13 specialized clinics, including prenatal, nutrition, and dental clinics for adults; 25 cents was charged for the first examination. Patients were referred by means of a steering blank, and written reports were returned by the social-service departments. A copy of a medical report is as follows:

WINNIPEG GENERAL HOSPITAL—SOCIAL SERVICE DEPARTMENT

MEDICAL REPORT

To Mothers' Allowances Commission.
Name: *Mrs. J. B.*
Address: _____
O. P. D. 25412
Diagnosis (please explain medical terms): *High blood pressure,* $\frac{190}{90}$.
Probable duration of illness? *Indefinite; should be on milk or buttermilk diet only.*
When will patient be able to work? _____
Is his line of work injurious? _____
Suggestions or remarks in respect to patient's condition: *Should have 2 quarts of milk daily for two weeks.*
(Signed)   L. M. T.
Date: *19/3/24.*

Outside Winnipeg there were 15 hospitals, 2 of which had clinical service and 1 of which had a medical social service department. Children and mothers requiring operations were taken to these hospitals, hospital care being paid for (under the hospital aid act) at a pro rata basis of $1.75 a day by the municipality and 50 cents a day by the provincial government.

The correction of serious physical defects was required by the commission and the visitors seldom found it necessary to threaten withdrawal of the grant to get these corrections made. Though intensive health supervision was carried on in Winnipeg and the suburbs, the great distances and lack of traveling facilities, the inadequate hospital facilities, and the inadequate staff made this out of the question through the rest of the Province. The families outside Winnipeg generally consulted private physicians and made their own arrangements as to fees; often only a nominal charge was made.

Public physicians could be secured in an emergency, and when they did not give their services or when long trips were necessary the municipality paid them.

Follow-up of special types of problems.

Tuberculosis.—It was the policy of the commission to require all contact cases of tuberculosis to be examined. The Winnipeg General Hospital maintained a tuberculosis clinic, and the five city tuberculosis nurses and the provincial public-health nurses visited tuberculous patients. It was also the policy of the commission to insist upon sanatorium care. Hospital and sanatorium facilities were adequate; a provincial sanatorium at Ninette, 15 miles from Winnipeg, cared for incipient and moderately advanced cases, and the King George Hospital in the city cared for advanced cases.

Venereal disease.—It was the policy of the commission to have Wassermann tests whenever there was reason to suspect venereal disease, and treatment was required if the results of the tests were positive. The provincial department of health maintained a genito-urinary clinic in Winnipeg and in four other towns in the Province; mothers' aid families in need of treatment were placed under the care of one of these. Two nurses did genito-urinary work, one in connection with the provincial department and one in connection with the genito-urinary clinic of the Winnipeg General Hospital.

Orthopedic and cardiac affections.—The only orthopedic clinics in Manitoba were in connection with four Winnipeg hospitals. The clinics of the Winnipeg General Hospital were available to anyone in the Province who could come to the hospital. The mothers' aid workers tried to secure orthopedic care for all children whom they knew to be in need of it. Braces or other apparatus were paid for by relatives or by a special grant through the mothers' allowances commission. The family visitor or the social-service departments of the hospitals followed up the cases.

There was no cardiac clinic. Cardiac cases were treated at the Winnipeg General Hospital, and patients could be accommodated at the Convalescent Hospital, though this was rarely used for mothers' aid families.

Eye, ear, nose, and throat affections.—The eye clinics conducted by the department of education and the Winnipeg General Hospital were generally used. The school nurses followed up such cases very carefully and frequently attended to obtaining the necessary treatment on their own initiative.

Medical work for infants and preschool children.—The bureau of child hygiene of the city department of health employed 14 nurses, who followed up the mothers of babies born in the hospitals, visiting at regular intervals during the first year of the baby's life. The bureau also provided milk and formulas.

A child-health conference, primarily for children under 2 years of age, was conducted weekly at the central office of the Winnipeg Department of Health; the commission encouraged mothers who had babies to attend these. Outside Winnipeg the public-health nurses conducted weekly conferences for children up to school age in 19 child-health centers. Dental clinics were conducted in connection with two such centers, and prenatal work was done also.

Forty-eight child-health conferences were held at agricultural fairs in the summer of 1923, and 2,000 children were given physical examinations. The babies were followed up if treatment was needed. As the nurses were expected to keep in touch with the families receiving allowances, their effort could be counted on to encourage these mothers to attend whenever a center was available. This was not a requirement, however, and it was not definitely known how many mothers' aid children were under the care of the child-health centers.

School medical inspection.—In Winnipeg it was the practice to give physical examination to all school children once a year. For the school year 1923–24 the children were divided into three groups for purposes of examination; namely, (1) those just entering school, (2) those found defective at a previous examination and those selected by the nurses as being in need of medical care, and (3) all children 10 years old and 14 years old. There were 14 school nurses, each supervising about 2,700 children. School inspections were made once in six weeks or two months. The nurses weighed and measured all school children once a year, and tested for vision; and if they found a defect the physician made an examination. Six dental clinics provided free dental care to all needy school children.

School children outside Winnipeg proper were inspected once a year by the 32 provincial public-health nurses. The yearly inspections included height and weight measurements. This provided for about half the school population of the Province outside Winnipeg; for the remaining rural sections there was no provision.

No plan had been developed for review of the school medical reports by the case workers on the staff nor for the follow-up of the school examinations. The school nurses were very active in having physical defects corrected, and this work was left to them unless there was some chronic trouble.

Malnutrition.—In Winnipeg if the school nurses in their annual inspection of school children found underweight children an entry was made on the medical card indicating that the medical inspector was to reweigh these children. A report was also sent to the parents. There were no nutrition clinics in the schools, but the nurses gave some individual instruction, and the Woman Teachers' Club was financing lunches of milk and crackers in one school that had a high percentage of undernourished children. The Winnipeg General Hospital and the Children's Hospital each conducted a nutrition class, and undernourished children were referred to these.

In the 19 rural municipalities and 11 suburban sections where the 32 provincial public-health nurses were stationed the underweight and undernourished children were formed into weekly nutrition classes after the yearly school examinations. The nurses visited the homes and instructed the mothers in regard to health habits and food, as did the staff workers and friendly visitors also. If children were seriously undernourished the nurses communicated with the commission in regard to extra diet. It was not known how many mothers' aid children were underweight or were attending the nutrition classes.

MENTAL HEALTH

Available facilities.

At the time of the study a psychologist was about to take charge of the psychological work in the public schools, the teachers referring children who were retarded or who seemed mentally deficient to this department for examination and assignment to a grade or to a special class. Physical examinations preceded the psychological examinations (the school physical inspection was sometimes considered sufficient). The psychological department had no social worker; the school nurses visited the homes of deficient children and secured family and developmental histories. It was expected that much emphasis would be placed on behavior problems, but at the time of the study the department had not yet undertaken this work.

Excellent facilities existed in Winnipeg for the diagnosis and treatment of mental defect and disease. The Psychopathic Hospital adjoined the Winnipeg General Hospital and each used the facilities of the other. Both the Psychopathic Hospital, which accommodated 50 patients, and the clinic maintained by this hospital were supported by the provincial government and thus served the entire Province. Follow-up work was done by one of the two psychiatric social workers connected with the clinic if this seemed necessary; or by a staff visitor, or by a friendly visitor, or by all three working together.

There were two other hospitals for mental diseases in the Province outside Winnipeg, also an institution for the feeble-minded. These hospitals did not maintain clinics, nor were there any traveling clinics in the Province.

Follow-up of special types of problems.

In Winnipeg and the suburbs it was a simple matter to secure psychological examinations and advice in regard to retarded and subnormal children, and it was the intention of the mothers' aid workers in Winnipeg to obtain expert advice on all such problems. If the difficulty seemed to be simply one of retardation the school psychologist was consulted; if mental defect or disease seemed to be involved the clinic at the Psychopathic Hospital was used. Children whose fathers had been or were insane were not examined as a matter of routine, but sometimes arrangement was made for examination at the psychiatric clinic, especially if these children were backward in school or showed symptoms of mental unbalance. The Psychopathic Hospital often knew the family histories of children whose fathers had been committed to a hospital for the insane, as such commitment could be made through this hospital. If children showed behavior difficulties an effort was made to interest them in club activities or to get the help of a "big brother" or a "big sister." If such methods were not adequate it was the policy of the commission to have these children examined by a psychologist or a psychiatrist.

Outside Winnipeg the reports from the ungraded schools rendered it difficult to diagnose retardation and the great distances prevented the use of the facilities of any of the hospitals for mental diseases. The only service that could be provided was that given by the friendly visitors, who might be helped by suggestions from a staff visitor.

A mentally defective child needing institutional care would be put on the waiting list for permanent custodial care.

HOUSING

Compared with the housing problem in many cities in the United States, the housing conditions in Winnipeg seemed excellent. The families both in Winnipeg and in the country lived in cottage houses with abundance of sunshine, fresh air, light, and play space. The wide streets and shade trees gave an impression of space and quiet beauty. The majority of the homes even in the city had a small flower plot or border, and the windows were full of blooming plants. In the country vegetable gardens were the rule.

No family occupied less than three rooms. Generally there were four or more. There was a living or sitting room, though sometimes a pleasant kitchen did duty for sitting room as well. In Winnipeg a few houses occupied by mothers' aid families had bathrooms, and the others had inside toilets; but outside the city the majority of the toilets were outside. There was no running water, gas, nor electricity in the Province except in the towns. Most of the mothers cooked with coal or wood, and some used oil stoves in summer. There was no great need of ice; the cellars were used for cooling.

In considering where a family should live care was given to the character of the neighborhood and the physical condition of the house. A family might be advised to move from a lonely country house to a hamlet or town for the sake of better educational or other community advantages. The maximum rent allowed for a mother and two children was $20 per month; for a mother and three children, $25 a month; for a mother and four children, $30 or $35 a month. However, a mother might take women boarders to make up the rent if it exceeded that allowed in the budget. There were 263 mothers who owned their homes in whole or in part and 113 others owned their farms in whole or in part.

The following case story illustrates the efforts made in regard to proper housing for mothers' aid families:

Mrs. H. had five children under 7 years of age and was expecting a baby in two months. The family was destitute because of the long sickness and previous unemployment of the father, and Mrs. H. in her extremity had sold her furniture. When her husband died her neighbors took her and the children into their homes, and all the payment she could promise was the remnant of bedding still unsold. At this stage the mothers' aid worker began to help. As it was essential that Mrs. H. have rest and special nourishment before her confinement, a furnished room was found for her and the youngest child, and the four older children were placed temporarily in a children's home. While Mrs. H. was in the hospital the ladies' auxiliary collected furniture and gave the mothers' aid visitor money to buy what was necessary, so that when Mrs. H. and her new baby were ready to leave the hospital a little comfortably furnished cottage was ready. The cottage had been thoroughly cleaned by two other mothers receiving aid; good fires and an appetizing meal completed the welcome home. Three days later the visitor brought home the four older children.

94535°—28——14

EDUCATION

COOPERATION WITH THE SCHOOLS AND FACILITIES FOR EDUCATION

Contacts with the schools.

The visitors planned to keep in close touch with the schools, and they could do this in Winnipeg and the suburbs. Visit to the schools were frequently made. In country districts the schoolteacher often was a friendly visitor as well. The teachers sent to the mothers' allowances commission every quarter a copy of their quarterly or monthly report to the parents. One of the city workers received copies of these reports monthly for each child in school under her supervision.

Provision for handicapped children.

The physically handicapped child.—The public schools had one sight-conservation class, but no provision for the education of deaf, crippled, or other physically handicapped children, nor were there any open-air classes. The Province maintained an institution for the education and vocational training of the blind.

The mentally handicapped child.—There were 26 special classes in the public schools in which children were enrolled on recommendation of the psychological department of the schools.

Provision for children wishing further education.

No scholarships were available except those in the four colleges, but evidently the commission made an effort to assist and to encourage children to obtain educational advantages and applied with careful consideration for individual cases the ruling requiring the equivalent of the child's wages after he was 15 years old to be deducted from the grant if he did not go to work.

One of the exceptions to the ruling that all children must go to work at 15 years or the equivalent of their earning capacity be made up in some other way is shown in the following case story:

Mrs. L., who had been a widow for five years, was living on a farm with her four children, the oldest of whom was 15-year-old Marie, when she applied for aid in 1921. She had made an unsuccessful effort to support herself and her children by selling milk to campers in the summer and raising vegetables to live on through the winter. She wished to sell her farm, pay her debts, and move to Winnipeg so that Marie might go to high school. When this was done Marie obtained work in a private family to pay for her room and board and graduated from high school. In 1923, at 17 years of age, she secured a permit to teach in the country at a salary of $90 a month. Of this she sent home $35 a month. In the fall she was told that the permit could not be continued; and as she had sent home all the money she could spare she could see no way of going to normal school. The mothers' aid visitor took the matter up with a member of the provincial department of education, who advanced Marie's tuition as a personal loan. The mothers' allowances commission made a special concession in permitting her to take the year's training without contributing to the family support, and they also increased the grant from $53 to $76. Marie, however, earned her room and board. The next year she passed her examination and was given a school in the country with the promise of one nearer home. She was planning to help a younger sister take the teachers' training course. The 16-year-old son was given special permission to attend school to make up for time lost when he was delivering milk on the farm. He earned his food and clothing allowance after school hours.

Several boys and girls were taking business courses in evening schools. Apprenticeship was not greatly encouraged except when a child had a special aptitude, because of the small wages earned while learning. Two boys were studying engineering in railway shops, and two were learning printing. Six boys and girls were taking day business courses, four in high school and two in commercial schools. A few children were taking piano lessons which were provided free or were paid for by money earned by the child or the mother by some extra work. The workers were eager to find such opportunities, and one visitor had secured free violin and piano lessons for three children in one family, all of whom played in a church orchestra.

SCHOOLING AND WORK OF CHILDREN 14 AND 15 YEARS OLD

The child-labor, compulsory-education, and mothers' aid laws.

The compulsory-education and child-labor laws [5] required school attendance from 7 to 14 years of age. Any school board having an attendance officer, however, might by by-law require children to remain in school until 15 years of age. School attendance was required between 14 and 16 years of age if the child was not employed in industry, on the farm, or at household duties. Boys 13 years old could obtain employment certificates permitting them to work in stores not more than two hours a day on school days or eight hours a day on Saturdays and holidays. The law did not allow boys under 14 or girls under 15 years of age to be employed in factories. In Winnipeg school attendance was required to the age of 14, and a child had to remain in school until the close of the school term during which he attained the full age of 14 years. There were no continuation schools.

The mothers' aid law did not specify the age at which grants should cease, but the mothers' allowances commission had ruled that they should be given only to the age of 15 years, regardless of the child's health or school grade. Until 1923 the commission had been liberal in permitting children to continue in school to the age of 16 years, but with the necessity for retrenchment the ruling that all children should go to work at 15 was applied. Furthermore, it was required that the child's contribution to the family in wages must be made up by some other member of the family or a relative if the child continued in school.

Children in school and at work.

There were 111 children (56 boys and 55 girls) 14 and 15 years of age in the families receiving aid; 76 of them were 14 years old and 35 were 15 years old. Of these 111 children 84 were attending school, 18 were working, and 9 were neither attending school nor working.

---

[5] Manitoba, Stat., Consolidated Amendments 1924, ch. 164, sec. 3, p. 1208; Rev. Stat. 1913, ch. 180, secs. 19–20, pp. 2641–2642 (Consolidated Amendments 1924, ch. 180, pp. 1338–1339), Rev. Stat. 1913, ch. 70, secs. 5–6, pp. 1052–1053 (Consolidated Amendments 1924, ch. 70, pp. 493–494).

Children in school.—Among the 84 children 14 and 15 years old attending school were 43 boys and 41 girls. The grade and type of school in which they were enrolled are shown in the following table:

Number of children 14 and 15 years old in school at the time of the study, by grade and type of school; Manitoba, Canada

| Grade or type of school | Total | Children 14 and 15 years old attending school ||||||
| | | Boys |||Girls|||
		Total	14 years	15 years	Total	14 years	15 years
Total	84	43	34	9	41	36	5
Elementary school:							
Second grade	1				1	1	
Third grade	1	1	1				
Fourth grade	1				1		1
Fifth grade	2				2	2	
Sixth grade	13	7	7		6	6	
Seventh grade	21	9	8	1	12	12	
Eighth grade	16	11	10	1	5	5	
High school:							
First year	21	10	7	3	11	9	2
Second year	5	4	1	3	1	1	
Third year	1	1		1			
Business school	2				2		2

The two 15-year-old girls in business school and the 15-year-old boy in the third year of high school had been given special permission to continue in school, and an allowance was being continued for a 15-year-old boy in the second year of high school who had just become 15 and had not yet found work; but no allowances were granted to two other 15-year-old boys in the second year of high school and to three boys in the first year of high school, although none of the five had yet been able to find work. The 15-year-old boy in the eighth grade was earning $12 a month for work outside school hours. The 14-year-old girl in the second grade was mentally defective, and the 15-year-old girl in the fourth grade was under the care of a tuberculosis clinic.

Occupations and earnings of the working children.—The occupations of the 18 working children 14 and 15 years of age were as follows:

	Number of children		Number of children
Total	18	Girls	8
Boys	10	Houseworker	3
Delivery boy	4	Factory worker	2
Office and messenger boy	3	Clerk in store	2
In printing office	2	Clerical worker	1
Clerk in bank	1		

All these working children were 15 years old except one delivery boy, who was 14. This boy and five others had left school in the eighth grade; another was in the sixth grade, four were in the seventh, and six were in the high school (four in the first year, two in the second). For one child the grade was not reported.

The monthly earnings of the working children were as follows:

	Number of children
Total	18
$15	4
$20, under $30	2
$30, under $40	8
$40, under $50	3
$50 or over	1

This list includes, however, the earnings of a 16-year-old boy for whom some data were reported and does not include one of the 14-year-old children, who was working as an apprentice in a printing office and receiving no wages. One of the four children earning $15 a month received her board in addition, and it is probable that two of the other three did also, as they were employed at housework, the fourth being a clerk in a country store. The amounts contributed by these children to the family support varied, the majority giving approximately half their earnings. Two of the three girls who were doing housework contributed $3 a month and one contributed $5 a month. The girl who was clerk in a country store and earning $15 did not contribute anything to the support of the family.

Children neither in school nor at work.

Among the nine children who were neither attending school nor working were two 15-year-old girls and two 14-year-old boys who were temporarily out of work. Two 14-year-old girls were staying at home to help their mothers, who were ill, and one 14-year-old girl who could not attend school on account of trouble with her eyes was also helping at home. One 14-year-old boy had to stop work on account of illness. For a 15-year-old boy no further information was obtained.

Illustrative case history.

The following case history illustrates the responsibility assumed by working children:

Mrs. M. was granted aid from November, 1918, to May, 1923, for four children aged 15, 12, 4, and 2. Thomas, the oldest boy, had started to work in a garage, and during the two years he had been at work he had not only contributed to the family the amount required by the commission but kept up the repairs on the house, buying the paint to repaint it and doing the work himself in the evenings. In the year prior to the study the side of the cellar had fallen in, so that it was necessary to rebuild it and repair the plumbing. Thomas had been saving to buy some new clothes and have a holiday; but he went to the bank, drew out all his money, and told his mother to call the workmen. His savings would make the first payment, and he would pay the rest monthly. The mothers' allowances commission granted a special allowance, however, and the boy started to save again for his clothes. When his wages were raised to those of the average working man he told the visitor that the family could manage without the grant, though there were still two children in school; and with the boy's promise to assist his mother until the younger children were able to take his place the grant was canceled. The visitor telephoned to Thomas's employer that the whole responsibility of the home would now be upon the boy's shoulders. Two weeks later the mother stated that Thomas had been given charge of a department and his wages raised. To make up for the lost vacation the boy's employers took him with them on a motor trip during which he had charge of the car; he had a good holiday and was treated well.

EDUCATIONAL WORK FOR THE MOTHERS

A few mothers were enrolled in English or sewing classes. Very few receiving aid could not speak English; these were encouraged, but not required, to attend classes in English.

RECREATION

The budget carried an item for recreation, allowing $1.25 a month for a family consisting of a mother and three children. This had to cover also such expenses as those incidental to health and education. Employed minors up to 18 years of age were allowed $5 a month for incidentals (not including clothing); those between the ages of 18 and 20 were allowed 20 per cent of their wages in addition to this $5; and the older brothers and sisters (21 years of age or older) were allowed 30 per cent of their wages in addition to the $5.

Outdoor sports in winter and summer were much enjoyed. The schools were not used as social centers in Winnipeg, though a few community clubs met in the schoolhouses. In the country the schools were used for all kinds of entertainment. Probably the most important source of social life, especially in the country, was the church. Every effort was made by the mothers' aid visitors to keep the church connections of the families close and well knit. Some memberships in the Young Men's Christian Association or the Young Women's Christian Association had been granted by the commission. Boy Scout and Girl Scout troops were organized in the large towns, but not many mothers' aid children belonged. There were not many libraries or playgrounds except in Winnipeg. A few families owned pianos or phonographs or had contracted for them before the father's death. Often the relatives would pay the balance due so that the family could keep them.

There were a number of fresh-air camps to which mothers and children were sent from Winnipeg for a two weeks' summer outing. The Roman Catholic organizations conducted one camp, the Jewish group maintained one, the Robertson Memorial Settlement had two cottages for mothers with babies, and one camp for boys and girls was maintained by the business men of the city. About 50 mothers' aid families were sent to these camps through the help of the city auxiliary of friendly visitors, who raised the funds for food and traveling expenses.

Family in America

AN ARNO PRESS / NEW YORK TIMES COLLECTION

Abbott, John S. C. **The Mother at Home:** Or, The Principles of Maternal Duty. 1834.

Abrams, Ray H., editor. **The American Family in World War II.** 1943.

Addams, Jane. **A New Conscience and an Ancient Evil.** 1912.

The Aged and the Depression: Two Reports, 1931–1937. 1972.

Alcott, William A. **The Young Husband.** 1839.

Alcott, William A. **The Young Wife.** 1837.

American Sociological Society. **The Family.** 1909.

Anderson, John E. **The Young Child in the Home.** 1936.

Baldwin, Bird T., Eva Abigail Fillmore and Lora Hadley. **Farm Children.** 1930.

Beebe, Gilbert Wheeler. **Contraception and Fertility in the Southern Appalachians.** 1942.

Birth Control and Morality in Nineteenth Century America: Two Discussions, 1859–1878. 1972.

Brandt, Lilian. **Five Hundred and Seventy-Four Deserters and Their Families.** 1905. Baldwin, William H. **Family Desertion and Non-Support Laws.** 1904.

Breckinridge, Sophonisba P. **The Family and the State:** Select Documents. 1934.

Calverton, V. F. **The Bankruptcy of Marriage.** 1928.

Carlier, Auguste. **Marriage in the United States.** 1867.

Child, [Lydia]. **The Mother's Book.** 1831.

Child Care in Rural America: Collected Pamphlets, 1917–1921. 1972.
Child Rearing Literature of Twentieth Century America, 1914–1963. 1972.
The Colonial American Family: Collected Essays, 1788–1803. 1972.
Commander, Lydia Kingsmill. **The American Idea.** 1907.
Davis, Katharine Bement. **Factors in the Sex Life of Twenty-Two Hundred Women.** 1929.
Dennis, Wayne. **The Hopi Child.** 1940.
Epstein, Abraham. **Facing Old Age.** 1922. New Introduction by Wilbur J. Cohen.
The Family and Social Service in the 1920s: Two Documents, 1921–1928. 1972.
Hagood, Margaret Jarman. **Mothers of the South.** 1939.
Hall, G. Stanley. **Senescence:** The Last Half of Life. 1922.
Hall, G. Stanley. **Youth:** Its Education, Regimen, and Hygiene. 1904.
Hathway, Marion. **The Migratory Worker and Family Life.** 1934.
Homan, Walter Joseph. **Children & Quakerism.** 1939.
Key, Ellen. **The Century of the Child.** 1909.
Kirchwey, Freda. **Our Changing Morality:** A Symposium. 1930.
Kopp, Marie E. **Birth Control in Practice.** 1934.
Lawton, George. **New Goals for Old Age.** 1943.
Lichtenberger, J. P. **Divorce:** A Social Interpretation. 1931.
Lindsey, Ben B. and Wainwright Evans. **The Companionate Marriage.** 1927. New Introduction by Charles Larsen.
Lou, Herbert H. **Juvenile Courts in the United States.** 1927.
Monroe, Day. **Chicago Families.** 1932.
Mowrer, Ernest R. **Family Disorganization.** 1927.
Reed, Ruth. **The Illegitimate Family in New York City.** 1934.
Robinson, Caroline Hadley. **Seventy Birth Control Clinics.** 1930.
Watson, John B. **Psychological Care of Infant and Child.** 1928.
White House Conference on Child Health and Protection. **The Home and the Child.** 1931.
White House Conference on Child Health and Protection. **The Adolescent in the Family.** 1934.
Young, Donald, editor. **The Modern American Family.** 1932.